Main Street.

J. R. R. E.

THE HISTORY OF NORTHALLERTON
From the Earliest Times to the Year 2000

by

MICHAEL RIORDAN

BLACKTHORN PRESS

Blackthorn Press, Blackthorn House
Middleton Rd, Pickering YO18 8AL
United Kingdom

www.blackthornpress.com

ISBN 0 9540535 0 8

© Michael Riordan 2002

Illustration Credits

The publisher and author are grateful to the following for help with
providing illustrations: Andrew Avery, Bodleian Library, University of
Oxford, Guildhall Art Gallery and National Portrait Gallery

Printed and Bound by the Cromwell Press
Trowbridge, Wiltshire

PREFACE

Any compiler of a definitive history of an ancient, substantial and vibrant locality such as Northallerton must have qualms about the end product. This author is no exception.

For example, with the in-depth research and garnering of information came the commensurate realisation of the comprehensiveness of the subject and how little one really knew. Then there is the question of balance with the vast transition between eking out the slightest scrap of detail from the time-misted earliest days (and oh what triumph of discovery of any ancient fact!) to the contemporary volume of a massive abundance of Northallerton information over the past two centuries and the consequent unenviable task of selection from this mountain of modern material.

Attendant too is the very conscious aim of achieving essential historical detail and accuracy whilst making the subject of interest and palatable to the general reader. And finally, the last history of Northallerton was published as long ago as 1885 – when the town nestled around the gas-lit, motor-less High Street where horses busily clip-clopped along; since which time a colossal social and technological revolution has taken place with a kaleidoscope of telling events including two World Wars interspersed.

Prior to the publication of this book there were four main Northallerton historians each of whom compiled a published history of the town: Roger Gale (1739), James Langdale (1792), Christopher Ingledew (1858) and Rev Joseph Saywell (1885). Roger Gale's "An Historical Account of the Borough of North Allerton" (1739) was only eleven and a half pages but it is of crucial importance because it was the first proper history of Northallerton and as such contained invaluable information. Gale was born in 1672 the eldest son of Dr Thomas Gale (1636 - 1702, of Scruton and the Dean of York) educated at Trinity College, Cambridge University and became one of the most learned men of his age being a first Vice President of the Royal Society of Antiquaries and Treasurer of the prestigious Royal Society.

He was MP for Northallerton on four occasions – 1705, 1707, 1708 and 1710. In 1713 he was made a Commissioner of Excise but deposed by Premier Mr Walpole who wanted the post for one of his supporters. He died at Scruton aged 72 on 25th June 1744 "universally esteemed and much lamented by all his acquaintances," and was buried in Scruton churchyard. He wrote his "North Allerton Account" in 1739 to be included in Mr Willis's "Nontitia Parliamentaria" (a survey of parliamentary boroughs) but this never materialised and it was finally published in Nichol's "Bibliotheca Topographica Britannica" in 1781.

In 1792 James Langdale tellingly prefaced his "The History and Antiquities of Northallerton" of eighty-eight pages with lines from Webster's "Duchess of Malfi" commencing:

> "I do love these ancient ruynes:
> We never tread upon them but we set
> Our foote upon some reverend history."

This was the first separate book produced on Northallerton and a second edition was published in 1813. Langdale was a popular printer and bookseller with his business on Northallerton's High Street whose life was ended in an unfortunate manner in 1823 when his horse drawn gig was hit by a cart in which the driver had fallen asleep. With the shock of the collision he ruptured a blood vessel near the heart and died the following day aged seventy-two.

Christopher J. D. Ingledew produced the first in depth historical exposition of Northallerton in 1858 bearing the same title as Langdale's – "The History and Antiquities of North Allerton." He was a barrister-of-law of the Middle Temple, had strong local family ties being born at Northallerton in 1823 and resided in a large house on Northallerton High Street immediately north of the present Midland Bank. His scholastic book was published by a subscription list, many of the sponsors being leading local people as well as several titled subscribers. Unfortunately he died aged only thirty-eight soon after his history was published having produced one further book – "Ballads and Songs of Yorkshire" (1860).

Finally in 1885 "The History and Annals of Northallerton" by the curate of Northallerton Parish Church the Reverend Joseph Saywell F.R.H.S. was published (price 5/-) having been printed in Northallerton by J. Vasey and Company. Saywell lodged at the house on the main street directly to the north of the "Tickle Toby Inn" (now occupied by the travel agents Lunn Poly) and was only in Northallerton for five years before moving in 1885 to become Vicar of Ackworth in south Yorkshire. His book was a veritable 'tour de force' of historical detail, description and anecdote concerning Northallerton, although in parts he relied almost verbatim on Ingledew and left his book with a very lengthy appendix of material not included in the main text. Nevertheless,

Saywell's historical contribution to the town is both considerable and invaluable, particularly because his history is the last one to be produced up to the present time.

An updated history of North Yorkshire's county town became long overdue as time elapsed. In my case some propitious basics were in place such as: a very close involvement with Northallerton and especially its people where I had been brought up and educated (latterly at the venerable Northallerton Grammar School); and an avid penchant for history which eventuated in reading for an honours degree in the subject at Sheffield University on leaving school in 1952.

However, my first real thrust into Northallerton's local history did not occur until 1964 with a posting as a Squadron Leader to nearby Royal Air Force Leeming when I was prevailed upon (not quite ordered!) as a 'local native' and editor of the station magazine 'Leeming Life' to produce articles of interest about the area for the vast majority of personnel and their families who were newcomers. Such was the stimulation awakened by this that on returning to live permanently again in the town in 1972 a vague notion of updating Reverend Saywell's monumental work of 1885 had formed.

Simultaneously came an acute awareness of the crucial need to become more comfortably familiar with the complex subject which encompassed almost two thousand years. In consequence virtually the next three decades were spent in pursuit of local historical information in a great variety of ways. This consisted principally of research in libraries and places of record both locally and up and down the land paralleled by direct personal information seeking: interviewing and talking to local people, reviewing buildings and places and generally studying and reflecting on all aspects of Northallerton and its environs, anatomy, social and economic fabric and metamorphosis over the centuries.

The purpose and mission statement of these activities was always "to write and have published a new history of Northallerton" but by-products just seemed to transpire. These included frequent public lectures and talks about the town; the conduct of historic town tours; increasing work for local civic bodies particularly Northallerton Town Council; continuous local history work with the children and students of all the town's schools – an especially illuminating and rewarding experience; and the writing and publication of six books between 1991 and 2000 concerning Northallerton and its people.

Thus after the travail and vicissitudes of the past few years the at long last production of this book – a personal "magnum opus" as it were – has brought a certain feeling of satisfaction but far outweighed by an enormous sense of relief!

Innumerable thanks are due in regard to its appearance. I am particularly bounden to the two main mines of reference and information – North Yorkshire County Reference Library and North Yorkshire County Record Office, both of which are fortuitously situated in Northallerton. In both places the staff were unfailingly helpful, friendly and painstaking in their attentions – often beyond the call of duty.

Other major sources of reference have been Darlington Reference and Local History Library, the "Darlington and Stockton Times" library and archives department, York City Reference Library, Durham Cathedral's library and archives departments, Scarborough Reference Library, Christ Church College, Oxford University Library, the Bodleian Library, Oxford, the Public Record Office, Kew, the British Library London, the British Library Newspaper Section, Colindale, North London and the Air Historical Branch, MOD (Air), London. Help and invaluable information was forthcoming in every case.

For sustained support for the enterprise over the years I am indebted to my family, friends and both individuals and organisations in Northallerton and district. Latterly, my publisher Alan Avery of Blackthorn Press has been most helpful, discerning and patient. Ultimately (as a rare modern-day computer dinosaur) for the last strenuous production of the printed word I am very much in the debt of Anne Smirthwaite who reproduced my hand-written text so assiduously and speedily that I was forced to keep up with her and finalise matters!

It is hoped that this book will fill an historic vacuum in Northallerton's civic infra-structure, promote an awareness of Northallerton's history, heritage and unique character and be interesting and useful to each individual reader.

At least it is felt that an historical edifice has been created upon which others can build in the future – because the history of Northallerton, ancient and modern, will not end suddenly in 2002!

CONTENTS

9. THE INTER-WAR YEARS (1918 – 1939)

10. THE SECOND WORLD WAR (1939 – 1945)

11. THE POST WAR REVOLUTION (1945 – 1974)

12. THE LAST MILLENNIUM LAP (1975 – 2000)

Football 439, Rugby 439, Hockey and Tennis 439, Memorial Baths 440, Other Sports and Games 440, Golfing Expansion 440, Equine Activities 441, Alan Hinkes-Mountaineer 441, Visits and Events 443, Viscount Northallerton 445, The Modern March 445.

BIBLIOGRAPHY

APPENDICES

INDEX

COLOUR PLATES

Plate 1 Copy of an oil painting impression of the Bishop of Durham's Palace.
Plate 2 "The Battle of the Standard" painted in 1893 by the historical painter Sir John Gilbert RA (1817-1897) in the Guildhall Collection, London.
Plate 3 Northallerton Parish Church
Plate 4 Old Northallerton – The Vicarage Wall and "Oddfellows Arms"
Plate 5 Northallerton Grammar School – rebuilt 1776
Plate 6 Dr Townsend's Vicarage of 1828
Plate 7 The Resplendent North Riding County Hall by Walter Brierley seen in 1909
Plate 8 Northallerton Market Place 2002

MONOCHROME PLATES

Plate 1 Castle Hills depicted in 1794 before levelling and dismantling took place especially in 1838 with the construction of the Great North of England Railway
Plate 2 Porch House
Plate 3 Dr John Radcliffe
Plate 4 Northallerton Church post 1779 and 1787 Restoration
Plate 5 "Vine House" 1789 – now the Rutson Hospital
Plate 6 Warrior's Yard – now behind Ottakers
Plate 7 Henry Rutson (1831-1920) – the Hospital Benefactor
Plate 8 Northallerton Shooting Club in the 1880s
Plate 9 John Hutton MP of Solberge and Sowber Gate
Plate 10 Northallerton Station 1841

A NOTE ON WEIGHTS, MEASURES AND MONEY

The weights, measures and monetary values used in this book are the ones contemporaries used. These may be summarised as:

Money:

4 farthings	=	1d (penny)
12d (pence)	=	1s (shilling)
1s	=	5p
20s (shillings)	=	£1 (pound)
21s (shillings)	=	1 guinea

Weight:

16oz (ounces)	=	1lb (pound)
1lb	=	0.45 kilograms
14lb (pounds)	=	1 stone
1 stone	=	6.35 kilograms
2 stones	=	1qr (quarter)
1qr	=	12.70 kilograms
4qr (quarters)	=	1cwt (hundredweight)
1cwt	=	50.80 kilograms
20cwt	=	1 ton
1 ton	=	1.02 tonnes

Volume:

2 pints	=	1 quart
1 quart	=	1.14 litres
4 quarts	=	1 gallon
1 gallon	=	4.55 litres
2 gallons	=	1 peck
1 peck	=	9.09 litres
4 pecks	=	1 bushel
1 bushel	=	36.40 litres
8 bushels	=	1qr (quarter)
1 quarter	=	2.91 hectolitres

Distance:

12in (inches)	=	1ft (foot)
1ft	=	0.305 metres
3ft (feet)	=	1yd (yard)
1yd	=	0.91 metres
22yds (yards)	=	1 chain
1 chain	=	20.12 metres
10 chains	=	1 furlong
1 furlong	=	201.17 metres
8 furlongs	=	1 mile
1 mile	=	1.61 kilometres

Area:

30¼ sq yds	=	1 perch
1 perch	=	25.29 sq metres
40 perches = 1 rood = 1210 sq yds	=	1011.56 sq metres
4 roods = 1 acre = 4840 sq yds	=	0.405 hectares

Table prepared by Stephen Harrison

1

The Beginnings (until 1100 AD)

Profile

Northallerton, the County Town of North Yorkshire, is of ancient origins, compelling annals, marked individuality and remarkable buoyancy. It has been a legal and administrative centre for over a thousand years (since Saxon times) during which it has flourished as a thriving market town situated centrally at the northern extremity of the Vale of York in a rich agricultural area between the Hambleton Hills and the river Swale on a stretch of sand and gravel adjacent to the confluence of two streams at Castle Hills, Sun Beck and Willow Beck, which flow into the river Wiske.

There has always been a strong air of centrality about the town; indeed it is largely to its position that Northallerton owes its development, history and importance. Astride the major eastern route south to north, England to Scotland and London to Edinburgh it was a natural route centre where in olden days the tracks were drawn together which are now represented by the key roads radiating around the town: from the south via York (Thirsk Road) and Boroughbridge (Boroughbridge Road which was part of the traditional Great North Road); from the west, the Pennines and Dales (Ainderby Road); from the north via Darlington (Darlington Road, again part of the Great North Road); and from the east (Stokesley and Crosby Roads). Additionally the main east coast railway line was constructed here by 1841 when Northallerton railway station was opened.

Prehistory

The other critical factor in the town's basic make up has been the rich alluvial deposits, ideal for cultivation and farming which the last Great Ice Age brought to the area 12,000 to 70,000 years ago.

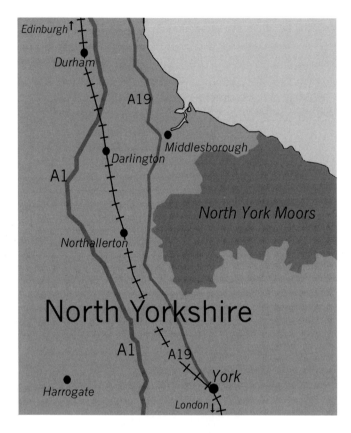

Map 1. North Yorkshire

Previously this part of Yorkshire had been a vast ocean (450 million years ago); part of a great desert (400 million years since) and a torrid tropical forest and swamp (100 million years past).

Prehistoric activity in the Northallerton vicinity is evidenced by two discoveries early in this century. A bronze leaf-shaped ancient British spear-head was found a little to the west of Castle Hills measuring 9½ inches (24 cms) in length and weighing 3¾ ounces (105 gms). In 1918 it was fully described in the "Yorkshire Archaeological Journal" by Edward Wooler, an eminent archivist who commented that "It is interesting to speculate how the spear-head came to be lost and discovered in the position where it was found." At that time the spear-head was in the possession of solicitor and bailiff of Northallerton John

Ingleby Jefferson of Standard House (the maternal grandfather of Grace Gardner).

Bronze Age Spear Head found near Castle Hills

Exactly the same could be said of the second prehistoric find a stone battle axe head which came to light around the same time on the Solberge estate one mile south of Northallerton to the west of Boroughbridge Road. It is made of basalt, has a cylindrical hole for the axe shaft, is noticeably heavy and is in excellent condition. It is in the possession of Mr John Willis a locally born and educated (Northallerton

Bronze Age Battle Axe Head

Grammar School) successful business man from nearby Sowber Gate who bought the battle-axe head for £80 in the 1980s at the sale of the Solberge Hall effects of the outgoing Talbot family who had succeeded the Huttons as the owners of Solberge in the 1920s. The axe-head was authenticated in 1998 by the Yorkshire Museum, York by the antiquities expert Dr Ceinwen Paynton who ascribed it to the later Bronze Age between 1800 and 500 BC.

The Roman Presence

The originations of human settlement at Northallerton are almost certainly Roman, and there is much evidence to substantiate this. Roger Gale the nationally renowned antiquarian wrote the first history of Northallerton in 1739 in which he asserted that "It is highly probable that it rose out of the ashes of an old Roman station whose name we have lost;" stressed the presence of the nearby village of Romanby (which is the only habitation in Britain with a combined Roman-Danish place name); and observed that the then great banks and entrenchments of Castle Hills "are thought by the judicious to have been Roman works."

Indeed Castle Hills to the west of the present town were believed traditionally to have been Roman, Gale's brother-in-law the Reverend Dr William Stukeley (1687-1765) the famed antiquarian and archaeologist holding strongly to this view, as did several eminent visitors to the site in the eighteenth century – Colonel Ainslie, Sir William Erskine and George William Duke of Argyll who called it the 'Roman encampment.' There is much more information to support the view that the Romans were present there.

Agricola the Roman general and his invading army according to Saywell (1885) encamped on Castle Hills in his campaign against the Scots in 82 AD and through the years a series of Roman coins and relics have been unearthed there.   The Reverend John Balguy Vicar of Northallerton (1729-1748) wrote the poem "From the ashes of a Roman urn dug up at the Castle Hills, near Northallerton AD 1743" which commenced:

'Trifling mortal tell me why
Thou has disturbed my urn.'

Then in 1788 a farm ploughman Lawrence Leadley turned up a large porous blue clay urn in a field near to Castle Hills containing innumerable Roman coins chiefly of the later Roman Emperors and in good condition. These several hundred coins soon went into circulation as currency tender in the Northallerton district becoming known colloquially as "Lawrie's farthings." It is possible that the hoard was the pay of a Roman soldier ("Aes Militarum") too ponderous to carry but for which the owner never returned. Around this time Francis Smythe FSA of Thirsk unearthed several Roman coins near the summit of Castle Hills whose owner William Metcalfe also discovered Roman coins there in almost pristine condition.

Overwhelming evidence of a Roman presence was afforded when the Great North of England Railway (which became part of the London to Edinburgh main railway line) was driven through Castle Hills. On 28th March 1838 workmen digging the foundations of the first railway bridge to the north of Northallerton (now Zetland Bridge) came across an urn of dark blue clay believed to be Roman, the foundations of a freestone drainage system and some Roman coins. Farther into the hill according to the reliable contemporary "York Herald" a supposed votive altar dedicated to the Roman Sixth Legion (which came to England in 122 AD) was unearthed which was inscribed: "INSTANE FLA. HYRO. LEG. V1. V." – 'Being present Flavius, Hyronimianus, of the Sixth Legion, Victorious.' It is believed that the altar was placed in the library of Durham Cathedral.

Both a well of dressed freestone of a yard (91 cms) in diameter and another well two yards square of strongly bound and dove-tailed blackened oak were found along with many interesting stones before the level needed for the railway line was reached with several yards still remaining to the bottom of the second well which would remain unexcavated. Widespread dispoilation unfortunately took place for many stones were broken up to fill up the abutments to the bridge and the oak wood was widely used for making snuffboxes and walking sticks. Roman spurs were discovered as well as coins of Antoninus Pius, Marcus Aurelius, Commodus, Severus, Geta and Constantinus.

There is little doubt then that a Roman encampment or station existed at Castle Hills and this would be appropriate from a strategic viewpoint situated as it was between two major Roman roads – Dere Street to the west from York (Eburacum) via Aldborough to Catterick and to the east from York to the Tees at Middleton-one-Row via Thornton-le-Street, Thornton-le-Beans and Bullamoor. It seems significant that the road from Zetland Bridge, the scene of Roman discoveries, leads directly from Northallerton to Catterick – the key Roman military fortress and encampment "Cataractonium". *[see monochrome plate 1]*

Castle Hills originally was high embankments and deep ditches in a concentric formation over twenty acres. It was lowered in 1801 (south) and 1807 (east) and divided into fields in 1811. The dismantling process was completed in 1838 by the building of the Great North of England Railway leaving only a scar on the east side.

It remains the enigma of the town's history – was it natural or man made – but there is little doubt that future archaeological investigations will reveal more of its secrets and that it was the original seat of Northallerton's human settlement. With the establishment of the military base at Catterick the Romans would have a continuing need for both food and hides (tents, uniforms and shields) for their soldiers. The Northallerton area would have a great potential for supplying these and it is quite probable that a Brigantes farming "colonia" could have emerged producing goods for Roman consumption.

Indeed Arthur Raistrick ("The Romans in Yorkshire" 1960) asserts that in the second century this area was established as a series of farms and estates ("colonia") which was settled by Romanised Brigantes and Romans "with Roman buildings on Castle Hills, Northallerton occupied after 150 AD." Captain JS Weston (Cambridge County Geographies 1919) also strongly concluded that based on York as the major defensive hinge behind Hadrian's Wall the Northallerton area would have a concentration of settled Roman veterans.

A final and intriguing footnote was added to the Romano-Northallerton speculation in 2000 by the archaeological survey promoted by TESCO on their new store site before its re-development at the south of Northallerton behind the east side of the High Street. This thorough investigative archaeological study was professionally and painstakingly carried out by "Pre-Construct Archaeology Limited" whose on site team was led by Mark Randerson over a six month period on either side of the New Year of 2001. The fundamental overall scenario revealed was that of a medieval post-Norman Conquest 'corridor' town, with property lines and 'dividers' running uniformly and distinctly east to west to the main road (now the High Street).

However, there was a most telling discovery which was an exception to the basic east to west pattern in the form of a ditch and gully which ran at right angles from north to south. This categorically pre-dated the overall medieval earthworks and was believed by the archaeologists to be the remains of Roman field works – field boundaries and a fence line. Some seemingly corroborative evidence was the finding in that vicinity of two sherds of Roman pottery one of which was a braided Samian piece of Roman table-ware of western Gaul which belonged to the first two centuries of the Roman occupation.

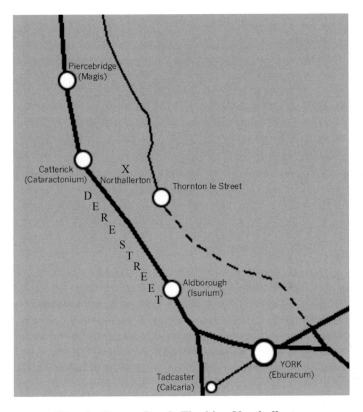

Map 2. Roman Roads Flanking Northallerton

Although tentative, the apparent discovery of Roman field works is of great importance as it is the first time that a Roman presence at Northallerton had been verified by "controlled modern archaeological excavation" in the words of Pre-Construct Archaeology's director Robin Taylor-Wilson. Conjecture about the location of the field works is interesting especially in its relation to all the other Roman discoveries at Castle Hills, with the main theories connected with road communications.

A salient suggestion is that the field works were part of a "mansio" – a minor Roman signal station – set up to facilitate the operation of imperial messengers who were part of the vital "cursus publicus" or Imperial Post. The credence of this is worthy of close examination when the exact location of the Roman field works are considered regarding the surrounding road configurations.

The field works were discovered adjacent to the north side of what was New Row only about forty yards (36 metres) in from the High Street. Thus they are in very close proximity to the junction at Romanby Road and the High Street of the two major national roads on the eastern side of the country – the York road and the Boroughbridge road (the old Great North Road). This would be a crucial communications point from time immemorial.

Additionally in realistic Roman terms there was the possibility of some sort of a linking route between the two Roman roads running on each side of Northallerton. In the eighteenth century it was believed that a Roman road ran from Thornton-le-Street via Romanby to Catterick but this has never been proved. Equally a route could be conjectured from a point around Thornton-le-Beans from the one road via the New Row area to Romanby road and Springwell lane to Castle Hills (of definite Roman connection) and thence to Catterick (Cataractonium). In any event it is likely that any Roman activity in the area of the field works finds at Northallerton would almost inevitably concern roads or communications.

The Dark Ages

When the Romans left Britain in the fifth century the country descended into the 'Dark Ages' about which little is coherently known. Successive and frequent invasions took place by the Angles, Saxons and Vikings with the land laid to fire and sword for long periods. The Angles and Saxons began to arrive in the fifth century and gradually settled only to be strongly challenged in the eighth century by Danish raids of a fierce nature.

The Northallerton historians agree that in 769 AD the tyrant King of Northumbria, Beornredus could have burned down Northallerton's church as he laid waste to Catterick (Roman - Cataractonium) and that in 883 AD King Alfred caused all the desolate area between the Humber and Tweed to be re-inhabited. Peter de Langtoft (an Austin Friar) wrote in the 1120's of the Danish invasions and King Alfred:

> "Tille Alfred our Kyng com tythings starke
> That fyve Kyngs and fyve earles ver comen of
> Denmarke
> That wild on him renne, and reve him the coroune,
> With alle ther grete folk, thei lay in Alvertoune."

Indeed because of its central position Northallerton must have been in the midst of the battles, skirmishes and multiplicity of comings of the invaders as the eventual local place names testify.

A Saxon Church

Further evidence of Northallerton's early existence is indicated by the history of its Parish Church. Dr Stukeley, stated in a paper read to the Antiquarian Society on 30th October 1755 that:

"Paulinus (the first Bishop of York in 630 AD) built many parish churches in Yorkshire...He built Northallerton Church now remaining."

Parish Church Saxon Stone Cross-Head

Thus it is possible that a wooden Saxon Church was in existence and it is unequivocal that a stone Saxon church lay on the present site as fragments of eighth and ninth century Saxon crosses (the oldest ascribed to 730 AD) and fabric were found during Church restorations (especially 1882/5) and are now preserved in the present Northallerton Parish Church. The dedication of the church to "All Saints" is indicative of

Saxon origins and at nearby Brompton Church, which was a satellite of Northallerton its "Mother Church," famous "hog-back" tombstones of Viking origin have been discovered, emphasising clearly that both the churches were existent in Saxon times.

Paulinus was certainly active around Northallerton because in a remarkable episode he baptised over 10,000 in the nearby river Swale (there being no existent churches) as described around 630 AD in Pope Gregory the Great's epistle to St Eulogius, Patriarch of Alexandria:

"On the day of Christ's nativitie, he (Paulinus) did regenerate by lively baptisme above ten thousand men, besides an innumerable multitude of women and children. Having hallowed and blessed the river, called in English Swale, the archbishop commanded by voice of criers and maisters that the people should enter the river confidently, two by two, and in the name of the Trinitie baptise one another in turnes... they were transported to the banke on the other side: and notwithstanding so deepe a current and channel, so great and so divers differences of sex and age, not one person took harm."

Saxon Settlement

Christianity in the locality was undermined by "the harrying of the heathen men" (the Anglo - Saxon Chronicle" regarding 793 AD) but after the Danes had been defeated by King Alfred at Edington in 878 AD, their leaders were baptised and Christianity restored throughout the country. At some stage during these times Anglo - Danish peaceful co-existence in the local habitations had commenced. Typifying this were the adjacent market towns, Northallerton (Saxon name ending) and Thirsk (Viking name ending) as too did the intermingled villages around Northallerton: Romanby, Ainderby, Danby Wiske, Kirby Wiske, Borrowby and Maunby (all Viking ending); and Brompton, Thornton-le-Beans, Thornton-le-Street, Thornton-le-Moor, Scruton, Morton, Great Smeaton and Cowtons (all Saxon ending).

The Town's Name

Northallerton's historians vary in their assessment of the derivation of the town's name. Roger Gale believed it was named after King Alfred but James Langdale thought it came from the Alder tree which were plentiful in the area, his thesis being supported by both Ingledew and

Saywell. Modern scholarship, however, has emphatically concluded that it is derived from the Old English personal name of 'Aelfhere' and the Saxon ending 'ton' (farm) so that Alverton means "Alfred's farm" (A.H. Smith 'The Place Names of the North Riding of Yorkshire,' 1928). The 'ton' was a fenced farmstead or enclosure which would develop into a village or in Northallerton's case a small town.

The name was spelt variously – Aluertune, Aluertun and Alverton in the "Domesday Book" (1086), Alvertona in the twelfth century and by the fourteenth century the prefix "North" was regularly used – North Alverton. It was demonstrably the northernmost of the other eight Yorkshire "Allertons" and "North" was added to distinguish it from these: Allerton Mauleverer, Chapel Allerton, Moor Allerton, Allerton Bywater, Allerton Grange, Allerton Gledhow, Allerton Lee and Allerton near Bradford all of which were listed by Ingledew. By the sixteenth century the reference in two words (North Alverton or Allerton) was completely common but it was not until the nineteenth century that the town was generally called by the single modern title of Northallerton.

The Saxon Town

The earliest town settlement was in the Castle Hills area and eventually in Saxon times a Saxon 'Great Hall' could have existed for the main leader (originally Aelfhere). Almost certainly this would have been situated on the site of what became the Bishop's Palace (now the older part of the Northallerton cemetery) where substantial Saxon earthworks were located in the nineteenth century.

The Saxon population would be grouped adjacently at what is now the North End with the dwellings distributed around the Green with the Parish Church on the south western side. It could well have been on the typical Saxon pattern of a central green surrounded by open fields where a resident had individual "strips" of land, beyond which were common pasture, woods and "waste".

By the tenth century Yorkshire had been divided by the Danes into Ridings ("Thirdings") and the Ridings into Wapentakes each with a central meeting place where courts were held. Northallerton was the headquarters of the Allertonshire Wapentake and thus has been an important local government centre for more than a thousand years.

Ancient Allertonshire derived its name from its centre Northallerton and contained the following other places: Birkby, Borrowby, Brompton, Brawith, Cotcliffe, Crosby, Deighton, Ellerbeck,

Foxton, Girsby, High Worsall, Holme, Hornby, Hutton Bonville, Hutton Sessay, Hutton Conyers, North Kilvington, North Otterington, Knayton, Landmoth-with-Catto, Lazenby, Leake, Little Smeaton, Norton Conyers, Osmotherley, Over Dinsdale, Romanby, Kirby Sigston, Sowerby-under-Cotcliffe, Thimbleby, Thornton-le-Beans, Thornton-le-Street, West Harlsey, West Rounton, and Winton with Stank and Hallikeld.

The stature of Northallerton in Saxon Times can best be gleaned from the "Domesday Book". Northallerton was described as "waste" after the 1066 Norman Conquest in the "Domesday" survey – "modo wastum est" – but before this in the Saxon era "Domesday" ascribed much prosperity and local importance to "Aluertune" where:

"there are 44 carucates of land (around 8000 acres) taxable which 30 ploughs can plough. Earl Edwin held this as one manor before 1066, and he had 66 villeins (freemen) with 35 ploughs.

To this manor are attached 11 outliers (berewicks): Bretebi (Birkby); Smidetune (Great Smeaton); Sourebi (Sowerby-under-Cotliffe); Smitune (Little Smeaton); Kirkebi (Kirby Wiske); Corketune (East Cowton); Landemot (Landmoth); Bergeby (Borrowby); Griftorentun (Thornton-le-Beans); Romundebi (Romanby); Jaforbe (Yafforth).

Now it is in King's hands. Waste value then £80.

There is there, meadow 40 acres; wood and open land 5 leagues long and as wide."

"To this manor belongs the jurisdiction ("soke") of these lands: Neuhufe (Newsham Grange); Wefthufe (Westhouse); Mannebi (Maunby); Werlegefbi (Warlaby); Eindrebi (Ainderby Steeple); Jadforde (Yafforth); Leifenchi (Lazenby Hall); Dignefhale (Over Dinsdale Grange); Runtune (West Rounton); Irebi (Irby Manor); Hereffaie (West Harlsey); Sigheftun (Kirby Sigston); Colebi (Cowesby); Timelbi (Thimbleby); Leche (Leake); Chennieton; Raueneftorp (Ravensthorpe Manor); Torentun (Thornton-le-Street); Croxebi (Crosby Grange); Otrientun (North Otterington); Romundebi (Romanby); Brunton (Brompton); Cheluintun (North Kilvington); Keneueton (Knayton).

"In all there are 85 carucates taxable which 45 ploughs can plough.

There is there, meadow 60 acres. There were 116 Freemen. Now it is waste."

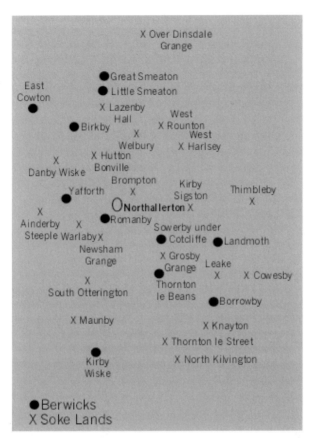

Map 3.
Saxon Northallerton. Dependent Berwicks and Soke Lands

Here then is categorical evidence that Saxon Northallerton was a town of some stature committed to agriculture with eleven berewicks and twenty-four sokelands dependant upon it. It was settled and thriving as too it appeared were all the reliant villages. And so why was the Northallerton manor and the surrounding settlements designated as "waste" in 1086 in the Domesday Book? The answer to this condition was most probably the infamous military excursion carried out by William the Conqueror and the Normans in 1069 known as the "Harrying of the North" in which Northallerton and its district were completely devastated.

The Harrying of the North

Following the Norman Conquest in 1066 William the Conqueror had great difficulty in subduing the North, illustrated by the murder of his successive appointees as Earl of Northumberland: Copsig was beheaded by the Northumbrians in 1067 and his successor Robert de Comines was murdered at Durham in 1068. The latter incident determined William to seek a "final solution" to the problem of the rebellious North and in Autumn 1068 he came from Wales with a cavalry force of approximately 700 and laid waste to the area from York to Durham. Men, women and children were annihilated and the means of existence destroyed – animals, crops and implements.

Northallerton faced the full force of the Norman onslaught and Symeon of Durham, one of the main chroniclers of events writing around 1164, stated that William the Conqueror encamped at Northallerton (presumably at the defensible Castle Hills) and also recounted an interesting tale involving the town. When the Norman advance had reached Northallerton, a great darkness descended which the Normans believed attributable to the spirit of the patron saint of Durham, St Cuthbert and they turned tail and in fear and panic returned to York. William who had not been with the army spurned superstition and led his men personally back north ravaging the country on all sides.

Symeon went on to graphically describe the Norman devastation:

"It was shocking to see in the houses, the streets and highways human carcasses swarming with worms, dissolving in putridity and emitting a most horrible stench; nor were any left alive to cover them with earth having perished by sword or by famine or had abandoned their native land. During the space of nine years the country lay totally uncultivated. Between York and Durham not a house was inhabited all was a lonely wilderness, the retreat of wild beasts and robbers and the terror of travellers."

It could be argued that Symeon was biased because he was a Saxon sympathiser but other chroniclers were equally condemnatory of William the Conqueror including the impartial Odericus Vitalis who had a French father and an English mother. He wrote that corn, cattle and every type of food was burned and famine raged with the survivors forced to eat rats and even human flesh. The land was strewn with unburied corpses, he estimated that 100,000 Christians died from hunger and he strongly condemns William for "such barbarous homicide." Certainly the "Harrying" blots the escutcheon of William the Conqueror who is said to have confessed the great sin of these brutalities on his death-bed.

The Northallerton – Durham Connection

Soon after the death of William the Conqueror in September 1087 his successor William Rufus in gratitude for the friendship and fidelity shown to his father and himself, granted to William Carilepho Bishop of Durham (1081-1096) and his heirs and successors the royal manor and soke (legal authority) of Allertonshire with all its rights and appendages. This initiated a Northallerton - Durham connection which lasted seven hundred and fifty years, except for two brief periods in 1100 and during the English Civil War (1646-60), until 1836 when the Bishop of Durham's authority passed to the Bishop of Ripon who was superseded by the Ecclesiastical Commissioners in 1857.

The early Yorkshire Charters (British Library) relate the grant by William II to William Bishop of Durham of the manor of Allerton: "Rex Willemus secundus dedit episcope Dunelmensi Alvertonam cum suis appendiciis cum terris et carucatis in villis ibidem scriptis."

At the same time in December 1091 William Carilepho Bishop of Durham granted to the Prior and monks of St Cuthbert's Durham the churches of Allerton, Sigston and Brompton with their tithes. King John confirmed this right in 1204 and despite a strong challenge to this privilege by the Archbishop of York in 1410 successive priors of Durham retained control of the Northallerton church until the dissolution of the Monasteries after which the Dean and Chapter of Durham Cathedral obtained the rights including the appointment of the Northallerton vicars, confirmed by Henry VIII in a deed of 1541.

This temporal (manor and land) and spiritual (church) Durham control had a great influence on Northallerton over the centuries and Allertonshire became an enclave of Durham in Yorkshire being called the Durham "peculiar." The town and its fairs and markets, the Grammar School, the Bishop of Durham's Palace and Northallerton Parish Church were major institutions very much affected by Durham's control. In the peculiars of Allerton and Allertonshire both the Bishop of Durham and the Dean and Chapter of Durham had "peculiars" in which they had ecclesiastical rights and jurisdiction.

Eventually, by the sixteenth century "The parishes and chapelries in the bishop's peculiar were:

Birkby, Cowesby, Hutton Bonville, Leake, Nether Silton, North

Otterington, Osmotherley, and Thornton-le-Street.

Those in the Dean and Chapter's peculiar were Brompton, Deighton, High Worsall, Kirby Sigston, Northallerton and West Rounton.

These places were also subject to visitation by the Archbishop of York" (Margaret McCallum).

2

Early Medieval Northallerton (1100 to 1300)

The Battle of the Standard 1138

Undoubtedly, the most famous event of Northallerton's early history was the Battle of the Standard which was waged between the English and the Scots approximately three miles north of Northallerton in what is now Brompton parish on 22nd August 1138. It became one of the most celebrated and chronicled battles of early England.

The political cause concerned the succession to the English throne after the death in Normandy of Henry I in December 1135 from a surfeit of lampreys. Henry had wanted his daughter Matilda (also known as Maud) to succeed but the Norman barons did not want a woman ruler and chose Henry's nephew Stephen as monarch, who was crowned on 26th December 1135 with the sanction of the Archbishop of Canterbury and the Pope. This was not acceptable to Matilda's supporters including King David of Scotland who hoped to gain Northumberland by allegiance to Matilda.

Anarchy, civil discord and lawlessness characterised Stephen's reign (1135 - 1154) and though the "succession question" was important the salient reason the English barons rallied together against the Scots was the sheer menace to their civilisation of the wild, blood-thirsty, ferocious and marauding Scots. An uneasy peace came to an end in March 1138 when King David crossed the Tweed with a motely of an army from all over his kingdom: "from the wild west and the Isles, Highlanders and Lowlanders both Norman and some English, Picts, Scots and Gaels."

There followed a campaign of brutal savagery the Galloway Picts "those bestial men" being the perpetrators of the worst atrocities and though King David was a humane man he was unable to control them. W. Grainge wrote: "Their progress across the country was marked by the most horrible cruelty and devastation, houses and churches were plundered and burnt, the greatest part of inhabitants massacred...". Saywell said, "It is related of them that they behaved after the manner of wild beasts slaying all who came their way." And P. Warner opined that "Nothing so dangerous had ever been seen in England." It was imperative that the unruly and undisciplined host of invaders should be stopped and English preparations to do this went ahead.

As King Stephen was occupied in the south with unruly subjects he ordered Thurstan, Archbishop of York, the Lieutenant of the North to deal with the Scottish menace. Although old and infirm and prevented from attending the eventual battle by illness, he was very astute in the preliminaries both uniting the many facets of the English baronial interests and depicting this as a "holy war" of the Christian defenders of religious faith against the barbarian hordes. He issued a spirited pastoral which emphasised the worthiness of the cause and that anyone dying for it would receive absolution from sins, and had this read by priests from all pulpits.

It is said that from towns and villages came streams of armed men headed by priests to join the "Holy War" and "It bore more the look of a holy pilgrimage than the preparation for a great battle" ("Yorkshire Archaeological Journal Vol 10" - Alex Leadman). To give this religious fervour a focus Thurstan invented the famed holy "Standard" which was taken into the fray, gave the Battle its name and entered the meaning "raising the Standard" into the English dictionary.

The Standard comprised a ship's mast from the Convent at Beverley mounted on a four wheeled cart bearing at the top a silver pyx containing the Blessed Sacrament and hung with the banners of St Peter of York, St John of Beverley and St Wilfred of Ripon. Hugo de Sotevagina the Archdeacon of York wrote this couplet on the base of the pole:

"Dicitur a stando standarum, quod stetit illic
Militiae probitas vincere sive mori."
("Standard, from stand, this fight we aptly call
Our men here stood to conquer or to fall.")

Rallying to Thurstan came the flower of the northern barony with their followers: Robert de Brus and his son Adam de Brus; Bernard de Baliol with troops direct from King Stephen; Walter le Gross, Earl of Abermarle; Richard de Curcy; William Fossard; Ralph Hanselyn; Robert de Ferrers with the Derbyshire men; Walter de Gaunt leading the Normans and Flemings; Walter L'Espec who later founded Rievaulx

Figures of the Standard

and Kirkham abbeys becoming a monk; Roger de Mowbray; Alan Percy; William de Percy; Robert de Stuteville; William Peverell who led the Nottinghamshire men; Gilbert de Lacy (the only English knight killed) and his brother Ilbert de Lacy; Eustace Fitz-John; and Ralph Nowell, Bishop of Orkney deputising for Thurstan.

The English army moved from York to Thirsk where Baliol and de Brus were sent forward to parley with King David. Their overtures were turned aside and the English army moved forward through Aluerton (Elfretun) to take up position three miles north of the town to await the battle. The battlefield was between the Darlington - Northallerton road (A167) and Deighton Lane on the site of Standard Hill Farm where the English army, according to early writers, were regaled by great rallying speeches from Walter de L'Espec, Robert de Brus and particularly Ralph Bishop of Orkney. A close wedge formation characterised the English army's main body drawn up around the "Standard" between Standard Hill Farm and Scots Pits Lane. Well-armoured Knights were the back-line, fronted by a line of spearmen, and the primary attacking line in the very front were archers with some spearmen and armoured foot knights. Finally to protect the open land to the west a troop of English cavalry was situated approximately on the line of the Northallerton - Yafforth Road north of Northallerton Church.

Facing the English to the north were the Scots with the front centre of their focus of attack the Galloway Picts whose leader Fergus Lord of Galloway had insisted they filled this key offensive position. Behind these 6000 Galwegians were cavalry under the King's son Prince Henry on the right of the line, footmen in the centre commanded by William Lord Allerdale and the Earl of Strathean, and on the left Lowland Scots led by Earl Cospatrick of Dunbar. King David stationed himself with his personal bodyguard on the left of the army just beyond the present Deighton turn.

The battle started in the very early morning - probably between 5 and 6 am and lasted for only two hours. It was crude with no strategy or tactics and the two armies rushing headlong at each other. The Scottish achilles heel was soon exposed - that of having the Galwegians in the forefront, because though they were fierce with reckless courage, they were armed only with short swords or pikes and were ill-clad as writers reported "with kilts leaving their buttocks half naked." They charged wildly forward yelling their battlecry "Albanigh! Albanigh!" but under-armed and ill-dressed they were no match for the better armed and clothed English in face to face conflict.

Additionally they found themselves under a hail of arrows from the English archers "who cut them down like standing corn in front of the sickle" (P.M. Turner). Aldred of Rievaulx who witnessed the battle wrote, "Like a hedgehog bristling with quills, so you might see a Galwegian bristling with arrows, yet still brandishing his sword." Every contemporary chronicler emphasised the devastating effect of the English arrows, as did Sir Walter Scott centuries later when he wrote about "Northallerton Field" in "Ivanhoe" making much of the English archers and the "good yew-bow":

> "To the right ear the cords they bring -
> At once ten thousand bowstrings ring,
> Ten thousand arrows fly."

Whilst the Scottish failure continued in the centre of the battlefield, Prince Henry and his cavalry were driving the English cavalry back towards Northallerton with some success. However, a rumour spread amongst the Scots that King David had been killed and with this added to the set-back in the centre, the Scots began to lose heart and to retreat. King David endeavoured to rally the Scots on the left of the line but this was to no avail and he and his retinue abandoned the field and retreated to Carlisle. Meanwhile Prince Henry engaged the English cavalry

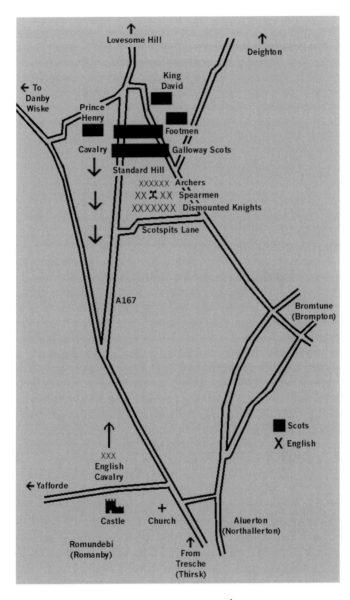

Map 4. Battle of the Standard 22nd August 1138

Battle of the Standard Monument erected in 1910

briefly but he too realising the hopelessness of the Scots' cause escaped from the battlefield and arrived at Carlisle three days later where King David anxiously awaited him.

Ultimately England's victory was complete and the routed Scots were pursued throughout Yorkshire and the northern counties, and evidence of Scottish troops being slain elsewhere has emerged such as the discovery of forty skeletons in 1855 at Kirby Wiske Rectory. The most conservative estimate of Scottish dead on the field or in flight was 10,000 with the norm being 12,000. Many of these were buried to the south behind the battlefield in the appropriately named "Scots Pits Lane" running from the Northallerton-Darlington Road towards Deighton Lane. This disposition of the Scots Pits Lane graves behind the English lines is one of the most intriguing features of the Battle of the Standard and several theories have been propounded regarding this. Obviously the answer is crucial to the course of the battle and the most tenable solutions are either that the Scots broke through the English lines or the English deliberately let the main body of the Scots soldiers through their ranks. In either case the battle would turn around with the Scots now fighting adjacent to Scots Pits Lane where they were slain and buried in pits.

Although the English were decisively victorious they did not press home their advantage and eventually in April 1139 by the Treaty of Durham King Stephen granted Prince Henry the Earldom of Northumberland excluding Newcastle and Bamborough, in return for which King David and Prince Henry swore fealty to King Stephen. Neither was the battle crucial in ending the English - Scottish warfare which continued for nearly three centuries.

Essentially, however, it did stop the Scottish menace which threatened northern English civilisation and it is still commemorated locally in various ways. A figure of the "Standard" is featured on the Northallerton Coat of Arms, and the Allertonshire School and Northallerton College badges. Finally, central to the battlefield on the Darlington to Northallerton Road, is the Standard monument erected in 1910 for £26 by public subscription on the initiative of Northallerton banker W S Charlton, and constructed by local craftsmen - Dan Oakley (stone work) and Charles Fowler (copper plate inscription).

Northallerton Castle

Impressions of the ruins of Northallerton Castle

By the time of the Battle of the Standard a castle stood at Northallerton, on Castle Hills but nearer to the town than the site of the Roman camp. According to John Leland, Henry VIII's historiographer who detailed the area in 1538, "W.N.W. from the Bishop's Palace (now the cemetery site) be ditches and the Dungeon Hille wher the Castelle of Alverton sum tyme stoode. No part of the Walles thereof now apperith." The castle was erected by Rufus, Bishop of Durham around 1130 and said to have been improved in 1142 by his successor William Cumin.

Hugh Pudsey, another Bishop of Durham greatly strengthened and extended Northallerton Castle in 1174 and it evidently awed contemporaries by its massive size astride Castle Hills, towering over and commanding the whole surrounding area. Henry II had a policy of removing all "adulterine fortifications" which threatened his power and his ability to control the barons. This certainly applied to Pudsey's castle at Northallerton particularly in view of its strategic position and prominence and indeed in 1177 according to Hovenden, a contemporary writer, Henry ordered the razing to the ground of "castellum novum de Alverton" (the new castle of Northallerton).

The Bishop's Palace

Stones and materials from the Northallerton Castle were undoubtedly used to build the Bishop of Durham's Palace, which was constructed on "motte and bailey" specifications - "At the left fide of Northallverton a little from the Chirche is the Bishop of Dyrham's Palace, strong of Building and well motid" (Leland 1538). Although no exact data is available it probably dates to around 1200, just after the dismantling of the larger Northallerton Castle and it served as a residence of successive Bishops of Durham until approximately 1600 in the form of a castellated manor house.

It is quite possible that a Saxon or earlier fortification existed on the Bishop of Durham's Palace site. On October 28th 1904 Edward Wooler FSA of Darlington an eminent local historian and archaeologist wrote to the "Darlington and Stockton Times" strongly protesting at what he entitled "Vandalism at Northallerton." The town cemetery had been laid out here in 1856 and Wooler was inveighing against the Northallerton and Romanby Burial Board filling up the ditches (which had been the Palace moat) on the northern side with rubbish "to my horror and indignation" because he asserted this was the location of

Saxon earthworks or even earlier fortifications. Having minutely examined the site Wooler was convinced of its ancient origins and rarity. Perhaps future archaeological research employing scientific modern methods will shed light on the originations of this intriguing site, which at present clearly shows evidence of a bailey surrounded by a moat with a "motte" (mound) on the south-western side.

King John, who would be a guest of the Bishop of Durham, visited Northallerton with his retinue on a tour of the Northern Counties on Friday 20th June 1212 leaving for Easingwold the next day. The King and his suite again resided at Northallerton on Saturday 1st September, remaining on Sunday and leaving on Monday for Darlington; the following Thursday 6th September the King and Court returned from Durham staying overnight at Northallerton before going to Knaresborough on Friday morning. King John and his retainers again stayed overnight at Northallerton on Monday 16th September 1213 going to Knaresborough early the following morning. In 1236 Henry III stayed twice whilst visiting Durham. It is quite probable that on these occasions the Kings resided at the Bishop of Durham's Palace as he did have a residence by then in Northallerton which is evidenced by episcopal charters issued by the Bishops of Durham "at Alverton," such as liberties being granted to the burgesses of Hartlepool by the Bishop "in situ" at Northallerton on 3rd October 1230.

At the end of the thirteenth century and into the fourteenth frequent royal visitors resided at the Bishop's Palace in connection mainly with the English - Scottish wars for which Northallerton was frequently used as a rendezvous for the various components of the English army before they went north to fight. Edward I was the most frequent royal visitor: 13th April 1291, 15th and 16th August 1292, 20th January 1293, 9th and 10th October 1296, in July 1298 (when the English army assembled at Northallerton prior to their victory at the Battle of Falkirk on the 22nd July) 7th March 1302, 27th and 28th April 1303 and 1st October 1304. On one of these visits the Bishop of Durham presented the King with a white palfrey and reference was made in the episcopal accounts concerning the upkeep of the swans which swam in the moat. Edward II visited 6th and 8th April 1312 and Edward III July 1327.

In 1317 the Bishop's Palace was attacked, rifled and occupied by Sir Gosselin Denville, a member of an honourable family from Northallerton, with a considerable band of ruffians assisting him. Denville became one of the most notorious robbers of his day. Rymer in "Records of Public Executions at York" says that he and his gang were only taken after a desperate conflict with the Sheriff and his 500 men and taken to York to the scaffold, amidst the general jubilation of the local people.

With peace restored the Bishop's Palace remained the town's foremost residence, with the Bishop of Durham occasionally staying there, until the sixteenth century. The most notable and best documented visit was from the 17th to 19th July 1502 when Princess Margaret, the eldest daughter of Henry VII, sojourned here with her extensive retinue en route to marry James IV of Scotland - an historic liaison as their grandson James VI of Scotland and James I of England united the Scottish and English crowns in 1603.

In 1534 "the scite of the mansion" was valued at £241.11s.3d. and of course John Leland described the Bishops Palace as strongly established in 1538. And yet a century later it was derelict and when Roger Gale wrote in 1739 - "now there is not a stone left, several houses in the town having built or repaired out of these ruins." Earlier in 1658 Richard Franck in "Northern Memoirs" had said it was "demolished with age and the ruins of time, and serving as a receptacle for bats and buzzards, owls and jackdaws."

The final death knell for the Bishop's Palace tolled on 26th September 1663 when in a letter to John Danby, Gent, the Bishop's steward, tenant of Hall Garth (which was adjacent to the north east of the Bishop's Palace and now the site of the newer part of the cemetery), Dr John Cosin, Bishop of Durham, authorised the use of the stone of the "mannour house" to be used to repair the decayed Castle Mills and:

> "to require you to suffer Thomas Lascelles,or some appointed by his order, to take downe and carry away from the said mannour house, one hundred and twenty fother, for the works afforesaid; as also for repairing some other defects in the markett place in North Allerton.
> And this shall be your sufficient warrant herein.
> Given under my hand and seal manuel, this 26th of September, in the year of our Lord God 1663 Jo Duresme."

Although the Bishop's Palace was dismantled over three hundred and thirty years ago many of its stones remain in the fabric of the town's older buildings and periodically stones are unearthed in the cemetery during grave digging operations which clearly belong to the Bishop's Palace. Mother Shipton the prophetess of Knaresborough born in 1487 has the last word on the Bishop of Durham's Palace at Northallerton. She forecast that the moat would be filled successively with water, trees and blood: it was of course abundant with water originally, in the last century trees have sprung up in it to fringe the old cemetery and if the reception of dead bodies into the cemetery is allowable the final part of her prophecy has been fulfilled!

Castle Soke Mills

A corn mill existed in Northallerton near to the Bishop's Palace in medieval times known as Castle Soke Mills which may have been in decline by 1664 because Bishop Cosin ordered John Danby, his steward of the manor of Northallerton to enforce all the citizens of "North Allerton and its Parish" to have their corn ground at these mills.

However, by 1812 the mills must have been defunct because according to Saywell "the foundations of the ancient Castle Soke Mills dam were discovered and many loads of good stone carried away." The exact location of these mills is unknown but they were almost certainly on Willow Beck bankside next to the Bishop's Palace on the eastern verge of Castle Hills.

Medieval Items

There were many important or interesting events and enactments concerning medieval "Allerton". In 1166 the soke of Northallerton was amerced (fined) ten marks (£6. 13s.4d) for putting a man to the judgement of water, without the knowledge or presence of the king's servants. Incidentally this was a barbarous legal process as the accused was bound and thrown into a pond - if he sank he was guilty and if he floated he was innocent!

Philip de Poitou in 1195 was chosen as Bishop of Durham by royal association and patronage rather than religious worth - he was a Privy Councillor and one of Henry II's favourites. He was elected at Northallerton in 1195 by the monks assembled there in the presence of Hubert Archbishop of Canterbury, which was confirmed by a ceremony in the chapter house at Durham Cathedral on 11th January 1196 and he was consecrated by Pope Celestine on 20th April 1197 in Rome. Despite some far-reaching deeds including the foundation of St James Hospital at Northallerton, when he died on 22nd April 1208 he was "buried like a dog" in unconsecrated land although he was later accorded Christian burial in Durham Cathedral.

Extracts from the Exchequer Rolls (royal financial statements) throw interesting light on medieval "Allerton." For example in 1197: "Alluerton owes £8.11s.0½d for a debt of the Bishop of Durham; Roger, son of Jukel de Aluerton owes 40s for a certain house; of the whole amount of £200.5s.10d of tallage 'the town of Aluerton renders account of £30 for this and it owes £19.3s.10d'; John de Romundeby has rendered one mare and owes half a mare."

Medieval "fines" were an easy method of placing on record a family settlement, a gift to a religious body or land settlements. Northallerton examples indicate a developed town and the names of some of the early local citizens. On the 25th November 1218 twelve men were chosen to decide a case concerning three carucates of land in Appleby and amongst these were John of Romundeby, Thomas of Lacel, Thomas of Oterington, Hugh of Watlas and Richard of Leyburn. At Westminster 20 October 1233 Dionise wife of William of Lasceles claimed from Geoffrey of Ocry forty acres of land and 105 acres of meadow as her dowry at Oteryngton; Richard, Master of Alverton Hospital, at Westminster faced claims regarding his advowsons of churches at Oterington in 1245 by Thomas of Oterington and Thornton-le-Street in 1247 by Geoffrey of Uppeschal; and in 1251 at York Adam Smith and his wife Anabel claimed a moiety of a toft in Alverton from William the Blacksmith of Alverton and Clarice his wife.

Several grants are of local interest including: 1153 - 57 Hugh Pudsey Bishop of Durham confirmed to the monks of Rievaulx land at Crosby with the mill, marsh and meadow; 1157-70 the monks of Durham granted to those of Rievaulx "tithes of thraves" of Cowton belonging to the church of Alverton amounting to three marks annually; Robert de Laceles (1154-59) confirmed by his heir Geoffrey with the consent of his brothers William and Robert granted a carucate of land to the monks of Rievaulx consisting of half the town of Morton Grange and all of East Harlsey and Bordelby (Borrowby) for 400 sheep, 10 cows, a bull and an oxen.

Medieval Roots

After the "Harrying of the North" Northallerton developed as a "corridor" town whereby it could be ringed defensively with cattle and livestock herded into the middle for safety. As can be seen from the medieval records it was a well-developed township by the thirteenth

Medieval Pits Excavations – TESCO site

century with the places of major importance to the north – the church and the bishop's palace but the population spreading to the south along the main thoroughfare. The more wealthy citizens dwellings were flanking the main street with boundary lines and property divisions running back at right angles east to west. The poorer classes habitations would be grouped to the rear at the edges or on the verge of the town as it were.

The urban pattern has recently been confirmed by the archaeological survey of "Pre-Construct Archaeology" which identified the distinct east to west divisions and boundaries in the twelfth and thirteenth century with the unearthing too of some structures, medieval pits and wells. It seems also that the settlement of the poorer people away from the main street (towards what is now East Road) was confirmed by pits with eel and fishbone fragments with some evidence of crude manufactures such as glue-making.

Thus the town had physically settled by the thirteenth century into its standard and familiar structure of burgage lines running back from the main street which was largely undisturbed until well into the twentieth century. The thirteenth century too saw the emergence of several crucial strands – the very roots of Northallerton's history concerning: religion; fairs and markets; health and hospitalisation; politics; and the town as a major centre on the main England – Scotland eastern route.

Religion

Norman Church Pillars

Religion was a vital medieval facet of Northallerton and of course the medieval world which basically centred around it. The parish of Northallerton consisted of the borough of Northallerton with the 'mother' church of All Saints, Romanby, Lazenby and the chapelries of Brompton, Deighton and High Worsall. Whether the Northallerton All Saints Parish Church building survived the "Harrying of the North" is unknown but by the beginning of the twelfth century it consisted of an aisless nave with three bays and only a small chancel. The "Victoria History" stated that at that time:

"The nave was probably about 39 feet long and occupied the western portion of the present nave, the chancel being much smaller in length and breadth."

The church was added to in 1120 the work being probably instituted by Bishop William Carilepho of Durham and completed by his successor Bishop Flambard. Remnants of this process now remain as the most ancient part of the present church situated at the north west of the building.

The patronage of the Bishops of Durham can already be seen as vital to the upkeep and development of Northallerton's church and was eventually reflected in the stateliness and grandeur of the present church with its outstanding landmark features for what was essentially a market town. It did indeed become a "Bishop's Church" in medieval times.

Hugh de Pudsey's Durham episcopate saw the addition of a south aisle to the nave and chancel in 1190 and in 1220 substantial alterations took place including the building of an Early English style tower and a new chancel to the east of this. The early thirteenth century too witnessed the incumbency of the first known Vicar of Northallerton, Gilbert de Vere, the presentation and appointment of the successive Vicars lying in the gift of the Prior and monks of Durham Priory.

In 1218 Gualo the papal legate summoned the local clergy to the Northallerton Church at Easter where he gave absolution to some, obliged others to repair to the papal court in Rome, and suspended or deposed others. Around this time the Northallerton Vicarage was built and on 16th June 1231 a Chapel of Ease was granted to Romanby.

There was a continuous dispute between the Archbishops of York and the Bishops of Durham regarding the suzerainty and visitation of several churches in Yorkshire in the Middle Ages. For example in 1281 Archbishop William Wickwane of York excommunicated the Durham churches including "Alverton" but Parliament eventually condemned him to the Tower and to pay a fine of 4,000 marks to the King. Later Robert Bishop of Whitby's dispute about the Church of Skirpenbeck was decided in his favour by the royal Justices who convened their commission in Northallerton Church.

Jewish "Starres" or documents dated 17th June 1237 concerned Aaron the Jew of York who held land in Northallerton. He was vastly rich and important and believed to be the original "Isaac of York" in "Ivanhoe". The Jews were persecuted in medieval times and the King had extracted the great sum of £2666. 13s. 4d. in silver from Aaron. The latter had possessed himself of his lands in Northallerton from Thomas the Steward of the Prior and Convent of Durham at Northallerton and the land was redeemed from Aaron by the Durham Prior and Convent between 1285 and 1289.

Fairs and Markets

Markets have been held at Northallerton from time immemorial and the earliest award of a market appears in a copy of a lease of tolls and premises connected with markets and fairs issued by the Bishop of Durham on 20th July 1772:

"Whereas, our Sovereign Lord King Henry the First, in the Twenty Seventh Year of his Reign, in the Year of our Lord 1127, Did Grant to Robert, then Lord Bishop of Durham, and his Successors, the manor of Allertonshire, with a market every Wednesday at North Allerton…"

Fairs and Markets were the keystones of medieval Northallerton's agricultural and commercial economy and King John in 1200 granted two fairs to Philip Poitou Bishop of Durham at Northallerton: at Candlemas held on 14th February for horses and cattle mainly lasting for a week but sometimes up to a month; and for the feast of St Bartholomew on 5th September for horned cattle and leather and 6th September for sheep.

Later two more Northallerton fairs were granted to the Bishops of Durham by the Crown. St George's Fair was given in 1554 by Queen Mary to Bishop Tunstall on 5th and 6th May for horses, cattle and sheep which became the "fancy fair" or "play fair" and a great resort for young men and the fair sex. Finally St Matthew's Fair was granted by King James I to Bishop William James in 1609/10 on 3rd and 4th October for cattle and sheep.

K.L. McCutcheon has observed that in the medieval times until the nineteenth century "the fair was one of the main links in the system of trade local, national and international…to all classes of people the annual or semi-annual fair was an event of outstanding importance... It was an institution of political, religious, judicial and above all commercial importance." And the weekly markets at Northallerton must be equally recognised as fairs, of which they were a minor version, playing as they did a critical economic role for the town and district. Significantly the market has remained until the present time as an essential feature of the modern town's commerce attracting many visitors to Northallerton weekly on Wednesdays and Saturdays.

During the Middle Ages the men of Northallerton held the town off the Bishop of Durham paying him forty silver marks to secure the profits of the local fairs and the right to hold assizes of bread and ale. Originally the fairs and markets would be held in the vicinity of the churchyard at the North End and the centre of activity was marked by a cross "as a signal for upright intention and fair dealing and designed as a check on worldly spirits."

Later the market moved south from the North End as did the market cross which by the sixteenth century was situated between the

"Shambles" and the Toll Booth, which were both demolished in 1872 and the market cross placed in Mr Jefferson's garden at his Standard House residence, North End. In 1913 the market cross was re-sited in the High Street to the south of the Town Hall, where it remained until October 1987 when it was placed a little to the south opposite the "Black Bull" when the High Street was refurbished.

Health - St James' Hospital

Spital Farm

The third major indicator to the town's future development occurred in the hospitals' sphere, the ethos of which is deeply embedded in Northallerton's character, commencing with the foundation of St James' Hospital by Philip de Poitou, Bishop of Durham 1197-1208. It was situated in the now parish of Romanby on the southern outskirts of Northallerton on the east side of the Northallerton to Thirsk road, the site now being occupied by the derivatively named Spital Farm, whose farmhouse building and surrounding walls contain fabric of the ancient medieval hospital.

Leprosy was a major scourge because of insanitation and overcrowding in towns and St James was principally a leper hospital where thirteen patients were maintained in small beds ("lectalis"). They were to be nursed by gentle female hands humanely and with tempting foods until health returned or death released them from their earthly suffering. Additionally thirteen local poor folk were "relieved" at the hospital gate every eventide with bread and pottage and needy travellers were lodged overnight at the "hospitum" near the gate. Caring for the district's poor and sick for over three centuries established a very firm base for Northallerton's hospital tradition and reputation.

Canon Raine printed three documents regarding the hospital and an Ordinance dated 27th October 1244 is believed to contain the fullest known description of an English medieval hospital. It was issued on the formal ordination of the hospital by Nicholas Farnham, Bishop of Durham who attributed its foundation to a predecessor Philip de Poitou and excused the delay of the ordination.

The ordination delineated the organisation and staffing: the government of the hospital was vested in a warden "custos" who was allowed a servant, two foot boys and three horses; two chaplains, each with his clerk, had charge of the spiritual welfare of the inmates; a baker and a brewer and a boy to help and a cook with his kitchen boy formed the household; five brethren who could be clerics or laymen - one porter or procurator of the poor who received people each night, one butler or keeper of the store, one granger, one larderer, and one gardener. Finally there were to be three sisters who wore the dress and followed the rule of the sisterhood, two of whom were to tend the sick at night and all shared in the household work.

The hospital's endowments were considerable - upwards of two thousand prime agricultural acres including valuable farms on the roads to Thirsk, Boroughbridge and Osmotherley the churches of North Otterington and Thornton-le-Street, half a plough land at Romanby, eight oxgangs at Otterington, the town of Ellerbeck and its mill, possessions in County Durham and elsewhere, and burgages in Northallerton.

The hospital was often the subject of pronouncements by senior ecclesiastics. A bull of Pope Gregory confirmed the hospital with the churches "de Ottrinton and Toruntun in Via" but in 1379 a visitation by Archbishop Alexander of York found the hospital in poor condition with only three infirm patients and almost a 'skeleton staff' their being only one priest, no brethren and two sisters one of whom Constance de

Fencoates was wearing secular dress and dwelling with the Master, William de Appleby! Things had improved, however, in 1397 when Pope Boniface IX confirmed John Hyldyard as Warden "of the hospital of Allerton." And well known local names appear often such as when in 1272 the Master of St James confirmed as the successor to Adam de Brompton as Vicar of "Thornton in Strata", John de Rostona (John Rutson).

In 1540 St James was dissolved with the "lesser monasteries" at which time there was "a Master, three chaplains, four brethren, two sisters and nine poor people with revenues valued at: £58. 10s. 10d. per annum in the whole and £56. 2s. 2d. clearly." (Tanner -'Notitia Monastica' 1744). With a duplicity common in such matters at the time Richard Morysine (Morison) who was one of Henry VIII's Privy Councillors was made the Master of St James Hospital which he surrendered to the Crown on 19th May 1540, it being referred to as: "Hospitalis Sancti Jacobi juxta North Allerton."

Richard Morysine (now the late Warden and soon to be knighted) was granted St James Hospital in 1541, leased it on 4 March 1545 to his servant John Combes at a rent of £52. 17s. 0d. and then conveyed it to Henry VIII on 7th July 1545 who included it among the endowments of Christ Church, the Oxford University College when he founded this in 1546. Christ Church became one of the most prestigious of the Oxford University Colleges and the episode concerning St James Hospital wherein Morysine had been awarded the hospital by the Crown and then given it to the King, prompted Bulmer to observe in his Directory of North Yorkshire 1890: "thus what was left for the benefit of the poor has been appropriated to the education of the rich."

The archives of Christ Church describe the 1546 endowment as: "In Yorkshire lately of Richard Morrysone and once of the hospital of St James (Northallerton) lands at Romanby, Osmundesley (Osmotherley), Silton, Nunhouse, Thornton, Northetringtone, Ellerbeck, Twyselle, Long Newtone." Down the years the estate was called "The Grange" and in 1759 the land at Romanby, Thornton-le-Moor, Thornton-le-Beans plus the churches at North Otterington and Thornton-le-Street were worth £362. 10s. 0d. rental per annum.

Land disputes sometimes occurred such as a Bill of Complaint in 1635 by the Dean and Chapter of Christ Church against locals including Richard Metcalfe, Francis Lassells, James Meeke and John Talbot. Property was usually let on a long-time basis but sometimes for a shorter lease of twenty-one years as in a notice in the "York Courant" of 22nd

September 1741 concerning the "Corn Tythe of Thorneton le Moore and Thorneton le Beans...and the farm called Spital Farm near Northallerton." Eventually the land and property began to be sold by Christ Church starting in 1817 with 865 acres in the Manor of Ellerbeck. Then within the last hundred years the bulk of the Christ Church holdings have been sold including:

The "Burgages" in Northallerton - 16 November 1898
and 19 November 1902
Street Farm   Thornton-le-Street, 44 acres,1921
Spital Farm   Thirsk Road, 195 acres, 1947
Watergate Farm Thirsk Road, 157 acres, 1947
Longlands Farm Thirsk Road, 115 acres, 1947
Thornton-le-Beans, 6 acres   and 17 acres, 1947.

By the late 1990s Christ Church still owned some land locally around Ellerbeck and their Dean and Chapter had remaining interests in the churches of North Otterington and Thornton-le-Street.

Lazenby Medieval Chapel

There was another medieval religious establishment near to Northallerton at Lazenby which was termed St Mary's hospital but was more probably a collegiate chapel. It was founded on 19th February 1290 by John de Lythegranes and his wife Alice for a master and six chaplains for the celebration of masses for the souls of the founders and other "Christian people", dedicated to the Blessed Virgin and endowed with the whole manor of Lazenby. A mandate was issued to its warden John Sleight by the Archbishop of York William Greenfield on 25th January 1314-15 – "Domine Johanni Sleght, custodi hospitalis de Leysingby" – to help to relieve the poverty of the convent Arden Priory near Hawnby.

However, whether the original intention of the hospital/college was ever fulfilled is uncertain for in 1443 because the endowment was insufficient, the Bishop of Durham obtained a royal licence to assign it to the abbey of Jervaulx which was to supply two chaplains to perform service in the chapel at Lazenby. The effect of this would seem to be that the establishment lost its collegiate character, the last master was Nicholas Hulme appointed in 1425 and it became a simple chantry chapel for two priests appointed by Jervaulx Abbey. This situation existed until and after the Dissolution of the Monasteries in 1535 with the chantry priests in a survey of 1546 John Wylde and Richard Woodenhall by which time Jervaulx had been granted to Matthew Earl of Lennox and his wife Margaret.

Members of Parliament

The fourth and historic milestone for Northallerton concerned parliamentary politics. In 1298 in the 26th year of Edward I's reign the Borough of Northallerton returned two members to Parliament, John le Clerk and Stephen Maunsell. This privilege was not taken up again for 342 years probably because of the monetary factor as all MPs wages and expenses had to be paid by the parliamentary borough's constituents. Eventually in 1640 two Northallerton MPs were returned, Thomas Heblewaite and Sir Thomas Cholmley, followed by two members continually until 1832 when the town lost a member with the passage of the Great Reform Act. Thereafter a single Northallerton MP was returned until the Northallerton constituency was merged into that of Richmondshire in 1885.

Route Centre

The fifth characteristic of Northallerton emphasised in the thirteenth century was the town's crucial role in national communications and human movement as a route centre, stopping place and military rallying point. Frequent royal visits particularly highlighted Northallerton's favourable position mainly in pursuance of the Anglo Scottish wars already noticed in connection with the Bishop of Durham's palace.

A prime example of Northallerton's central involvement in the Scottish - English wars was the prelude to the Battle of Falkirk. Some nobles had sworn allegiance to the Scottish king and refused to attend an English parliament at York. Determined to bring the rebel nobles to book Edward I ordered his army to assemble at "Allerton" from whence he led his army northwards to gain a decisive victory over the Scots at Falkirk in 1298.

The north-south journey and travelling are indicated in the description of a party conveying Robert de Insula from Durham to London in 1274 to seek the king's confirmation of Robert's recent election as Bishop of Durham. They took fifteen days to reach London from Ketton in Durham County and ten days to return. The route was via North Allerton and Boroughbridge which even then was part of the major road south to north which became the Great North Road. Four wheeled ("carectae") and two wheeled ('bigae') vehicles were used drawn by horses and the time taken was probably greater than usual because of the conveniences they would be afforded - for example a stock of herrings was despatched from North Allerton to Doncaster ahead of the party's arrival there.

3

Late Middle Ages (1300-1485)

The Anglo-Scottish Wars

The outstanding and indeed cataclysmic feature of Northallerton's history in the fourteenth century was the Anglo - Scottish conflict. Although the Battle of the Standard of 1138 was important in its own right, it solved nothing in the long run concerning the extreme antipathy and consequent bitter hostilities between the English and Scots. Even after the actual warfare ceased in the 1400s it was an uneasy peace and the antagonism did not end finally until the 1745 rebellion of "Bonnie Prince Charlie" and his Scottish army's defeat at Culloden in 1746.

Edward I's frequent Northallerton visits were prompted by the Scottish - English warfare and several "arrays" or calls to arms were made such as that in 1303 when Harsculpa de Cleasby and his fellows were ordered to assemble at Allerton with 1400 footmen. On 6th and 8th April 1312 Edward II dwelt at the town and at Alverton on 14th January 1315 Sir John Gower, priest, preached to the English army on its way to Scotland at Northallerton.

Meanwhile on 24th June 1314 the Scots under King Robert the Bruce had won a famous and decisive victory over the English at Bannockburn. After this battle an expedition in 1318 under Sir James Douglas made a dash at York, ravaging the country with fire and sword. They were given 1000 marks (£666. 66) to save Northallerton by its citizens, but they still sacked the town and burned the church. The Scots mercilessly devastated the north of England and only the castles and walled towns escaped.

It seems likely that the town was again laid waste both in 1319 and 1322 when the English were defeated at Myton on Swale and Byland respectively. Direct proof of the town's plight was its exemption in 1319 from paying the King's taxes on the basis that it had been ruined by his enemies and in 1323 the proctor of Northallerton Parish Church was given licence to collect alms throughout the country for rebuilding the church burned by the Scots. Edward II issued a commission in 1323 to every place in the wapentake of Alverton to duly array every available man between sixteen and sixty.

When Edward III (1327-1377) succeeded to the throne although only fourteen he immediately marched against the Scots and the writ to raise the troops was dated at Alverton in 1327. This was his first visit to Northallerton followed by others in 1331, 1333 (with his Queen Phillipa) and 1356. The tide of the Scottish wars turned in England's favour in 1333 when the Scots were defeated - at Halidon Hill where the ruthless efficiency of the English longbow was first demonstrated. Levies continued to be called for and those of 1334 and 1336 were ordered to rendezvous at Northallerton. It is hard to imagine how Northallerton and the other North Riding towns survived this dislocation to their life which was essentially agricultural and market orientated and indeed in 1336 the benefices of Northallerton and Allertonshire were among those in the North unable to pay the tax of the quadrennial tenth.

The last heavy Scottish attack came in 1346 when David Bruce penetrated as far as York. Northallerton's fate was not recorded but Hollinshed says "foure tounes only" were exempt from burning: Hexham, Corbridge, Durham and Darlington. So Northallerton again could have been subject to sacking. A more peaceful existence is indicated by the apparent rebuilding of the Northallerton Church between 1345 and 1381 (though this could have been later that century). However, as a virtual "border" town in these troublesome times, the fear of the Scots must have been endemic in generations of Alvertonians.

The Scottish menace remained the major disruptive influence of the fourteenth century and perhaps the last word on this appears in medieval ecclesiastical tax assessments before the Scottish attacks in 1292 and after in 1318. In 1292 Northallerton was the richest settlement in the area paying the highest taxes of 1467 shillings for the "Valor of Pope Nicholas" but by 1318 this had been reduced to 533s. Allertonshire's tax assessment of 1.47 pence per acre in 1292 had sunk to 0.66 pence in 1318, although despite its privations Allertonshire was the most prosperous wapentake in the North Riding.

All Saints Parish Church

In the 1318 Scots' sacking of the town and church the latter suffered serious damage. The chancel, north transept and aisle were partly destroyed and the tower fell, scorch marked stones in the church particularly at the base of the rebuilt tower still bearing witness to the fiery ruination. After the royal licence in 1323 to collect restoration funds nationally the aisle was rebuilt and lengthened in 1330.

Because of the incidence of bubonic plague "Black Death" nothing further was accomplished in the fourteenth century but the present commanding tower was built in 1420 at the behest of Thomas Langley Bishop of Durham (1406-1437) somewhat to the north east of the previous tower. The old stairway was retained and also parts of the old tower to act as cores to the new one. By 1440 the south aisle exterior was reconstructed, the south aisle widened, the south porch added in its present familiar form, the north aisle was rebuilt and the transepts equipped with wide windows. *[Colour Plate 3]*

The accounts of Durham Priory with regard to the revenue collected from their various parishes in the case of Northallerton give strong indications of the economic vicissitudes and situation of both the church and its lay hinterland. Before the Scots sacking the receipts were £88. 0s. 0d in 1293 but had fallen to £66. 13s. 4d (£66.66) in 1348. Around the onset of the bubonic plague they were £71. 1s. 2d (£71.05) in 1350 declined to £59. 6s. 8d (£59.33) in 1392 and to £51. 0. 0. in 1420 and thereafter slumped further to £38. 13s. 4d (£38.66) in 1446 when there was a levelling out which continued into the next century to £36. 6s. 8d (£36.33) in 1537.

Early Education - Northallerton Grammar School

As often during desolate times something worthwhile arises from the ashes and in Northallerton's case these years saw the establishment of Northallerton Grammar School and two medieval friaries - one Carmelite and the other Austin friars. In total contrast to the warfare, education came to Northallerton in 1322 when "Robert Colstan, clerk was appointed to be rector of Allerton Grammar School to hold at pleasure: datis Dunelmie die St Cuthberti in Marcio AD 1322". The school which is one of the oldest Grammar Schools in the country is notable therefore for great longevity and its continued existence and stability were confirmed by the appointments of three more Masters in the fourteenth century: Robert Drybeck "Magistrum Scolarum de Alverton" was mentioned in 1349; John Podesay was appointed for five years on 5th October 1377 and William of Leeds, Chaplain, for three years on 15th December 1385.

Willelmus Prior Ecclesie Dunelmensis dilecto sibi in Christo Roberto Colatan de Alverton, clerico, salutem in auctore salutis.

Fusis pro te precibus favorabiliter inclinati, regimen scolarum nostrarum de Alverton, te ad eas regendas testimonio quorundam idoneum reputantes, tibi conferimus intuitu caritatis ; Ita quod circa pueros instruendos sub debito iuramenti nobis praestiti diligenciam adhibeas efficacem.

In cujus rei testimonium sigillum nostrum praesentibus apponi fecimus usque ad nostrum beneplacitum duraturis Datis Dunelmie die S. Cutberti in Marcio A.D. 1321.

William, Prior of the Church of Durham, to his beloved in Christ, Robert Colatan of Alverton, clerk, health in the author of health.

Giving favorable attention to the petitions made on your behalf, we confer on you, with a view to charity (intuitu caritatis) the Headmastership of our school (regimen scolarum nostrarum) of Alverton, thinking you, by the testimony given, fit to be Head of it ; so that you use sufficient diligence in instructing boys, as you ought, by virtue of your oath to us.

In witness whereof we have caused our seal to be affixed to these presents, to remain in force during our pleasure. Dated at Durham on S. Cuthbert's Day, in March, in the year of our Lord 1321. i.e. 20th March, 1322.

Northallerton Grammar School Manuscript of 1322

The school was designed as a "Grammar and Song school" attached to Northallerton Parish Church, the masters appointments were by the Durham Convent and Priory (after 1540 the Dean and Chapter of Durham) and all the early appointees were clergymen. From its original foundation the Grammar School was situated until 1909 immediately to the south of the Church on the High Street the site now being occupied by the solicitors' firm Place, Blair and Hatch. From early days it was possible for the brighter pupils to progress to Oxford University for in 1381 Bishop Hatfield issued statutes for eight students to be sent annually to Durham (now Trinity) College - four from Durham city and two each from Howden and Allerton. In the selection of candidates "the influence of the local patron was supreme" (RB Dobson, "Durham Priory").

Unfortunately the careers of the selected Oxford University students from Northallerton Grammar School are unknown, but the school remained for many centuries in a key role in the town producing some famous and a multitude of successful people.

The Northallerton Friaries

Northallerton's medieval friaries make a complete factual contrast: about the Carmelite Friary we know much but about its Austin counterpart very little. The Austin Friary was endowed in 1340 with eight acres by William de Alverton and built on the site of the present "Fleece" inn and the two adjacent houses to the south. It is believed that some fabric of the present "Fleece" belonged to the Friary but there specific knowledge ends although generally, these friars wore a white gown with a black hood, they were a mendicant order (received alms and gifts), they laboured for the first part of the day and spent the remainder in reading and devotion, they had to observe the strictest chastity and on Sunday they were allowed to drink wine - alcohol thus having been drunk on the "Fleece" premises for 650 years!

Information on the Carmelite Friary, the site of which now occupies the Friarage Hospital, is abundant. It was established on the east side of Northallerton in 1356, the foundation being ascribed to John Yole a Northallerton merchant, Thomas Hatfield the Bishop of Durham and Edward III. To found the Friary John Yole gave a croft called "Tentour" and a pasture of three acres and one rood which was confirmed by Edward III and it is believed that the next year Thomas Hatfield gave six more acres. Edward III who stayed at the Bishop's

The ancient 'Fleece' inn on the Austin Friary site

Palace Northallerton in 1356, carried out a commission to build the Friary and Lord Randolph Neville built a complete church within it, in which Helena the wife of John Yole was buried.

The Carmelite Order was founded in Palestine in 1122 and eventually there were thirty-seven Carmelite houses in England. To emphasise the Northallerton Friary's prestige Walter Kellaw its first Prior was also Provincial (leader) of the Carmelites in England, he being buried at the Northallerton Friary in 1367, as later was an Earl of Westmorland. This could have been Earl Ralph de Neville whose will of 1440 benefited the Friary and there were nineteen other known benefactors including Sir John Clervaux of Croft (1390), Richard Lord Scrope of Bolton Castle (1400), Lady Isabella of Fauconberg (1401), Sir Thomas Boynton of Acklam (1402), Sir Alexander Neville (1457) and Sir Fitz-Randolph, Lord of Middleham (1457). Amounts bequeathed varied and in return the Carmelites prayed for men's and benefactors' souls.

These benefactions and "alms" received were the basis of the Carmelites' existence for they were a mendicant order reliant on gifts and possessing only the Friary land. They were called the "White Friars" because they wore white hoods and cloaks, they were vegetarian,

A Carmelite Friary skeleton unearthed in 1954 – Priory Close

dined communally and shared everything. A very strict order, they rose early, kept silence for long periods, remained in separate cells in meditation and one source reported that they slept in coffins. The Prior was elected by the "freres" and the order was dedicated to St Mary.

For nearly two hundred years the Carmelite Friary was a notable institution in the town but like St James' Hospital and the Austin Friary its days were numbered with Henry VIII's "dissolution of the lesser monasteries". On 22nd December 1539 William Wommefray the Prior and nine friars surrendered the Northallerton Carmelite Friary to the Crown. In 1553 the site was granted to Richard and Henry Vavasour and has been held variously since by Robert Raikes Fulthorpe, William Wailes, John Dixon (1858), William Thrush Jefferson (1880), Cuthbert Wilson, James O'Malley, North Riding County Council (1939) and the Ministry of Health (1948).

The Friary site extended from the present location of the Friarage

Hospital across Brompton Road (which three centuries ago was a minor track called Brompton Lane) to the High Street to include the Rutson Hospital area. By 1858 "no vestige remains save the modern wall of the stone from old fabric" wrote Whellan about the Friarage and this applies today with the most recent disappearance, the original stone entrance gate on Brompton Road leading to the High Street which was demolished in 1958.

From time to time relics of the Carmelite Friary have been unearthed. In the mid nineteenth century when a gravel pit was commercially developed on the site off the south east of Brompton Road, cartloads of human bones were taken away, a part of the Carmelite graveyard having been disturbed. Similarly in 1887 six perfect skeletons were discovered along with stained glass and glazed tiles which were undoubtedly from the Carmelites' Church. More human bones have been found on the site during excavations in 1938 and 1954. By a great coincidence of time exactly four hundred years after the Carmelite Friary which existed to save souls closed in 1539, a hospital aimed to save lives was developed on the exact site in 1939 – the start of the Friarage Hospital.

Medieval Information

Three vital sources in the fourteenth century give a good insight into medieval Northallerton, its constitution and its people: an Inquisition held in 1334; a 1358 Table of Pontage; and the Poll Tax of 1377.

Inquisition of 1334

Firstly a most important Inquisition was held in 1334 (7 Edward III) because Anthony Bek the Bishop of Durham 1284 - 1311 had levied £20 yearly on the town not as a right but by extortion and a similar exaction against the town had been made when the see of Durham was vacant and in the King's hands. Northallerton appealed against the impositions and the subsequent inquisition (which ruled in Northallerton's favour) shed much light on the medieval town. It was in the hand of Ralph de Neville who conducted the proceedings and entitled "Inquisito De Libertatibus Villae De North Alverton."

The inquiry found that: the men of this town were free and of free condition ("liberi et libera conditionis"); they held the town with its "tofts" and "crofts"; they held the market and fair thereof with all the profits of the Bishop of Durham at an annual rent of 40 marks of silver; and in all the pleas of lands and tenements within the town, the townsmen would form a jury.

Alvertonians had the right to have the "Reve" present if they were impleaded in the court of the Bishop of Durham; the latter had plea of "hymsoken" (forcible entry), "bludewite" (bloodshed), "replevin" (recovery of goods) and amends of the assize of bread and ale; and he also had liberties in the Court Leet and Court Baron, which had many copyholders paying a moderate fee.

The findings regarding the Northallerton complaint were that Anthony Bek, Bishop of Durham deceased, and the late and present King had taken £20 from the townsmen by extortion or against their will. It is of interest that the markets and fairs were so well established and that the Toll-Booth played a key role with courts and standard measures held there. Here in 1334 the Toll-Booth was the first official civic public building mentioned in Northallerton's history.

This royal inquisition was of particular interest because it highlights the role of the Bishop of Durham in relation to Northallerton and also indicates the inherent independence, attitude and spirit of those who led the town. Although the Bishop of Durham was the over-lord of Allertonshire much of the land was held as sub-tenants directly to the Crown and in 1315 he only held direct control over seven vills – Romanby, Brompton, Borrowby, Knayton-cum-Brawith, Thornton-le-Beans, Osmotherley and Sowerby-under-Cotliffe with the latter being awarded to Sir James Strangways in the 1490s leaving six vills. Additionally, although his chief officers the Steward, Bailiff and Receiver were always in place they were all local people and with Durham's distance away (probably a two days' journey) Northallerton essentially was virtually self-governing.

As Christine Newman asserts in "Late Medieval Northallerton": Northallerton was "the focal point of the administrative, economic and social activity within the liberty (of Allertonshire)" and the royal inquisition of 1334 confirmed its rights and indicated "an increasingly assertive community."

1358 Pontage Tolls

Secondly in 1358 a table of "Pontage Tolls" (Bridge tolls) concerning Northallerton discloses much information as to the actual goods, food, raw materials and animals the town dealt with. Also it is significant in connection with the importance of the Great North Road running through Northallerton, that the King (Edward III) gave a grant of pontage for the "North brigg" (North Bridge) at the north entrance to the town in 1358.

Table of Tolls			
Northallerton Pontage (North Bridge) 1358			
Herring	3d (boatload)	10 pigs	1d
Grain load	¼d	10 goats	1d
Seafish load	½d	10 hams	½d
Lamprey doz	1d	5 salted pigs	½d
Sturgeon tun	1d	Malt load	¼d
Salmon fresh or salted	¼d	Salt quarter	¼d
Cod salted	¼d	Goods over 5s	¼d
'Hard Fish' 100	2d	Goods over 10s	½d
10 Fleeces	¼d	Brushwood cartload	1d
1 Sack Wool	2d	1 wey of grease/tallow	1d
Cloth Pack	3d	Garlic 2000	1d
Cloth Load	½d	Wine tun	2d
1 whole cloth	1d	Wine pipe	1d
100 worsteds	2d	Ashes load	½d
100 worsted coverlets	1d	Wood quarter	1d
100 'Aylesham' linen	1d	100 boards	½d
1 clothof silk/samite/		Timber cartload	1d
brocade	½d	Millestone	½d
1 cloth of plain silk	½d	Honey load	1d
1 horse/mare	½d	1 cwt brass/copper	1d
1 ox/cow	½d	Bark cartload	1d
1 hide/salt/tanned/fresh	¼d	Faggots 100	¼d
1 bale 'cordewain'	2d	Cwt avoir dupois	1d
100 wool fells	1d		
100 skins lambs/rabbits/			
hares etc	½d		

Northallerton North Bridge tolls of 1358

Poll Tax 1377

Thirdly an idea of the population of Northallerton can be gleaned from the Poll Tax of 1377. The Poll Taxes of 1377, 1379 and 1381 represented a new concept of taxation because whereas before taxes were assessed on lands or goods, now the Poll tax was money payable on "heads." The 1377 Poll Tax was levied at a flat rate of 4d per head on males and females fourteen and over in a town and was more useful than the 1379 and 1381 returns because there was less evasion. Caution is of course necessary too with the 1377 figures with evasion and other reasons but it is a reasonable comparative guide to the population.

According to the Poll Tax in 1377, London had 23,314 taxpayers, York 7,248 and Allerton (Northallerton) 372. Richmond in 1377 was 370, Helmsley 282 and Pickering 420 whilst figures for such other North Riding market towns as Thirsk, Stokesley and Easingwold are not available. Brumpton was 114, Romandby 78, Dighton 62, Wynton 25, Ellerbeck 34, Themylby 57, Ossemonderley 55, North Otryngton 21, Beroghby (Borrowby) 104, Ainderby wyth the steple 51, Morton 65, Thrintoft 49, Warlaghby 29, Jafforth 54, Newby Wiske 40, Danby Wiske 100, Sandhoton 42, Croft 157, Dalton super Tees 58, Smeton 62, North Couton 37, South Couton 49, East Couton 83, Eryom (Eryholme) 82, Welberi 76 and Est Harlsaay 84.

An estimate of the population based on the 1377 Poll Tax gives Northallerton 744 persons (372 taxpayers), Romanby 156 (78), and Brompton 228 (114). It is interesting to note the importance of the Great North Road which passed through Northallerton as reflected in such populations for that time of Great Smeaton 124 (62), Dalton-on-Tees 115 (58) and Croft particularly 314 (157).

The Black Death

The "Black Death" bubonic plague carried by rat fleas had arrived in England in 1348 and exterminated over a third of the population according to some sources. Regarding Yorkshire it appeared at Hull in May 1349 and spread immediately to York. By the end of the summer it affected the whole county and the scourge continued for several years with devastating effects. For example in 1361-62 a third of the clergy in Richmond and Catterick deaneries died and in the North Riding "vacant holdings and abandoned fields" abounded. No record of Northallerton's plight remains but it must have suffered losses in common with the rest of the county.

The 1377 Poll Tax figures were arrived at after the worst Scottish effects earlier in the century and the onset of the bubonic plague which had serious and ongoing effects. From all the evidence available it is impossible to estimate the Northallerton and Allertonshire population by the end of the century and early Tudor times but it is probable that by then it had not risen above the 1377 level.

Late Medieval Military Scene

In the fifteenth century England was torn by the long drawn out civil war termed the Wars of the Roses because it was fought between the Houses of York and Lancaster vying to control the throne. Remarkably because of its strategic position and its proximity to both of the armies Northallerton had no known involvement in the conflict. Saywell, however, says "It is very probable, that the town was directly or indirectly the scene of various skirmishes, military gatherings and levies." This though is only conjecture and Northallerton and district experienced much more settled times than previous centuries.

There were only two militaristic movements recorded in the fifteenth century before the Tudor rule and both were of a minor nature. Firstly in 1405 the followers of Mowbray and Archbishop Scrope assembled at Northallerton and twice in July of the same year Henry IV (1399-1413) stayed at the Bishop's Palace in the town whilst reducing the North to quietude. The other military involvement was in 1456 when Sir William Plumpton rode through Northallerton with forces mustered by Henry Percy, Earl of Northumberland to make an incursion upon the Scottish Borders. Sir William had secretly married Joan Wintringham and lest he was killed in battle he notified Sir Robert Littester of his secret at Northallerton!

Records and Documents

Bishop Langley, the Lord Bishop of Durham (1406-1437) had a "strongly fortified palace at Northallerton" ("Yorkshire Archaeological Journal") and his Registers made many references to "Alverton." Some of these concern St James' Hospital which in 1409 the Master John Newton, reported to be in a "ruinous state." Others confirmed the grants in wills to the Carmelite friars of Northallerton: Robert Wyclyf, Rector of Hutton Rudby XXs in 1423, Robert Conyers of Stockton 6s. 8d. (1431) and John Palman a "towell de werke" (1436). Very significantly the Bishop issued several edicts from "Alverton" when he was resident there in his Palace such as the appointment in November 1430 of Richard Corston as Master of St James' Hospital on the death of Henry Strangways.

Other documents of the period have some significance especially with the old local family names referred to. For example in 1424/5 4th February "lands in the territories of Northallerton and Oversilton" were granted to Robert Marshall, William Fencotes of Ripon, Robert Busei of Berughby (Borrowby) and John Grenewood. Drawn up at "Northalverton" it was witnessed by William Lascelles, John Knayton, Thos de Kylvyngton, Thos Spycer and Peter Multon. Some wills are worth recalling for their quaintness: on 6th April 1499 Johanna Smyth de Northalverton bequested - "a towel to the high alter, a brass pot to the church, to Elizabeth Scrube my daughter, tway dublers, and a dash of pewter, a mat, one pair of sheets, a gowne, and a ketyll, to Robert Seroby a brass pot."

Fifteenth Century Buildings

Two important buildings were established close to the south of the Parish Church on opposite sides of the main street – the Guild Hall on the east side in 1444 and the Maison Dieu on the west by 1476.

There was a "Gild or Fraternity" established in Northallerton Parish Church and on 9th June 1441 Cardinal Kemp, Archbishop of York granted an indulgence of 100 days relaxation of penance to all who liberally contributed to the honour and conservation of this Gild or resorted to it on account of devotion to those saints in whose honour it was instituted. Interestingly in the Middleham Household Book of Richard III a sum of "xiiis iiid" is set down to the gild of Alverton" which is the only known recorded link between that king and the town.

The Guild Hall or "House" belonging to the Guild was erected in 1444, being attributed to Cardinal Kemp. Situated on the site of the present Jefferson and Willan solicitors' premises, in an old document held by the late John Boston the Guild Hall was detailed as the place the Northallerton Guild met with the interior containing some curious apartments and their ceilings adorned with coats of arms. In its hey-day it was the scene of North Riding Quarter Sessions and other important events such as the trial of rebels by Sir George Bowes in 1570 after the Rising of the Northern Earls. It acquired much local notoriety after it became the Northallerton Parish Workhouse in 1720 and was finally demolished in 1862.

'Maison Dieu' (House of God) was a medieval hospital established in accordance with the will of Richard More a wealthy Northallerton draper. It existed in 1436 when letters of indulgence were granted of forty days by the Bishop of Durham Thomas Langley regarding the institution but is more commonly dated to 1476 when an indenture conveyed the trusteeship for it to Sir Thomas Strangways. This showed it to be extremely well endowed with about thirty properties of land and tenements given to maintain: the 'Maison Dieu' for thirteen poor people of either sex who were to find two beds for poor travellers, make daily chants and pray for the souls of the founders; and a Chantry set up at the altar of the Trinity in the Northallerton Parish Church with provision also for a chantry priest.

The Richard More charity was under the stewardship of the Earl of Carlisle in the seventeenth century and in 1788 (by which time it was overseered by the Northallerton Select Vestry) the "Maison Dieu" was rebuilt on its original site adjacent to the north of the "Pack Horse Inn" (now occupied by the Wesleyan Chapel) consisting of alms-houses for poor widows. By 1851 six widows were housed there which continued until the 1960s when the last resident widow died and the almshouses became defunct.

At the end of the fifteenth century John Fisher, the Vicar of Northallerton (1491-94) caused a new Vicarage to be built and during this much more settled century it is most probable that housing in the town was increased and improved. The ordinary houses would have slate or thatched roofs and were of the "cruck" rather than "timber posts" construction, the farther north they stood in the Northallerton area.

A schedule of repairs exists dating to around 1450 concerning the Bishop of Durham's peasants' houses in the villages of Knayton, Thornton-le-Beans, Sowerby-under-Cotcliffe, Romanby and Brompton. Ninety buildings belonging to sixty-five tenants were listed, many for minor repairs but thirty five needed major structural alterations and eleven completely rebuilding. Ten "cruck" houses were measured: six had two bays (three pairs of "crucks") and four had one bay (two pairs of "crucks").

The table overpage analyses some of the village houses.

Local Government

The Strangways of Harlsey were the most powerful family in Allertonshire in the fifteenth century. Their ascendancy in the area had been initiated by Justice James Strangways who died in 1442 but was noted by John Leland, Henry VIII's chronicler in his "Itinerary" of 1538 as "Strangwaise the judge" who built the "praty castelle" at West Harlsey, the manor of which he had held since before 1423. Successive Sir Thomas Strangways were the Stewards of Allertonshire for the

Village	Cruck Buildings	Timber framed Buildings	Total
Knayton	9	6	15
Thornton-le-Beans	1	2	3
Romanby	5	-	5
Sowerby-under-Cotcliffe	5	-	5
Brompton	7	-	7
Total	27	8	35

Bishop of Durham with the second Sir Thomas Strangways the Speaker of the House of Commons in 1461. The third Sir James was granted the manor of Deighton by Yorkist Richard III in 1484 which was confirmed by Tudor Henry VII in 1485 and held the Stewardship of Allertonshire for well over thirty years. His death without issue in 1521 marked the end of the Strangways dominance in the area.

By the fifteenth century much more is known about Northallerton's local government than in previous centuries. The town was held of the Bishop of Durham as a mesne borough at a fee farm ("firma burgi") and was granted annually to various townsmen. In 1344 the fee was fixed at 40 silver marks or £26. 13s. 4d (£26.66), which was lowered to £7 in the sixteenth century. The rights included income from the toll booth and profits from the shops therein, all the rents in the "vill of Allerton", income from tolls, tallage, stallage, picage and passage in the time of market and fair and other times and the issues, profits and amercements of the Borough Court.

The administration of all criminal justice in both Northallerton and Allertonshire was in royal hands but the Borough Court at Northallerton regulated the town's tenurial, economic and social affairs. It was held in the toll-booth upper storey (the shops were below) with ordinary sessions held every Friday and conducted by the clerks of the court. The two key meetings were those of the Chief Borough Court which were held on the first Thursday after Michaelmas in September and again at Easter. At the Michaelmas sessions the officials for the year were

The old toll booth at the head of the main street

elected by the joint jurisdiction of the bailiff and a jury made up of freemen of the town held under the Steward of Allertonshire. The town bailiff (the most important official) and four bye-law men, two constables to enforce law and order, two officials to supervise the assize of bread and ale, and two to regulate the selling of meat and fish were elected.

Thus the court was strongly in local hands with the jury of "Magna Inquisito" as it was termed, vested with much authority. The Borough Court greatly influenced the day to day running of Northallerton and in essence the actual effective control of the town was essentially localised.

Emergent North Allerton

And so Northallerton was emerging from the medieval world with a more settled and compact format with a fully re-built church, a well-established grammar school, a medieval hospital and two friaries, steady trade and commerce, and a strongly independent borough and people. The bubonic plague cast a dark shadow as it did over the nation as a whole but a crucial factor had been the cessation of the Anglo-Scottish wars and the dislocation of normal affairs – which may have meant less colourful historic times but resulted in a more stable, urbanised and prosperous town.

4

The Tudors (1485-1603)

National Visitors

Sixteenth century Tudor Northallerton was splendidly ushered in by the royal visit on 17th July 1502 of Princess Margaret, daughter of Henry VIII, progressing to Scotland to marry their King James IV which eventually merged the English and Scottish crowns in 1603 under their grandson James VI of Scotland and James I of England. She was under the protection of the Earl and Countess of Surrey and accompanied by a magnificent royal retinue on her journey via Newark, York, Newbrough Priory, Northallerton, Durham, Newcastle and Berwick to Edinburgh where she was married amidst great pomp and feasting on 8th August 1502 in the chapel of Holyrood House.

John Young, the Somerset Herald, vividly described Princess Margaret's progress north and her marriage celebrations and his still surviving manuscript depicts the Northallerton stage of the bridal journey:

"The XVIIth day of the said Monneth (July) the Quene departed from the said Newbrough to Allerton, and at the Intrynge of the said Place, she was received by the Vicayr and the folks of the Church with the Freres Carmelites in Processyon, and the Bishop Morrey did as before (revested the Princess with the cross at the gate of the Church). From that place she was conveyed, as Custom was, to the Manayar of the said Byschop of Durham.

The XIXth day of the said Monneth, the Queene departed fro Allerton, in sayr Aray and noble Companyd; and Sir James Straungwysch, Knight, Sheryff of the said Lordschyp for the said Bishop, mett hyr welle accompayned."

It is interesting to note here the ancient and close Bishop of

55

Durham – Northallerton connection and his representative Sir James Strangways of Harlsey Castle.

The preparations for the famous Battle of Flodden in 1513 saw another illustrious visit to Northallerton when the Duke of Surrey encamped with the English army here prior to inflicting a decisive defeat of the Scots who lost their King James IV who was killed along with an estimated 11,000 of his countrymen. By coincidence the Scots had crossed the border into England on the 22nd August exactly three hundred and seventy five years to the day since the Battle of the Standard, emphasising Northallerton's long involvement with the English - Scottish warfare.

How exactly the able-bodied males in Northallerton and district were affected by the "call-up" to the army is uncertain but "commissions" were issued in the North Riding to muster men against the Scots' attacks in the preceding centuries. In 1547 Sir William Strickland conducted 600 soldiers from York to Alnwick (passing through Northallerton) of whom 227 were raised in the North Riding, 11 of these from Allertonshire. "Each man received a coat value 3s 4d, 8d a day and ½d a mile conduct money from the place of assembly in his wapentake to Alnwick." Previously Henry VIII had passed an Act in 1512 enforcing practice with the long bow which in Northallerton's case would have centred around the Church Green with arrows probably sharpened in the still very prominent grooves in the Northallerton Church porch and the north western wall.

Cardinal Wolsey the then all-powerful Chancellor of Henry VIII (1509-47) was the third national figure known to visit Northallerton early in the sixteenth century but he caused consternation and retributive repercussions for the people of Romanby on his episcopal visitation in 1523, shortly after his elevation to be Prince Bishop of Durham. Whilst he was "sitting" at Northallerton Wolsey's authority was questioned by the Northallerton vicar, Leonard Hutchinson, a very strong character who had been Master of the University College, Oxford University. Such was Wolsey's wrath that he ordered that Northallerton Church's parochial chapel-of-ease at Romanby should be pulled down and obliterated. This was subsequently carried out with the wall fabric and glebe land of the chapel sold thus destroying an ecclesiastical institution of three hundred years.

The Reformation and the Tudor Church

The original Carmelite Friary doorway on Brompton Road

Shortly after this sorry chapter in Northallerton's ecclesiastical history it suffered further great losses when the Carmelite and Austin Friaries were suppressed as well as St James Hospital in 1539-40 with the dissolution of the "lesser monasteries" by Henry VIII. The Church and the appointment of the Vicar were in the gift of the Prior and monks of the Durham Priory. The latter were expunged by the "dissolution of the monasteries" and the Church and Vicar's incumbency were conferred on the Dean and Chapter of Durham Cathedral as confirmed by Henry VIII in a Latin deed of 1541:

"Patent Roll 33 Henry VIII Part 9, m.30 (15) Dated 33 Henry VIII, Grant to The Dean and Chapter of Durham of a yearly Rent out of the Rectory of Northallerton with the Avowson of the Vicarage of the same in the County of York"

The old Vicarage originated by Dr John Fisher (1491-94)

Northallerton had a strong connection with the Reformation in England which saw the Church of England substituted as the Established Church with the monarch Henry VIII as its head. Dr John Fisher the martyr of international recognition was Vicar of Northallerton from 1491-94 and during his incumbency rebuilt the Northallerton Vicarage with remnants of the west wall destroyed by the Scots in 1318 being retained.

He progressed to become Bishop of Rochester in 1504, helped Henry VIII to write his book against Martin Luther which gained the King the title of "Defender of the Faith", but refused steadfastly to acknowledge Henry VIII's supremacy in ecclesiastical affairs as head of the Church of England. In 1534 he was imprisoned in the Tower of London and refusing to betray his conscience was beheaded at Tower Hill on 22nd June 1535 which subsequently became commemorated as a Roman Catholic 'feast day', in recognition of Cardinal St John Fisher.

Robert Askew was Northallerton's Vicar from 1533 to 1547 when

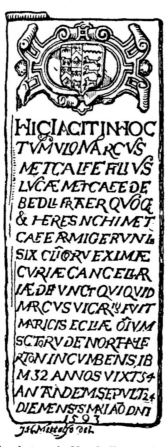

The Oldest Tombstone in Northallerton Church 1593

the break with Rome took place but except for the Pilgrimage of Grace rising in 1536 there is no evidence to quantify the effects of the Reformation in Northallerton. Sunday still remained as sacrosanct in Tudor times as it had been previously. This was indicated by a court ordinance of 1498 which ordered butchers to keep their shutters closed on Sundays and to attend church on pain of a one shilling fine on non-compliance.

There were several examples of continued piety: in 1546 a chantry to St Laurence existed a thousand yards from the church; a priest John

59

Blaisdaille was paid by Thomas Markenfield to say a mass or hold a divine service in the church or at Romanby; and in the sixteenth century a cottage in Northallerton was made responsible for founding and maintaining a light in the Parish Church.

At one stage Northallerton church seemed to be in need of repair as a visitation in 1535 stated: "the chancell at Northallerton in decaye". Locally born Mark Metcalfe, the son of Luke Metcalfe of Bedale is notable because of the length of his incumbency as Vicar of Northallerton 1561 to 1593 and that his tombstone is now the oldest one in the church. Francis Kaye who succeeded him was the last Tudor and first Stuart Vicar of Northallerton (1593 to 1624) and he too was buried in the church at his request "in the Queire". His will bequeathed forty shillings to the local poor (North Allerton 20 shillings; Brompton 10 shillings and Romanby and Deighton 5 shillings each) as well as maintaining four widows in clothes annually.

Leland's Itinerary

A vital visit to Northallerton was that of Henry VIII's antiquary John Leland in 1538 having been given a royal commission in 1533 to make a search for English antiquities. For six years to fulfil this he travelled around the country including much time in Yorkshire eventually producing his "Itinerary" which included the first factual description of Northallerton in such detail never recorded before. The main extracts regarding Northallerton are:

> "The Broke caullid Coddebek rifing yn the Browes of Blake
> More therby commith by Tresk and after goith into Willowebek
> River
> From Kirkeby Wiske to Northalverton a 4 Miles by Pafture
> and Corne Ground ----------
> The Towne of Northalverton is yn one fair long Streate
> lying by South and North.
> The Paroch Chirch of it is large, but in it I faw no
> Tumbes of Noble men yn it.
> There was a Houfe of …Freres in the Eft fide of
> the Toune.
> And yn the fame Cofte but a Mile or I cam ynto the
> Towns I faw the Hofpitale of S… foundid by…
> Biffhop of Dyrham.

60

At the Weſt ſide of Northalverton a litle from the Chirch
is the Biſſhop of Dyrham's Palace, ſtrong of Building and
welle motid.
And a 2 flite Shottes Weft Noth Weft from it be Diches
and the Dungeon Hille wher the Castelle of Alverton ſum tyme
ſtoode. No part of the Walles therof now apperith.
There cummith a very little Bek through the Toun of
Northalverton as from Est to Weft, and is communely caullid
Sunnebek.
A little by North without Alverton Toun is a Bridg of one
Arch of Stone, through the which cummith a bygger Broke
then Sunnebek, and riſing partely out of …cummith
toward the Weft, and paſſith through the Medowes by twixt
the Castle Hilles and the Biſſhopes Palace, and ther about
receyvith Sunnebeck into it, and within half a moile lower goith
into Wisk.
Northalverton ſhir is holey of the Dition of the Biſſhop of
Dureſme, and such Gentilmen as have landes there be of the
Holde of the Biſſhope.
Theſe Gentilmen be of moſt Name in Northalvertonshire:
Straingwaife of Harleſrey, wher Straingwaife the Judge buildid
a praty Caſtelle,
Malory, Coniers, Vincent in Smithon Paroch a little beyond
Smithon Bridge,
Thwaites, whose Houſe I ſaw on the lift Hand, a little a
this fide Smithon Bridge.
There is very litle Wood yn Northalverton ſhire: and
but one Park at Huten now without Deere
The Place caullid Cowton More, wher, a ſum ſay, was the
field of the Standard betwixt the Engliſeh Menne   and the
Scottiſeh, is, as I lernid, a 4 Miles by North Weft by Alverton.
There is good Corne in Northalverton, yet a great Peace of the
Ground that I ſaw at hand bytwixt Northalverton and Smithon
Bridge is low Paſture and Mores, wherof Part beere ſum fyrres.
From Alverton to Smithon Bridge a 6 Miles, wher Wisk rennith
cumming a 6 Miles of by Efte from Smithon."

Leland's description is invaluable for excepting spasmodic
visitors' comments, Northallerton was not delineated again until 1739
by Roger Gale. It is significant that "good Corne" is mentioned because

agriculture has always been the essence of Northallerton's existence and that the town "is yn one fair long Streate" succinctly describes Northallerton even up to the present day when the same High Street is the hub of the town. The main historical discrepancy is the siting of the Battle of the Standard at Cowton Moor, whereas modern scholarship is united in its location at Standard Hill, three miles north of Northallerton.

North Riding Quarter Sessions

An event of real importance in the town's progress to become the official County Town of the North Riding of North Yorkshire occurred in 1558 when the North Riding Quarter Sessions were held at Northallerton's Guild Hall. Although initially sporadic they were accommodated at the Guild Hall until 1720, Vine House 1720-1770 and the Toll Booth 1770-1785. Finally from 1785 every North Riding Quarter Sessions was held at the successive purpose built Court Houses at Northallerton until October 1971 when the Quarter Sessions system gave way to that of Crown Courts. Thus North Riding Quarter Sessions were a feature of Northallerton life for over four hundred years.

Tudor Rebellions

There were three risings against the Tudors which involved Northallerton and district the first of which was of a lesser nature. Discontent of varied strands in the North against the new Tudor King Henry VII resulted in the murder at South Kilvington on 28th April 1489 of the Earl of Northumberland the major royal magnate of the region. On 5th May around two thousand discontents converged on Northallerton but in the face of the royal army led by the Duke of Surrey the rebels dispersed. Forty-four were indicted (with one of the juries of "Allerton" men) but of these only two were from Northallerton and they survived the condemnation.

The other two northern rebellions against the Tudor government were much more important: the Pilgrimage of Grace 1536 and the Rising of the Northern Earls in 1569. Northallerton was involved to quite a degree with the latter but only to a limited extent with the former.

The Pilgrimage of Grace was a conservative demonstration with several causes, the most powerful of which was the suppression of the monasteries with the demand for these to be restored. Robert Aske, a

Yorkshire lawyer led the movement which affected mainly the East and West Ridings of Yorkshire and Lincolnshire though North Riding and Northallerton men were involved.

On 17th January 1537 two messengers of the rebel Sir John Bigod were taken - one near to Northallerton - and in another incident seized papers showed that rebel brothers Sir John and Sir Ralph Bulmer were to meet at Northallerton during the uprising. At one stage 40,000 had joined the insurrection but support melted away and the Duke of Norfolk's force defeated the rebels whose leaders including Robert Aske, and the abbots of Fountains and Rievaulx were executed at York. Foremen of two juries trying accused insurgents were local gentry Sir Christopher Danby of Thorp Perrow and Sir James Strangways of Harlsey. There were no records of North Riding hangings.

The Rising of the Northern Earls was a much more dangerous affair for the Crown led as it was by the two most powerful nobles in the North, Thomas Percy Earl of Northumberland and Charles Neville Earl of Westmorland who raised their rebellion by entering Durham City on 14th November 1569 under arms, demanding the return of Catholicism and Mary Queen of Scots as monarch. Both the leaders of the rebels and the royalists stayed at Northallerton at various times with the main centre of the revolutionaries more to the north-west especially at Richmond.

In November 1569 Northumberland and Westmorland stayed at Northallerton and Sir George Bowes the Queen's representative, who also later made his headquarters in Northallerton, in letters to fellow high ranking Royalists described the rebel actions regarding the town. Bowes warned the Earl of Sussex of the threat to the town by the Earl of Westmorland who had stated that if Northallerton did not send him "one hundred men tomorrow, to Leaming or at the furthest, that night, Ryppon, he, on his return would burne and spoile the towne." Shortly afterwards Bowes informed Captain Drury about the rebels: "Thursdaye they went to Allerton, and in their waye forced the whole people to follow them, muche against most of their wills." This alleged coercion of reluctant Alvertonians to join forces against the Crown is quite characteristic of Northallerton which was strongly and traditionally Royalist throughout its history.

The Earl of Sussex was the Commander-in-Chief of the Queen's army and having advanced from York to North Allerton with his army growing more numerous continually, he wrote from North Allerton on 14th December 1569 to Sir William Cecil the Queen's chief minister that with the martial strength now available "If the rebells offer the fyght, I wyll not refuse it." Conversely, however, the rebels' support was dwindling and they were so intimidated by the royalist army numbering nearly 20,000 that they dispersed without a fight. Their leaders fled to the Continent via Scotland but eventually the Earl of Northumberland was captured and beheaded in August 1572 on the pavement outside St Crux Church at York.

Sir George Bowes was directed to try and execute the guilty rebels, one of the centres selected for this being "Allerton" on the 16th January 1570 included in a "circuit" from 13th to 23rd January when Bowes held brief and expeditious proceedings at various venues. The judgements were comparatively lenient as Bowes wrote to Cecil on the 13th January 1570 from "Alverton" that many rebels had been coerced and not revolted willingly. It was an historic court held by Sir George Bowes at the Northallerton Guild Hall (now the site of Jefferson and Willan, solicitors) on the 16th January ending with the hanging of seven local rebels - the last recorded hangings in the town. Those executed at the front of the Guild Hall were: "Allerton - Xpor Hancock, Richard Wynde, Randall Horner, Robert Heckley, Henrye Thompson, Allan Lynsley, William Taylor."

Xpor Lambe was the hangman and three who were found guilty "in absentia" were: "William Markenfield - Romanbye, Thomas Mabson - West Roughton and John Prest - Borowbye." Other judgements against Cleveland rebels to be executed were given at "Allerton" on the 18th January 1570.

Porch House - 1584

Leland described the Bishop of Durham's Northallerton Palace as substantial in 1538 and "the scite of the mansion" was valued at £241. 11s. 3d in 1534. However, in 1584 a building to rival and then replace the Bishop's Palace as Northallerton's premier residence was erected on the east side of the High Street close to the Parish Church - Porch House. *[monochrome plate 2]* Richard Metcalfe was its originator and first occupant with his wife Margaret - their initials were discovered during alterations in 1844 engraved on an oak beam: "RM 1584 MM." Porch House was to have an illustrious future and the Metcalfes became a major family in Northallerton's history, commencing with Richard who was the great, great grandson of Thomas Metcalfe of Nappa Hall, Wensleydale who was the son of Thomas Metcalfe, a Captain at

Agincourt in 1415 for Henry V who gave him lands in Wensleydale for his services. Margaret, Richard's wife, was the daughter of Roger Wilson of Danby Wiske.

The Tudor Grammar School

Northallerton Grammar School continued to flourish in Tudor Times and a 1546 Commission referred to "landes gyven for the fynding of a Grammar Scole in Northallerton" by "certen well disposed persones, to the intent and for the better bringing up of the towne children and others of the inhabitants of the country." In 1548 the King's commissioners Sir Walter Myldemaye and Robert Kelway gave Bedale and Northallerton Grammar Schools good reports. In Northallerton's case the "Scole is very mete and necessary to be continued" and that John Foster, "Scholmaster there" should have his stipend "and wages yerelie, £5 1s. 8d".

Another 1570 Commission by Edmund Archbishop of York at the command of Queen Elizabeth I again found favourably for Northallerton Grammar School and its Schoolmaster John Foster as did a report in 1571 by the Archdeacon of Cleveland, Ralph Cowton which said the school was "in a proper place and it had been duly kept since the first year of Queen Elizabeth's reign with a great attendance of scholars."

North Allerton Tudor Scene

It appears that in 1559-60 Queen Elizabeth I seized Allerton and Allertonshire worth a yearly value of £218 9s. 1¼d from the Bishop of Durham but returned it to that See in 1566. This was recorded by Thomas Rymer historiographer royal to William III in his book "Feodora". Rymer was born at Appleton Wiske and one of a series of boys of ordinary backgrounds educated at Northallerton Grammar School in the seventeenth century who reached national prominence.

The records and accounts of the Bishopric of Durham are a major source of information about Tudor Northallerton. For example in Bishop Richard Fox's episcopy (1494-1501) mention is made of the re-equipping of the mansion (Bishop's Palace) with towels, cushions and napkins, excavating the moat and attending to the great stable and the great granary as well as attention in the town to the church, toll-booth, shambles, market cross, stocks, gaol and common pond. Mention too is made of the watermill next to the mansion house let to Thomas Milner at £8. 0. 0. yearly and also the windmill to him at £1. 6s. 8d. per annum.

The bishop's woods at Clack near Osmotherley and Cotcliffe were well maintained as befitted their obvious importance. He had fisheries at "Cotebeck" (Cod Beck) and Borrowby becke, a plaster quarry at Brompton and a slate quarry at Osmotherley. The overall revenue from Allertonshire in 1500-1501 was £260 to £270 with the major expenditure of £25.18s. 5d. on officials of which the Steward (then Sir James Strangways) was paid £10 per annum.

It is interesting to note the enclosures in the Bishop of Durham's six villages which would benefit the major tenants with more compact land-holdings but disadvantage the lesser tenants. Osmotherley was enclosed by 1550 except for a large proportion of the Open Field, Knayton 1570 except for the Commons and Romanby 1596 followed in the next century by Borrowby, Thornton-le-Beans and Brompton.

In Romanby in 1496 the Bishop had fourteen leading tenants who were able to be arrayed "as well in harness as in horse" which was reminiscent of the Scottish wars and in Northallerton he had lands which are still well known tenanted by leading townsmen who tended to occupy and rent the land near to the town. For example, Castle Hills was tenanted by Thomas Metcalfe in the 1490s, the Great Applegarth by William Ampleforth and Motehill Close by Edmund Skarlett whereas Greenhowsike farther out was held by various tenant farmers in the long-strips configuration of the medieval "Open Field" system.

A survey of 1596 canvassed the oldest inhabitants and found that the North Moor had long been common land used by the townspeople at 4 pence for a full year and 2 pence per half year. Agriculture of a mixed nature was of course the major occupation and the townspeople often had a dual role such as John Stevenson a smith whose will in 1498 disclosed that he left wheat, rye, barley, peas and hay as well as a horse, three cows, sixteen sheep and six pigs.

Edmund Skarlett apart from holding land was also the bailiff of Northallerton and the receiver for the Bishop of Durham for many years from 1506 followed by his son Thomas. Edmund's wife Agnes was also involved in brewing and bread making. Indeed he exemplified an elite of business and tradesmen who had emerged from the peasantry to run the town through the borough court keeping law and order, regulating trade and social behaviour by serving as officials and on the juries. Dr Christine Newman described "a strong spirit of community which was rational, coherent and politically pro-active in terms of its own interests."

Other than agriculture the identifiable occupations were: butcher, brewer, baker, smith, slater, wheelwright, plumber, mason and plasterer. Then there were those associated with Northallerton's time-immemorial leather industry: tanners, saddlers, glovers and shoemakers. Finally came the weaving trades which even as early as the fourteenth century were established commercially in the town: weavers, tailors, shearmen and dyers. There were shops other than those in the toll-booth and the Wednesday markets were bustling and even occasionally disordered. An emphasis here is that they were attended by villagers and country folk from several miles around to buy and sell and in fact the economy of Northallerton and its hinterland operated on an inter-dependent basis.

Northallerton was granted another fair in Mary's reign in 1555 – "Saynt George's faire" – in May which still survives today as the "May Fair". In the preamble of application it was stated that Northallerton was:

> "a very populous town with many franchises and liberties but on account of the poverty of its inhabitants is now in great ruin and decay."

It is certain that trade had slowed and possibly the economy had somewhat stagnated but the plea was probably over-stated to ensure its success. Whatever the situation, by 1586 in 'Britannia' William Camden the Elizabethan antiquarian is enthusing about Northallerton's St Bartholomew's fair of September, "it was the throngest beast fair that I ever saw." And throughout the following three centuries Northallerton was famed for its fairs, cattle and horses.

The social problem of vagrancy was on the increase as the sixteenth century unfolded possibly partly as a result of the bubonic plague ("the great pestilence") and the enclosure movement. There were frequent court ordinances regarding "rogues and vagabonds" and a particular unease was felt about itinerant Scots (a historic and prevailing anxiety) with court orders to match such as in 1513 when the borough court renewed a prohibition of harbouring Scots on pain of a £1 fine.

There were several cases involving prostitutes both in the nearby villages and the "Backsyde" area of Northallerton (possibly the back of the High Street east area). Although only one inn "The Swan" is known by name it is certain that ale houses were on the increase and to curb cards, gaming and the "harbouring of young men" a 9 pm curfew was invoked in 1511.

Debt and trespass were the highest on the courts' lists but affray and assault were well represented. To sports lovers a borough court case of affray in 1495 would be of interest when Robert Appleton and Edward Garsdale of Northallerton were each fined 3s 4d (16p) for causing an affray during a game of football in the Applegarth. Football was then banned with a 6s 8d fine cited and the fine for carrying a football within the town was £1. The Applegarth's association as a playing field thus dates to five hundred years, as does football in the town.

Travel

The independence and assertiveness of Northallerton's people was not the result of insularity and remoteness as it was a great thoroughfare being on both the Great North Road and the York road to the north. Consequently it would have constant visitors from London and elsewhere in the country, would be abreast of national happenings and receptive to new ideas.

Leaving London from Bishopsgate the Great North Road passed through Islington, Enfield, Hoddesdon, Ware, Royston, Huntingdon, Stevenage, Grantham, Doncaster, Wetherby, Boroughbridge, Northallerton, Darlington, Durham, Newcastle, Alnwick, Berwick, Dunbar, Haddington and Edinburgh. Inns offering good accommodation, food and ale abounded "en route" which applied to Northallerton as a major "stopping-place." Innumerable horses would travel the road daily and it is no coincidence that Northallerton had two "Horse Ponds" for refreshing the horses on the now Prison and Friarage Hospital sites.

There were no coaches at the start of the sixteenth century and only a few at the end, with most travellers going by foot (often driving animals) and the rest by horseback. Travel was slow, arduous, expensive and dangerous with robbers abounding. The journey from London to Edinburgh took the ordinary traveller a fortnight and it cost one shilling, or three days' agricultural wages, to hire a horse. Not surprisingly then except for the wealthy, those forced to seek work elsewhere or the few adventurous characters seeking their fortunes, the majority of people would never leave their native Allertonshire in Tudor times. However, there were movements of workers at harvest-time and recent research by Dr David Severs of Northallerton has revealed a Northallerton worker as far away as Warwickshire in 1581.

Local Citizens

Information is limited regarding individual local Tudor citizens and most of this is contained in wills and legal documents. For example the will of Lady Joan Hastings, widow of Sir Richard Hastings, dated 19th March 1504 directed that a priest should sing in the chantry founded by her father Sir Richard Welles, Lord Willoughby in Northallerton Parish Church before he was executed for rebellion by Edward IV. The cost would be met from her manor in Romanby as would 6s. 8d. allocated to her servant William of North Allerton. Others personally named Allerton found in documents included Thomas de Allerton who made a Pilgrimage to Rome in 1507 and Matthew de Allerton who in 1509 bequeathed land in Northallerton to Byland Abbey.

John Henisle "tailour of North Alerton" was granted sanctuary in St John's of Beverley and interesting wills were those of: Cuthbert Pepper (1566) East Cowton gent, Tomes Smythson (1543) Cowton Grange, Robert Thompson (1551) Morton-on-Swale and Lancelot Gayle (1566) Scruton. Robert Thompson, a gamekeeper left to his brother "Rayff": "my setting spanyell doge, with all the netts and geyr pertenying to it." Roger Gale the Northallerton MP and historian was the grandson of Lancelot Gale who, in keeping with the merriment which was a feature of our ancestors' funerals, instructed that he wanted his friends and neighbours to have a dinner at his Scruton house on the day of his funeral.

Probably the two best known local Tudors were Edmund Gheast and Roger Ascham who both rose from modest beginnings to achieve national stature. Gheast was born in Northallerton the son of Thomas Gheast in 1514 and after receiving his early education in the town – most probably at Northallerton Grammar School – he went to York School before he went to Cambridge University becoming a Fellow of King's College. He became Bishop of Rochester (1560) and Almoner to Queen Elizabeth thus being in charge of the royal finances. Eventually he became Bishop of Salisbury and was interred in the choir of this cathedral when he died in 1577. He was the major compiler of the Liturgy of the Church of England which was in general use until the twentieth century.

Roger Ascham (1515-68) from Kirby Wiske was the son of the Steward of the local manor and showing great early academic promise he was admitted to Oxford University. Bulmer (1890) ascribed his early education to Northallerton Grammar School and though there is no direct evidence of this, the proximity of the school to his home, the known attendance at the school of 'bright' boys from his area and the school's tenancy of scholarships to Oxford University, give credence to this claim. He eventually became a senior Fellow at St John's College, Cambridge and Public Orator at that University. He was an authority on archery writing a book on the subject entitled "Toxophilus", enjoyed music and chess, was a dedicated gambler, a great frequenter of cock-fighting and the hunting field and was very widely travelled.

However, his greatest claim to fame was as an erudite academic, versed exceptionally in Latin, Greek and foreign languages, who was the Tutor for sometime from 1548 of Lady Elizabeth at Cheshunt, Hertfordshire before she became Queen Elizabeth I. She became Ascham's "brightest star" of the many tutees in his career, being gifted and fluent at French, Greek and Latin and such an assiduous student, who studied history three hours a day and carried a book with her constantly, that Ascham feared she might burn herself out. He wrote "Scholemaster" regarding teaching which was frequently reprinted and was widely acclaimed but despite his national fame he never forgot his early days in his native North Riding of Yorkshire, memories of which he treasured as the happiest days of his life.

5

Northallerton under the Stuarts 1603 - 1714

The English Civil War

Conclusively the most important event in seventeenth century England was the Civil War (1641-1646) between the Royalists ("Cavaliers") and Parliamentarians ("Roundheads") which brought the execution of Charles I in 1649 and monarchless rule until the restoration of Charles II in 1660.

It has been said that many ordinary English people were unaware of the Civil War but this certainly was not the case at Northallerton where troop movements were frequent - Royalist, Roundhead and Scottish. North Riding Quarter Sessions were cancelled totally in 1643 and 1644 because "the North Riding has bene sore trobled with severall armyes of soldeirs." Northallerton suffered greatly with armies billeted on the town particularly at the hands of the Royalists in 1641 and the Scots in 1644 and 1646 - on each occasion crops, cattle, victuals and useful goods were seized and the local resentment was marked against the military.

There was only one Royalist - Roundhead clash in the vicinity of Northallerton which occurred in early 1644 when, serving with Colonel Tempest's Royalist regiment of foot, Lieutenant Colonel Gerard Salvin was slain in a skirmish with Parliamentary troops. However, as would be expected on the Great North Road the town was a major military stopping place as exemplified when in September 1640 the King's army concentrated at "North Allerton" where the Earl of Stafford, commanding the army, wrote to Sir George Radcliffe with utmost pessimism about the Royal forces.

Charles I at Northallerton

The most important Northallerton visitor, however, was the King himself, Charles I, who according to Parliamentary Records in 1641 stayed at Porch House on his way to York as a guest of the Metcalfe family headed by George Metcalfe, who died soon afterwards. It is very likely that Charles passed through the town during the Civil War but the next time he stayed there was in February 1647 again at Porch House as a prisoner of the Parliamentary Commissioners - three lords and six commoners led by the Earl of Pembroke - en route from his captivity under the Scots at Newcastle to London and his eventual execution on 31st January 1649. There is an ageless Northallerton legend that he tried to escape unsuccessfully from a southern window (now "bricked up") aided by the now parentless Metcalfe children but there is no corroborative evidence of this whatsoever.

Charles' Ransom

Charles' captivity generated Northallerton's involvement in a major political event resulting from the Civil War. On 5th May 1646 Charles surrendered to the Scots at Newark and was taken to Newcastle via Topcliffe (and presumably Northallerton) as a prisoner. After negotiations the English Parliamentarians agreed to pay £400,000 ransom for Charles to the Scots and made immediate efforts to raise the money ("House of Commons Journal"). The first moiety of £200,000 conveyed in 36 carts containing £1000 bags was sent on 16th December 1646 from London to York arriving there as late as the 3rd January 1647 "the waies being very bad and monies overturned."

At York the money was counted and the first moiety of £100,000 dispatched on 16th January by convoy to Northallerton arriving in three days on 19th January. It was received by the Scots on 21st January and the document of receipt signed, dated and annotated "Northallerton". The second moiety of £100,000 was similarly dealt with on 3rd February.

The first £100,000 remained at Northallerton from 19th to 27th January before being transported North heavily guarded with the horse captains receiving £100 and foot captains £50 for the safe conduct of the money to Scotland. It was said "how the bonny Scots laugh and fling up their caps at the sight of the money!" Northallerton gained an unfair reputation as the town that had sold the King and the Scots received great approbation:

> "Traitor, traitor Scot
> Sold his King for a groat"

went the popular cry.

Also regarding Charles I and Northallerton, the town's MP in 1660 Francis Lascelles (1612 - 1667 of Stank Hall and Northallerton) was one of the Yorkshire Commissioners appointed for the trial of Charles in January 1649 and though he refused to sign the warrant of execution he was excluded from the House of Commons in 1660 on the Restoration of Charles II because of his part in the trial. Finally, Charles I's major opponent Oliver Cromwell was also in the Northallerton district as he stated in a letter of 11th September 1648 to Lord Fairfax that the widow of one of his slain leaders Lieutenant Colonel Cowell "came to me near Northallerton much lamenting her loss."

The Inter-Regnum (1648 - 1660)

When the Parliamentarians took over the country one of their earliest actions was to abolish the episcopacy and sell the bishops' lands. This greatly affected Northallerton the manor of which belonged to the Bishop of Durham, with the lands being sold between 1648 and 1650 to various people including Thomas Lascelles, James Danby, Richard and Robert Metcalfe, Henry Darley and John Wastell, the latter two buying Northallerton Borough in 1650 for £237. 3s. 2d. After the Restoration the Northallerton lands and Borough were successfully re-claimed by the Bishop of Durham John Cosin, who accused Thomas Lascelles of destroying "a grate fish pond of several acres."

Thomas Lascelles during the monarchless period had typified the stern and uncompromising attitudes of the Puritanical magistrates. A typical illustration was at the Northallerton Quarter Sessions on 22nd July 1656 when he brought Thos Thorpe and Rich Purslaw for "travelling on the Lord's Day" before the Court which "concurs with him therein 'and thinckes fitt that Mr Lascelles doe issue his warrant to levy 10s of each of them, and...the said parties to sitt six hours in the stocks."

Such extremist and harsh punishments became common-place with "whipping" for example greatly increasing: in 1652 a Romanby woman was whipped for a minor crime and at the July 1656 Northallerton

Sessions a woman was sentenced "to be whipt" for stealing two sheets; and the previous July at Northallerton five accused had been whipped for minor offences.

Games and Christmas were abolished and a series of arbitrary actions explained why the Parliamentary regime was so unpopular and the Republican government so short-lived. Royalty was discountenanced with all Arms of the late King ordered to be taken down in 1650 and drinking Royal "toasts" banned; in 1656 with Northallerton's Frances Lascelles and Leonard Smelt on the Sessions bench "eight men were to be whipt being Common Players of Interludes" which had happened to four actors whipped in 1652. Crimes of immortality were a major quarry of the Puritanical JPs: in January 1657 a man and woman who confessed carnal knowledge of each other were gaoled for three months; and a woman admitting to fornication was gaoled for three months at the 1657 Northallerton Sessions.

To the gratification of Northallerton in common with many of the nation in 1660 Richard Cromwell the Lord Protector abdicated which was effective when General Monk submitted to the Crown having marched his army from the North via Northallerton to London. Evidently General Lambert, one of Cromwell's ablest Generals, "disbanded his army and parted with his officers at Northallerton in tears." This was in total contrast to the Northallerton joy at the Restoration of the King which was celebrated thereafter annually by the pealing of the Parish Church bells on the monarch's birthday.

However, there were some local anti-Monarchists and a serious affair was the 1663 Farnley-Wood plot in Yorkshire after which twenty-one plotters were hanged and quartered and their heads displayed at York, Leeds, Doncaster and Northallerton.

The Plague

The bubonic plague of Asiatic origin knew no bounds of centuries and between 1348 and 1671 it periodically devastated English communities. Despite its situation on the Great North Road with frequent visitors Northallerton appeared relatively unscathed by the plague in Tudor Times but in 1604 the area was badly affected and "dyed in York 3512 persons in 1604." In Northallerton church-yard 54 were buried in 1604 "who died of the plague" between 18th January and 28th May and in 1605 from 16th July to 21st November ninety people are recorded in the Northallerton Parish Register as dying of the "Great Plague."

The Guild Hall – Quarter Sessions venue until 1720

Frequently taxation was levied throughout the North Riding by the Quarter Sessions to relieve the stricken communities which happened for Thirsk (in 1605 when it must have been harder hit than Northallerton) "Leminge" (1626) and "Bedall" (1636). Places suffering the epidemic were quarantined with people not allowed to trade or travel which applied to Leeming in 1626. When the Great Plague ravished London in 1665 the alarm and justifiable trepidation of the North Riding was reflected by a 1665 Quarter Sessions order "that a strict and sufficient day and night watch be kept in every township within the said Riding to prohibit all manner of persons, as well as travellers suspicious to have come from London or other places infected."

North Riding Quarter Sessions

An invaluable insight into the affairs of the North Riding and its constituent towns like Northallerton are found in the proceedings of its Quarter Sessions during the "troublesome times" of the seventeenth century. They commenced around 1350, met four times annually and were made up of Justices of the Peace who by 1600 had enormous powers dealing with 300 statutes. James I had a very low opinion of JPs calling them "Idle-Low-Bellies" but in fact they were the backbone of law and order and civil and criminal jurisdiction in England.

The first full Quarter Sessions held at Northallerton in the seventeenth century was that of 12th January 1609 before five JPs including Sir Thomas Lascelles and Will Mauleverer. Gradually because of its central accessibility the Quarter Sessions were held more here, and after 1699 the Midsummer Sessions was always held there. The 1785 centralisation of the Quarter Sessions with a purpose-built Court House was of critical importance in Northallerton's progress to become the North Riding of Yorkshire's county town with officials and local government housed here.

Alehouses

Amongst a myriad of Quarter Session responsibilities a main area was the upholding of the various licensing laws and Northallerton featured prominently in proceedings. In July 1605 at "Richmonde" Roger Robinson, Gabriel Coates, Anthony Marshall, and Will Lendrawe all of Northallerton were arraigned for keeping unlicensed alehouses. Thomas Cotes of Northallerton was accused of "keeping a common house of play with cardes and other games" in April 1606, around that time Cuthbert Kearton of the town was fined "for using much drinking with men's servants in the night tyme" and in 1609 Northallerton Alehouse keepers Phillip Dean, Roger Lambe and Will Nelson were found guilty of "suffering excessive drinking."

Roger Vitty and Henry Atkinson of Romanby at the Northallerton Sessions of 10th July 1612 were indicted for "illegal brewing" and at the same Sessions eleven Northallerton ale-house keepers were charged with "harbouring rogues" - the number of licensees involved indicating the large number of ale-houses in the town. Throughout the century licensing cases continued to abound many of an interesting nature, for example: Robert Suttle at Northallerton on 12th January 1609 of Leeming Lane, was accused of harbouring highwaymen - "badde fellowes, who very suspiciously ryde in the high street called Leeming Lane, as we suspect for robbing;" publicans were supposed to offer hospitality to travellers and an alehouse keeper of Streete House (Thornton-le-Street) was reprimanded in 1624 for refusing Rob. Blackbeard lodging who "almost perished by the weather;" and in 1677 a Knayton publican was found guilty of sheep stealing being punished by whipping, suppressed from brewing and having his sign pulled down by the Knayton constable.

Rogues and Vagabonds – Poor Law Act 1601

In the enforcing of the Poor Law of 1601 there was a real fear of "rogues and vagabonds wandering the country" and real causes of unemployment and hunger were ignored in favour of the easier and cheaper method of repression. Harsh measures were encouraged by the government and innumerable cases of stringent (barbaric in modern terms) punishments were meted out to "sturdy beggars," rogues and vagabonds by the North Riding magistrates. For example at the Northallerton Midsummer Sessions of 1610 four men and three women (including Anne Latham of Brunton - Brompton) were found guilty of "being rogues and vagabonds" with the men being sentenced to be branded with the letter R on the left shoulder in open Court and the women were to be publicly whipped at Northallerton.

The 1601 Poor Law Act made parishes responsible for their own poor which caused much inter-town dissension the many disputes being settled in the Quarter Sessions instanced by: in 1670 a "poor" child was ordered to be "conveyed" to Richmond from Northallerton; Northallerton Parish in 1674 found the hamlets Romanby, Lazenby, Bankhead and Crosby Cote refusing to pay their poor rates and eventually at the Quarter Sessions in October 1680 Romanby's refusal to pay the £4 annual poor rate was upheld because "the poor of Northallerton do increase, and the poor of Romanby are much diminished."

Poaching and Games

Strict measures operated regarding poaching and the playing of games especially on a Sunday. In 1606 Will Rainold and John Hutchinson of Brompton were charged with "killing hares in snow-time;" Charles Scarlett of "Romandby" appeared for shooting doves at Romanby in 1605; James Kendroe and Will Nelson of Northallerton in 1612 were arraigned for playing "Nyneholes" on the "Sabaoth daie;" Rob Hackforth of "Dighton" was arraigned for "playing Baules in the Churchyard;" whilst in 1613 Chr Knowles of Exilby was indicted for "playing cardes in his house on the Sabbath and keping a common football for young men of the town to play contrary to the law." On the other hand the law constrained men to practise with the long bow and in April 1612 Richard Rymer Junior and Tho Walker of Northallerton were brought to book "for that they do not exercise shootinge off the long bowe."

Punishments

Whipping and branding were frequent punishments but there were also other extreme methods of retribution - gaol, transportation, the pillory, stocks and "ducking" stool. Thornton-le-Moor and Catterick were upbraided for lacking a pillory or stocks which were required by law in every township. Northallerton's pillory was assigned to Henry Buttry of Northallerton in July 1606 found guilty as an extortioner, fined £10 and made to stand in "the pillorie" with a paper on his head stating his crime.

In 1654 three JPs including Leonard Smelt and Francis Lascelles of Northallerton sentenced Mary Outhwaite of Firby "to be set in the ducking stool and publiquely ducked for being an incorrigible and notorious scold, and abusing her neighbours." Transportation was a regular sentence an example being at the Midsummer Sessions in 1674 when a Brompton man having already being burned in the shoulder as an incorrigible rogue was committed to York Gaol "until he shall be transported into some of the English plantations beyond the seas."

Witchcraft at Northallerton

The most remarkable case concerning Northallerton was heard at Thirsk in October 1623 when Elizabeth Cleary of Northallerton was found guilty of witchcraft. She was charged –

"for exercising certain most wicked arts, inchantmentes and charmes, on a black cow (value 50s) belonging to Edw. Bell of Northallerton, by which the cow was sorely damaged and the calf in her totally wasted and consumed."

The verdict by the Jury of 12 Yeoman (10 from Thirsk) –

"Who find Elizabeth Clearey guilty of the most wicked and diabolical arts, called inchantments and charmes. To be committed to prison for a year, and once each quarter to stand in the pillory, and when released to be bound to the good behaviour for a year, and then to appear at the next Sessions." Subsequently it was decreed that the "convicted witch is to be sett on the pillorie once a quarter in some markett towne in the Ridinge upon some faire daie or markett day."

Soldiers' Pensions

"Lame Soldiers" - soldiers wounded in the national cause - were paid pensions by the Quarter Sessions and Francis Lascelles, Northallerton from 1605 was the "Treasurer for Lame Soldiers". The money for the pensions was levied throughout the Riding - £468 in 1662 just after the Civil War for example. At the Northallerton Sessions in July 1610 there were five "lame soldiers" eligible for pensions which ranged from £7 to £2 per annum. During the Inter-Regnum (1646 - 60) the Parliamentary "lame soldiers" were pensioned such as Thomas Holmes who received £2 annually.

Rates and Payments

Rates were estreated according "to their ancient rents and customs" across a whole range of County needs and sometimes for individual items such as the highways in "North Allerton" at the Midsummer Sessions, 1693 which ordered the payments to be made by the "inhabitants of land" and estate holders. The county beacons were assessed in 1612 and 1688 when "Bullamoore" was named as the Allertonshire beacon. Individuals distressed by fire loss and damage were aided such as Thomas Coates of Northallerton, given 66s 8d in 1612 and when twelve houses in Northallerton were destroyed by fire in 1655 in what was the most destructive fire in the town in modern times, the North Riding Quarter Sessions awarded the town £5.

Morals

Individuals straying from the moral path were upbraided. At Northallerton in 1609: "James Cootes of Barton, a fornicator that hath had a bastard...but is often drunken and doth lye harkening under mens' windowes"; a woman was convicted of being a "night walker" and the Governor of the House of Correction was ordered "to give her due correction by whipping until the next Quarter Sessions."

Wages, Apprentices, Trades

The regulation of wages, work, trade and apprenticeships was a final important function of the Quarter Sessions. In 1658 wage rates were set for artificers, labourers and servants "thorow the North Riding and especially in every markett towne." For instance; a carpenter, mason, thatcher and mower were to be paid daily "with meate 6d without meate 12d;" a taylor and reaper of corn (male) "4d with meate and 8d without meate;" a reaper of corn (woman) "3d with meate and without 6d;" and servants annually - male £3, cook/maid £2, dairy maid £2 and ordinary maid 30s.

Apprentices were strictly indentured for seven years but equally Masters' obligations were also enforced. Thus in 1673 John Raper of Northallerton was released from his apprenticeship with "Will Durham Bedall" butcher because of his Master's incompetence and in the same year apprentice John Gamble of Northallerton was released following the prolonged absence of his Northallerton Master, Will Moore ropemaker.

Professional trades were strictly upheld. For example in 1605 Will Nelson of Northallerton was indicted "for using the art and mystery of a glover" but proved at the next Sessions that he was qualified. Several Northallerton cases followed - a grocer "using the art" of a brickmaker (1675), and in 1676 one yeoman using the trade of a mason and another a wright.

Trade was also firmly regulated. Frances Lascelles in 1605 was charged with "buying great sommes of barley in Thirske Markett than the market will beare" and eight farmers were arraigned at Northallerton Midsummer Sessions of 1679 for selling old butter with five others charged for selling butter without the weight stamped on the firkins.

JP Power

The power and attitude of the magistrates was illustrated in a dispute in 1616 between the JP Will Mauleverer of Ingleby Arncliffe and Christopher Lazenby a prominent Northallerton citizen who called Mauleverer "a knave and a badd Justice of Peace." Lazenby was then called "a man of dissolute behaviour" and Mauleverer "an ancient and renowned JP" by the Quarter Sessions who continued that it is "not thought fytting by this Court to be tollerated and suffered without some punishment or reproofe in a man of so leaud condition as the said Lazenby is." Finally they issued a warrant for Lazenby's appearance at a Higher Court - the next Assizes at York.

North Riding Military

In 1640 there were four regiments of the King's Party in North Yorkshire: Richmondshire, Langbaurgh, Pickering Lyth and Northallertonshire, the latter commanded by Sir Robert Strickland and then Sir Thomas Strickland. 1688 saw the raising of the Green Howards in the West Country - the regiment which was to have the closest of links with the North Riding and Northallerton and also in that year Colonel John Darcy's Regiment was formed in the North Riding the third part of which concerned Allertonshire being commanded by Colonel Sir Roger Strickland.

Because of its vital position on the Great North Road troops were constantly billeted on Northallerton which would welcome the North Riding Quarter Sessions stipulation in 1690 of the cost of billeting soldiers: a trooper – "6d meat 6d hay and straw per night; a foot soldier - 4d meat a night; and 2d ale or strong beer for all troops."

The Borough of Northallerton

In 1298 John le Clerk and Stephen Maunsell became Northallerton's first MPs but the privilege of sending representatives to Parliament was waived until 5th December 1640 when a motion was made in Parliament to restore the ancient privilege of membership to "Malton and Allerton" which was passed on 11th December 1640 (Commons Journal). The burgage tenants of the borough of Northallerton had the privilege of voting and they returned Thomas Heblewaite and Sir Henry Cholmeley. Two members were then sent continually until 1832 when the Borough lost a member, followed by one representative until 1885 when the Borough was merged with Richmond into the Richmondshire constituency.

The Lascelles (later Harewood family) were a crucial influence on the seat until the mid-nineteenth century. Thomas Lascelles (1624 - 97) of Stank Hall and Northallerton was the Borough's MP in 1688, 1690 - 95 and 1695 - 97.

Sir Gilbert Gerard, MP for Northallerton 1678 to 1685 was notable for incurring the personal displeasure of Charles II by asking the King for a sitting of Parliament in January 1679 and being the subject along with his fellow Northallerton MP Sir Henry Calverley in 1680 of a congratulatory and laudatory 'Leter of Thanks' from the Borough of Northallerton. This was signed by sixty-two leading citizens and is still preserved in the British Museum being upheld at the time as a magnanimous letter to deserving MPs which could be taken "as an example for the whole nation."

Population and Property

The Hearth Tax was introduced after the restoration in 1660 to provide income for Charles II, occupiers being charged 2s per hearth annually. Evasion was rife making conclusions as to wealth and population difficult but indicators are feasible as to the situation of Northallerton and district.

"North Allerton Towne, Romanby and Brumpton" Hearth Tax returns were collated in 1673 showing that: Northallerton possessed 451 hearths belonging to 188 occupiers, Brompton 130 hearths for 81 people and Romanby 54 for 35. Larger and more sophisticated housing was indicated in Northallerton borne out by the occupiers with three or more hearths: Northallerton had 70, Brompton 12 and Romanby 4, the latter showing a "village pattern". Northallerton was a built up comparatively wealthy town which is in keeping with contemporary accounts.

Most important information was a list of names of persons in the town over three hundred years ago and the more wealthy of these: Thomas Lascelles (5 hearths), Dr Jo Neale (6 - the Vicarage), Alice Bradley (5), Christopher Lazenby (5), Wd Merrington (4), Richard Pearce (9), Thomas Smelt (6 - the Grammar School), and George Metcalfe (5 - Porch House).

Trade and Industry

Trade and industry crucial to the town, were strictly regulated accordingly and even featured in petitions to parliament from the "ancient borough of Northallerton." One in 1697 stated that "quantities of lead, butter and other commodities are daily carried from thence (Northallerton) to Burrough-Briggs; and thence by water upon the river Ouze to several parts of this Kingdom and beyond the seas; but in case the rivers Ayre and Calder be made navigable as is intended by a bill in the House; it will drain the river Ouze, and deprive the petitioners of the benefit they receive thereby; And pray, that the said rivers may not be made navigable."

Another petition to parliament in 1698 came from the shoe-makers of Northallerton against the export abroad of tanned leather. Tanning of

Seventeenth Century High Street Shop – W R Green (1930)

course was a major local industry as was spur making in the seventeenth century, which were probably accentuated by the greatly increased military movements.

The town appeared to have a natural reputation for the brewing of strong ale and a poem was published in York celebrating "North Allerton the ale town" in 1697 entitled "In Praise of Yorkshire Ale."

"Northallerton, in Yorkshire, does excel
All England, nay all Europe, for strong ale,"

ran this rollicking poem's most quoted couplet with Mrs Bradley's "humming stuff" the most potent brew. The author given by Saywell was Giles Morrington an Attorney at Law but a person of that name remains so unidentifiable that it is thought that the composer could be George Meriton a Northallerton Attorney who wrote poems such as "Landlord's Law." Public houses in the main street abounded many of them on the known sites of present or previous hostelries.

Tradesmen's tokens were used as legal tender and one of these was for "Thos Redmayne, King's Arms Northallerton" depicting a Post Boy at full speed, indicating that in 1668 this inn was concerned with delivery of post and mail. Other tokens were of Edmund Barstow 1667, William Hutton, Hatter 1669 "His Half Peny" and Francis Rymer, Mercer, 1670 "His Half Peny."

Fairs and Markets

As in medieval times markets and fairs were the keys to Northallerton's commerce, with markets on Wednesday and three fairs annually until the town was given a fourth by King James I in 1611 after an enquiry by Sir Francis Hildesley in October 1609. This St Matthews Fair was granted to William James Bishop of Durham, Lord of the Manor of Northallerton for 3rd and 4th October and also every other Wednesday from Lammas (1st August) to Christmas for cattle dealing. This was important as Northallerton was on one of the main drovers' routes from Scotland into England, down which came droves of cattle and sheep. Another famous nearby drovers' road passed near to Osmotherley through Slapestones where the "Chequers Inn" became a popular resting place.

Northallerton had a national reputation for its Fairs as evidenced by a succession of visitors on their nationwide travels. In 1638 Richard Braithwaite with the pseudonym of "Drunken Barnabee" wrote:
"Thence to Allerton, rank't in battell
Sheep, Kine, oxen other cattell...
But I made my fare the cellar."
Marmaduke Rawdon journeying from York into Scotland in 1664 recorded in his diary that on the night of 25th August: "lodged att a faire market towne called North Allerton. This hapened to be a faire day for

oxen, kine and sheepe, the greatest in England."

Some records of transactions at Northallerton are available. In the Household Books of Lord William Howard of Naworth Castle (on the English/ Scottish borders) appears:

"CATTEL SOLD 1633 September 24 Rec. of William Grayme for 60 steers and 9 runtessoulde at Allerton (all charges deducted) CCLVII £ xviii vid." (£257.91)

It is interesting to note the distance the cattle were driven for sale - an endorsement of Northallerton's reputation.

But things were not always straightforward as the following extract from "The London Magazine" in 1647 shows:

"Bloody news from Yorkshire: or the great robbery
committed by twenty highwaymen upon fifteen
butchers as they were riding to Northallerton fair."

One of the robbers was rumoured to be the notorious highwayman Nevison, hanged at York in 1684 and the incident emphasises the highwayman menace to travellers.

The Church

The Church continued to be central to Nothallerton affairs and by virtue of the emergence of the Select Vestry of the Parish Church with its increasing powers gradually became the chief executor of local government in the town and parish of Northallerton.

There were some colourful incumbencies as far as the Vicars of Northallerton were concerned with the benefactor of the poor Francis Kaye being succeeded in 1624 by John Craddock whose short stay until 1627 was nothing less than sensational. He was a pluralist being Vicar of Northallerton, Rector of Gainford, co Durham and Vicar of Woodhorn, Northumberland simultaneously. A complaint was made against him in Parliament for extortion (House of Commons Journal) and he died abruptly from poison in 1627. His wife was accused of the crime, stood trial and was acquitted.

Controversy too centred on the incumbency which followed, filled quite legitimately according to the church records on 17th May 1628 when Thomas Blaikeston was "properly inuested into the vicaridge of

Northallerton Church Font of 1662

Allerton". Notwithstanding this he was publicly and dramatically ousted as Vicar in 1640 by Thomas Mann who replaced him by entering the Church when Blaikeston was reading a lesson during divine service, claiming the living by producing a document, turning Blaikeston out of the Reading Desk and Church and delivering a long prayer and longer sermon.

This usurpation took place shortly before the start of the Civil War but even when this ended and Charles II was restored in 1660 Thomas Mann was confirmed legitimately as the Northallerton Vicar on 22nd September 1660 wherein he remained until his death in 1669. The present font in the south western corner of the Parish Church dates to 1662 being built on the same column of the former one and bears the initials of the Vicar Thomas Mann along with those of the four church wardens of the time. The wooden pyramid cover hanging above the font was formerly suspended from the Singing Gallery.

Dr John Neile, whose father was the Archbishop of York, escaped narrowly with his life at the hands of the Roundheads at Scarborough Castle in the Civil War but was rewarded for his Royalist loyalties being appointed as Chaplain to Charles II and then Vicar of Northallerton

(1669-75). His son William Neile (1675-86) followed him making a unique Vicar father and son succession in Northallerton Church history.

The Select Vestry

By the end of the seventeenth century the Select Vestry of Northallerton Parish Church had become the major ruling body of both the church and the town. Eleanor Trotter declared that "the origin of select vestries is in many cases wrapped in obscurity" and this aptly fits Northallerton. Here twenty-four men comprised the Select Vestry with the Vicar as Chairman and its composition self-perpetuating as vacancies (usually caused by death) were filled by the Select Vestry itself. Gradually the reins of local government were taken over completely by the Select Vestry which dealt with the church, poor and highways, levying rates to offset the cost of these.

Early 1600s West Prospect Northallerton Church

The Churchwardens' Accounts were a main area of rates and in 1687 payments were led by Thomas Lascelles £3.10s.0d, Richard Peirse £3. 0s. 0d and William Metcalfe £2. 16s. 0d. Disbursements by the Churchwardens in 1687 included for: Ringers St George's Day;

"Candles and Lyte 1s. 2d;" Load of Lime (Churchyard) 9s. 9d; "a Syth to mow the Churchyard 1s. 0d;" John Coulson Plummer £8. 11s. 6d; "Breade Wine for Communions £1. 3s. 10d;" Surplice washing 3s. 0d. Similar entries continued until the end of the century. Finally, to emphasise the autocratic way the Church was run in favour of the better off, there are regular entries in the Churchwardens' Accounts of the granting of pews to the individuals for private use "having paid for the same according to custom."

Bishops of Durham

The Bishop of Durham still featured often in Northallerton affairs although it seemed with a decreasing influence especially with the growing power of the North Riding JPs, the Quarter Sessions and the Northallerton Select Vestry. The Court Halmot and Courts Leet and Baron for Allertonshire of the Bishop of Durham were held in Northallerton every Michaelmas and Easter to carry our the bishop's tenants' business including receiving fines and rents, surrenders and admitting copyholders. From the mid 1500s a High Steward presided over the courts but after Lord William Burghley in 1614 they do not appear in the court rolls whereas 'Learned Stewards' are then frequently named who conducted the courts and in many cases were legally qualified.

Charities

Several charities were bequeathed to Stuart Northallerton the first by John Eshall and his wife who by indenture of 28th July 1612 conveyed annually 40s to the Northallerton poor and 20s to the Master of Northallerton Grammar School, both of which continued into the nineteenth century.

Francis Kaye - Vicar of Northallerton favoured the local poor in his will of 1624 (see page 60). John Cosin Bishop of Durham left Northallerton's poor £2 in 1671 (his remains incidentally resting overnight in the town en route from London to burial at Bishop Auckland). Northallerton was one of four towns to receive bibles for the use of the poor in 1688 by Lord Wharton the money for which was to be raised from the Swinithwaite estate near Leyburn.

Northallerton Grammar School

William Palliser Archbishop of Cashel in Ireland was born in 1644 at Kirby Wiske and educated at Northallerton Grammar School before going to Trinity College Dublin at fifteen where he enjoyed a brilliant academic career which included fellow, medical fellow, holy orders (1670), Professor of Divinity and Doctor of Divinity. By 1694 he had become Archbishop of Cashel and when he died in Dublin in 1726 he left "twenty pounds yearly and every year" to the poor of Northallerton, thus endorsing his great regard for his "alma mater," Northallerton Grammar School.

The school also produced another eminent churchman and lavish local charity donor in John Kettlewell (1653-1695). Much is known of him because of the writings of George Hickes - another Northallerton Grammar School prodigy who became Dean of Worcester. Kettlewell was born at "Lowfields" farm Brompton owned by his father and attended "ancient Northallerton Grammar School" under the formidable Master, Thomas Smelt. He went to St Edmunds College, Oxford University at seventeen, was elected Fellow of Lincoln College in 1675 (in succession to Dr John Radcliffe, another Northallerton Grammar School tyro) ordained in 1677 and became Rector of Coleshill Warwickshire in 1678.

He refused to take the Oath of Allegiance to William and Mary in 1689 believing in the "Divine Right of Kings" as opposed to parliamentary monarch making and was deprived of his Coleshill living. As a non-juror who refused to compromise his opinions he became well known and admired nationally.

When he died of a harsh illness at 42 he left Lowfields farm Brompton after the death of his wife, with its rents and profits to the poor of Northallerton and Brompton with certain stipulations the bulk of which were typically educational: bibles and prayer books for the literary poor; £4 for the education of poor children; £6 for an Apprentice to learn a trade; and sending a worthy candidate to Oxford or Cambridge University. "Kettlewell's Charity" continued in various forms until the present day.

William Palliser and John Kettlewell were just two of a galaxy of successful pupils in the seventeenth century of Northallerton Grammar School which had such a good reputation that the gentry from near and far sent their sons there. A good example of this was Robert Grey born in 1610 the younger son of Sir Ralph Grey, who after attending Northallerton Grammar School went to Christ's College, Cambridge

University, became a Doctor of Divinity in 1660, was Rector of Bishopwearmouth for over fifty years and died 100 years old. This colourful character in 1617 was placed on a table in Northallerton Grammar School by the local gentry to give a loyal oration to James I who was progressing to Scotland via Northallerton.

Thomas Burnet was born at Croft in 1635, studied at Northallerton Grammar School before going to Clare Hall, Cambridge University in 1651 to become a Doctor of Law and eventually Master of Charter House, London where his portrait by Kneller hangs as well as the British Museum. He achieved the highest scholastic reputation writing several valuable works being particularly versed in elegant Latin composition. When he died in 1715 he was interred in the Charter House chapel.

Thomas Rymer born at Appleton Wiske in 1638 was in the same Grammar School class as George Hickes and then went up to Sidney College, Cambridge University and thence to Grey's Inn. In 1692 he became "Historiographer Royal" to William III and wrote many pamphlets and books the best known of which was "Feodora" which was recognised as a classic of its kind. He was buried in St Clement Danes Church in the Strand in 1713 and his manuscripts are now in the British Museum being invaluable for legal and antiquarian information.

George Hickes hailed from Newsham, being born there in 1642 and attended Northallerton Grammar School before entering St John's College, Oxford University at seventeen. After a distinguished academic and ecclesiastical career, which included Fellow of Lincoln College, Oxford 1664, he became Chaplain in Ordinary to Charles II in 1681 and was installed Dean of Worcester in 1683. He was deprived of the latter when he refused to sign the Oath of Allegiance to William and Mary (1689) and after a period of retirement he finally became Bishop of Thetford.

During his lifetime he was a prolific writer of treatises, pamphlets and books - his "Thesarus" and other works being nationally famous especially those concerned with old northern languages and antiquities, at both of which he was particularly adept. He also enjoyed a high reputation as a preacher, one inspired sermon being at the Yorkshire Feast, Bow Church London in 1682, a very prestigious honour during the course of which he revealed his great pride in his Northallerton - Yorkshire roots:

"Our County, as the curious observe, is the epitome of England: whatsoever is excellent in the whole land being to be found in proportion thereto."

Dr George Hickes – Dean of Worcester

He performed the last rites on diaryist Samuel Pepys and when Dean Hickes died in 1715 he was buried at St Margaret's Westminster. His portrait in canvas is in the Bodleian Library, Oxford.

John Hickes, George's brother was also born at Newsham and educated at Northallerton Grammar School but there the resemblance ends for after going to Trinity College Dublin he eventually became a Nonconformist minister and was continuously in trouble with the authorities. He joined Monmouth's abortive rebellion (1685), fled seeking refuge with Lady Alice Lisle who was beheaded for sheltering him and Hickes was hanged at Glastonbury in 1685.

The last of Northallerton Grammar School's eminent prodigies of the seventeenth century was John Radcliffe who is the best known because of his bequests to Oxford University which bear his name. He was born in 1650 and educated at Wakefield and Northallerton Grammar Schools, the authority on this being Robert Nelson (1656 - 1714) a pious, learned and prolific author. Radcliffe at fifteen went to University College, Oxford University, took his BA in 1669, became a Fellow of Lincoln College, Oxford, turned to study in the medical faculty taking his MD in 1682 and two years later removed to Bow Street, Covent Garden London where he established an extensive medical practice which made him a rich man. *[monochrome plate 3]*

His wit, repartee and bold insolence made tales of Radcliffe legion - a particularly well known one being in addressing William III about his legs: "I would not have your Majesty's two legs for your three kingdoms." He was royal physician to William III and Queen Mary, and Princess Anne and though he lost royal favour his practice flourished despite it was said "a devotion to the tavern and bottle." In 1713 he became MP for Buckingham but died the next year, being buried at St Mary's Oxford and Kneller's portrait of Dr Radcliffe was hung in the Bodleian Library at Oxford University.

After making generous provision for his family he gave £5000 to University College, Oxford and £40,000 to the University of Oxford out of which the university library was built (Radcliffe's Camera) and his trustees used part of the money to build a scientific library by 1794 which became known as Radcliffe's Tower. Amongst other benefactions were £600 per annum for travelling scholarships and funds to the still famous St Bartholomew's Hospital and the John Radcliffe Hospital, Oxford.

The mentor and inspiration of several of these pupils was Thomas Smelt who became Master of Northallerton Grammar School in 1651 moving from a highly successful mastership at Danby Wiske. It was said that in his Danby Wiske time he was an intemperate drinker being intoxicated for days on end but he gave up alcohol and "became a monument, and pattern of strict Temperance and Sobriety to his dying day".

Smelt was an excellent Greek and Latin grammarian and a strong character who was interested not only in the boys' academic progress but their personal development too. He influenced them with his own views - particularly his strong Royalist beliefs. George Hickes and many others felt highly indebted to the start that Smelt gave them and Hickes especially praised his rejection of alcoholism: "it redounds to his honour - the reformation of himself from a sin from which so few reform." He died amidst universal local regret on 19th November 1686 being buried in the churchyard adjacent to his beloved Grammar School with the Parish Register bearing this epitaph: "Thomas Smelt 'vir eruditus' schoolm., buried."

Catholics and Nonconformists

A traveller's assertion that there were no "dissenters" in Northallerton was almost correct for there is little evidence of Catholics or Non-conformists in the district. The town was overwhelmingly Royalist in the Civil War and there were only a few papish Recusants (those who refused to attend the Church of England service) - at the Richmond Quarter Sessions in July 1614 there were no Recusants named at Romanby and Brompton and only seven at Northallerton, and the Northallerton Sessions of October 1617 called purely to list Recusants recorded none at Northallerton.

There were some isolated cases of religious non-conformity: William Meade and his son-in-law Roger Lambe in 1628 for refusing to take the oath before Ralph Hutton, the official of the Dean and Chapter of Durham were sentenced to stand before the Minister in Northallerton Parish Church "in submissive manner for one hour, and to pay unto his majesty 20£;" and in July 1679 John Andrews was imprisoned for seven years for allegedly "exercising the office of a Romish preist at Romanby, att one Mrs Metcalfe's house" and administering the Sacrament to about ten people. But such instances were minimal and extreme religious intolerance never visited Northallerton.

Some separate churches were set up in the district, a Quaker Conventicle being reported in 1669 at "North Allerton," a Presbyterian Meeting was licensed near "North Allerton" on 23rd December 1672 and at the Northallerton Sessions of October 1689 Quaker Meeting Houses were sanctioned at places they existed: "North Allerton, Borrowby, Harlsey, Ellerbecke, Thimbleby, Ingleby, Osmotherley, Harlesey Castle, Winton, Morton and Rownton."

At Northallerton the Quaker Meeting House was on the east side of North End adjacent to what is now Quaker Lane with a nearby burial ground (human bones have been found here during building developments) which probably dated to the eighteenth century, because in June 1698 two Quakers were buried in the Parish Church graveyard.

Land and Enclosures

The land holding situation was in a fluid state in the seventeenth century with for example the sale and then re-possession of the Bishop of Durham's extensive lands. Some land was enclosed - "Overton meadow was inclosed in ye yeare 1634," and the Glebe Terrier (description of church land) of 1685 mentions "old inclosures," that "some pasture had recently been enclosed" but that there were still Open Fields at Northallerton.

There were also illegal enclosures as shown in the Quarter Sessions Records: in 1634 two yeomen had stopped up the road between Northallerton and Stokesley; and a Thornton-le-Beans man had closed the highway at "Oxe-pasture" in 1637. A protracted land dispute was waged between Christ's Church College, Oxford and various Northallerton men including Francis Lascelles, Richard Metcalfe and James Meeke regarding the former holdings of St James' Hospital with the dues and ownership eventually being resolved in favour of the College.

Travel

Roads were so bad that travel could only be by mounted horse or foot in the seventeenth century, although stage-coaches were introduced, and contemporary conditions can be illustrated by the Royal Mail.

In Tudor times selected innkeepers maintained a stable of horses capable of servicing the Royal Post and Mr J Carter was the Northallerton Post Master. In 1603 when James I ascended the throne carrying of letters from London to Edinburgh (via Northallerton) became important but the system was spasmodic and in July 1635 a public postal service was introduced to carry Charles I subjects' mail. This was carried out by runners carrying postbags and a stave - to leap streams and obstacles - but by 1700 mounted riders were used to carry the post bags. Some Northallerton Postmasters were Thomas Redmayne (1667), of the "King's Arms" G Harlow (1685), R Richardson (1690) and Mary Richardson (1694) - their son Robert Richardson is believed to have rebuilt the present "Golden Lion" around 1730.

Early Maps

Northallerton was featured unequivocally on the Great North Road on the early maps, one of the first being "performed" by John Speede in 1610 and included North Alverton, Romanbye, Yafford, Brunton (Brompton) and Thornton iny Beans. The best travellers' early map was "Itinerarium Angliae" by John Ogilby of 1675 concerned with "the Post Road for conveying Letters to and from this Greater Center (London)" the local route being York, Burrowbriggs, Topcliff, Northallerton and Darnton (Darlington).

Stuart Journeys

A traveller on the route in 1639 was John Aston in the service of the King who noted in his Journal that he had lodged at Yorke and then gone north:

> "That night 27th April I came to North Allerton and lodged in a poore house, the toun being filled with troupers before me. Yet I found indifferent accommadacion both for my selfe and horses, good meate for 6d, and good provender beanes and oates for 8d a peck. The dearest provision was beer at 4d a small flaggon. But there had beene all the foote (in their passage) quartered before us, which occasioned that scarcity of drink."

John Cosin the Lord Bishop of Durham's Household Book described his journey south on Friday 12th July 1667. They stopped at Smeeton for a drink at Mr Wharton's (1s), paid 4d "to the poore there" and 6d for greasing the coach. At Northallerton they stayed overnight paying "Mrs Wilson the housebill for meate £2. 1s. 6d, coach horses 13s. 7d. and saddle horses 15s;" Hugh Finch was paid 6s for 6 horses that night and his oastler 1s; and

> "Given the poore there 5s; Given to the ringers there 2s. 6d.
> Payd for mending my Lordes coach 2s. 6d."

Stage Coaches

The first known stage coach advertisement that concerns Northallerton appeared on 5th April 1658 in the "Mercuricus Politicus" with the coach going from the George Inn Aldersgate, London to various cities and towns at rates and times mentioned…

> "…To Yorke: in four days for xls…
> Every Monday to Helperby and Northallerton for xlvs
> To Darnton and Ferryhill for 1s. To Durham for 1vs
> To Newcastle for iii£. Once every fortnight to
> Edinburgh for iv£."

This presaged an era of travel dominated by the stage coaches but in 1659 they were described as "hellcarts" with several charges levelled against them: they undermined the breeding of good horses and prejudiced the art of horsemanship; trade was lessened by fewer horse-riders and their needs of boots, spurs, saddles and bridles; the king's revenues would suffer; and inns would suffer that the coaches did not call at. Thus there was much opposition to the first Act of Parliament in 1662 for making turnpike roads and the major approach roads to Northallerton were not transformed by turnpikes until after the middle of the eighteenth century.

Roads and Bridges

The keys to Northallerton's eminence as a route, agricultural and administrative centre have always been its communicating roads and bridges. In the seventeenth century each town and village was responsible for the roads' upkeep and the frequent orders of the Quarter Sessions for habitations to mend the roads is indicative of the state they were in. For example in 1607 Northallerton was fined 10s. "for not scouring the King's high waie in a lane at a place called Warebank Lane adjoyning Viccars Croft" (now Bullamoor Road adjacent to the Friarage Hospital).

Ainderby Steeple in 1609 was to repair the road between Bedale and Northallerton; and "Thornton le Strete" was ordered in 1612 to mend the road between "Thirsk and Allerton Markett." So that the highways could be properly maintained the 1693 Quarter Sessions levied highway rates at Northallerton of 5d in the £ on all inhabitants of land and 5d in £20 of every personal estate.

Bridges were also critical to Northallerton's accessibility and listed as "county bridges" (those built and repaired by the North Riding) at the Quarter Sessions in 1676 were: Allerton, Cattiericke, Becke

Romanby Pack Horse Bridge

(between Knayton and Borrowby), Croft (south side), Leeming, Morton, Topcliffe, Wiske and Yafforth. Northallerton North Bridge was crucially on the Great North Road spanning Willow Beck had been mentioned in 1358 as receiving a grant of pontage for repair, by John Leland in 1538 as being "one arch of stone" and in the seventeenth century as only needing occasional small repair.

Romanby was a "pack horse bridge" and at the October 1620 Sessions £22. 15s. 0d. was ordered for its repair. At Morton a ferry was used to cross the Swale in the fourteenth century followed by a wooden bridge and then in 1618 the magistrates ordered a stone bridge to be built by the "not employed" - the first time the use of the unemployed for temporary work was referred to. The Wiske bridge was described as "an usuall high waie for the King's post...but in great decaie" in 1620. Finally Otterington Bridge, formerly wooden and known as "Newby Plancks" then, was in great ruin in 1623 but in 1684 Edward Saltmarsh was granted £100 by the North Riding magistrates "for building a stone bridge for carts at Newby over the Wiske."

Some Characters

When Henry Jenkins of Ellerton-on-Swale died on 9th December 1670 he was attributed with the astonishing age of 169 based greatly on his early memories including taking a cart-load of arrows to the English army at Northallerton before the battle of Flodden in 1513. His death was recorded in the Bolton-on-Swale Parish register as a "very aged and poore man of Ellerton was buried here" but in 1743 two monuments were erected in the Bolton on Swale church and churchyard to him, both giving his age as 169: one was a simple monument to "Henry Jenkins the oldest Yorkshireman;" the other was a black marble tablet bearing a eulogistic epitaph by Dr Thomas Chapman, Master of Magdalen College, Cambridge in high flown language beginning -

"Blush not marble to rescue from oblivion the memory of Henry Jenkins."

A field at Yafforth Road, Northallerton was named in his memory "The Jenkins" where skating regularly took place in the nineteenth century, but modern opinion universally rejects the extremity of his age. Nevertheless, the stories about him are legion such as that of a visitor to Ellerton seeking Jenkins who was directed to his cottage where he encountered an old man with flowing white hair in the front garden. "Hello Mr Jenkins I'm pleased to meet you", he said. To which the old fellow replied - "I think it's my faither ye want. He's at back chopping wood."

George Calvert, Lord Baltimore was born at Kiplin near Northallerton in 1578 and died in London in 1632. He was knighted in 1617, became James I's Principal Secretary of State but became a Catholic and though he resigned his office, James made him Baron Baltimore. He is best remembered as the founder of the Catholic State of Maryland, though the grant of Maryland was given to his son Cecil Calvert after Lord Baltimore's death. Firm ties now exist between Maryland and Kiplin Hall which is one of the most historic buildings in the district.

Anne Stringer of Northallerton was born in 1613 and lived until she was 108 and the most dissolute Northallerton character was William Maw who was born in 1660 and went to London giving up his trade as a cabinet maker to live by illegal means and being burned in the hand in April 1710 for his offences. Undeterred he continued his criminal ways, concocted his death and funeral to escape further punishment but eventually was apprehended on five counts including three of highway robbery and hanged at Holborn on 29th October 1711.

6

Eighteenth Century Northallerton (1714 – 1800)

Historical Sources

In the eighteenth century source material concerning Northallerton becomes abundant and the histories of Roger Gale (1739) and James Langdale (1792) are invaluable and give the first detailed descriptions of the structure of the town.

Gale wrote that Northallerton "consists of one wide street about half a mile in length...it is very open and spacious from one end to the other, and it is now almost new paved...from side to side and several good houses of stone and brick erected on it." Situated on the High Street, he continues, are the Toll Booth, where the July Sessions and Bishop's courts are held, the Cross on "four ascents" and the Shambles, all of which belong to the Bishop of Durham who leases them out with the tolls at £8.

"It is a great thorough-fare to the North, with good inns for accommodation of travellers." He mentions two stone bridges over Sunbeck for foot passengers and horses, and the Registry of Deeds built in 1736 - "a handsome house and office." Initially he emphasises the handsome church "covered in lead" and the spacious churchyard.

By the time Langdale wrote in 1792 the town had developed: "It is well paved from side to side and several good houses being erected in it, it has become much more beautiful and commodious than formerly" except for the ugly Toll Booth. "From its situation on the Great North Road, it has always been a considerable thoroughfare and contains several good Inns for the accommodation of travellers." Importantly he cites the North Riding Buildings - the Register Office and sixty yards to its east "a magnificent building erected within these few years for a Session-House, House of Correction etc."

The first plan of Northallerton was drawn up in 1793 by W Jefferson and Son (Solicitors) and shows the town completely centred on and confined to the main street with burgage houses stretching down each side and yards or gardens running back from the majority of these houses. Substantially the main property owners were Mrs Peirse and Lord Harewood who controlled many parliamentary votes as the privilege of voting rested with burgage house tenants. Friarage Street was named Thorn Gapp and Quaker Lane, Jesseygate Lane with the Quaker Meeting House at the north-western end of the latter adjoining the main street.

North Riding Quarter Sessions

In 1720 the North Riding Quarter Sessions was moved from the Guild Hall to the Toll Booth at Northallerton, thence to "Vine House" in 1770 and finally to the purpose built North Riding Quarter Sessions House in 1785. All the Quarter Sessions were permanently held in the Court House from 1786 with all the prestige and custom this brought.

The Justices were all powerful and dealt harshly with offenders. For example at Northallerton in July 1719:

"George Testiman, convicted of larceny, to be conveyed to the Castle of York and transported to some of his Majesty's plantations in America for seven years"; and in 1777 John Anderson was found guilty of stealing a handkerchief worth 10p and sent to "some of his Majesty's ships of war."

County rates were simple: when £100 was estreated by the North Riding Sessions, Allertonshire contributed £8. 12s. 4 ½, of which Northallerton paid 12s. 8 ½, Brompton 11s. 10 ½. and Romanby 7s. 2d. In 1786-1787 money was raised thus to defray the expenses of the North Riding which were £3765. 1s. 8d. some of the major items being: Bridges £1582, York Castle £629, Prosecution of Felons £374, Conveying Vagrants £315, House of Correction £195, Clerk of the Peace £143 and Coroners Inquiries £138.

County Buildings - Registry of Deeds

As well as the centralisation of the Quarter Sessions the other crucial factor in Northallerton becoming the North Riding county town was the siting of the North Riding county buildings, the first of these being the Register of Deeds office in 1736. An official Register Office

North Riding Registry of Deeds – High Street Entrance

existed at the "Fleece Inn" in Thirsk in 1726 and deeds could also be deposited at Mr Straker's "Kings Head" Northallerton. However, an Act of Parliament in 1735 decreed that a Register of Deeds should be established in the North Riding.

Will. Turner was the first Register of Deeds for the North Riding elected by the Quarter Sessions at Northallerton on the 17th July 1735. In September 1735 the Justices by a majority decided to establish a register office at Northallerton as "the nearest markett town to the centre or the middle of the North Riding." Suitable land was obtained on 28th September 1736 from Will. Wood and his father Humphrey and by 11th April 1738 John Wade had completed the building for £400. Additionally rooms "for the reception of a family" were ordered by the JPs which were built by Will. Peirse for £108. 17s. 7d. and finished on 30th October 1738.

Registers of Deeds were elected by the North Riding Freeholders, the elections being always held at Northallerton which again added kudos to the town, with some very strongly contested such as that of 1782. Then William Chaloner, Henry Pulleine, John Cayley, Samuel Skelton, Richard Peirse and Matthew Butterwick were in opposition with Butterwick the successful candidate who then held the post for forty-five years. The successive Registers became important and familiar characters dwelling in the Register House and it is interesting in view of the eventual North Riding/North Yorkshire staffing levels at the County Hall that the original office consisted of the Register and one clerk!

Additions to the North Riding buildings at Northallerton commenced in 1782 with John Carr of York the architect - famous for his many Yorkshire buildings including Harewood House. Firstly the Register House was enlarged which enabled the old Register's offices to be used as his home with a yard, a good garden and entrances from both the High Street and Zetland Street. Next, proposals were made in 1784 by the North Riding Justices for the building of a Court (Sessions) House, Governor's abode and House of Correction.

Land for this was purchased at the east end of Zetland Street from the Bishop of Durham John Egerton on the stipulation that the Bishop's Courts would be held there in perpetuity. It was low-lying swampy waste land called Priest Garth of 1.2 acres, which had been used as a "receptacle for rubbish" by the townsfolk and in the middle was a "Horse Pond" for the cleansing of "post and stage" horses.

The new Court House appeared to be "in situ" by October 1785 with "the Governor's House below and the Sessions House above" and the House of Correction by October 1787 with George Parkin becoming its first Governor. John Carr was paid £200 for his entire professional services. This establishment of a cluster of County buildings and the centralisation of the Quarter Sessions confirmed Northallerton indisputably as the North Riding County town - a position it has never relinquished.

Church Affairs

Around the same time as the construction of the county buildings, Northallerton Parish Church was partially re-built but according to a future curate Rev Saywell writing a century later with displeasing results. In 1779 the chancel was re-erected in the unattractive "Assembly Room" style of the period and then in 1787 the high pitched roofs of the nave, aisle, trancepts and chancel were lowered to obtain the lead. "Instead of the three distinct roofs which covered the nave and aisles, one monstrous slated roof was substituted" wrote Saywell who went on to condemn "this wholesale spoilation" being effected he maintained for the price of the lead (£320. 15s. 0d) to balance the books of the churchwardens who had an outstanding debt of £332.10s. 5½d. The great restoration of 1882-1885 to Saywell's pleasure restored the architectural lines and stateliness of the church. *[monochrome plate 4]*

In 1787 new galleries and oaken pews were installed and the courtyard was levelled during which an ancient stone coffin was unearthed. This was placed near the south porch where it was used as a drinking trough for horses and though having long lost this utility, remains there to this day.

It is interesting to note that in 1777 there were no trees in the churchyard and that the church possessed 95 acres of glebe and terrier land in and around Northallerton along with 28 acres in Romanby and 26 acres at Deighton. 4239 acres in the Northallerton parish were subject to the annual payment of tithes to the church – a situation existent from time immemorial. The Vicar paid £16 yearly in rent to the Dean and Chapter of Durham Cathedral.

The church was overwhelmingly the town's most dominating influence in the eighteenth century with each successive Vicar chairman of the now all-powerful Select Vestry of the Northallerton Parish Church. Some of the Vicars attract particular notice and glimpses of their lives reflect their day and age.

John Balguy (1729-1748) who it will be recalled wrote an ode to a Roman urn in 1743 was a Vicar of eloquence and learning who published several religious tracts and played a leading part in the major ecclesiastical dispute of his time – the Bangorian Controversy. Possibly his most dramatic religious confrontation, however, was when a Quaker, Anne Flower burst into the Church one Sunday morning on 20th July 1735 in the middle of the matins service and began to strenuously hold forth. Reverend Balguy dealt with her courteously and probably saved her from the anger and zeal of the mob that had gathered outside.

When Robert Pigot (1748-1775) was Vicar, entries in the "Book of Excommunications" reflect the moral clime of the time and the uncompromising sternness of the church. For example Thomas Powles and Mary Robson who had cohabited were excommunicated for incest Mary being Thomas' niece; and Mary Jackson was excommunicated in 1755 for the crime of fornication.

Benjamin Walker (1775-1814) was the longest serving Northallerton Vicar of all time and he and his wife (formerly Miss Warren) had eighteen children. In keeping with the hazardous conditions of pestilence and disease of the times which took no account of age and rank four of the children died young. Of the survivors two became Church of England ministers, one a Ripon solicitor, another a Captain in the Royal Navy and three officers in the army – two Colonels and a Major General.

Reverend James Wilkinson surpassed Reverend Walker's clerical longevity at Northallerton because he was curate at the Parish Church for forty-two years (1772 to 1814). He hailed from Uckerby near Scorton where he owned a farm of four hundred acres and throughout his curacy he was also Vicar of Hutton Bonville. Finally, he was not only the Master of Northallerton Grammar School for a record forty nine years (1771 to 1820) during which time he taught countless boys including the renowned Byerley brothers John and Thomas, but he also initiated and organised the complete re-building of the Grammar School in 1776.

The Select Vestry

The Select Vestry of "the four and twenty" was the main organ of Northallerton's government and management until the formation of the Northallerton Poor Law Union (1834) and the Local Board of Health (1851). Although its power was undemocratically based it dealt benevolently with many of its cases as exemplified in the "Orders of the Vestry" records.

Churchwardens and Constables' Books

The Select Vestry appointed the Churchwardens and Constables and levied rates to defray the costs of their activities which were documented in their "Books". Obviously, the Churchwardens' main concern was the Parish Church and their books had a colourful variety of items: in 1705 church wine cost £5. 2s. 7d; in 1706 Thos. Walker saddler, was "to have the pew opposite John Todd's;" a clock for the church tower was donated in 1714 by the Northallerton MPs Cholmely Turner and Leonard Smelt which was to be taken care of by Thos Hepton (1776); the "Singing Gallery to be enlarged" (1775); and "the North Door of the Church to be walled up" (23rd September 1797).

Bell-ringing occasions were illuminating: "Rining" on the Gunpowder Treason 1705, 13s; 1722 to celebrate Charles II Restoration and King George I's birthday, £1; 1781 Cornwallis' success over the American rebels in South Carolina, 5s; 1797 ringing twice on the Duke of York passing through the town, 8s. 10d; and 1798 for Admiral

Northallerton Fire Engine "1736" (served 1742 to 1893)

Nelson's victory at Aboukir.

Payments concerning the Constables were also interesting: in 1739 "for whipping Jno Malloy which was dumb and Thos. Thompson a sailor 1s. each prisoner"; repairing the Stocks 1744 and 1753; 1760 Mr Richardson's "Golden Lion" given 2s. 8d. for accommodating "1 Shoulger"; the Bell-man James Lakin paid 2d. for two "Cries" in 1760; "a coppey put on the Church door" of a Militia list in 1762 for 2s.

The Constables in 1797 were paid 2s. for taking a man at the "Raceground" (Broomfield) and for "searching the town in Racetime." A journey from Northallerton to Easingwold cost 25s. 6d. " chaise 19s., Post Boy 2s. 6d. and Tole Bars 4s." in 1799; letters were carried in 1798 to Leeds (3s.), Bradford (3s.) and Masham (2s.); and an enigmatic entry was the payment of 1s. on each of three days to the Constables for "attending at Mr Hirst's door on account of rioting" in 1798.

Under the control of the Constables was the Newsham's Fire Engine purchased for Northallerton in 1742 and in 1750 it was "oyled and cleaned" by Leonard Hebden for 6s. 0d. Its origination date of 1736 was emblazoned on its side and it was horse drawn, operated by hand and lasted miraculously until 1893 when a ferocious fire at the linoleum factory emphasised its inadequacy.

Assessments

Expenses for local activities, mainly for the Church, Constables and Poor, were also the responsibility of the Select Vestry. From 1707 to 1714 the Church rates were 4d. in the £ with the Peirses Thomas (£4. 13s. 4d.) and Henry (£4. 7s. 4d.) leading the list in 1714 which included the Duke of Leeds £1. 13s. 4d, and Richard Metcalfe £1. 13s. 4d., Cuthbert Mitford 10s. 11d. and Lord Crew 1s. 4d.

Rates applied for the "Constables of Allerton" in 1738 contained familiar places: Castle Hills was assessed at 3s. Porch House 5d., and the Quaker Meeting House 5d; and in 1797 Applegarth 2s. 11d, "Ston Cross" 2s. 8 ½, "Black Bull" 9s. 7d. (Mr Sidgwick), "Pack Horse Inn" 3s. 9d, "New Inn" 2s. 6d. (J Carter), "Tickle Toby" 2s. 1d. (Peter Kemp), "Flice" 3s. 4d, and "Golden Lion" 15s.

The Poor

The Select Vestry estreated 6d. in the £ in 1781 as a Poor rate and earlier on 26th January 1756 had placed "£100 at Interest on the Security" of the turnpike road from "Burrowbridge to Durham" (the Great North Road via Northallerton) to produce revenue for the Poor but this was withdrawn in 1788 to be used to repair the Maison Dieu houses.

Northallerton's Poor were sub-divided into those in the Workhouse and the others subject to "out-door relief". From 1720 the Guild Hall was used as the Workhouse of the Parish which operated the Workhouse with an average weekly total of twenty two inmates until 1783 when responsibility for the Poor was let to a private individual by advertising - "Poor To Be Let." William Chapman as a result was chosen as Workhouse Master by "five open votes to three" and took the annual contract of £165, remaining Master for several years when the average weekly occupancy was twenty-four inmates.

An important step forward was the appointment of "a Medical Man" for the poor in November 1776 with Dr Richard Dighton the first incumbent at an annual salary of four guineas, which was increased to ten guineas in 1796. The appointment was "called" by the Bellman in the town down to the last detail of the terms.

Such enlightenment was not unusual for the Select Vestry in their treatment of the Poor in which they often showed great benevolence: Anne Wilford was given one guinea to go to London to better herself with wealthy relations (1779); Widow Margaret Robson was given "a horse cart load of coals and a peck of wheat." (1782); "Geo Scarlett with straw to thatch his house" (1784); Thomas Byerley allowed 5s. to seek work (1785); Richd Garbutt's wife given 10s. 6d. "having five small children in Small Pox" (1785); Rachael Wilford to be conveyed to York "for the benefit of the Infirmary" (1786); Robert Gamble's house to be fitted up as a Blacksmith's shop (1786); "10s. to be paid to Thoms Rowland to Convey him to Scarboro for Benefit of Sea-Bathing." (1787).

Charities

Several charities were used by the Select Vestry to benefit the "outdoor poor" including Kay's Charity and the Maison Dieu for poor widows which was "in danger of falling down" in 1787 and repaired the following year. There were two new charities the first couched in the will of Lady Mary Calverley widow of Sir John Calverley on 10th May 1715 leaving the dividends annually from £1500 at interest to the poor of Darlington and Northallerton and the in-between villages. Mrs Elizabeth Raine's of 1737 was the second new charity with money being given to the poor of Romanby and Northallerton. The main clause was for £6. 4s. 6d. for loaves of bread to be distributed from Mrs Raine's graveside at the Eves of Christmas, Easter and Whitsun by the Vicar and Churchwardens. Mrs Raine's gravestone is still prominent opposite the South Porch in the churchyard.

Apprenticeships

Apprenticeships were still deemed vital to the regulation of trade and were protected as in 1728 when Will Johnson of Northallerton was released from his indenture by the Select Vestry because his Master Joseph Bedlowes barber "has run away." The Select Vestry tried to apprentice as many poor boys as possible but the policy was different for poor girls very few of whom were apprenticed with most entering domestic service.

Living Conditions

Atrocious weather conditions characterised the 1780s and 1790s bringing great hardship to the poor with the Tees freezing over in 1779/80 and prolonged frosts with deep snows at Northallerton in

1783/84, 1784/85 and 1788/89. Food prices were high and with a bad 1785 harvest the Select Vestry provided bread and potatoes for the poor families in 1786. Things worsened in the 1790s with the deepest snow ever known in the North Riding which prompted Edward Lascelles to distribute £50 to the poor in his manor of Northallerton the "York Herald" commenting on this on 11th July 1795 that "never had the poor called out more loudly for relief nor when was relief more generously offered."

The century ended with 1799 being "the most unfavourable year in the memory of man": a severe frost and snow in the early months was followed by incessant rain from April to December finalised by deep December frosts. To counter high prices the Select Vestry bought wheat and sold it cheaply to their poor at Northallerton. Emigration acted as a safety valve but there is little evidence of a major exodus from the Northallerton area where as in the rest of the North Riding "Privation was undoubtedly a recurrent feature in the lives of the poor who even in normal circumstances, lived close to subsistence." (R P Hastings)

A saving grace in Northallerton and district was that in both the domestic and agricultural spheres working men and women were hired annually and lived in with their employers who were responsible for their upkeep, thus being cushioned from the most devastating conditions. From a sustenance viewpoint the potato was introduced into the North Riding in 1760 and by 1800 was the main item of the lower classes' staple diet.

Health

It is little wonder that in the prevailing conditions worsened by the cramped and often noxious living quarters that health was poor, epidemics frequent and the visitation of death constant. Except for those "living in" with their employers, the lower classes in Northallerton were mainly herded in the dark, dank, narrow yards leading off the High Street in cottages usually "one room up and one down" to accommodate the entire family. Additional to the overcrowding was the sheer squalor of the yards where overflowing privies and dung heaps existed side by side with the living quarters and drinking wells. And though the burgage houses fronting the Main Street had vastly superior living conditions, such was the virulence of diseases and epidemics that no-one was invulnerable.

Ingledew cites longevity at Northallerton with 63 persons from the

1. Castle Hills depicted in 1794

2. Historic Porch House

3. Dr John Radcliffe

4. Northallerton Church, post 1779 and 1787 Restoration

5. "Vine House" 1789 - now the Rutson Hospital

6. Warrior's Yard - now behind Ottakers

7. Henry Rutson (1831-1920) - the Hospital Benefactor

8. Northallerton Shooting Club in the 1880s

New Row Yard – now the Tesco site.

town and Romanby living to over 90 between 1721 and 1857 but this is far outweighed by early deaths and the general death rate. In a normal year in the eighteenth century the average burial rate at Northallerton was 25-30 which was well exceeded in some years of probable epidemics: 1746 - 63, 1760 - 56 and 1770 - 48. 1784 saw 74 deaths inclusive of 19 small pox, 3 fever and 2 whooping cough. Two victims were Richard five months and Elisabeth nine months the children of the town Doctor, Richard Dighton.

Friendly Societies

After 1760 "Friendly Societies" were established promoting self-help and thrift which protected the working-man to some degree against unemployment, injury and death. Between 1763 and 1799 seventy-one "Friendly Societies" were registered in the North Riding with one each at Brompton, Borrowby, Osmotherley and Appleton Wiske and four at Northallerton including the Northallerton Amicable Society and the New Friendly Society.

Vagrancy

In the light of social and employment factors it is no surprise that vagrancy was one of the major problems of the time for which extreme punishments were meted out. The amounts recorded for "the conveyance of vagrants" speak for themselves in the numbers involved and at the Northallerton Quarter Sessions of July 1713 the magistrates perceived "the great abundant and wandering concourse of beggars" and ordered the Constables to be more severe in dealing with them.

Proven rogues and vagabonds were harshly treated by the Quarter Sessions at Northallerton: in July 1739 Jane Hood was imprisoned and sentenced "to be whipt" twice at Bedale; "Jas Mason to be publicly whipped as a sturdy rogue and vagabond" (July 1749); Joseph Stuart "an incorrigible rogue" in 1775 was sentenced to be whipped twice at Richmond, imprisoned for six months with hard labour and sent to "His Majesty's land or sea forces."

Enclosures

It is likely that continued enclosures of land contributed to the vagrancy situation to the detriment of the small landholder. "Watlass Moor an open common field of 390 acres" was enclosed by the Sessions at Northallerton in 1754; the common lands and moors of Osmotherley were cited for enclosure in 1755; Yafforth Moor was to be enclosed in 1788 with interested parties meeting at the "Golden Lion" Northallerton; and Knayton Moor was due for enclosure in 1796.

Of great importance to Northallerton was the proposal to enclose the "Northallerton Playing Fields" as initiated by a notice in the "York Courant" on 27th August 1765. Entitled "Northallerton Township Playing Fields" it desired "The several Proprietors of the three

Township Fields lying at Northallerton called Greenasike, Turker, and Knottabottom to meet at the house of Mr Robert Richardson, the "Golden Lion" in Northallerton on Thursday 5th September at 10 am. to consider proper Ways and Means for dividing and enclosing the same." It is probable that the enclosure plan succeeded with the town losing its common playing fields with the exception of Greenhowsike which was unenclosed and in "strips" of land on the Northallerton Tithe Map of 1844.

Agriculture

New methods of farming were a feature of the later eighteenth century and a good example of this in the Northallerton district was the better breeding of animals by Thomas Booth of Warlaby who in 1789 founded the famous Warlaby Shorthorn herd by buying and hiring from the herds of the Colling brothers of Hurworth near Darlington and Henry Pierse of Bedale. Booth's herd of large hornless cattle on his Warlaby farm became nationally and even internationally renowned for the next century.

Earlier in 1725 Daniel Defoe in a "Tour thro' the Whole Island of Great Britain" had waxed lyrical over the area's animals - "the best and the largest oxen and the finest galloping horses." He mentions Northallerton's "Fair once a fortnight for some months" and that the animals were taken to the Fens to be fattened for the London market. Another visitor in 1763 stated that Northallerton's "Fairs for horned cattle, horses and sheep are the most thronged in England, incredible numbers, particularly of oxen being bought at this place."

Great droves of animals would arrive in the town for the Fairs - the "Durham Ox" was a known drovers' inn - and to the east of the town near to Osmotherley the "Highland Drovers Road" had its hey-day with an estimated 24,000 head coming down from Scotland annually on the route, the animals being driven an average of ten to fourteen miles a day. A drovers' resting place was the "Chequers Inn" at Slapestones having a well known sign with the motto: "Be not in haste; step in and taste: Good ale for nothing - tomorrow." Which never came! As the century progressed the use of fodder crops (turnips) to keep animals alive throughout the winter rendered the Fairs less important but they, along with the markets, remained an integral part of the town's economy

The government gave subsidies to farmers, in 1781 passing an Act for the "Encouragement of the Growth of Hemp and Flax."

Beneficiaries in this respect were all to the east of Northallerton at Ellerbeck, Brompton, Ingleby Arncliffe, Deighton and Thimbleby and connected with the hemp and flax production was the bleaching of linen cloth at the bleachfields of Matthew Bovill at Swainby (circa 1782) and John Flanders (circa 1789) at Crathorne.

Cattle Plague

A most serious occurrence was the cattle murrain or plague which broke out in the Northallerton area in 1748 to such a virulent extent that the Quarter Sessions for five years were concerned largely with the plague and the regulation of the sale and movement of cattle. In 1748 with the cattle distemper raging all fairs and markets in the North Riding were suspended.

At last in 1753 the plague abated and at the Northallerton July Quarter Sessions it was "ordered that all fairs etc within the Riding to be henceforth opened." A postscript recalls the composition then of a "Cattle Plague Psalm" which was sung at Osmotherley Church a typical verse being:

"No Christian's bull nor cow they say
  But takes it out of hand;
And we shall have no cows at all,
  I doubt within the land."

Evidently it was sung with such feeling that five farmers at the Service burst into tears! Indeed it had been a disastrous time for local agriculture.

Commerce

Local trade was as formerly centred around agriculture and the importance of the skinners' trade was emphasised by a petition presented in 1718 to Parliament by the skinners of the borough of Northallerton praying that the abuses butchers and others do to lamb and sheep skins should be redressed. Early in the century the spurriers still flourished and with the stage-coach era dawning in the second half of the century the leather industry boomed with tanneries springing up at the North End of the town. Stabling had added importance in all the "coaching" inns such as the "Black Bull" and "Golden Lion." Before the factory system several "cottage" industries were engaged in such as nail, basket, rope and candle making with evidence that weaving was the most predominate of these in Northallerton.

The "shop economy" was now well established and advertisements appeared regularly regarding shop property, apprentices and goods. For example in a 1792 "York Herald" Mr J Langdale Bookseller, Printer and Druggist, Northallerton advertised a "fresh Supply of Spilsbury's justly celebrated Antiscorbutic Drops." Some shops were multi-purpose like Langdale's but most dealt with specific areas like butchers, grocers and drapers, by this time the entire High Street being developed with shops and businesses.

North Riding Bank

As a result of the increased prosperity, economic advancement and more complex commerce a bank was opened at Northallerton on 7th February 1793 called the "North Riding Bank" with its security underwritten by Richard Peirse, Warcop Consett, Edward Topham and Thomas Walton. Initially it was successful but was forced to close in the dire economic circumstances of the country in the early nineteenth century. Nevertheless, its foundation was an important financial milestone in Northallerton foreshadowing the modern banks.

Roads and Travel

Trade and travel were facilitated by the improvement of the roads and the onset of the "coaching era" in one of the most colourful stories of the century. At the outset the roads were as deplorable as they had been in the seventeenth century and Arthur Young the agriculturist drew wide attention to their fearful state. The times of journeys were interminable: in 1749 two stage coaches lumbered from Newcastle to London taking three days to get to Northallerton where they stayed overnight; and John Matthews, a lawyer in 1753 travelled from Yarm to London on the Great North Road via Northallerton in fourteen "stages" there and eighteen back by private post chaise. The Northallerton outward stage from Yarm cost: chaise 14s 3d, breakfast 1s 4d, ostler 8d and hay/corn 6d and the overall London return journey £24. 6s. 5d.

Travel costs were exceptionally high but Northallerton evidently had an unwanted reputation as an expensive place to stay. The Rev. Sidney Smith wrote to the Countess Grey in 1762 advising her against being laid up at the "Black Swan" Northallerton where "your bill will come to a hundred pounds."

The North Riding Quarter Sessions constantly referred to the roads and bridges. In 1743 Northallerton North Bridge was "a County bridge - very much out of repair and dangerous for travellers" but this was repaired with the Great North Road to Darlington to carry forward the English army under the Duke of Cumberland to Culloden in 1746. Smeaton, Masham and Morton bridges were mended between 1710 and 1714 and the Justices issued many warrants against erring townships for not repairing their roads.

Turnpike Trusts

Turnpike Trusts were the great movement forward in the betterment of the roads, when by Act of Parliament a body of Trustees were enabled to improve a stipulated stretch of road and subsequently charge specified tolls for the use of this road. By 1745 at least some of the Great North Road between Boroughbridge and Durham had been turnpiked as evidenced by Quarter Session proceedings which also in 1749 earmarked "Jas. Hird, Surveyor of the Northallerton turnpike road" for £50 of the £163. 2s. 9d. cost of building Newsham Bridge. The two main local roads had been turnpiked before 1750: Boroughbridge to Durham via Northallerton and York - Thirsk - Northallerton.

Their Turnpike Trustees met annually to auction the tolls, at the "Golden Lion," Northallerton for the Boroughbridge Road and "Three Tuns," Thirsk for the York Road.

Examples of the Let of the Tolls:

Boroughbridge - Durham

Toll Gates	Feb 1774	Feb 1795
Darlington	£ 250	£ 300
Croft	280	402 (including Lovesome Hill)
Entercommon	500	350
Lovesome Hill	131	
Newsham	141	169
Topcliffe	184	200

York – Northallerton

	1778	1796
Purgatory	£ 170	£ 213. 10s.
Stockill Green	188	382. 10s.
Skelton	295	511

An illustrious name associated with the continued improvement of the Great North Road was that of John Carr the eminent York architect who reconstructed the North Bridge at Northallerton in the 1790s at the behest of the North Riding magistrates.

The other local road of note was Boroughbridge to Piercebridge which was recognised as another branch of the Great North Road with toll bars at Butcher House Bar, Leeming Bar, Catterick and Piercebridge.

Coaching

Between 1763 to 1774 four hundred and fifty two Turnpike Acts were passed and the great coaching era had commenced which vitalised Northallerton with a constant flow of coaches including those of the Royal Mail which began its mail "run" by stage coach from London to Edinburgh via Northallerton in 1786. Some of the regular coaches were; "High Flyer" ("Kings Head"); "Edinboro' Mail" and "Diligence" (both "Black Bull"); "Wellington" ("Golden Lion," Godfrey Hirst); "Leeds and Shields Royal Mail" ("Old Golden Lion," William Cariss). The "Royal Charlotte" in 1788 ran "Well guarded and at Reduced Prices" from Newcastle to Holborn, London in two days, being horsed at the "Golden Lion" with the Northallerton - London fare £2. 8s. For "short" journeys the cost was 3d per mile "inside" and 1 ½d "outside".

The Thirsk to Northallerton route had grand stretches of road thirty yards from hedgerow to hedgerow and Northallerton to Great Smeaton also had "fine flowing hedgerows and a spacious roadway" (Thomas Bradley, "Old Coaching Days"). At Northallerton a thriving coaching industry saw all the main hotels and pubs stabling horses (sixty at the "Golden Lion"), changing teams of two and four, washing horses at the two Horse Ponds on the sites now of the prison and Friarage hospital and resting them in nearby fields (the "Golden Lion" field was on the present site of Northallerton College).

It was a great thrill for the Northallerton townsfolk as the clarion call of the approaching coach pealed out and the coach swept into the High Street with a rattle and a bustle. "The stage coach," wrote Bradley "with its beautiful team, and the Royal Mails having driver and guard in scarlet were a thing of beauty and of joy which brought the people of Northallerton rushing to their doors."

There were of course adverse aspects to the coaching story. "Outside" passengers in bad weather travelled in conditions of deep

"The Golden Lion" – premier Great North Road coaching inn

privation and there was a constant threat of highwayman - for instance the Newcastle to London coach was robbed by two highwayman on the night of 16th May 1774. Driving in "opposition" included driving rivals off the road in this commercially orientated industry.

Accidents were frequent and often drivers were cited for "furious driving". Although coachmen were generally of a good character and many were well known personalities they numbered some extremists such as Ralph Soulsby who driving his coach the "Wellington" in opposition to another coach from Great Smeaton to Northallerton killed three out of his four horses. It is alleged that two horses died approaching Northallerton, the third expired outside the Parish Church and he arrived at the "Golden Lion" with one horse.

But despite its drawbacks the coaching era, which was at its height from 1780 to 1840, brought excitement, colour, employment and economic benefit to Northallerton. It was no coincidence that when the coming of the railway (the "Iron Horse") ended the stage-coach operation to all intents and purposes in 1841, that the town's population reversed its continual upward trend of many centuries:- 1841-3092; 1861 -2870.

Swale Bedale Brook Navigation

Canals were also the subjects of national improvement and in the Northallerton district there was a scheme to make the Swale navigable from Morton Bridge. The latter would become an inland port with barges plying down the Swale to the Ure, the Ouse and beyond which would have greatly affected Northallerton's trade pattern. Mooted in December 1766 the plan was called the "Swale and Bedale Brook Navigation" because it also involved Bedale Beck, but though its commissioners met several times between 1767 and 1770 and the matter was strongly advocated, the fifty sponsors necessary were not forthcoming to form a committee and the project was abandoned in August 1770.

Religious Creeds

Controversy still surrounded religion in the eighteenth century and at the Northallerton Quarter Sessions of July 1702 the Justices avowed that they would "put in the strictest execution of the laws against all persons guilty of the neglect of the worship and service of God on the Lord's Day." Certificates had to be produced, such as that of Richard Metcalfe of Romanby in 1701, that individuals "had received the Lord's Supper." "Registration of Papists Estates" in the North Riding in a 1719 Quarter Sessions filled 139 pages of the Order Book but there were no Catholics registered at Northallerton, Brompton and Romanby.

Religious tolerance was much more marked, however, than in the previous century as evidenced by the number of non-conformist houses allowed by the Quarter Sessions: the house of John Janson, Northallerton (1705), Thomas Forster, Borrowby was allowed a Quaker Meeting House (1727) and "the house of John Wood at Northallerton to be licensed for Dissenting Ministers" (1732).

Non-conformism was undoubtedly on the increase at Northallerton particularly Quakerism which flourished at the North End of the town, with a Meeting House which was referred to in various Parish Books: 1710, 1747 when Joseph Flanders was in charge and 1759 under James Wood being called then the "Elder House". Near to the Meeting House was a Quaker Burial Ground where internments occurred until 1790 when the last burial was Elizabeth Burn who had been visiting her relative Dr John Lincoln a Northallerton physician. By the end of the century Quakerism seemed confined to a few zealous adherents in the town.

Methodism gradually prospered in eighteenth century Northallerton with meetings being held in private houses licensed for the purpose until in 1796 the Wesleyans built a chapel on "Bakehouse

Corner" (at the junction of East Road and Friarage Street). John Wesley on his wide ranging evangelistic travels preached at Northallerton three times and visited Osmotherley on many occasions it being one of his favourite places. On 15th April 1745 Wesley paid his first Northallerton visit "when I preached at the Inn ("Old Golden Lion")" where he found the townsfolk to be "a noble people". He visited again on 12th May 1755 with his wife and for the last time on Saturday 3rd June 1780 when he held a Service and delivered a sermon in Jacky Wren's yard - now the yard of the "Buck Inn" - Wren being a pious weaver whose house was licensed for Services. In his Journal Wesley recorded that it was a large congregation but a "careless people", which contrasts hugely with his 1745 opinion!

Politics – MPs

Northallerton's status was demonstrated and enhanced by its possession of two Members of Parliament but it was a "Pocket Borough" controlled by its largest property owners who owned the majority of the "burgage houses" which carried a vote each for the tenants in the Borough. In 1739 the town had 194½ burgage houses according to Roger Gale, mainly owned after 1750 by the Peirse and Lascelles families which was reflected in the identity of the Northallerton MPs: from 1713 when Henry Peirse became an MP, successive Henry Peirses represented Northallerton throughout the eighteenth century (except from 1754-1775); Henry Lascelles became a Northallerton MP in 1745 and he was followed by Lascelles family members for an unbroken sequence of 85 years. As a blatantly "Pocket Borough" Northallerton was a target for the parliamentary reformers but did not lose an MP until the Great Reform Act of 1832.

Military Affairs

Northallerton's key position on the Great North Road made the passage and billeting of troops both frequent and inevitable. Very often the town was full of soldiers and in 1734 this situation was reflected in the Parish Registers when the number of illegitimate children directly related to soldiers caused much consternation. Generally, however the military influxes caused few problems except for isolated cases as in 1795 when the Officers of the Duke of Gloucester's regiment caused such affront to the townspeople that a subsequent Quarter Sessions found them with a charge to answer and their prosecution was only avoided by Officers paying a sum to the Northallerton poor.

The military movement of the greatest moment in the century was the encampment of the English army commanded by the King's second son the Duke of Cumberland on Castle Hills in 1746 before going north to heavily defeat the Scots at the Battle of Culloden. Miss Annie Crosfield, the daughter of the town's leading attorney, Thomas Crosfield, eulogised the event in her poem "Castle Hills" and a local who rode express post from Northallerton to Newcastle-on-Tyne for the army was Robert Simpson the ostler at the "Old Black Swan" and later landlord of the "Packhorse Inn".

With the outbreak of the Napoleonic War in 1793 extra "county business" of meetings of the Lieutenancy and Magistracy of the North Riding took place in Northallerton at the "Golden Lion" or Court House. For example on 3rd April 1794 such a meeting occurred chaired by the Lord Lieutenant Earl Fauconberg to "take into Consideration the plans proposed by the Government for augmenting the Internal Force of this Kingdom." Detailed proposals were decided and published later concerning the North Riding Militia, extra militiamen to be called up, volunteer companies including coastal batteries at Whitby and Scarborough and the county rate to pay the cost.

The Clerk for the Lieutenancy meetings was Henry Hirst who lived at the "Friarage" (the present Northallerton Divisional Police Station) and was responsible for the Orders of the Lieutenancy. The next General Meeting at the Court House, Northallerton regarding the "National Defence against any attempt at Foreign Invasion" composed of the Nobility, Gentry, Clergy and Freeholders in May 1794 started a Subscription List to defray expenses in raising a militia and aiding General Defence. Earl Fauconberg led the subscribers' with £200 and others were Warcop Consett £100, Sir Thomas Dundas £100, Henry Gale £50, Thomas Coore £21, Matthew Dodsworth £100, John Wharton £100 and Leonard Smelt £20. By September 1794 the list stood at £7122. 10s. 6d.

Northallerton Grammar School

Northallerton Grammar School continued to produce eminent men from humble beginnings. *[colour plate 4]* Colonel William Lambton (1756 – 1825) was a poor boy of humble parents from Crosby Grange who obtained one of the four annual free places at Northallerton

Colonel William Lambton

Grammar School. He progressed to gain a commission in the 33rd Regiment of Foot commanded by Sir Arthur Wellesley, the future Duke of Wellington. When the regiment was stationed in India Major Lambton undertook a mathematical and geographical survey of India between 1802 to 1823. His work as the Originator and Superintendent of the Great Trigonometrical Survey of India has been acclaimed as a stupendous feat of courage, perseverance and ability.

John and Thomas Byerley the sons of a Brompton joiner also

gained free scholarships to Northallerton Grammar School and went on to remarkable careers. John (1780 – 1837) went into the literary sphere producing plays, essays and poetry. He was knighted in 1819 and as Sir John Byerley received an annual pension of £200 from the Prince Regent, later to become George IV. He also invented 'oleagine' a substance used in woollen cloth production.

Thomas Byerley (1788 – 1826) also went to London and carved out a remarkable career in the literary sphere with a meteoric rise in journalism to become editor of the 'Literary Chronicle', 'Evening Star' and 'Mirror' and to move in the society of many of the leading figures of the day. His early death at thirty-eight was very much lamented.

In 1776 Northallerton Grammar School was entirely rebuilt by public subscription the list of which was virtually the "Who's Who" of the late eighteenth century Northallerton. A direct reference to the school's antiquity is that even then the building "to be pulled down" by William Mudd (the appropriately named builder!) was called "the old Grammar School".

The new building which now forms the main structure of the offices of Place, Blair and Hatch solicitors, was constructed at an overall cost of £137. 14s. 8½d. This left a good sum spare and the decision taken by the Vicar Reverend Benjamin Walker and churchwarden Will Squire as to what best to do with the residual amount gives an idea of the prevailing educational philosophies. It was decided to build an additional room adjoining the west of the school "to serve for the punishment of scholars in"!

On 4th October 1776 an advertisement in the "York Courant" to attract would-be pupils proposed to board "Young Gentlemen" and instruct them in English, Latin, Greek, Writing and Arithmetic for £14. 3s. 6d. per annum at the 'lately rebuilt' school. In 1781 at a visitation by the Archbishop of York it was stated – "We have a Grammar School endowed with about three acres of land and the sum of five pounds and twenty pence annually. Taught by the Curate of the Parish James Wilkinson."

Other Schools

What is believed to be the first Sunday School in England was started at Catterick in 1763 and the Methodists opened the first Sunday School in Northallerton for upwards of thirty children in May 1780. The Northallerton Parish Church Sunday School was opened in the vicinity of the Vicarage for sixty poor children in May 1787, its first teacher being a schoolmaster, John Ward.

There were various village schools in the nearby communities and the "village schoolmaster" became rather an epic figure in the eighteenth century. A good example was Joseph Tennant of Ainderby who served as "Master" of the village school for over sixty years. Bedale Grammar School advertised for a Schoolmaster at £20 an annual salary and at Harlsey Rev J Steele operated a private school for boys under twelve.

Property

Durham House – built mid 1700s by John Carr

Interesting notices abounded in the newspapers for Northallerton property: "the Corn tythe of Thornton-le-Moor and Thornton-le-Beans...along with Spittal Farm" belonging to Christ Church College, Oxford (September 1741); a good house for a tanner "at the North End of the West Side of Northallerton" (1742); a "Burgage House newly new" near Northallerton Market Place with several dwellings in the backyard (1768); Ware Banks, 14 acres bounded by the Common Field Turker (the now Friarage Hospital site) and "a Common Field called Greenhowsike" (1770); the tile sheds and tile kiln of John Hutton,

Sowber Gate was let in 1795; and a modern built dwelling house fronted with free stone and covered in Westmoreland slates (December 1798) - Durham House on the High Street when Northallerton was advertised as "of a mild and healthy climate, a cheap market and good neighbourhood, and possesses all the conveniences of a thorough fare between London and Edinburgh."

Hostelries

In the sixteenth century Camden ascribed to Northallerton " an exceeding good inn or two" and this reputation still applied in the eighteenth century. The "Golden Lion" was the leading hotel being rebuilt from a smaller hostelry around 1730 by its then owner Robert Richardson who also had a "Cock Pit" for cock-fighting at the rear. It became one of the major coaching inns on the Great North Road in the stage-coach hey-day with a national reputation controlling all the "coaching-ground" to the north and south of the town. Robert Richardson died in 1769 and was succeeded by Godfrey Hirst who was followed by his son Francis Hirst (deceased 1835) who made a fortune out of the coaching industry.

One of the first newspaper notices concerning the "Golden Lion" was a Sale there of "Wiskemore Farm" in 1739 and as the century progressed it was the constant scene of important Sales and Meetings of high calibre (Magistrates, Lieutenancy and Clergy of the North Riding) making it one of the premier hotels in the County. Rivalling the "Golden Lion" in the later part of the eighteenth century was the "King's Head" in coaching and other aspects such as the registration of horses for the Northallerton Races and the holding of the "Race Ball" and similar prestigious events in its large Assembly Room. In 1770 its owner John Carter claimed it as the Northallerton Post-House but with the cessation of the stage coaches its trade dwindled and it had closed by the 1860s, its site now being occupied by the Central Arcade.

The "Black Bull," "Old Golden Lion," "Waggon and Horses," "King's Arms" and "Black Swan" were the other coaching inns but all the other public houses had stabling which was completely full especially at "Fair Times" and Northallerton Races. The latter had its attendant public houses at either end of Racecourse Lane which paralleled its northern boundary - the "Unicorn and Turf" to the east and the "Horse and Jockey" (renamed "Railway Hotel" then "Station Hotel") to the west. The other best known eighteenth century " pubs"

123

were the "Durham Ox," "Nags Head," "Tickle Toby," "Fleece," "George," and "Pack Horse Inn."

Sports

Northallerton was reported in the eighteenth century as well-known for "quoits, cricket, and 'spell and knur'." The latter has died out but was formerly a popular northern game played between individuals the object being to strike with a bat a small ball ("knur") thrown up by a spring trap ("spell") as far as possible. It was usually played on wide open spaces which would probably be at the Greenhowsike town fields or possibly the Applegarth.

Another popular sport which had its hey-day in the eighteenth century was cock fighting. On 27th November 1744 a "York Courant" notice advertised a "Cock-Match, at the PIT of Robert Richardson, Northallerton between the Gentlemen of Northallerton and the Gentlemen of Kirkby Malzeard" on 14th, 15th and 16th January 1745." It appeared that by December 1746 when the Northallerton and Darlington Gentlemen engaged in a Cock Match Richardson's pit was "newly covered" and it was still in operation owned by H Richardson in 1790 when it held the "Northallerton Cockings". Northallerton Races held "cockings" annually but the last notice extant of "Northallerton Cockings" was in 1794 and the activity seems to have ceased before the end of the eighteenth century.

Horse Racing

Horse racing flourished at Northallerton from 1765 to 1880 on the Broomfield racecourse where a meeting of a high standard was held annually in early October spanning three days. At its zenith it was one of the highest rated race meetings in England, this being before it was reduced in size by the intrusion of the Great North of England Railway built partially through the western part of the course.

Notices of "Northallerton Races" appeared in the York newspapers each year from 1765 onwards for what became not only a racing but a social occasion with outsiders flocking into the town. "Searching the town during race-time" appeared regularly in the Constables' Books with pick-pockets, "card sharps" and welching bookmakers abundant. The horses were registered at the "Golden Lion" or "King's Head" and all the stables in town were full as too were the hostelries.

The races themselves were often hurly burly affairs with the narrowness of the track necessitating starting the horses in rows of three abreast - once it took a starter 27 attempts to get the horses "off"! Results were published in the "York Courant" and there were usually five races on each of the three days' racing. A Silver Cup value £50 was awarded in 1769 by the Stewards to the winner of a "Maiden Race" on the Friday and this was carried out yearly until the end of the century shortly after which a 100 Guineas Gold Cup was also raced for.

Certainly the Silver Cups were highly prized as evidenced when Mr Coates' chestnut mare "Melpomene" won on Friday 12th October 1770. Mr Coates sold "Melpomene" to P Wentworth in 1770 for 500 guineas - a very high sum for the time, which reflects the standard of horse racing at Northallerton. Immediately after his win Mr Coates "carried" the Silver Cup from local town to local town with it being liberally filled and eagerly emptied by celebrating admirers!

Individuals

When George Augustus, Prince Elector of Hanover, was made a Peer of England in 1706 by Queen Anne one of the titles he was accorded was Viscount Northallerton, which he retained after becoming Prince of Wales in 1714 but divested with his other titles upon becoming George II in 1727. He was the last English King to lead his army into battle - against the French at Dettingen in 1743. Viscount Northallerton reappeared in the Royal family during the twentieth century amongst the dignities of the Duke of Teck.

The first Duke of Northumberland (1712 - 1786) Hugh Smithson was born at Northallerton on the west side of the High Street at the house opposite the Toll Booth of Robert Mitford (a relative his mother was visiting) on the site now occupied by Barkers of Northallerton. His mother Philadelphia was the daughter of William Reveley who built Newby Wiske Hall and Hugh was christened at Kirby Wiske Church.

His father Langdale Smithson predeceased his grandfather Sir Hugh Smithson and when the latter died in 1729 the young Hugh took the title. He married the heiress of the Percy family, Lady Elizabeth, and on the death of his father-in-law in 1750 there being no lineal male successor, he succeeded to his titles of Duke of Somerset and Earl of Northumberland and finally was made Duke of Northumberland in 1766 by George III, the only Duke that monarch created. He had many influential positions and was strongly connected with London hospitals.

Former Lascelles Chapel – Northallerton Church

A popular story concerned the famous vine growing outside "Vine House" Northallerton (now the Rutson Hospital) - reputed to be the largest in Europe and of great longevity having been planted before 1600 according to Thomas Rymer. *[monochrome plate 5]* Passing through his birthplace in 1775 the Duke of Northumberland observed from his carriage that the vine was damaged and leaking liquid. Immediately he dispatched his head gardener from his Northumberland seat Alnwick Castle to tend the ailing vine. The expert saved the vine by sealing the base with lead and by 1790 it covered 139 square yards.

The Lascelles connection with Northallerton was long-standing – back to medieval times – but a most significant link was forged on 22nd August 1672 when Daniel Lascelles of Stank Hall (1655 - 1734) married Margaret Metcalfe of Porch House at Northallerton Parish Church, where he was eventually buried after a distinguished career including MP for Northallerton (1702) and High Sheriff of Yorkshire in 1719. His wife Margaret unfortunately died in 1690 bearing twins – Hannah and Henry – at Northallerton.

Although the Lascelles had been active in Barbados for half a century it was the twin Henry as Collector of Customs in Barbados who founded the family fortune. It is difficult to assess the amount but in 1836 when the slave owners were given compensation for their slaves "the heirs of Henry Lascelles were recorded as owning four plantations and 933 slaves in Barbados and two plantations and 344 slaves in Jamaica." ("Harewood" Carol Kennedy).

In 1739 Henry Lascelles moved from Northallerton to the Harewood estate in Wharfedale which he bought from John Boulter, but kept his links with the town being Northallerton MP (1745-52) and was buried there on 19th October 1753 after committing suicide in London. His sons were left fortunes - Daniel £284,000 and Edwin £166,000 - and the latter set out to build elegant Harewood House, designed initially by John Carr and added to by Robert Adam, it being commenced in 1755 and inhabited in 1771.

Again Edwin kept strong ties with Northallerton representing it as MP in 1754 and 1780 - 90, before becoming the first Lord Harewood. He died without an heir in 1795 aged eighty-three and was succeeded by his cousin Edward Lascelles (born in 1740) who was raised to the peerage as Baron Harewood in May 1796 and became Viscount Lascelles Earl of Harewood in 1812. Edward had very close relations with Northallerton being its MP for twenty-two consecutive years (1790 - 1812) and from his marriage to Anne, daughter of William Chaloner of Guisborough, in 1761 the later and present Harewoods are directly descended.

The other main property owning family, the Peirses played a prominent role as almost constant MPs for Northallerton in the eighteenth century. Their family seat was at Bedale Hall which frequently was the scene of their celebrations and munificence: for example on 19th September 1775 Henry Peirse, already a Northallerton MP, had a convivial 21st birthday party with 200 guests attending a "Coming of Age Ball" in an illuminated Bedale Hall, with the different Bedale inns "treating" the Peirse tenants by arrangement with Henry.

Hugh Pannell (1721-1788) was the most eminent and prolific clock-maker in Northallerton's history coming to the town from Stokesley in 1750, producing fifty-five long case clocks to become a successful businessman, property owner and member of the Select Vestry. His son Joshua was born in Northallerton in 1757 and went into business with his father making nine long case clocks before he died in 1803. Family longevity in Northallerton is characterised here because in 1776 Hugh Pannell was a contributor to the 'subscription list' whereby Northallerton Grammar School was rebuilt and nearly two centuries later his direct descendants brothers John, David, Keith and Peter Severs attended Northallerton Grammar School in the 1950s with David going on to produce an erudite book in 1998 portraying his ancestor Hugh's life and work.

The Tragic and Unusual

Every Northallerton traveller to and from the south on the Great North Road from 1702 encountered the macabre sight of the remains of Tom Busby on the gibbet and gallows by the roadside at "Busby Stoop Inn". He had been hanged and gibbeted in that year for murdering his father-in-law Daniel Auty, a fellow criminal counterfeiter - but the thieves had fallen out, and Busby's mortal remains hung there with a lolling skull and knotted rope still around his neck for many years to deter others.

To the north of the town another local murder gained notorious fame as the events became popularised in a poem. William Stephenson, 27, a grocer of Northallerton was hanged at Durham on 26th August 1727 for the murder of Mary Fawdon (or Farding). Mary was pregnant by him but he was already married and he took her to Hartlepool and then flung her into the sea to her death near Maiden's Bower, Hartlepool in June 1727. A subsequent sentimental ballad was entitled "The Hartlepool Tragedy - the confession and dying words of William Stephenson" which he was alleged to have uttered on his death bed.

A most unusual tale recounted by Saywell concerned a chimney sweep Robin Horton living in Northallerton around 1765 who had two club feet, with a wife with one club foot and a grey horse similarly deformed! As a team they successfully burgled local mansions until a robbery carried out in snow left tell-tale club foot prints back to their abode! Robin and a son were found guilty and transported but the mother and the rest of the family continued to rob, until eventually they were caught and transported.

The most compelling and ghostly mystery of the district's eighteenth century was that of Mary Ward in 1759 in local folk lore known as "The Romanby Tragedy" the title of a poem of the event. Mary was a servant at Romanby to one of a band of illegal coiners and she stumbled upon some secret apartments used for the coiners' criminal practices. She told an acquaintance about this who unwittingly repeated it to her master who determined to get rid of Mary forever.

On a Sunday evening an unidentified horseman arrived at her master's mansion with the news that Mary's mother was dying. Mary left hurriedly for home which was eight miles from Romanby via

Morton Bridge but never reached home as she was slain on a heath adjacent to Morton Bridge. Mary's ghost is claimed to distressfully haunt around the vicinity, with the strongest testimonies to seeing apparitions between Romanby and North Otterington.

Two marriages are of interest, the first a "Gretna Green" elopement printed in the "York Courant" on 24th March 1778; "On Thursday set out on a Matrimonial Jaunt to Gretna Green Mr Ewbank, mercer in Northallerton with Miss Richardson of the same place; an agreeable young lady with a genteel fortune."

The second marriage is so unusual that its veracity is borne out by its factual transcript in the Northallerton Parish Church records and its subsequent appearance in the meticulously researched "Yorkshire Archaeological Journal". In Northallerton Parish Church on 25th August 1782 George Lumley of Northallerton aged 104 married Mary Dunning also of Northallerton aged 19. The betrothal was entered in the Parish Registers with the signatories Rev James Wilkinson, the curate, who officiated and the witnesses Thomas Robinson and WM Gibson. Nothing further can be traced of the couple whose married life therefore dwells in the realms of the unknown!

7

The Nineteenth Century

The Age of Reform (1800 – 1900)

General Situation – Pre 1830

Some early Northallerton population figures show a steady increase attributable to a thriving agricultural, commercial and nodal town on the Great North Road at the height of the colourful Stage Coach era:

> 1791 - 1960
> 1801 - 2138 and 502 families
> 1811 - 2234 and 517 families
> 1821 - 2626 including 1303 males, 1323 females, 557 houses and 562 families

The populations of the rest of the Northallerton Parish in 1821 were: Brompton 1223, Romanby 294, Deighton 134 and High Worsall 154.

However, underlying this apparent uniformity and settled prosperity were serious inadequacies both in the political and social spheres. Politically before 1832 only 211 males had the parliamentary vote and the Northallerton borough was a totally undemocratic "Pocket Borough" with the two members of parliament being selected by the grandly influential families of Lascelles and Peirse. Additionally local government was in the hands of the Select Vestry of self-perpetuating membership and the elite of the Justices of Peace attended to the judicial and administrative matters of the North Riding.

Worse than anything were the deplorable living conditions of most of the working classes who lived cramped together in the narrow, ultra unhygienic yards running off the High Street (then called the Main Street). Health was affected and epidemics broke out regularly of small pox, cholera, typhoid, diphtheria and scarlet fever. Finally the old Workhouse to which the destitute were consigned when they were no longer able to maintain themselves was in a dilapidated, dirty and generally deleterious state.

The Napoleonic War

The matter of great moment in the early 1800s was the Napoleonic War which lasted, except for a short interlude of peace, until 1815. The main occurrences connected with the war at Northallerton were the important meetings of the North Riding Lieutenancy which was responsible for the carrying out of government policy and edicts concerning the war. All the meetings were held at either the "Golden Lion" or in the North Riding Court House and vital deliberations took place regarding such matters as the "Defence of the Realm" and the Local Volunteer Forces.

When the Duke of Leeds as Lord Lieutenant and all of the Deputy Lieutenants came to town all was hustle and bustle particularly around the "Golden Lion" and Court House with excitement in the air.

Some examples indicate the work and deliberations of the Lieutenancy. At a meeting on 13th June 1803 of the "Lieutenancy and Magistry" the assembled designed "A humble Address from the Lord Lieutenant, the Deputy Lieutenants and the Magistrates of the North Riding, expressive of their attachments to his Majesty's Person and Government, and a solemn pledge to co-operate with their fellow subjects to resist French invasion." Drawn up at Northallerton the address was presented to King George III by Lord Pelham. In August 1803 Northallerton itself sent a similar Address to His Majesty when "the Burgesses and other Inhabitants met at the Court House for that purpose."

In 1803 it was proposed by the Lieutenancy to start a War Subscription List and amongst the many subscribers Sir Samuel Crompton gave £365 including £50 to the Northallerton Volunteers. The latter had been formed for some time and their existence is memorialised today by the commemorative plaque in the south transept of Northallerton Parish Church to their Commanding Officer Samuel Peat who died aged 47 on 17th October 1802. On 3rd October 1808 at the "Golden Lion" the Lieutenancy united all the North Riding Volunteers units by decreeing that the Local North Riding Militia would be formed into a Regiment of 700 to 1200 men to comprise a "Permanent Military Force."

Little is known about what part the ordinary Northallerton citizen played in the war but several served their country in the warfare such as William Simpson who was blinded in battle and became "an honest cow-keeper". With its position on the main eastern route Northallerton

To the Memory of
SAMUEL PEAT, ESQUIRE,
Late Captain commanding the Northallerton Volunteers,
He departed this life 17th October, 1802,
Aged 47 Years.

Why hallowed dust, should friendship seek to tell
That merit here ! thy life has spoke so well :
Thy powers departed now with " here he lies,"
Points to the spirit wafted to the skies !
Teach us to follow dear departed worth,
To rise with him above the grovelling earth.
Eternal Father ! at whose awful throne
We bow, let " Thine Almighty will be done."

Samuel Peat Memorial

saw the continuous movement of regiments some of which stayed in and were billeted on the town.

Guy Fawkes night was always celebrated on November 5th with a great enthusiasm - many said too enthusiastically - and the town gained a reputation for this. In 1804 General Hewgill who was stationed with his regiment in Northallerton tried to stop the Guy Fawkes activities but with mud and mire thrown at him he was unable to read the Riot Act and forced to retreat. This episode had an ironic outcome because a detachment of the 52nd Regiment was sent to Northallerton from Whitby to quieten the town. The troops were quartered on the publicans until June 1805 and the result was that no fewer than thirteen women married soldiers: Ann Hedley;   Ann Dunn, housekeeper to R Bearpark; Margaret Brown; Isabella Gowland; Betty Gowland; Ann Blades; Betty Sedgewick; Mary Prince; Miss M Hoggart, a farmer's daughter; Sarah Wood; Isabella and Mary Rigby; and Ellen Fearby (cook at the "Kings Head").

The Booths

Henry and Charles Booth, Northallerton brothers and officers were heavily engaged in various actions in the Peninsular War under their Commander-in Chief, Arthur Wellesley - later Lord Wellington. One of the most brilliant battles the "Combat of Coa" was graphically described in correspondence from Henry Booth, then a lieutenant in the 43rd Regiment to his brother in England, a battle in which his other brother Lieutenant Charles of the 52nd was also engaged. Henry Booth became a Lieutenant Colonel and commanded the 43rd Regiment from 1830 until his death from natural causes at Northallerton on 6th May 1841. His memory is perpetuated on a commemorative marble tablet in the north transept of Northallerton Parish Church.

Victory Celebrations

Joyful and celebratory peals at Allied successes in the war were supplied by the Northallerton Parish Church bell-ringers recorded in the Churchwardens Accounts: ringing in 1805 for the great naval victory of Nelson at Trafalgar 15s; as a total exception on Thursday 9th January 1806 dumb peals greeted Nelson's sad interment; Sir Arthur Wellesley's success at Talavera 15s 17th August 1809 (after which battle Wellesley was designated Lord Wellington); Wellington's victory of 1814 15s; entry of the Allied army into Paris 15s; on the proclamation of peace 1815 15s.

The war ended with the defeat of Napoleon at Waterloo in 1815 but Northallerton with confident aplomb had already celebrated the Allied victory some fourteen months previously! A meeting of inhabitants had resolved at the "Golden Lion" in April 1814 that a celebration dinner starting at 4 p.m. on 2nd May 1814 at the "Golden Lion" and costing one guinea per head to "CELEBRATE THE CESSATION OF HOSTILITIES BETWEEN FRANCE AND THE ALLIES" should take place. The dinner was duly held on the appointed day.

Much Ado About Politics

Parliamentary Reform was the next vital national issue which raised excitement and feelings throughout the land - not least in Northallerton which had its own significant part to play in the mosaic of Britain's fervour. The Great Reform Act of 1832 invaded a political system which had been the stronghold of the privileged classes who had controlled the entry to parliament and MP's seats.

In 1832 Northallerton was a typical "Rotten" and "Pocket" Borough. The town had first sent two members to parliament in 1298 and since 1640 there had been a continuous representation but with the seats dominated for decades by the Lascelles and Peirse families and in 1831 only 211 having a vote out of a population of 3004. Apart from its own constituency Northallerton and district also had an interest in the North Riding County parliamentary seats. In the famous North Riding County Election of 1807 between Viscount Milton, the Hon. Henry

Lascelles and William Wilberforce, which cost the first two gentlemen over £100,000 each, the following numbers of locals voted at York, the hustings centre:

Northallerton (55), Brompton (25), Romanby (2), Osmotherley (14), Thornton-le-Beans (8), West Rounton (12), Birkby (3), Borrowby (5) and Brawith Hall 1 (Warcop Consett). From Northallerton all but Fletcher Rigge, Dr William Bayley and James Wigfield voted for Lascelles as did all the Brompton voters.

At the time the two main aspects the reformers were fighting against were the voting system believing more men should be enfranchised and the unequal electoral districts whereby a growing town of thousands may not be represented whereas a market town like Northallerton had two members. Although Northallerton stood to lose a member reform was popularly favoured and when Earl Grey's Administration failed to get the Reform Bill through, a Public Meeting called by the reformers at the "Black Bull" on 14th May 1832 indicated public opinion by its large attendance and high feelings. The Reform Bill was passed on 4th June 1832 when Northallerton, under Schedule "B" of the Act, lost one member in the redistribution of seats but had its voters increased from 211.

A most interesting Government document is the "Report on the Borough of Northallerton" by H.W. Tancred in 1831. It states that: "The Town consists of little more than of two rows of houses, facing each other on opposite sides of the Great North Road", but because of the Quarter Sessions being held here "it is necessarily a great thoroughfare - - - - - - There are no manufactures carried on in the town - - - linen manufacture is the only one existing in the neighbourhood with its chief seat at Brompton." It describes "the strips of ground" at right angles to the principle houses which have been built upon (the yards) and details the houses of £10 value and upwards: Northallerton 189, Brompton 80 and Romanby 25.

The 1832 Election

The prolific descriptions of the Northallerton election in December 1832 following the passage of the Great Reform Act are symptomatic of the contemporary involvement and drama. In a determined effort to throw off the political yolk of the powerful landowners a zealous group approached Captain George Boss RN of Otterington Hall who was married to the cousin of Prime Minister Earl Grey to stand for

Northallerton Parliamentary Borough – post 1832

Parliament and thus "open up" the Borough. Captain Boss graciously acceded and from June 1832 a terrific campaign followed involving as the other candidate William B. Wrightson who though he had stood as a Liberal for Hull was considered at the time to be part of the "establishment" of landed families whose support he had.

Two symbols were designed to indicate the aims of Boss's supporters - a giant gilded key "to open up the Borough" and a great broom "to sweep it clean." Brompton was the local epi-centre of the fervent and vociferous enthusiasm for Boss's candidature and on Monday 25th June 1832, the day chosen to commemorate the passage of the Reform Bill, a great open air party and procession took place at this spirited village: "a day such as the oldest person in the village never witnessed and which the rising generation will cherish in their remembrance to the last hour of their existence" *(York Courant).*

For a massive feast on Brompton Green a whole fat ox had been roasted, a battery of field guns repeated staccato salvoes through the day and the flags the "Union Jack" and the "Royal George" fluttered from masts with all the village festooned with banners and favours. At 11 a.m. one thousand people formed a procession to Northallerton. A rousing band led the procession in which everyone wore a yellow favour or sash.

The great column then returned to Brompton for the dinner which was preceded by the arrival of Captain Boss amidst a cacophony of sound, swirling hats and great acclamation. The meal took place on three massive trestle tables with an estimated five hundred. Numerous toasts were made commencing with the Health of His Majesty and culminating with that of Captain Boss. On conclusion he was given huge cheers and with his horses removed from his carriage he and his wife were dragged by the Bromptonians to Northallerton. To set the seal on a memorable day three hundred ladies who had prepared and served the dinner, sat down at Brompton to tea and plum cake.

The electoral campaign was strenuously waged until the election of 10th December 1832 which took place with the Committee Rooms of the parties - the "Black Bull", Liberal and the "Golden Lion", Conservative - flanking the "hustings" which were in between. On a show of hands the Returning Officer, J.S. Walton declared Captain Boss the winner but Mr Wrightson requested a poll which by 6.0'clock resulted as follows:

Captain Boss   108
William Wrightson   97

Amidst wild enthusiasm Captain Boss made a victory speech from the "Black Bull" window.

The following day saw the "Chairing" of Captain Boss accompanied by totally memorable scenes as the chair carrying the gallant Captain was placed in his carriage and processed around the constituency. A band led the procession which was followed by four thousand people. They moved three times round the Market Cross, then to Romanby and thence to Brompton where the greatest welcome imaginable awaited Captain Boss of cannons, bells and "every manifestation of joy." The "Chairing" occupied three hours.

Although it was a glorious victory the Captain Boss story was tinged with tragedy. In the middle of his election campaign his wife Charlotte died at Otterington Hall on 11th September 1832. He did not stand for re-election in 1835 and died at Otterington Hall aged 56 in October 1838 less than five years after his great triumph.

Further Elections

By contrast his defeated opponent in 1832 William Battye Wrightson was returned unopposed in 1835 for Northallerton and embarked on a long and honourable parliamentary career remaining as Northallerton's MP until 1859. He was returned unopposed in 1837 when the Conservative candidate Hon. Edwin Lascelles withdrew.

1841 saw a very vigorous election when Wrightson (Liberal) was opposed by Hon. Edwin Lascelles (Conservative). Wrightson received a tremendous reception at Brompton which was "like a triumphal procession rather than an electioneering canvass - - - and we can only apply the same language to the village of Romanby" ("York Herald"). When voting took place on Wednesday 30th June 1841 the already high excitement was maximised by the arrival of the voters from the villages of Brompton and Romanby who marched into town "en bloc". The voting resulted in a victory for Wrightson with 128 votes to Lascelles' 114.

In both 1847 and 1852 Wrightson was unopposed. March 1857 turned out to be a very different proposition, however, because of the emergence of a strong Conservative candidate Hon. Egremont Lascelles, one of the late Earl of Harewood's sons. The election was as close as could be with only three votes separating the candidates: Wrightson 129 Lascelles 126.

There was renewed political excitement two years later in April

1859 when another contested election was fought out between Wrightson and C.H. Mills of London who had the powerful support of the Harewoods as the brother-in-law of Hon. Egremont Lascelles. By the narrowest margins Wrightson defeated Mills 138 to 136 votes. The colour, fervour, skulduggery and complete involvement of the population in the election was typical of the Northallerton seat which had a reputation now for its electoral exploits and atmosphere.

William Battye Wrightson was by this time something of a local legend having been Northallerton's MP for the Liberal influence for twenty two years and a "Great Liberal Meeting" in August 1859 at Brompton commemorated the seventh successive return to parliament of Mr Wrightson. A sixty yards long marquee bedecked with banners and slogans housed one thousand guests at five huge tables, with Hoggart's brass band of Darlington and the "Brompton Glee Singers" in attendance.

The Iron Horse Cometh

The arrival of the railway at Northallerton on what was to be the main line from London to Edinburgh was one of the most crucial happenings in the town's history. It contributed essentially to Northallerton's development as a route, administrative and agricultural centre and indeed it was one of the first market towns in the world to be served by a railway for both goods and passengers.

Coaching Demise

Sadly, for nostalgic contemporaries the coming of the "carbon snorting steam horse" caused the rapid demise of the exciting and colourful stage-coach with its booming trade. The "Golden Lion", "Black Bull", "King's Head" and the "Old Golden Lion" were still the main coaching inns in the nineteenth century and the coaches serving the town were prolific: the "High Flyer", "Royal Mail", "Wellington", "North Briton", "Cleveland", "Eclipse", "England Rejoice", "Trafalgar" and "Royal Telegraph". Some people became rich on the proceeds notably Francis Hirst proprietor of the Golden Lion who held the "ground" on each side of the town until his death in 1835.

Illustrative of the advances in times and efficiency are the London to York post:

Thomas Layfield

coach times : 1761 - Winter 96 hours - Summer 72 hours;
1796 - 31 hours; 1836 - 20 hours.

Analogous to this was the great improvement of the roads by the Turnpike Trusts one local example being the reconstruction of the Great North Road at Boroughbridge Road as it entered Northallerton in 1835 which was re-routed, straightened and widened.

Advanced speeds meant more accidents which were often put down to "furious driving" especially when the coaches were running in "opposition" to each other. In 1821 the "Edinburgh Mail" on its way to Northallerton crashed at Sunderland Bridge killing two outside passengers and a stage coach driven by Anthony Welsh through Northallerton killed a child on 23rd June 1806, a verdict of accidental death being brought in with the coach proprietors ordered to pay £10 to the Crown.

Much was written about the end of the "Stage Coach Era." Drinkwater Meadows wrote in "Bentley's Miscellany" about Northallerton in 1842 - "The railroad has removed its traffic and covered its pavement with grass. The Church standing in the centre of the town, surrounded by its elevated burial ground, is no longer agitated by the passing to and fro' of the 'Wellington', 'High Flyer' or the 'Royal Mail'; the guard's horn or coachman's whip no more disturbs the devotion of the assembled congregation."

Tom Bradley in "The Old Coaching Days in Yorkshire" (1889) described the last journey in 1844 of coach driver Thomas Layfield of Northallerton: "At last, starting from Newcastle on its southwards journey, the coach drove into Darlington, empty; into Northallerton empty; into Thirsk empty. As its driver, with bowed head, drew up at each successive stage, the proprietors saw that the end had come and the old 'Wellington' went off the road forever."

A telling commentary of the stage-coach situation is to be seen in the toll rents:

The Great North Road: (Boroughbridge to Darlington via Northallerton)

	1826	1861
Topcliffe Gate	£ 630	£ 210
Newsham Gate	410	105
Entercommon Gate	1020	125 (plus Lovesome 95)

With the disappearance of the stage coaches came the loss of employment for drivers, ostlers, post-boys and saddlers. The "King's Head" which had been the other main coaching inn along with the "Golden Lion" closed, and for the first time since records were kept, Northallerton's population decreased: 1841 - 3088; 1851 - 3082; 1861 - 2870. However, once the town had settled down to the new regime and the railway became an increasing asset the population trend reversed upwards (1871 - 3164 and 1881 - 3692) a situation which has continued until the present day.

Railway Construction

The application to Parliament by the Great North of England Railway Company to build a railway from Hurworth (the Tees) to York was made in November 1836, a petition having been drawn up in its favour signed by land - owners, gentlemen and other residents in

Northallerton and district numbering over four hundred. Royal assent for the subsequent Act of Parliament was given on 12th July 1837 and the first sod was cut at Croft on 25th November 1837. Digging at Castle Hills to commence the construction of the railway in the Northallerton area started on 28th March 1838. This was Contract "No 7" for work from Castle Hills to the south of Northallerton (Huttons' Wood) - 2 miles 836 yards.

Roman finds made the initial work at Castle Hills highly exciting and bore witness to Roger Gale's firmly held theory that there was some sort of Roman encampment here. On the second day of work, on excavating the foundations of the first bridge to the south of the hill (now Zetland Bridge) part of a dark blue urn, believed to be Roman was unearthed. Almost immediately several Roman coins were discovered and further into the hill a "Votive Altar" was found which indicated that this had been a Roman station occupied by the Sixth Legion which came to the north of England in 122 AD.

In August 1839 further Roman coins were found by boys playing on the periphery of Castle Hills adjoining the great railway works which were mainly of Severus and the later Emperors and very corroded. Undoubtedly contemporaries then believed the Castle Hills to be Roman - for example the "York Herald" referring to the railway maintained that it would pass "over Castle Hill plains, formerly an ancient Roman encampment."

The large and extensive embankment which took the railway through Northallerton and Romanby was made up mainly of the soil and material from Castle Hills and apart from the building of Croft Bridge was the most difficult engineering feat in the York to Darlington programme. A phenomenal amount of 252,641 cubic yards of soil made up the embankment which gives an idea of the size of Castle Hills before it was dismantled.

A setback occurred at 6 o'clock on Wednesday evening 18th July 1838 when the bridge being built to take the railway over Willow Beck collapsed with a rumbling roar. Fortunately, the workers had all left the site. Shortly afterwards in November 1838 the Railway Company were faced with a strike by the Masons' Union mainly engaged at Croft Bridge: they discharged the offending masons and advertised for more!

Finally there was a social factor causing temporary unrest in the local countryside with large numbers of railway labourers quaffing great amounts of ale leading sometimes to "riots" as at Scorton in October 1838 when three labourers were imprisoned and three fined. It was officially stated that the commitments to Northallerton Gaol were greater than ever "owing principally to the large influx of persons of loose and disorderly habits connected with the public works now being carried out in the district."

When the Darlington - York railway of 44 ½ miles was completed in September 1840 it had cost £20,000 per mile. Other aspects were pertinent regarding the railway at Northallerton. The handsome iron bridge over which the Great North of England Railway crossed the Great North Road at Boroughbridge Road "is the greatest span of any iron bridge on the flat principle" ("York Herald" June 1840). A coal depot had been erected by Mr Robson of Northumberland at Northallerton by 4th January 1841 when the railway coal trade from Durham began. Finally a railway station at Northallerton had been contracted for in June 1840 and was completed before the railway opened, the architect being Mr Green, Darlington.

It is noteworthy that the railway then ran "out of town" as South Parade was not developed and the built up area ended around the "Nags Head" at the south of the main street.

Grand Opening

Amidst "the intense interest of all classes" the Darlington to York Great North of England Railway was opened on 30th March 1841. With 150 guests in open carriages each with a red tuniced postillion the train "Puffing Billy" set off from Darlington at twenty to ten (forty minutes late!) arriving at York station at five minutes to one. After lunch the party returned to Darlington carried by two trains - one of twelve and the other of eleven carriages leaving at quarter to three with a shrill whistle.

"Northallerton was reached at a quarter to five" reported the 'York Herald.' "The station, which is commodious and elegant being built in the Elizabethan Gothic style, was crowded with the inhabitants of the adjoining town - - - - Near this station a colossal work had been completed - the removal of Castle Hills, which many of our readers know was a stupendous mound of earth, and was of great antiquity, the prevailing opinion being that it was artificially formed in the time when the Romans occupied the northern part of this island."

The trains arrived at Darlington Bank Top station at quarter to six, though the normal Darlington - York journey would take two hours and it was merely a question of time before this would be the mid-way stretch on a completed east coast route from Edinburgh to London. The Great North of England Railway was opened to the public on Wednesday 31st March 1841.

Railway Expansion

In 1845 a Bill was obtained to form a Leeds to Stockton line by the Leeds Northern Company which was extended to Hartlepool in 1846. Owing to a dispute with the rival company the York, Newcastle and Berwick Railway which by amalgamation had taken over the Great North of England Company, another act was obtained to build a Melmerby to Northallerton line which was finished on 15th May 1852.

With two rival companies in the early 1850s Northallerton had two passenger stations with the Leeds Northern Company siting one at the North End of the town, with the other existing main line station at the South End. However, this disputatious affair ended with the amalgamation of the York, Newcastle and Berwick with the Leeds Northern Railway Companies, along with two others, to become the North Eastern Railway Company. K Hoole describes this as "the most important event in the history of the railways in the North East."

As far as Northallerton was concerned the unified system brought the logical set-up of one passenger station at the South End and a Goods station at the North End. There were eventually five platforms at Northallerton station which continued to develop its facilities throughout the nineteenth century including: a ticket office, telegraphist department, first class, second class and ladies waiting rooms, a restaurant, a bookstall, station master's and station offices, with the whole enveloped by glass domes on iron pillars on both the south and north bound platforms.

Meanwhile other lines had been constructed at Northallerton the first being the Bedale branch line which met the main line at Castle Hills on 6th March 1848 and was extended to Leyburn on 19th May 1856 and finally to Hawes Junction on 1st October 1878. For several decades the line was the main artery of movement for people, animals and goods of Wensleydale. This railway had great scenic beauty and the stations read like a tourist hand-book: Northallerton, Ainderby, Scruton, Leeming Bar, Bedale, Crakehall, Jervaulx, Finghall-Lane, Constable Burton, Spennithorne, Leyburn, Wensley, Redmire, Aysgarth, Askrigg and Hawes Junction.

The Castle Hills inner junction curve into the west side of

Northallerton's northbound platform was completed in 1882 to ease the traffic hitting the main line. The average speed then of the Dales train was 18 mph and the fares from Northallerton to Bedale Return were: 1st Class - 1s 6d; 2nd Class - 1s 0d; 3rd Class - 8d.

Rail Accidents

On the debit side, however, accidents occurred with much frequency. The first of any magnitude recorded in the Northallerton area was just north of Cowton in October 1845 when part of a train became detached and the first class carriages derailed with "Mrs Whitehead so hurt she may not recover." In December 1860 a Bedale cattle train was hit by the "beef train" from Newcastle and the main line blocked for four hours. This pattern continued with Northallerton having various accidents and on the 4th October 1894 the worst one when the "Flying Scotsman" crashed into a goods train near Castle Hills on a foggy night at 3.a.m., Driver Adamson receiving fatal injuries and Driver Clark having his arm amputated.

By far the most fearful accident in Northallerton's vicinity, however, happened at 4 am in thick fog at Manor House signal box on the North Eastern Railway up line on 2nd December 1892 between Otterington Station and Avenue junction. A goods train from Middlesbrough to Starbeck was allowed to run from Northallerton High Junction but was stopped at Manor House by the signals and thundered into by the duplicate 10.30 pm express passenger train from Edinburgh to Kings Cross running twenty three minutes behind the scheduled train. Ten people were killed and many injured.

Signalman James Holmes in the Manor House cabin had tragically forgotten that the goods train was in the section and had fatally given the "line clear" signal to the express. At the inquest before the North Riding Coroner Dr Walton of Northallerton the jury brought in a verdict of "manslaughter" against signalman Holmes who was formally committed to York Assizes where he was eventually found guilty but with a strong recommendation for mercy which was acted upon by the Judge Mr Justice Charles with Holmes liberated having entered into recognisances of the sum of £50.

The crux of the situation of the accident attributable to Holmes' 'human error' was that he had previously applied for relief from duty on the grounds of unfitness for work because of the illness of his young daughter. The whole tragic event caused a great out-swell of

Northallerton Station Mart and Racecourse 1874

sympathy for all concerned including the unfortunate James Holmes.

There were also many individual accidents. The most advertised death was that of the popular John Clay the landlord of the "Golden Lion", Northallerton in July 1870. He paused to glance at his watch on the Northallerton main line station crossing and was struck by a passing train receiving injuries from which he died in the evening. Mainly as a result of this fatality an underpass tunnel was constructed to reach the north and west platforms without crossing the line.

Railway Assets

Over all the railway was a great boon to the developing market town where soon the loss of the stage coach economy was a thing of the past. In 1880 as many as 102 trains called at Northallerton a weekday, great numbers came by rail every year to both the Northallerton Agricultural Show and later the "Carnival", and agricultural trade boomed with animals so easily transported by rail to and from the town. In 1873 the Station Mart was founded adjacent to the station and a decade later the Malpas Mart was opened only a short distance away from the station off Malpas Road.

Finally, there is little doubt that having a main line station has been a potent factor in the selection and retention of Northallerton as the county town of North Riding (1889) and North Yorkshire (1974).

More Ado About Politics

The next highlight in Northallerton's political history was really a "lowlight" because the borough not only lost its remaining MP as a result of the Third Reform of Parliament Act in 1885 but also its constituency name which was acquired by Richmond.

Northallerton Borough

Before this, however, the Northallerton constituency had a rumbustious ending with several bitterly contested elections. In the 1865 election C.H. Mills carrying the Harewood influence for the Conservatives and the Liberal Jasper Wilson Johns contested a more than lively election which Mills won by 239 votes to 190. Immediately the Liberals objected to Mills' nomination on the basis of bribery and in April 1866 a House of Commons Committee met to consider the case of Jasper Wilson Johns v Charles Henry Mills.

It is remarkable according to the evidence given to the Committee at the lengths the Conservatives went to secure votes. It seemed that they controlled the "Golden Lion" (the Committee Room of Mr Mills was there), "Harewood Arms", "Oak Tree", "Waggon and Horses" and "Kings Arms" all of which dispensed drinks freely to voters. Another vote gaining gambit was that concerning land and rents. Thomas Lightfoot was assured he could go rent free if he gave his vote to the Tories. James Archer a pig dealer was offered "yon field of his for nothing." There was also the accusation of 'birking' regarding Snowdon Stainthorpe who it was alleged had been plied with drink and locked in the Harewood Arms on polling day so that he could not vote!

The upshot was that C.H. Mills was disqualified from becoming a Member of Parliament, a new writ was issued for the borough of Northallerton and William B. Wrightson (Liberal) and Egremont W. Lascelles (Conservative) the brother of the Earl of Harewood came forward.

One of the most tempestuous elections in Northallerton's political

Sir,

      Mr. GEORGE W. ELLIOT begs to draw your earnest attention to the following

INSTRUCTIONS TO VOTERS.

1. Vote **EARLY**, to prevent your opponents voting in your name.

2. On going into the Polling Booth you will be asked your name and where you live. A Ballot Paper will then be given you, and you will have to go into a private box, where you will find a pencil. You must then place a ✄ on the **RIGHT** hand side of the Ballot Paper, opposite the name of Mr. ELLIOT, (being the first name on the paper) as in the form below.

3. You must, on no account, make any other mark on the Ballot Paper. If you do, your vote will not be counted.

4. Fold up the Ballot Paper and put it into the Ballot Box.

5. If you should accidently spoil a Ballot Paper, you must give it to the Presiding Officer, and he will give you another.

FILL UP THE VOTING PAPER THUS :

1	**ELLIOT,** (GEORGE WILLIAM, Langton Hall, Northallerton, Yorkshire; and Penshaw House, Fence Houses, Durham).	**X**
2	**WRIGHTSON,** (WILLIAM BATTIE, Cusworth Park, near Doncaster, Yorkshire).	

The Election will take place on **TUESDAY**, 3rd February.

1874 Election Poster

history followed in 1866 for when election day dawned the proceedings at the hustings erected in Northallerton market place took four and a half hours of a most stormy character. Eggs, oranges and herrings were thrown from the Conservative side of the crowd at the Liberal supporters. The final declaration of Lascelles 224 and Wrightson 201 at the hustings was greeted by constant fights with the noise preventing anyone from speaking and as the fighting redoubled it was ultimately quelled by the police.

John Hutton of Solberge Hall stood as Conservative candidate for Northallerton in 1868 at the tender age of twenty one. He was opposed by Jasper W. Johns (Liberal) and amidst great excitement Hutton was declared the winner by the very narrow margin, 386 – 372. There followed the almost inevitable objection by Johns to Hutton's victory which the Liberals said had been achieved unfairly by "treating", bribery and corruption. It took until April 1869 to hear the case because parliament had fifty-eight such objections before it! The trial was held in Northallerton at the Court House and John Hutton was cleared of the charges and "duly elected" to the enormous delight of a great crowd that had gathered outside the Court House.

In 1874 Hutton retired as it turned out to be temporarily from the House of Commons and he was replaced by the popular local magnate George William Elliot who lived at Langton Hall. He had been instrumental in forming the Northallerton Tarpaulin and Brattice Cloth Factory in the 1860s which in 1890 started to produce linoleum. His opponent was that doughty Liberal fighter William Battye Wrightson who was contesting the seat over forty years since his first campaign in 1832. The result was a "very close run thing" with Elliot 388 votes winning by only nine votes - Wrightson 379 - at which the latter fine old political "long staying horse" at last went out to grass!

The April 1880 election was notable and historic locally because it was the last occasion that Northallerton sent its own MP to Parliament and as befitted the occasion the town kept up to the end its reputation for animated elections. George Elliot the sitting member was opposed by the extremely able Liberal Albert Rutson of Newby Wiske who was wanted in Liberal parliamentary circles to bring his prowess to bear in the House of Commons.

Polling day was Thursday 28th April 1880 and "Northallerton had earned for itself the name of being a stirring town during elections and although a big fight broke out and sticks were flying the aggression was not as marked as usual." ('Darlington and Stockton Times').

148

The Town Hall was the Polling Booth from which W.T. Jefferson the Returning Officer announced the result - Elliot 483, Rutson 383, Majority 100 - amidst deafening cheers. George Elliot was carried shoulder high to his hotel, the "Golden Lion" and he made a speech from the "Golden Lion" balcony, saying that if ladies had had the vote they would have won by 500! "The scene of wild revelry that night in Northallerton public houses has not been known in that town for many a day." ("Darlington and Stockton Times")

Northallerton lost its MP and was absorbed into one constituency with Richmond under the Redistribution Bill of 1884. With the massive growth of many urban areas without representation this seemed equitable, especially as it was sharing the fate of eighty other boroughs. Even then its omission from the parliamentary roll after continuous representation since 1640 and the first appearance of Northallerton MPs in 1298 was galling for many locals.

The Richmondshire Constituency

There was a strong fight between Northallerton and Richmond as to which town would give its name to the new constituency. Richmond's argument was based on the fact that it had had two members from 1584 to 1867 and Northallerton's on its position as the County Town of the North Riding and as a communications centre. The Boundary Commissioners found in favour of Northallerton but on 15th April 1885 the House of Commons in Committee reversed the decision of the Boundary Commissioners and changed the name of the Parliamentary Division to Richmondshire.

Next came a determined movement to make Northallerton the "Returning Town" for the Richmondshire Division - this to be decided by the magistrates of the North Riding. When the North Riding Quarter Sessions met to consider the matter on 15th July 1885 John Hutton proposed that Northallerton to be the centre of elections: Richmond was a "fallen off" town compared to Northallerton's progress; Northallerton's population rise was 484 to Richmond's 184; 102 trains stopped at Northallerton a day compared to Richmond's 6; and Northallerton was the capital of the North Riding which for many years had transacted county business. Despite Hutton's arguments Richmond was chosen as the election centre by 43 votes to 28. Northallerton was despondent but only a few years later became the division's nomination and returning centre basically because of its central position and as the county town.

The first election of the Richmondshire constituency in December 1885 resulted in the return of the popular Liberal Sir Frederick Milbank of Thorp Perrow who had been an MP in the locality for twenty years. He defeated the Tory G.W. Elliot by 4869 votes to 4320 but unfortunately illness forced him to resign the seat and another election took place in July 1886 with George Elliot and Edmund R. Turton of Upsall Castle in opposition. On this occasion George Elliot won by 4810 votes to 3859.

A vast concourse awaited the result in Northallerton Market Place and when it was announced cheer after cheer lustily rose up and "the whole town was in a state of jubilant excitement" ("Darlington and Stockton Times"). Elliot appeared on the balcony of the "Golden Lion" with his leading adherent John Hutton and after prolonged acclamation and victory speeches he was dragged around the town in his carriage by enthusiastic supporters.

G.W. Elliot and E.R. Turton again opposed each other in the 1892 election and Turton greatly reduced Elliot's majority the voting being Elliot, Conservative 4340 and Turton, Liberal 4181. At the end of this parliament's life (1895) George Elliot, who had become Sir George W. Elliot on his father's death in December 1893, resigned as MP on account of ill-health caused by a hunting fall. He went to Nice to recover but contracted typhoid and then pneumonia dying in November 1895.

John Hutton again as the Conservative candidate won the July 1895 election against the ever-persistent Edmund Turton by 584 votes - Hutton 4555, Turton 3971. Tremendous enthusiasm greeted him at Northallerton with his horses being unyoked and his carriage dragged down South Parade to the North End and back to the "Golden Lion" where John Hutton made a speech to "one mass of people which presented an enthusiastic scene which has scarcely been exceeded in Northallerton." ("York Herald")

This was to be the last election of the century in which Northallerton had obtained a widespread reputation for its lively election proceedings. John Hutton again succeeded in Richmondshire in 1900 obtaining a majority of 1456 against Geoffrey Howard (Liberal).

Law, Order and Local Government

Of great moment were the changes wrought in local government in particular the formation of: the North Riding County Police Force (1856); the North Riding County Council (1889); and the Northallerton

Urban and Rural District Councils (1895). All were centred at Northallerton the county town.

At the start of the century law and order was preserved by Parish Constables elected by the Select Vestry, along with the community, all answerable to the Quarter Sessions. This was augmented in Northallerton by the "Northallerton Association for the Prosecution of Felons" (1802) and the "Northallerton Association for the Prosecution of Poachers and Preservation of Game" (1810). In 1812 "in these restless times" a regular night watch was posted and a full time Constable was appointed at Northallerton.

A North Riding magistrate Joshua Crompton wrote to the Home Secretary in July 1839 of his disquiet about keeping the peace:

"The County is perfectly unprotected. The township constables are of no earthly use and with the exception of the police constables, one at Thirsk the other at Northallerton supported by subscription it is entirely devoid of defence."

The North Riding Constabulary

The passing of the County and Borough Police Act in 1856 enabled the JP's of the North Riding to create the North Riding Constabulary on 14th October 1856, Captain Thomas Hill having been selected on 4th October as the first Chief Constable. The Police Force consisted of the Chief Constable and fifty men of all ranks which was increased to 105 by September 1857. The boroughs of Richmond and Scarborough were separate entities to the North Riding Constabulary and had two and six men respectively. The original uniform of the North Riding Policeman was frock coat type of tunic, trousers, great-coat, "pork pie" hat, cape and waist belt.

Captain Thomas Hill

Captain Hill's appointment was crucial to the North Riding Constabulary which he headed from1856 to 1898 with dedication, efficiency and acumen. He came from Thornton-le-Dale, Yorks, and became a Captain in the North Yorks Rifles. In the magistrates' election for the post as Chief Constable he easily defeated his opponents: Hill 82, Major Straubenzee 23, Captain McBean 10 and George List 5.

One of Captain Hill's first actions was to purchase 16 horses and

Captain Thomas Hill

10 "carts" (traps). And although the Constabulary has since undergone massive technological change, horses are still on the inventory. Regarding police equipment in October 1897 when PC Hardy of South Otterington captured horse thieves in Ripon using his private bicycle it was speculated in the local press as to whether the bicycle might one day be used as official police equipment! Captain Hill took the force through many changes not least the building of the North Riding

Constabulary Headquarters in East Road next to the Court House in 1880 - now the building is no more being demolished in the early 1990's.

When Hill retired aged seventy-five on 31st September 1898 he was the longest serving Chief Constable in the country, receiving gifts of a silver case plus a cheque for £189. 6s. 6d. from the magistrates and a silver tray worth £50 from his officers. It is maintained that even after retiring he visited the Police Station daily to check that matters were proceeding well!

Major Robert Bower

Fortunately for the North Riding it acquired another renowned "character" of great ability and longevity as its new Chief Constable in Major Robert Bower who served from 1898 to 1929. Major Bower was already somewhat of a celebrity because of his doings in Africa particularly on the Nile and Sudan expeditions (1882 - 85) with the mounted infantry commanding the "picked shots"; and in Ibadan Tomba Country as British Resident where he heroically saved a magazine from exploding but received severe injuries. His exploits caused Edgar Wallace to model his legendary hero "Sanders of the River" on Major Bower who eventually became Major Sir Robert Bower KBE CMG.

North Riding County Council

A most momentous occasion for Northallerton was the formation of the North Riding County Council and its situation at Northallerton which substantiated the process started in 1736 which saw a Registrar with his clerk, ending with the present day when the County Council at the County Hall alone has around a thousand employees and is by far Northallerton's largest employer.

The first full meeting of the North Riding County Council was held on 1st April 1889 in the Court House with J.C. Dundas Chairman when the County Council effectively took on board the civil and administrative duties of the North Riding Quarter Sessions.

At the second Council meeting on 3rd July 1889 a pattern emerged which was to be common of discussions and reports under various headings at future meetings:

Hon J.C. Dundas (Chairman); Surveyor (Walker Stead); Registry (C.L. Ringrose); Contagious Diseases (Captain T. Hill); Public Analysis

(Thomas Fairley); Finance; Sanitary Committee; Weights and Measures; Rating Committee; North Riding Asylum; Closure Question - members could not speak for more than two minutes.

It will be of interest to all ratepayers that the North Riding estimates for the year April 1889 to April 1890 was £62,000 of which only £54,675 was spent!

The major and ongoing issue which concerned Northallerton was the "proposed new County Buildings". With the increase in work and creation of departments all the available space was being used in the Court House and Registry and buildings elsewhere in the town. Although the Standing Joint Committee set up a committee to look into the subject in 1891 it was not until twelve years later that the foundation stone of the new County Hall was laid. The real issue was as to whether to have the building on an entirely new site at the south of the town at Broomfield or an extension of the older County buildings down Zetland Street.

Demaine and Brierley of York were selected as the Architects in 1895 but haggling as to the building's site continued. In May 1898 a vote was taken on the site, a tie ensued and the Chairman John Hutton by his casting vote ensured that the new County Building would be built on the old Racecourse at Broomfield.

Northallerton UDC and RDC

In the meantime at local level a new administrative situation had evolved in 1895 with the formation of Northallerton Urban District Council and the Northallerton Rural District with Parish Councils at village level. The first elections for these were in December 1894 and caused great excitement and enthusiasm particularly for the Northallerton UDC where twenty seven candidates came forward.

Seven out of eight of the old Local Board were elected (Walker Stead, the County Surveyor missing out) and for the record this was the first elected Northallerton UDC:

T. Barker * 318, C. Palliser * 255, J. Guthrie * 240, Dr J.S. Walton * 223, G.J. Robinson * 209, G.J.E. Gardner * 189, W. Rolley 165, J. Ward * 153, T. Hill 141, M. Baines 129, H. Clidero 128, F. Skilbeck 128. (* denotes old Board member).

The sheer number of townspeople seeking election adequately expresses the keenness of those wishing to be involved in local government and in April 1898 the working- man appeared in the person of the besooted Richard Shuttleworth the local chimney sweep and a great "character." He did not get elected but representing the working man his candidature was a very important mile-stone.

Another step into the future was the election of Miss Annie Guthrie as a Northallerton representative on the Northallerton Rural District Council in December 1894 - the first woman Councillor of any description in the town. Around the same time she became the first woman elected to the Board of Guardians, and she thus achieved an historic and memorable "double". The first two Chairmen were C. Palliser, UDC and Colonel A.F. Godman RDC. Polling for the Councils took place at the National Schools and elections were spiritedly contested until the end of the century.

An appraisal of the Northallerton UDC accounts for 1896 - 97 gives some indication as to its main activities:

Income   £4213. 17s. 6 ½d including :
Rates £3049. 1s. 7d. Water Rates £631. 17s. 2d.
Use of Fire Engine £66. 2s. 1 ½d.

Expenditure:
Sewage Works £32. 13s. 2d. Footpaths Flagging £129. 19s. 10d.
Road £900 (including £73. 17s. 5d. scavenging and watering)
Waterworks £230. 10s. 3d. Public Lighting £399. 11s. 1d.
Fever Hospital £143. 17s. 2d. Salaries £160.

North Riding Quarter Sessions

Although the North Riding County Council took over control of the county's administrative and civil affairs in 1889, the North Riding Quarter Sessions dealt with all county matters until then and even after 1889 it had criminal aspects under its jurisdiction.

At the start of the century sentences remained severe with transportation being used quite liberally often for trivial offences: Thomas Metcalfe of Thirsk transported for seven years in 1811 for stealing a cream jug; Anne Chapman (1815) who purloined "wearing apparel" received a similar sentence. Whippings were also very frequent at the commencement of the century particularly concerning vagrants. In January 1819 John Dickens, a vagrant was sentenced to be publicly whipped in Northallerton Market Place.

The treatment of young people is especially hard to come to terms with in our modern day and age. John Hunter (15) of Scruton was transported for seven years for stealing a pocket handkerchief and in May 1834 he left York Castle to join one of the "Hulks" to begin his sentence. In 1846 Mary Davison (12) of Romanby stole 4s. 6d. and was sentenced to two months imprisonment. As the century unfolded, however, sentences became less harsh - the last Bastardy case was in 1839, whippings were no longer operative after the middle of the century, the stocks seemed to fall into disuse and transportation ended in 1867.

On the "civil" side the Quarter Sessions were very active before 1889 carrying on the North Riding's government with every decision affecting the county taken at Northallerton. Prominent were the passing into effect of the Highway Act in 1867 which divided the Riding into Highway Divisions; the formation of the North Riding Constabulary in 1856 and the selection of Captain George Gardner as Governor of the Gaol in 1862. Certainly the Quarter Sessions brought much animation and importance to Northallerton.

A final item of crucial importance was the Finances of the county with the Treasurer's post being an honorary one but eventually becoming one with a stipend as the monetary turnover increased, until the North Riding County Council took over with a full time professional County Treasurer.

Northallerton Gaol

The North Riding House of Correction was continuously under the jurisdiction of the Quarter Sessions with its delegation of Visiting Justices shouldering this responsibility. In 1802 Dr Neill described the prison as inadequate but by 1820 many changes had been wrought. A hospital had been built essentially to isolate contagious diseases, a separate section for females with nine sleeping cells was constructed in 1818, a new boundary wall 23 feet high was built and the infamous tread-mill for the prisoners to grind corn was installed. Foss was the architect.

In 1845 considerable improvements were planned for the prison which were completed in 1852, which before these alterations housed 296 prisoners in 68 cells. A new three storey block was built making 173 cells including the old ones and the old hospital was demolished with its replacement containing four spacious rooms at the end of the East Wing. A new chapel was erected and a new treadmill which could accommodate 94 men. The female department was enlarged by adding another wing with 40 sleeping cells with the total female accommodation now 60.

Illness continued to be rife amongst the prisoners. One of the major problems was the prisoners' health when they entered the gaol (especially from Tees-side), apart from the sanitation hazards of the time and town. Pulmonia, rheumatics, diarrhoea and dysentery occurred regularly and cases of fever such as typhus (1830), cholera (1832), and small pox (1865 and 1885). In the three months ending 31st March 1849 there were 128 cases of fever and 78 of diarrhoea in the prison.

Religious and moral instruction was given by the Prison Chaplains. The denominational make up of prisoners in Northallerton Gaol in August 1867 was:

	M	F	Total
Established Church	101	21	122
Roman Catholics	22	2	24
Wesleyan Meths	2	1	3
Baptists	1	0	1
Presbyterians	3	0	3
Primitive Methodists	2	0	2
Totals	131	24	155

By 1865 a schoolmaster and schoolmistress were in daily attendance at the gaol. Solitary confinement and whipping were the main forms of punishment especially in the first half of the century. The whip was a lethal instrument called the "cat o' nine tails" because it had nine tongues of 21 inches whipcord with knots in each. The prisoners in 1865 arose at 5.30 am in the summer and 6.0 am in winter retiring at 9.0 pm. The food was sparse with bread and water for the first week being improved gradually. The treadmill - a hated instrument - was replaced at Northallerton in 1863 by two hand mills for grinding corn but those sentenced to "hard labour" still had to work on the treadmill until late into the century, it being nationally abolished in 1898.

Expenditure varied but in 1864/65 the prison cost £3271. 7s. 2d. per annum with the annual cost of each prisoner being £21. 2s. 3d. Apart from the Constabulary the House of Correction in the latter half of the century was always the most costly item on the North Riding Quarter Sessions' budget. Lastly in the gaol organisation was the "prison bus - a melancholy vehicle" which plied regularly from the railway station to the gaol by the "backway" (the then undeveloped

Racecourse and Grammar School lanes) bringing its latest consignment of miscreants.

A host of interesting incidents concerned the prison during the century. Sensational at the time was the escape of five prisoners on Tuesday morning 22nd July 1817 and the matter was widely reported in the newspapers. Four were recaptured but the ringleader, John Wetherell, was never apprehended.

In 1836 a scandal occurred with the Chairman of the Visiting Justices Rev. William Dent of Crosby Court being accused of using meal from the prison for ten years to feed his dogs. A censure motion against Dent was lost by 15 – 17. The matter received wide publicity and was even taken up in London by the "Morning Star" which was so indignant that it stated that North Riding magistrates "were unfit persons to hold office."

William Martin and eleven other Chartists mainly from Sheffield and the West Riding in October 1840 were imprisoned at Northallerton after alleged subversive activities. The Secretary of State ruled that Martin should not "labour" but the North Riding magistrates decreed that all prisoners in the gaol should be dealt with equally which meant Martin would work. The impasse was resolved by Martin being transferred to Lancaster which was less stringent. The Chartist movement incidentally never really affected Northallerton though there is evidence of some strong support in Brompton, as ascertained by the research of Harry Fairburn of Northallerton.

Three Governors almost spanned the century at Northallerton Gaol: Thomas Shepherd from 1799 - 1826; William Shepherd who succeeded his father and was in office 1826 - 1862; and finally the redoubtable Captain George Gardner 1862 to 1898. The Shepherd family were unique nationally in the Governors' sphere. Thomas Shepherd died in 1832 and was buried in the north aisle of Northallerton Parish Church. All his four sons became Governors of Yorkshire gaols simultaneously: James - York Castle; William - Northallerton, North Riding; Thomas - Wakefield, West Riding; and Samuel - Beverley, East Riding.

Captain George Gardner of Balaclava

Captain George Gardner came to Northallerton in 1862 as Governor of Northallerton Gaol shortly after the Crimea War. He had already become a legend in his own lifetime as one of the survivors of the Light Brigade at the Battle of Balaclava immortalised by Tennyson:

"Cannons to the right of them
Cannons to the left of them
Into the Valley of Death
Rode the Six Hundred."

George Dudley Gardner had risen from the ranks in the 13th Hussars to become a Captain by the time of the famous charge from which his Company emerged with only nine survivors.

He at once brought efficiency to the Gaol and showed his wisdom by "establishing photography in the prison" by 1864 when he was complimented by the Quarter Sessions as to his method of discipline and labour. Fundamental, however, was his compassionate attitude to the prisoners which characterised his twenty nine years term as Governor during which an estimated 37,500 men, women and children passed through his hands. When he retired in 1891 at his presentation he said "he felt more impressed than he was at the roll call after the Charge of Balaclava."

The Captain had taken a full part in life too in the town, being for example the President of Northallerton Cricket Club and an abiding contemporary memory was of his popular and dignified figure being borne around the town by a mighty white charger – itself a survivor of Balaclava. His grave in Northallerton cemetery bears this simple telling epitaph:

"One of the Six Hundred."

The Gardner name lives on in Northallerton in the form of the Grace Gardner Trust incepted by the Captain's grand-daughter Grace Gardner in her will of 1966 which bequeathed most of her wealth for the benefit of the senior citizens of Northallerton.

North Riding Court House

The North Riding Court House was used for purposes other than the Quarter Sessions and the North Riding County Council. It also housed: the North Riding Bankruptcy Court; the Northallerton County Court which dealt with the civil cases of the district; the Northallerton Police Court meeting most Wednesdays to deal with petty offences and remand the more serious crimes to the Quarter Sessions and the Court Halmote, Court Leet, and Chief Court Baron of the Lords of the Manor of Allerton and Allertonshire.

The Lords of the Manor of these Courts were the Bishop of Durham (to 1836), the Bishop of Ripon (1836 - 57) and then the Ecclesiastical Commissioners continuously. In former days these Courts were very important locally. However, by the end of the nineteenth century the proceedings were usually only of about an hour during which several admittances to copy-hold property would be made. Following this the Courts' members repaired to the "Golden Lion" when everyone including the Jury was entertained to lunch.

North Riding Registry of Deeds

The North Riding Registry of Deeds was the final cog in the local government wheel and it was of course the oldest of the County organisations in Northallerton and the nucleus around which the others developed.

There was an election for the first time in over a hundred years for the position of Registrar in 1872 with George A. Cayley of Hovingham defeating Robert Crompton by 581 to 351 votes. Finally in 1885 only magistrates could now vote according to the Yorkshire Registries Act of 1884 and Charles Ringrose a London Barrister recorded 72 votes against Darcy Bruce Wilson's 52 in an election of that year.

In May 1841 it had been decided at the North Riding Quarter Sessions to enlarge the Registry Office, purchase several houses adjacent to the Registry and demolish these to make a fine spacious new street to the Sessions House. The magistrates bought the old houses for £2000 and in 1846 these were pulled down and an excellent approach to the County buildings was constructed in the form of Zetland Street which was hailed as "an adornment to the town."

Northallerton Volunteers

In 1860 the Volunteer Battalions were formed up and down the country in the wake of the fear of a French invasion and by August 1860 the Northallerton Volunteer Rifle Corps contingent of the 19th North Yorkshire Rifle Volunteers Battalion numbered 54 led by Lieutenant Henry Rutson and Ensign William Fowle the officers, who eventually became Colonel and Major respectively. They were H Company of the

Battalion, already had a good band conducted by bugler William Fawcett, and were a colourful and prominent part of Northallerton life until the turn of the century.

In 1861 the Volunteer Battalion had a Shooting Contest at Jeckelow and soon they were competing annually in shooting matches at the Northallerton Greenhowsike range - in 1870 for example the Battalion numbered 800 with 102 from Northallerton and by 1895 had risen to 866 competitors. The Northallerton Volunteer Corps was often inspected on the Racecourse (Broomfield) and annual camps of a week's duration were a popular feature. After rifle shooting and parades the Volunteers would repair to the "Black Bull" or the "King's Arms" and the excellent Volunteers' Band now conducted by Bugler Albert Barker was constantly in the public eye. An impressive Northallerton Volunteers Rifle Company had been produced and when in 1908 the Territorial Army was formed there was a good basis for H Company of the Princes Alexandra's Own Yorkshire Regiment (the Green Howards) which went to war in 1914.

South African Wars

In South Africa various wars were waged in the latter part of the Nineteenth Century and on 22nd January 1879 the Zulus completely annihilated the British force at Isandula, wiping out the 24th Regiment which included Sergeant Milner of Hutton Bonville.

Lieutenant Alan Hill VC (Monochrome Plate 11)

A singular honour was accorded to a local soldier when on 15th March 1882 it was announced that "the Queen had been graciously disposed to signify her intention of conferring the Victoria Cross for bravery in the Transvaal War on Lieutenant Alan Hill." The action had taken place at the battle of Majuba Hill on 27th February 1880. In storming the Boer position Alan Hill had tried to save a fellow officer and then, though badly wounded, had picked up another soldier and ridden him to safety through withering fire regardless of his personal safety.

Alan Hill of the Northamptonshire Regiment was the son of Captain Thomas Hill of Romanby House, the North Riding Chief Constable and he had been already accorded a hero's welcome at Northallerton railway station when on his return from South Africa on

7th August 1881 a huge crowd and the Volunteers Band greeted him. He remained a celebrated and popular local figure, becoming a Major and changing his name to Hill-Walker upon his marriage to Miss Walker of Maunby Hall.   When he died in 1944 he was the oldest recipient of the VC and remains the only local person to have been accorded that honour.

The Boer War

The century ended as it started with a war. The Boer War broke out in 1899 and several Northallerton men were at the "front" in that year including Lieutenant E. Caffin, the son of the former Vicar Rev B.C. Caffin, and George Barker, a bandsman. The Jingoistic climate of the time is well measured by the "Darlington and Stockton Times" Editorial at Christmas 1899:

"we look forward hopefully for the bright tomorrow which will see British honour and glory undimmed, and our flag still the emblem of civilisation and progress, and Liberty and Right whenever it is unfurled."

Agriculture and Commerce

In agriculture lay the key to Northallerton's economy and so the agricultural vicissitudes of fairs, markets, shows and marts were of the utmost importance. Looking at agriculture generally Tuke wrote in 1800 that "in the best part of the Riding few open fields remain."

The Napoleonic War had given the North Riding farmers added prosperity with the need for beef and mutton for the army and navy and a Board of Agriculture Report talked of the pre-eminence "of North Riding cattle, sheep and horses". New methods in farming were being constantly utilised - Christopher Crowe at Kipling, the Rutsons at Newby Wiske and the Huttons at Solberge Hall being some enlightened examples. Animals of an advanced type also existed at Warlaby with the Booth's fine herd of shorthorns and Bedale where Henry Pierse began his breed of large hornless cattle.

A vital factor was the increase in markets for agricultural produce - the industrialised West Riding of 591,000 in 1801 had grown to 1,366,000 by 1851, to the north east Darlington, Stockton and the south Durham coalfield was another ready market as was Middlesbrough which rose from a hamlet to a booming town between 1831 and 1870.

And of course the arrival of the railway at Northallerton in 1841 revolutionised the movement of animals and agricultural produce at home and even to abroad.

Agricultural Shows

Agricultural Societies were set up in several market towns, Northallerton's being founded in 1840 when the Yorkshire Agricultural Society held its third Show since its inception in 1838 at Northallerton. The 1840 Yorkshire Show was sited at the 'Golden Lion' Field (now occupied by Northallerton College and Mill Hill School) and from the early morning Northallerton "presented an appearance of the greatest throng." It was said the horses and cattle excited much attention "particularly the short - horns for which this district is famed and which in numbers and excellence exceeded anything of the kind ever seen in this country." ("York Herald") Earl Spencer President of the Show took the chair at the dinner held in the Court House under a marquee holding 1300 guests.

The next Yorkshire Shows held at Northallerton were at the Friarage Fields (1858) and the Racecourse (1878). By 1858 the railway was well established and people flocked to the Show to the extent that 11,000 attended on the third or "shilling" day (so called because of cheaper admission). Prize money over the three days 3rd, 4th and 5th August was the then princely sum of £902 and Lord Bolton was President sharing his time with eight Lords, four Honourables, four Knights and four MPs! A similar scenario occurred in 1878 at the Broomfield, Racecourse site and it was hailed "as one of the most successful exhibitions of stock and implements ever held."

Northallerton Agricultural Society's early Shows were held at the "Golden Lion" Field before they were moved to the Racecourse and then to Friarage Fields to what became known as the Showfield where Shows were held until the 1930's. The Shows were well patronized and in 1843 it was claimed to have surpassed any other local society in the land. "The Black Bull," "King's Head" and "Golden Lion" alternated as the convivial Show dinner venues. A Silver Cup for the best hunter was donated in 1867 by John Hutton of Solberge worth £25. It was an appropriate prize because horses dominated the show and in 1887 there was a record entry of 300 horses. The Dinners were now held in the "Golden Lion" and even more latterly in a marquee erected on the Showfield with the "choicest viands of the season."

163

Apart from the "Northallerton" many other local villages had "Shows" which developed excellent reputations for buoyancy and hospitality. These included Osmotherley, Scorton "Feast", Brompton (Whitsuntide Sports), Borrowby and Kirkby Fleetham. Other Northallerton bodies held regular shows or displays later in the century: Northallerton Ploughing Society; the annual Show of foals and yearlings (started 1852); and the Northallerton Horticultural and Floriculture Society. Regular Horse Shows were staged below the Town Hall to the Church and of course there were perennial markets, fairs and eventually marts.

Markets

Northallerton Market goes back beyond written records but it can be safely back-dated to 1127 when the Crown granted the market rights to the Bishops of Durham who in turn vested these for a fee in the hands of the Northallerton people. In 1857 the market rights passed to the Ecclesiastical Commissioners who sold them in 1872 to the newly formed Northallerton Town Hall Market and Improvements Company.

In the nineteenth century the horse held sway as the main conveyance of the farmers and their wares to the weekly Wednesday markets with traps the chief vehicles and carts for the bulkier goods. The horses were rested in the stables which were behind all the public houses and the latter were the bartering places of the farmers, salesmen and dealers, where bargains were struck and business was lubricated by Northallerton's strong ale. Livestock was driven to market and with this and all the other goods the Market Place was a most animated scene.

Fairs

It was a similar environment but on a larger scale on "Fair" days with normally sheep, cattle and horses being shown and sold on different days. Because of their contemporary importance in the nineteenth century there is a profundity of information about the Fairs. The 1810 Candlemas Fair was typical for its horse element: "The show was plentifully supplied with horses for the army, coach, road and draught. The town is well-calculated for a show of this kind and contains stabling for upwards of two thousand horses." (*York Courant*) 1821 saw "the town crowded to excess" at Candlemas with dealers from all over the kingdom as well as Russia and France and in 1833 the Duke

Fun of the May Fair in the 1890s

of Cumberland, the King's second son, bought a horse for £200. A great demand for Army horses occurred in February 1871 - English, French and German.

The practice of exporting horses abroad went on until the end of the century and there were numerous examples of the sales of outstanding local horses including those by S Wilkinson of Romanby to Chile, Frances Heugh, Broomfield Farm to the USA and Stephen Furness, Otterington Hall to Sweden.

The horse was undoubtedly in its hey-day and at the 1895 Candlemas Fair there was an enormous throng when even Northallerton's extensive stabling was filled to excess. Amongst the buyers were Messrs Oppenheimer (Hamburg), Olds (Hamburg), Bartlett (Paris) and various English buyers from London, Leeds, Lincoln, York, Newcastle and Derby. A portent for the horses' future was that in the following year a motor car was seen in Northallerton for the very first time!

The May Fairs were ebullient. In May 1885 there was a great horse show on Monday dominated by foreign and national buyers including: London, Leeds, York, Mr Stevenson (for the London Tramway Company), Mr Laing (for Brazil) and Mr Skellington (for the French Army). There was a vast show of cattle and a small show of sheep on

Wednesday. May Fairs had two extra aspects - the "Play Fair" ingredient and the "May Hirings."

The "Pleasure Fair" always took place on the first Saturday in May with amusements, side-shows, entertainments, stalls and roundabouts powered by steam traction engines as the century progressed. These were all housed in the High Street with the living vans of the "Fair-folk" grouped on and around the Church Green. On "May Days" it was almost impossible to move in the crowded High Street, with the railway contributing to this: in 1881 on May Fair Day 2500 arrived by rail into Northallerton. "Fun of the Fair" was had by all - particularly those "hired servants" whose last opportunity for leisure it would be for many months.

There was a growing disquiet about the "Hirings" system operated in May and November which was increasingly thought to be ignominious. The women outside the "Black Bull" and the males at the Market Cross were herded together like so many animals for the hirers to look over them. At least by 1882 the women had been assembled indoors in the Town Hall. An example of the hiring wages per annum was:

6th May 1889 –Foremen £18 -£22; Ploughmen £14 - £17; Farm Boys £8 – £11. Head Girls £17 - £20; Second Girls £12 - £15.10s; Servant Girls £6.10s.

St Bartholomews (September) and St Matthews (October)the other Charter Fairs seemed to thrive at the start of the century but to decline in numbers and quality, especially in comparison with centuries past. Two factors especially motivated against these fairs: the adaptation of new methods of farming especially the use of fodder crops to feed the animals over the full year and prevent their sale and slaughter in autumn; and the commencement of the mart system and weekly sales which in terms of sheep and cattle sales eventually saw the end of animal fairs in the twentieth century.

Marts

The advent of the railway, with its capacity of carrying animals made regular marts inevitable and it was no coincidence that the first two permanent marts established in Northallerton were situated at and near the railway station respectively, and an animal gantry with access to the trains was built at the end of the southbound platform. David Atkinson, auctioneer, in 1873 opened the "Station Mart" adjacent to the railway station. The official name was the Northallerton Live Stock Mart Company and it became very successful.

"Malpas Mart" opened in 1888 at Malpas Field between the High Street and the Railway Station with the full title of the North Yorks Farmers Stock Mart Company, run as the name implies for the farmers. This mart too was very successful and was especially renowned for its Christmas Show and Sale when the primest local meat was provided for north eastern England and the west riding of Yorkshire.

Cattle

Another traditional method of selling cattle was by "droving" - driving animals on the hoof long distances and this gradually disappeared with the railway's capability of cattle transport. The main "droving inns" at Northallerton were the "Nag's Head" and the "Durham Ox" - the latter gaining its name from the famous animal the "Durham Ox" which was born in 1795 and in 1801 embarked on an unending national tour under the auspices of its owner John Day. Day constructed a wooden carriage for the animal which transported him from town to town, one of which included Northallerton.

Cattle plague broke out in the area in 1865 and though it wasn't on the same scale as that of 1747 it was a most worrying time. By February 1866, 2145 animals had been attacked and 1449 killed in the North Riding. But the epidemic abated and seems to have disappeared by 1867.

Emigration

Agricultural depressions occurred periodically and one of the most prolonged was in the early 1880's. Emigration then became a major consideration of both farmers and farmworkers and after a public meeting at the "Golden Lion" Assembly Rooms, J.B. Booth was commissioned to go to Canada to assess prospects. On 2nd April 1881 the "Darlington and Stockton Times" reported that because of the protracted agricultural depression and unsatisfactory farming prospects: "a considerable number of tenant farmers in the Northallerton area, have left, or are about to leave, the country for various fields of emigration". The emigration numbers for Northallerton itself do not seem to be high but in the surrounding villages some widespread departures took place, particularly to Canada and the USA.

Commerce and Industry

The commerce of Northallerton was geared as always to agriculture, and the population of the town and the surrounding villages. By the start of the nineteenth century the main shops were of a sophisticated nature and shops were a mainstay of the town.

In the 1860's a major factory was erected at Northallerton on the south west of the town near the railway station for the manufacture of tarpaulin, sack cloth and brattice cloth. George Elliot MP, became the chief shareholder and the factory was extended in 1890 to include the making of linoleum. The factory was now called the "Northallerton Linoleum Manufacturing Company", it employed 100 men several who had come from another linoleum factory at Kirkcaldy in Scotland and lasted until 1938.

There were important agriculturally based industries at the North End of the town. Two tan yards operated on the west side of the street and these were owned by Marmaduke Sidgwick and Thomas Hunter. Later in the century the tannery at North Arch became owned by John Walker who in 1902 had the house "Oak Mount" in Thirsk Road built as his private residence ("the house built for a tanner!"). The Provident Corn Mill was started around 1850 being situated on the east side opposite the Goods Station. It employed forty men and showed a steady profit throughout the century.

Apart from the large businesses small firms existed in some quantity such as the watch and clock makers - George Tesseyman (1823 - 66), George F. Clarkson (circa 1866), William Hepton (until 1840) and William Thompson Cade (circa 1850). Others were John Hardwick (pre 1836 Coachmakers), Hindmarsh's saw mill (1862), Northallerton Gas Co. (1841 onwards), North Riding Chemical Works (1863), Northallerton Co-operative Society (1893), William Bell (aerated waters 1888), T.W. Elleray (plumber1891), George Barker (iron and brass foundry 1899), Henry Dale (chains 1889) and Henry Rymer (saddler and harness maker). The latter carried out orders for Queen Victoria and the Csar of Russia.

Banks

Banks backed the agricultural and commercial enterprises in the Northallerton area, the first of which was the North Riding Bank which unfortunately suffered with the economic vagaries of the times and was liquidated in 1815. Better times were ahead when the Northallerton

Savings Bank opened in 1841 with 567 depositors by November of that year. In 1861 it was decided to have a new bank built on the site of the Old Workhouse (now the site of Jefferson Willan, Solicitors). It was opened on 17th May 1862 and had a capital of £35,300. 2s. 6d. and 1177 depositors. A little later the Yorkshire Banking Company opened a branch in Northallerton.

Messrs J Backhouse and Co opened a branch of their bank at Northallerton in the 1830s and this was managed from 1847 until his retirement in 1894 by Robert Morton Middleton (1808 – 1898) who was a leading citizen of the town giving particular support to the building of the Wesleyan Chapel in 1865 and to that church throughout his life. He lived in the Bank House adjacent to the north of 'Vine House' where Backhouses Bank business was conducted.

He was succeeded in 1894 as manager of Backhouses Bank by another long-lived denizen of Northallerton Thomas Russell (1861 – 1957) the son of Northallerton grocer and businessman Nathaniel Russell (1821 – 1896) and brother of Nathaniel Russell junior. Thomas Russell who had been with Backhouses Bank since 1871 became the first manager of Barclays Bank at Northallerton when Backhouses was taken over by them and the present Barclays Bank building (then the Bank House which housed the bank and its manager with his family) was built for him. He retired in 1919 after being with the bank forty eight years to live at Hatfield Road, Northallerton.

Insurance Firms

Firms concerned with insurance and fire set up branches in Northallerton: Phoenix (agents George Scott and Suzanne Todd) opened in 1803 and insured the Vicarage against fire in 1828; Newcastle and Tyne Fire Office 1803 (JS Walton); Globe Insurance 1804 (Peter Rigg); Royal Exchange 1804 (John Carter); Union Fire Office, London 1806; Albion Fire and Life Insurance Co 1808 (H Hirst); Yorkshire County Fire Office 1818 (Robert Hare); Guardian Fire and Life Assurance Co 1831 (Robert B Walton). All the agents were Northallerton residents several belonging to the legal profession.

Industrial Action

Of course the paths of agriculture and industry did not run on an even tenor. In the case of industry some strikes occurred one as early as 1818 when the Brompton weavers struck unanimously for higher wages, the matter ending when four men were sentenced to three months hard labour for joining an illegal combination. April 1825 saw the Brompton and Northallerton weavers strike for and obtain an increase from their masters.

Friendly Societies

But generally speaking the workers rather than join trade unions formed Friendly Societies for workers' benefits and self-help. The four earliest were: the Northallerton Friendly Society; the Northallerton Amicable Society charging 1.0s per month in 1850; the Northallerton New Friendly Society; and the Northallerton Female Benefit Club.

By 1875 the Ancient Order of Oddfellows had a branch at Northallerton and another Society was Standard Hill (No.449) Court of the Ancient Order of Forresters which was formed in 1886, had its Lodge Room at the "Black Bull", with 395 members and assets of £1671 on 31st December 1889. In 1896 the Providential Sick Society had 108 members and £2,183 and the Ancient Free Gardeners Friendly Society in 1898 met at the "Rose and Crown".

Apprenticeships

As in previous centuries Apprenticeships were prized and subject to strict binding conditions on both the Apprentice and Master. Usually if an Apprentice defected a notice would appear in the local press describing him and usually offering a reward for his return. Such notices appeared regarding Thomas Hepton who had run away from his apprenticeship with his father William Hepton clockmaker in November 1810. It is of interest that the majority of apprentices lived in with their masters and this applied to William Barker the founder of "Barkers of Northallerton" who moved to Northallerton from the family farm at East Cowton to serve his apprenticeship at the age of fourteen in 1882 with John Oxendale, draper with whom he lodged at South Parade throughout his apprenticeship.

Village Industry

Boddy's corn mill next to the main railway line embankment was the sole industry in Romanby though the village did grow with the influx of railway workers after 1850. Brompton had been a "weaving"

John Oxendale Advertisement 1881

village traditionally with the work being done domestically in the homes and it is likely that this industry would have died out as it did in Northallerton, but for the entrepreneurs Benjamin Wilford and William and John Pattison who in the 1850s built factories harnessing the weaving into a factory system. Weaving remained Brompton's major industry and in fact dominated the village.

Commercial Conditions

Weights and measures were introduced in 1826 responsibility lying with the North Riding Clerk of the Peace's Office. In 1831 a Weighing Machine for carts and waggons laden with bulky items was installed on what is now Grammar School Lane.

On an entirely different note the working conditions of the shop employees were ameliorated commencing in 1866 when the employers agreed to close at 7-o'clock in the evenings (except Saturdays) "to give their young men enlarged facilities for their mental improvement." In 1886 an experiment in the utility of a weekly half holiday for the shops was so successful and popular that from 1887 onwards the "Half Day Holiday" was secured with shops closing at 1-0'clock on Thursdays.

The New Town Hall in 1875

Northallerton Town Hall

The Town Hall, Market and Public Improvements Company, having acquired the market rights from the Ecclesiastical Commissioners swept away the disgusting old butchers' shambles and the dilapidated ancient Toll Booth and replaced them with the Town Hall. Nicholas Pevsner the architectural critic has dubbed it "irredeemable" and "joyless, utterly ignorant" but in fact from its official opening on 22nd December 1873, the Town Hall has given Northallerton sterling service.

The Improvements Company took the profits made from Market and Town Hall sources and the Directors drew a dividend. A typical year was 1897/98 when the market tolls amounted to £154, the Town Hall hire £93 and the Town Hall shops' hire £100. An anomaly was that some of the Directors of the Company were also Urban District Councillors, a situation that was not resolved until 1925.

The New Workhouse – Sunbeck House

Social Conditions and Health

Poor Relief - Workhouse and Guardians

A vital innovation in the social fabric of Northallerton was the formation of the Northallerton Poor Law Union run by an elected Board of Guardians in 1837, in accordance with the Poor Law Amendment Act of 1834. The Union was responsible for dealing with the destitute and able-bodied poor, thus replacing the Select Vestry in one of its main functions. In 1838 Northallerton and fifty two other places comprised the Union but by 1881 this had been reduced to forty members and these places:

> Ainderby Steeple, Appleton Wiske, Birkby, Borrowby, Brompton (2 members), Cotliffe, Crosby, Cowton East, Cowton South, Danby Wiske, Deighton. Ellerbeck, Guedable, Harlsey East, Harlsey West, Hornby, Hutton Bonville, Kiplin, Kirby Sigston, Langton Great, Morton upon Swale, Northallerton (3 members), Otterington North, Osmotherley, Romanby, Rounton West, Smeaton Little, Silton Nether, Silton Over, Sowerby under Cotliffe, Thrintoft, Thimbleby, Thornton le Beans, Warlaby, Welbury, Winton, Yafforth.

Important was the fact that the Poor Law Commissioners appointed by the Government were to oversee the Board of Guardians giving an element of external control. Totally memorable was that the Board of Guardians was to be democratically elected - the first time this had happened at local level - in total contrast to the self-elected and perpetuating Select Vestry.

In fairness to the Northallerton Select Vestry, however, it must be said that it was comparatively progressive and by contrast the Board of Guardians in their first few years were retrogressive. For example the Select Vestry in 1822 leased a two acre field to employ the labouring poor. On the other hand the Board of Guardians solidly resisted the very necessary replacement of the obviously dilapidated and decadent old workhouse for a new building until 1857.

Benevolence

Private benevolence was frequent throughout the century largely from the landowners such as the Earl of Harewood who in 1823 carried out his usual custom by permanently reducing annual rents and giving food and clothes to his tenants including those at Northallerton. The "York Herald" reported on 22nd December 1838 - "That truly benevolent English gentleman Peter Consett of Brawith Hall near Northallerton has during the last week presented £50 to Brompton and £10 to Romanby to be distributed to the poor of the respective townships."

Another feature at Northallerton was the "Soup Kitchen" which was provided for the poor in the cold depths of winter becoming an annual feature in 1831. The soup was 1d per quart with usually over two hundred quarts distributed at each session and it was paid for by voluntary subscriptions.

The Workhouse

In the Northallerton Union the outdoor poor were dealt with by the Relieving Officer and the destitute poor entered the Northallerton Workhouse. The old Workhouse built in 1444 by Cardinal Kemp as the Guildhall in 1720 became the Parish Workhouse. By the nineteenth century it had deteriorated to dilapidation, was nicknamed the "Bastille" and was roundly condemned by the Poor Law Assistant Commissioner, Sir John Walsham in 1841 as "execrably bad - - - a disgrace to the Guardians - - - one of the most wretched poor houses in England" and "with a medical man fully qualified but seldom ever sober."

At last in 1857 building started on a new Workhouse which was erected by 1858 situated at the southern end of "Friarage Fields" on the site of the former Carmelite Friary, covering 1.7 acres called Ware Banks which included the Horse Pond where the stage coach horses from the bustling nearby Great North Road had been washed and refreshed. With the stream Sun Beck running down Bullamoor Road parallel to the Workhouse, the latter became called Sunbeck House.

W.L. Moffat of Doncaster was the architect of the building costing £5,000 which was originally of red brick with a slate roof. By 1881 it served a population of 11,626 and housed 33 males and 33 females (including 9 boys and 7 girls) as well as a quota of itinerant vagrants or "tramps", the latter posing a large problem throughout the nation.

Teeming with incident and harbouring colourful characters, the Workhouse was a main centre of interest in the town. One of these "characters" was Mary Cornforth who had walked from the West Riding to live at Brompton and still liked "a bit of a crack" when she was 100 in 1901! A perennial item in the local press at the festive season was the Christmas dinner of roast beef and plum pudding washed down by quantities of good ale.

The "Union Contracts" are interesting - in 1880/81 contracts were awarded to: C. Fairburn (beef and mutton) H. Carter (milk) J.S. Winn, J. Boston and W. Collitt (groceries) G. Moon, Osmotherley (Flour and Meal), J. Weatherill (shoe making) Wheldon Bros, George Oxendale, John Oxendale and J. Ward (drapery) and T. Brockhill and G. Render (tailoring).

In July 1948 "Sunbeck House" became part of the Friarage Hospital complex with the new National Health Service, and with a white rendered front the workhouse building stands sturdily at the entrance of the Friarage Hospital.

Living Conditions

In the nineteenth century, the plight of the poor, the condition of the working classes, the health of the town and local government reform are inextricably bound together. Although much needed to be done by the end of the century some amelioration had been achieved.

Northallerton consisted entirely of the High Street with yards branching off to east and west which were dank, dark, airless, narrow and crammed with people. The small dwelling houses (predominantly one room up and one down) and drinking wells were adjacent to privies and dung heaps, pig sties, cowhouses and often slaughter-houses and manufactures. The town was in an entirely noxious condition.

Public Health Report

The best indication and direct evidence of this is to be found in the Report to the General Board of Health published in 1849 and produced for the Government by W. Ranger Superintending Inspector "Into The Sewerage, Drainage, And Supply of Water, And The Sanitary Condition Of The Inhabitants Of The Town Of NORTHALLERTON."

The Vicar Theodosius Burnett Stuart denounced the "open drain which runs from the east side of the town to the west, receiving into itself the sewers of many public and private buildings in its passage." This of course was Sun Beck: "its bottom consists of a filthy deposit of stinking mud, and its stream consists of discoloured, offensive liquid - - - the lower part of the vicarage garden is rendered useless through the exhalation from it." Two surgeons, Mr Hodgson and Mr Walton, were united in their condemnation of the town's sanitation which mainly concerned the appalling state of the yards where nearly half of the town's population lived.

The overcrowding in "sleeping rooms" (bedrooms) was staggering as some random examples show. It existed in fifteen yards including: in Rymer's yard, a man, wife and two children 8 and 11 slept in one small bed and in a second house a man, wife and seven children (16 down to 2 years) slept in one room; in Warrior's yard a man, wife and three children 20 (a man), 17 and 15 (two girls) slept in one bed; in Post Office yard a man 3 children (boy 16, girl 13 and boy 10) slept together; in New Row a man, wife and six children slept in one small room.

The plan of Gaine's or the "Tickle Toby Inn Yard" produced by Ranger's Report adequately profiles a typical insanitary yard: the dwelling houses are near to the pig sties, stables and a dung heap with the drinking tubs and water pump all in close proximity. A slaughter house flanks one dwelling house and a stable another, whilst a burial ground adjoins the bottom of the yard which also housed the fire engine!

Northallerton's average age of life was forty two years and three months and details were taken by the Report of the causes of death from 1st September 1847 to 11th October 1849 which totalled 184 including: 54 deaths - infectious diseases; 33 - tubercular diseases; 22 - diseases of the brain, spinal marrow, nerves and senses; 17 - age; 13 - dropsy and cancer. The main killers in the infectious category were: cholera 2, diarrhoea 6, fever 6, typhus 15, measles 9, scarlatina 3 and small pox 4. There were frequent epidemics - typhus (1830), cholera (1832), small pox (1885) and diphtheria in Brompton as well as typhoid in Northallerton (1893/94).

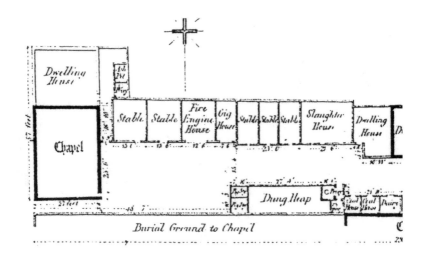

Detail of Tickle Toby Inn Yard – Plan 1849

And death by disease was not the unfortunate prerogative of the poor because several doctors and clergymen lost children, two sons of the Earl of Harewood died of typhus fever in March 1845 and disease killed the Vicar of Osmotherley Rev WC Burgess and four of his children in mid-century.

Burials

A main part of the Board of Health's Report concerned the burials particularly in the Northallerton churchyard elevated around the Parish Church where internments had taken place from time immemorial. The number of burials is impossible to gauge but an exact figure of burials from 1681 to 11th October 1849 was 8334 and at the latter date there were 314 headstones, 77 tombs and 1544 mounds. Reports of bones being thrown up when new graves were dug were legion and W. Firbank a gravedigger stated that he had once removed five skulls in digging one grave.

Obviously this situation could not continue and acting on the Board of Health Report, the Local Board purchased a new cemetery in 1856 the site chosen being that of the old Bishop's Palace. Initially the cemetery was confined inside the ancient moat of the Palace with two neat chapels of rest erected - one for the established Church (to the east) and the other for Dissenters. The cemetery was consecrated on Saturday 20th September 1856 by the late Bishop of Madras, Dr Spencer. Mary Thornton (80), the widow of George Thornton was the first person interred in the cemetery on Sunday 21st September 1856. The Northallerton and Romanby Burial Board administered the cemetery.

Local Board of Health

Another vital recommendation of the General Board was that Northallerton should have a Local Board of Health of twelve resident ratepayers elected by the property owners annually. Thus a Northallerton Local Board came into being in 1851 and of all its deliberations until 1894 the main one was about a water supply for the town, which had been the first conclusion reached by Mr Ranger's Report: "it is indispensably necessary to secure to the inhabitants an abundant supply of pure water conveyed into every tenement upon the constant system, for domestic use, cleansing and other household purposes."

Analagous to the need for a fresh water supply were the eternal problems of the dreadful sanitary arrangements: the hideous sewage system which permeated the town and homes with nauseous odours especially during the warm weather; and the proximity of refuse, and human and animal excreta to the drinking wells. Dr Lumley the Local Board's Medical Officer of Health in 1885 surveyed the wells (there were about 200 in the town) and of the 66 examined 23 were good, 22 were unsatisfactory, 13 bad and 8 which should immediately be closed. In this grave situation it is no wonder that infectious diseases were a constant part of life.

Water Supply

The Local Board continuously addressed "the Water Question" but failed to act conclusively despite the insistence of the Medical Officers and the wealth of evidence weighted towards the need of running water. It was not that the board did nothing - the problem was that they were divided and inconclusive about which method of supply to adopt. Eventually it was decided to obtain a supply from Oakdale near Osmotherley by building a reservoir and piping the water to

"Cutting the First Sod" – 22nd April 1892
Northallerton Water Works

Northallerton. Northallerton Water Bill finally passed the House of Commons on Thursday 2nd July 1891.

A jubilant telegram was sent to the Northallerton Local Board and the water supply was functioning by 1894 at a cost of £14,000 with Mr Fowler the engineer. The operation commenced with water from Jenny Brewster's spring being piped to Oakdale reservoir and then to a service reservoir near the "Fox and Hounds" at Bullamoor, 215 feet above and 1 mile 30 chains from Northallerton.

Sewage Works

The sewage works was instituted by the new Northallerton Urban District Council which had replaced the Local Board of Health in January 1895. Again it was a rather protracted process because the decision was made in September 1896 to implement the plans of the Oxygen Purification Sewage Company Scheme but the plant was not working until 22nd August 1898. The cost of the scheme was £1200 including £250 for the land.

So the century ended on a high note from a sanitary viewpoint with a piped water system and a sewage works. However, the town was still wanting healthwise because in 1900 there were 24 cases of typhoid and Dr Baigent the UDC Medical Officer of Health expostulated "The Yards are appalling, disgusting, unsanitary and indecent."

The elections for the Local Board were hard fought with many of the most influential men in Northallerton competing for places with the electorate equally keen. This pattern continued when the Urban District Council took over in 1895 with even more rivalry for places.

The Cottage Hospital

In the meantime a great amelioration in the medical well-being of the town had occurred with the opening on 11th October 1877 of the Cottage Hospital in the historic building of Vine House famous for the vine which had enveloped it in the eighteenth century. It is likely that Vine House dated back to Tudor times and also the vine. This building could tell so many tales - it was originally almost certainly the site of part of the Carmelite Friary which spread across Brompton Road (then a track called Brompton Lane) and during renovations in the nineteenth century stones believed to be those of the Carmelite Friary were found in the fabric of Vine House.

Northallerton medical men had expostulated the need for a hospital and in 1872 a young man of vision came forward to champion the cause - John Hutton of Solberge Hall the then MP for Northallerton. In December 1872 a circular signed by John Hutton MP and the Rev T.W. Mercer, Vicar of Northallerton, was sent to possible benefactors including Christ Church College, Oxford University who still retain their copy of the letter in their archives. Subscriptions were to be paid to the "St James Hospital Fund" and a telling passage was:

> "The promoters are anxious so far as possible to restore the foundation of the ancient Hospital of St James and the new Hospital will, it is hoped be as great a boon to the poor, only more in accord with the age in which we live."

Enough financial support was forthcoming to start the hospital in 1877 which saw John Hutton as Honorary Secretary, and Emma Butler the first matron at £60 a year. By 1879 the hospital was run by the sisters of North Ormesby until 1886 when Georgina Atkinson took over as Lady Superintendent until she retired in 1910. A commemorative plaque in the hospital records her great dedication, as does one to John Hutton the founder.

Two important developments were the opening of the Fever Hospital - a cottage in the hospital grounds - and the building of the "Dundas Memorial Wing" extension in 1894 for the accommodation of the hospital staff, £600 being raised to the memory of the Hon. John Charles Dundas, late Chairman of the North Riding County Council. The Fever Hospital was relocated to a house on the west side of Thirsk Road in 1893 and then was moved again to a house at the top of Sandy Bank where it remained until the 1950s.

The numbers admitted to the Cottage Hospital increased from 30 in 1878 when it only had six beds to 99 in 1898 when 13 patients a day could be accommodated. The rudimentary nature of the Cottage Hospital is exemplified by the announcement in December 1884 that "This establishment for sometime in want of a bath, Mr C. Palliser of Thirsk terrace has generously presented one." Indeed it relied entirely on voluntary help holding such things as; Garden Fetes, Bazaars, and "Pound Days" when people were able to contribute a pound of any description to the hospital. It seemed like a Godsend, when the hospital obtained a most generous benefactor in Henry Rutson of the well known Newby Wiske family. His attention was drawn to the hospital when he was admitted as a patient with failing eyesight. In 1905 he donated the Vine House building to the Hospital Management Committee. The Cottage Hospital took his name in 1905 and he went on to secure and donate the building adjacent to the north as well as giving £350 in 1907 and £1225 in 1908.

Church of England Affairs

The nineteenth century was crucial and memorable in many respects with regard to Northallerton Parish Church. After over seven hundred and fifty years the link with the Bishop of Durham was broken when Northallerton Church was transferred to the new see of Ripon in 1836 until 1857 when it was placed under the Ecclesiastical Commissioners where it has remained since. At the same time the appointment of the Vicar was retained in the gift of the Dean and Chapter of Durham as it had been since 1541.

Another important change was wrought by the Tithe Commutation Act of 1836 which modernised the tithe system, financial amounts being subsidised for the former payments in wheat, animals and so on to the church. Finally the Select Vestry of twenty four of Northallerton Parish Church lost its position as the premier executor of local government when it was supplanted by the Board of Guardians (1837), the Local Board of Health (1851) and the North Riding County Council (1889) along with the Northallerton Urban District Council (1895).

St Thomas Brompton

Elsewhere within the parish there were notable happenings. Throughout the centuries Brompton Church had been a chapel of ease for the "Mother" church of Northallerton in whose parish it was, but in 1843 Brompton became a parish in its own right. Extensive re-building and renovations followed of St Thomas' parish church in 1868 during which ancient crosses and five hogback tombstones were unearthed, which are some of the best Anglo-Danish specimens discovered nationally. This evidence of its pre-Conquest existence validated the ancient origins of its Northallerton 'mother' church. The restored St Thomas' church was re-opened with both the Archbishop of York and the Bishop of Ripon in attendance on 21st December 1868.

St James Romanby

A Romanby chapel had existed since 16th June 1231 when John de Romanby, his heirs and the men of the "vill" of Romanby were granted a perpetual chantry there, but this was suppressed in 1523 by Cardinal Wolsey. This was rectified on 7th June 1881 when the foundation stone of a new chapel of ease was laid at Romanby by John Hutton of Solberge Hall and then on Whit Tuesday 30th May 1882 the new St James Church Romanby was consecrated by the Archbishop of York, Dr Thomson who delivered a powerful sermon with the Northallerton curate J L Saywell reading a lesson.

Memorable Vicars

Reynold Gideon Bouyer, Vicar 1814 – 1826, was the great pioneer of education for the ordinary and poorer classes in the town. In 1811 he published a treatise on the education of the "infant poor" and instituted the first day school in Northallerton (1815) in the coach house of the Vicarage where the pupils were initially instructed at a sand-desk each equipped with a stick. Soon afterwards he opened a school of the

St Thomas Church Brompton

St James Church Romanby

183

"National Society" with 100 children of each sex the school prospering until the establishment of the National Schools in 1843.

Vicar Bouyer's successor Dr George Townsend (1826-39) wrote many learned treatises and rebuilt the Vicarage by 1828 but his most celebrated involvement was in 1850 after he had left Northallerton to become a canon at Durham Cathedral, when he had an audience with Pope Pius IX in the Vatican conducted in Latin and lasting three quarters of an hour. The main theme of Dr Townsend's message was the need for an ecumenical church and the uniting of all Christian sects – a far sighted and futuristic plan. He was much impressed with both the Pope's total simplicity and his patience.

Whilst still at Northallerton Dr Townsend had Cardinal Fisher's vicarage dismantled in 1827 and a new building erected a little to the south west to replace the old one. Completed in 1828 with its castellated roof, Latin inscription over the door and distinguishing fire mark of a black eagle Townsend's vicarage became a familiar Northallerton landmark until it was demolished in 1988 to be replaced by the modern Applegarth Court housing development. The ancient Vicarage wall still remains running down to and bordering Sun beck at the Applegarth – one of the few invaluable building relics in an increasingly modern structured town.

Church Atmosphere

Stringed instruments accompanied singers in the early church music until a barrel organ which could render thirty tunes was installed in the eighteenth century. This organ was sold for £11 when it was replaced by a "fine tuned instrument" which did sterling service until it too was superseded by another new organ on 26th Mar 1887 which was reconstructed by Messrs Draper and Rushworth of Liverpool in 1948.

William Smithson a Northallerton bookseller and printer (1833 – 1925) not only produced the invaluable annual digests of Northallerton "Smithson's Almanack" from 1869 through into the twentieth century but also an intriguing pamphlet in the 1890s entitled "Northallerton Fifty Years Ago" which gave an insight into Northallerton affairs including the church at Queen Victoria's celebratory Coronation Service on 28th July 1838. The Vicar (Dr Townsend) was led by the magnificently dressed long-gowned Sexton armed with a silver knobbed black staff into a church with two small galleries and a large one which was heated by a coke stove and lighted by candles mounted on metal hoops lowered by ropes from the ceiling. The pews which were purchased as property were high-backed with the old and infirm seated down the centre aisle.

Theodosius Burnett Stuart

Decisive changes were made by the Vicar Reverend Theodosius Burnett Stuart (1839 to 1849) with the church being installed with gas lighting in March 1840 and most importantly the time immemorial custom of purchased pews by the more privileged was literally swept away in 1847 with parishioners able to enjoy the pews equally. All the pews except in the chancel were cut down equally and divested of doors and the seating numbers was thereby increased from 780 to 1011.

Other vital projects which distinguished Burnett Stuart as a Vicar of memorable public good were: his granting of glebe land at 'Vicar's Croft' as allotments to be cultivated by the 'industrious poor' of Northallerton in 1843; and in the same year the momentous creation of the National Schools again at Vicar's Croft for the education of the girls and boys of the town. At the foot of the official record of this truly historic venture in Northallerton's social history is Reverend Stuart's own hand-written postscript: "Remember me, O my God, for good."

Thomas W Mercer

Reverend Thomas Warren Mercer of Trinity College, Oxford University was Vicar from 1850 to 1876 and he signalled perhaps a changing role of the vicars with additional involvement in lay public affairs by acting as a JP on the Northallerton magistrates' bench for a considerable time becoming its Chairman. He was the first Northallerton vicar to be interred in the new cemetery and during his incumbency two new bells were added to the bell-tower in 1872. These were cast in 1871 one in F sharp and the other in F natural by John Warner and Sons of London and extended the original six to now give a peal of eight bells.

Church Bells

The church bells were an ancient and important feature of Northallerton life and the other original six bells were:

"All glory bee to God on hee" B flat 1656. Re-cast in 1871;

"Jesus bee our speed" C sharp 1656, but probably as old as the tower 1420;

"God save His church" D flat 1656, but supposed to be the oldest bell. Called the "Shriving Bell" because it was rung every Shrove Tuesday;

"The Mount Grace Bell". Re-cast in 1802 and 1871. Believed to have hung in the bell-turret of Mount Grace before 1540 and having then fallen was rescued and re-hung at Northallerton. In E and called the 'Curfew Bell' rung formerly every evening at eight o'clock. Bears the legend – "In multis annis resonet campana Johannis";

"The Fire Bell" but not rung as such. 1802 G sharp;

"The Passing Bell" the tenor bell in the key below F sharp 1827 – the hour strokes from the clock are struck upon it and for funerals as it is especially deep and solemn.

Great Restoration – Benjamin Caffin

The great restoration of 1882 - 85 renewed the church's great beauty, largely bringing back the architectural lines of the old church. Reverend Benjamin Caffin the incumbent Vicar (1877 to 1894) incepted the operation which was directed by a distinguished Durham architect C. Hodgson-Fowler MA, FRIBA, the contractor for the stone work being J. Dodgson and the wood-work Joseph Wilson, both of Northallerton. Work started on Monday October 31st 1882 and the restored and beautiful nave, aisles and south transept were re-opened with divine worship on 6th September 1883 and similarly the tower and north transept were re-dedicated and opened on 22nd February 1884, the sermon being preached by the Archbishop of York.

In March 1884 the churchyard was levelled around the chancel which was then demolished, a fine Saxon cross head of an early date and Early English crosses being discovered in the process along with other discoveries of historical interest. A Masonic ceremony of elaborate ritual accompanied the laying of the corner stone of the new chancel by the Acting Provincial Grand Master of the North and East Ridings of Yorkshire Freemasons Dr Bell on Tuesday 1st July 1884, the Northallerton Band leading the Masonic procession from the "Golden Lion" Assembly rooms to the Parish Church and back.

George Grange superintended the building of the chancel (the fifth in the church's history) with Thomas Carse as Clerk of Works and it

DESIGN FOR NEW CHANCEL AND RESTORATION OF NORTHALLERTON CHURCH. C.HODGSON FOWLER, F.S.A. ARCHITECT

Northallerton Church restored 1882 – 1885
Architect's Plan

was completed by Whitsuntide 1885 when choral services celebrated the Restoration, Dr Thomson Archbishop of York preaching the sermon at the morning service. He also spoke at the Public Luncheon in the Town Hall which followed at one o'clock chaired by the Vicar and including all Northallerton's most notable citizens. The whole restoration had cost £6,300 most of which had been donated by its completion which was augmented by two gifts which are still exceedingly prominent in the Church, a new tower clock given by William Emmerson in April 1885 and a magnificent lectern presented by John Hodgson, The Lodge, South Parade.

When Benjamin Caffin died of pneumonia in 1894 his congregation mindful especially of his exceptional church restoration efforts immediately opened a fund by which the beautiful stained glass window now adorning the eastern and south chancel windows was installed in his memory. Depicting "Our Lord surrounded by All Saints" it was dedicated by the Archbishop of York on 20th July 1895.

Church Charity

Finally, the consistent work of the church on behalf of the poorer classes throughout the nineteenth century is worthy of emphasis. It has been seen how the church directly started the first Northallerton schools for all classes and in the 1880s the vicar and curates also brought education to the ordinary people by giving lectures at various houses in the town. Money was regularly collected for the poor such as in January 1883 when the amount given to them in food and coal was £37. 16s. 15½d. and the vicar and church-wardens were always at the fore in the Soup Kitchen.

Raine's charity was constantly operated – at Whitsuntide in 1886 sixty two supplicants were given bread – and apart from being Chairman of the benevolent Select Vestry which controlled the Maison Dieu occupancy, the vicar was Chairman of the Cottage Hospital Management Committee from its opening in 1877. Successive vicars and the Church gave great support to this institution.

Other Christian Creeds

The Quakers had a Meeting House at Northallerton built in 1691 and James Backhouse has shown that Northallerton was an important Quaker centre in 1773. However, in 1811 the Meeting House down North End east row was sold and despite later attempts to revive Quakerism in the town these failed.

The old Methodist Church (1796) was vigorously supported through the first decades of the nineteenth century when it was decided to build a larger chapel and the foundation stone was laid by Thomas Sadler of Bedale on June 23rd 1864 on the site of the demolished "Pack

Horse Inn". The chapel of red brick Victorian design was opened the following year. Previously Thirsk ministers had regularly visited Northallerton between 1774 and 1835 and Northallerton in 1815 was placed sixth in the Thirsk Circuit. By 1860 it had reached second place and in 1866 Northallerton was awarded its own Circuit.

The Independent Chapel or Zion Congregational Church was built in 1819 at the behest and cost of a Mr Hammond who had been born and bred in Northallerton but had gone to London where he made a fortune out of cheese. The cost was £2000 and the Chapel was situated almost opposite Zetland Street and to the west was its burial ground which stretched into the Applegarth and was closed in 1856.

Baptists had worshipped from the eighteenth century in Northallerton at first in some strange places including one venue on condition only that they gave it up for some part of the year so cock fighting could take place! In 1858 they had a meeting house down Marshall's Yard. They moved to the Bake House corner chapel vacated by the Methodists in June 1865 when their preacher was a real "fire and brimstone" zealot William Stubbins who had come to the area in 1844 from Retford with the belief "he was divinely prompted to undertake evangelistic work." Later the chapel was bought and put in trust for the Baptists and the premises were renovated in 1897.

A new Wesleyan Chapel was built at Lovesome Hill in the Gothic style with an adjoining stable for the preacher's horse. This building on the left side of the Northallerton to Darlington road became used as a squash court in modern times.

Since the eighteenth century the Primitive Methodists had worshipped in the town at first in a house off Quaker Lane and then in the 'Bark Room' down Tan Yard (now North Arch). In 1834 they took over the old "Theatre Royal" (built in 1800) at the end of the "Tickle Toby" yard where they worshipped for nearly sixty years.

Eventually a new site was purchased from Miles Soppet on the South End east side of the High Street for £275, and the Theatre was sold to Mr Mason a butcher. The foundation stone for the new chapel was laid on 22nd April 1889 which was opened for worship in 1891. Later it became known as the South End Methodist chapel and thrived until it closed in 1964 when the Romanby Methodist church was opened.

Although there was no official minister or Catholic Church until 1871 in Northallerton, in the area several Catholic Gentry - Pinkneys, Conyers, Dodsworths and Meynells - and some villages - Kirby Sigston,

Leake, North Otterington and Thornton-le-Street kept the old Faith alive. Until 1871 Northallerton came under Aiskew for its Catholic ministrations but by 1886 there was a regular service under Father O'Halloran in a building which became the Catholic Church off to the north east side of Malpas Road, known as St Mary's Catholic Church.

In July 1889 the Bishop of Middlesbrough Dr Lacy held a confirmation at the Northallerton Catholic Church when Father Butler was the Catholic incumbent, dividing his duties between the town and the Prison of which he was Catholic Chaplain. On Sunday 7th December 1890 Father Butler gave the Benediction of the Blessed Sacrament for the first time in Northallerton since the Reformation, in the Roman Catholic Chapel. Lady Herbert of Lea presented sacred vestments and a sanctuary lamp in honour of the martyred Bishop of Rochester, Cardinal Fisher the once Vicar of Northallerton.

The arrival of the Salvation Army in Northallerton was described thus by Saywell - "On September 10th 1881 a detachment of the Salvation Army invaded the town of Northallerton, since which time many converts have been made, chiefly from the 'lowest of the people'." In October they attracted so many inhabitants that they couldn't get into the Town Hall for the formal addresses and service. Similar enthusiastic scenes followed for the next decades and the 209th Corps Northallerton detachment sometimes attended services at the Parish Church in a disciplined well ordered way. But it must be added not always was it "sweetness and light" because on several occasions men heckled during Salvation Army meetings and had to be restrained by the Police.

Educational Progress

Northallerton Grammar School

Although education made great progress in nineteenth century Northallerton by contrast Northallerton Grammar School declined from its standards of excellence of former centuries except intermittently when enlightened masters were in charge. One of these was Johnathan Horner who took over the Grammar School in 1844 having had a school in "Flag Yard" on the east of the High Street for thirteen years. He refurbished the decaying school at a personal cost of £300. From then until his retirement in 1874 he ran the school on good and positive lines.

Normally there were 30 boys present who were well drilled in

English and Commercial Mathematics, the school being characterised "by respectable orderly routine but not by intellectual life of any kind" (*British Schools Report 1868*). The boys came from a variety of parental backgrounds, there was no playground and the boys played in the Town Street.

After Johnathan Horner left, the Grammar School fell again into a slough and various incidents did not improve its image. For example when the Master Rev W.F.N. Allen (Master 1874 - 1877) died on 27th March 1877 his personal effects contained documents and a full set of papal vestments which confirmed him as a priest of the Roman Catholic Church. The school ended the century in the doldrums.

Private Schools

In the meantime there were several other local boys' schools to which the affluent could send their offspring on a day or boarding basis. Some of these schools were: Ainderby Academy, Burneston Grammar School, Scorton Free Grammar School and Catterick Academy. From the 1850's onwards for several decades there was a flourishing boarding school at Mount Pleasant a large house on the northern edge of Northallerton and later to be the area's Maternity Hospital. The school had two successive headmasters Rev Edwin Bittleston and Edward Delanoy Little with normally thirty boys: some from abroad including India and Canada; others from elsewhere in England; local boys and even the aristocracy in the person of Lord Grey of Falloden.

For the local boys of the well-to-do businessmen, farmers and professionals the main private school was Samuel Jackson's West House School at the southern entrance to the Applegarth. This well conducted school lasted almost to the end of the century. Jackson had a dedication in educating his pupils which he did with great success and his ex-pupils such as John Boston and George Hird led the way in the commercial and social development of the town in the earlier twentieth century.

Young ladies education was also catered for in Northallerton starting with "Mrs Mitchell's Seminary for Young Ladies" in 1815. Romanby House in 1849 was an "Establishment for Young Ladies". Durham House on the east of the High Street was converted into a boarding/day school for girls run by Adelaide Forster in the 1860's and 1870's. The final girls school to open was that of Miss Nelson's at Essex Lodge, South Parade in 1893.

Public Education

The public education sphere saw the British School established (at the southern west end of Brompton Road in a building now forming three residential houses) in 1811 by the enterprise of the Church of England aided by the National Society. Rev Gideon Bouyer the Vicar of Northallerton was the driving force behind it and he exulted in 1815 that "A hundred children of each sex will now be admitted into it." Stone flags covered the floor and with only one fire at the end of the great hall in the winter the scholars had to clap and stamp their feet to keep warm. The older pupils ("monitors") taught the younger children.

The National Schools 1843

In 1843 the National Schools were built at the northern end of East Road to replace the British School, the schools (boys and girls were segregated) being opened for the education of the children in January 1844. Erected on Church glebe land called Vicar's Croft, the schools cost £917. 2s. 2d. which was partially defrayed by the sale of the old school for £155.8s.0d. and a government grant of £330.0s.0d. The Vicar Rev. Theodosius Burnett Stuart was the inspiration organising the whole scheme and he was the sole trustee.

In 1870 there were 115 Boys, 102 Girls and 150 Infants totalling 367 on the rolls and a great addition came in November 1898 when the Wesleyan School children entered the school. The latter had been taught since 1844 in the old British School when it was vacated by the Church of England children who transferred to the National Schools. The Wesleyan School was continually in financial trouble and it gave up a losing battle in deciding to close its school and send all the two hundred plus children to the National Schools.

Thus the augmented numbers in the National Schools in November 1898 were 217 Boys, 138 Girls and 201 Infants - a total of 556. Edward Clark (boys) and Miss Catherine Dalkin (girls) were the Head teachers, with other teachers and older, abler students being employed as "pupil teachers" to teach the younger children, some of these eventually becoming fully fledged teachers. Truancy was a problem particularly at "high times" - harvest, fairs and markets - and an Attendance Officer was a very busy official.

Romanby School

An 1881 Report by Her Majesty's Inspectors gave all the elements of the National Schools - Boys, Girls and Infants - very satisfactory credentials. The same applied to Romanby Church of England School where the "well conducted school ---- obtains an excellent proportion of passes and is of a high quality throughout." This must have given great satisfaction to the citizens of Romanby who had banded together in 1870 determined to build a school which happily came to fruition in 1873.

Brompton School

At Brompton a Committee had been formed to build a school which was opened on Monday 18th September 1841 when "230 smiling children" arrived to be educated by a Mr Arundel. The Government Grant was £150, Messrs Tutin gave school land and some of the main subscribers were W.B. Wrightson MP (£100) John and Benjamin Wilford (£50) and Thomas Walker, Maunby (£20). At a foundation dinner John Wilford gave the toast "The diffusion of Education amongst the Working Classes" and this is a fitting motto to describe the development of public education in the Northallerton area which was one of the most enlightened and fruitful aspects of the century.

Victorian Northallerton

Until the middle of the nineteenth century Northallerton's physical appearance remained much the same as it had in Langdale's 1790s time. In the 1840s, however, things began to change with first the installation of gas lighting with forty lamps on lamp posts spread through the town by the suppliers Malam and Parker at a cost of £7. 12s. 5d. in September 1840. Next came the impingement of what seemed the everlasting sameness of the main street in 1846 with the spacious new road of Zetland Street, constructed by the North Riding magistrates to give an imposing access to its county buildings – the registry of deeds, court house and gaol.

Soon came an even more fundamental change which is still proceeding into the twenty first century – the movement to provide housing away from the main street which was started in 1860 by the erection of a house for Miles Soppett mid-way on the west side of what was to be South Parade which had been widened in the 1830s. In the next two decades South Parade was fully developed with houses flanking the length of each side, many occupied by the major professional and tradesmen of Northallerton with 'living in' maid servants and sometimes male apprentices lodging who served in their Northallerton businesses like JW Clapham and William Barker when in their teens. By the end of the century the housing away from the High Street included Malpas Road, Gladstone Street, Romanby Road and Victoria Terrace – many of the houses rented to workers at the linoleum factory and the railway.

Central Northallerton had been enhanced by several sturdy Victorian buildings – the Workhouse (1858), Post Office on Friarage Street corner (1858), Savings Bank (1862), Wesleyan Chapel (1865) and Town Hall (1873) as well as the imposing Parish Church chancel in 1885. Cobblestones were still in vogue in the main street but a strong movement to asphalt the pavements had largely been effected by the 1890s, though it should be stressed that this only applied to the side-walks – the market place and surrounds were still cobbled well into the twentieth century. Finally near to the end of the century in a joint North Riding County and Urban District Councils' venture Sun Beck was culverted and made to under-pass the High Street.

Thomas Thompson, a native of Northallerton, became a skilled master builder of high reputation and was involved with the building of the Savings Bank, Wesleyan Chapel and the Town Hall. His son Robert was born at Northallerton in 1845 and after receiving his early education in the town he joined the Civil Service. Displaying outstanding abilities he rose through the Civil Service ranks to be appointed the Treasury Valuer and was eventually knighted to become Sir Robert Thompson.

Population Synopsis

The population of Northallerton rose considerably in ninety years (1801 – 2,138: 1891 – 3,302) – striking progress for what was predominantly an agricultural market town. A synopsis of the population according to the 1881 census is interesting:

Northallerton 3692, Romanby 414 and Brompton 1295
South Parade 303 people and 64 houses;
Gladstone Street 101 people and 22 houses;
The Gaol 126 inmates (113 male, 13 female, 21 under 21);
The Workhouse 66 people (33 male, 33 female including 9

boys and 7 girls);

The Cottage Hospital 7 patients; Maison Dieu 5 widows;

The Mount 38 boys; Golden Lion 9 servants; Railway Hotel 6 servants;

Domestic Female Servants "living in" 115;

905 people lived in "Yards" including – New Row 78 people 16 houses; Union Yard (=Market Row) 36 people; Flag Yard 59 people.

Going, Going Gone

HIGHLY VALUABLE FREEHOLD INVESTMENT.

FIRST-RATE HOTEL, AT NORTHALLERTON

MR. BOWMAN is Instructed by the Proprietor to offer for SALE BY AUCTION, at the GOLDEN LION HOTEL, in Northallerton, on WEDNESDAY, the 5th Day of JANUARY, 1853, at THREE o'Clock in the Afternoon (subject to such Conditions as shall then be produced), the above well-known HOTEL, containing 44 Bed Rooms, several good private Sitting Rooms, Commercial Room, elegant Smoke Room, large Kitchen, Laundry, Larders, &c., &c.; together with the extensive area behind, and range of Buildings thereon, consisting of Superior Stabling for Fifty Horses, Corn and Hay Chambers above, Lock-up Coach-houses, Brewhouse, and numerous other Out-Offices; an ASSEMBLY ROOM, capable of Dining 150 Persons conveniently, with the GARDEN, &c., now in the occupation of Mr. John Clay. And also the LARGE ROOM, above the Assembly Room, now occupied by the Poor Law Guardians.

The House and Buildings are in most complete Order and Repair. This far-famed Hotel being the only one of its class in the Town of Northallerton, cannot fail to command a thriving Business under judicious management, which it now does, not only during the Quarter Sessions, Fairs, Races, Balls, Markets, Public Meetings, &c., but at all times. In fact, it may be truly said, that the "good old times" have returned to this Old-established Family Hotel, Commercial Inn, and Posting House, and a more profitable Investment (now a rare thing) could not be offered to the notice of the Public.

For further Particulars, apply to Mr. JOHN TUTIN, of Northallerton (the Owner), or

Mr. JEFFERSON,
Solicitor, Northallerton.

Northallerton, November 15th, 1852.

"Golden Lion" Sale

Innumerable sales took place in the nineteenth century property market some of the many interesting being: seven eighteenths part of Greenhowsike and Turker (1804) – indicating its 'Open Field' strips nature;

Mount Pleasant (1810); Castle Hills – 43 acres (1815);

The Applegarth – 5 acres (1815); Broomfield Farm 'newly erected' 1817;

Houses on the main street belonging to Mrs Pierse – several thatched - "Northallerton is situated on the Great North Road" (1834); Crosby estate "beautiful and much admired (1844);

"A grocery shop, eighteen dwelling houses and school-room in the yard behind" (1847). Owner Lancelot Marshall. Flag Yard";

Wind and Corn Mill south end (1837) – Mill Hill;

24 cottages called New Row belonging to the trustees of Henry Neisbitt (1871);

"Standard Hill" farm 64 acres (1898) sold to A Clark, Brompton

£1115;

"Langton Hall" estate worth £1,300 annual rents income sold in London for £24,750 (1887).

Northallerton the 'Ale Town'

In keeping with its long held reputation as the Yorkshire 'Ale Town' in popular lore, Northallerton had twenty eight public houses in 1850 many of which stood at the head of 'yards' each being the social focus for the neighbouring people and as such central in the fabric of life which made up the town. They were especially busy at market, fair and race times and almost without exception had 'living in' servants and stabling for horses.

Some of the hostelries seemed to be frequently in the news often regarding drinking and one outstanding example was the "Sun" at the North End immediately to the south of Quaker Lane. In 1887 its landlady Isabella Dixon (53) died through an excess of alcohol and previously according to the magazine "Home and Companion" of 10th December 1853 it had lost a landlord in the same way as it reported the following unusual epitaph on a gravestone in Northallerton churchyard:

"Hic jacet Walter Gunn
Sometime landlord of the Sun
Sic transit Gloria munday!
He drank hard on Friday,
That being a high day
Then took to bed and died on Sunday."

The subsequent re-arrangement of gravestones with few inscriptions visible renders the veracity of this impossible to establish! Certainly the evils of drink and the consequent strong temperance movement were features of Victoriana to which Northallerton was no exception. A Northallerton Temperance Society was formed in July 1833 which by August 1834 had four hundred members. Fifty years later twice weekly meetings were being held in the Temperance Hall and a juvenile branch of the society had been formed. The non-conformist churches took a strong lead in the anti-drink campaign and in the early 1880s a Temperance Hotel was built and run by a Mr Laws this being the last building to the south on the east side of South Parade.

Virtually all the 'pubs' that are now non-existent were subject to sales in the nineteen century: the "Unicorn and Turf" (Thirsk Road); "Leopard" (Romanby Road); "New Inn", "Star", "George and Dragon", "Waggon and Horses", "Three Tuns", "King's Arms", "Black Swan", "King's Head", "Oak Tree", "Old Golden Lion" (all in the High Street); "Rose and Crown", "George", "Sun" and "Railway Hotel" (all at the North End).

Public houses which exist today were also subject to sales: in 1808 the "Black Bull" was advertised for sale (landlord John Smith) which included "a pew in Northallerton Church" as a possession; and in the same year Robert Thompson lately of the "Nag's Head Inn" let it be known that he had taken over the "Durham Ox", and was particularly welcoming to Graziers having "Good stabling and Grass for any quantity of cattle."

The Golden Lion Hotel

The "Golden Lion" remained as the pre-eminent Northallerton hostelry. With the Quarter Sessions now established in town and the permanent County buildings in such proximity the "Lion" was frequented constantly by those on County business as well as being the headquarters of the local parliamentary Conservative Party. The Assembly Rooms hosted County and major town meetings, numerous sales and important dinners. In 1846 it had 44 bedrooms and stabling for 76 horses.

Obviously one of the main roles of the "Golden Lion" was to accommodate guests and situated on the Great North Road it was nationally known and had auspicious visitors. On 12th December 1816 the Grand Duke Nicholas, (1796 – 1855) heir to the Csar and later Csar Nicholas I of Russia stayed at the "Golden Lion" overnight on a Grand Tour of Britain. His entourage included Sir William Congreve, Baron Nicolay, General Kutusof, Monsieur Mansell, General Waronsoff, Admiral Perowsky, Monsieur Clinkar and Dr Crechton. When they proceeded the next morning at 11 O'clock Mr Hirst set them off with eight excellent horses each mounted with a post boy, all dressed alike with scarlet coats and jockey caps.

His Royal Highness, the Duke of Connaught, Queen Victoria's son, on Tuesday 18th July 1876 stayed at the "Golden Lion" en route to Edinburgh with a detachment of the Connaught Rangers who were billeted on the town. He had dinner at the Registry House in the evening with Sir George Cayley the Registrar with the band of the

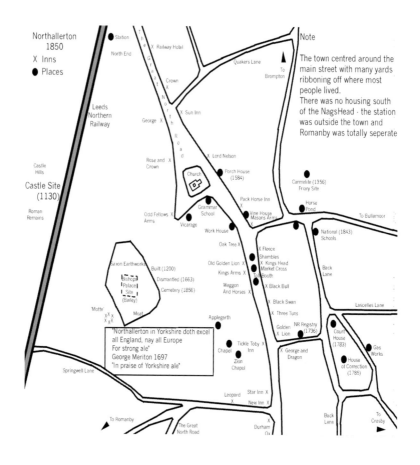

Northallerton 1850 – Inns and Places

198

Connaught Rangers playing for several hours at the gates fronting the High Street. There was a great show of patriotic loyalty the next day when he departed, a very large crowd gathering to cheer him and his Rangers on their way.

Andrew Carnegie (1835-1919) the Scottish/American ironmaster, millionaire and philanthropist arrived at the "Golden Lion" with WS Blaine, the recent Republican candidate for the Presidency of the United States of America in a splendid coach and four accompanied by their suite in June 1888. They stayed for a full weekend and on leaving on Monday morning they "were saluted with cheers which they recognised with frequent bowing." *(Darlington and Stockton Times).*

Leisure and Sports

William Smithson recalls leisure activities in the 1830s: skating on the 'Horse Pond' (now the entrance to the Friarage Hospital); spell and knurr; bows and arrows; skittles and quoits; fives against the buildings at the back of the town; greyhound coursing; cricket matches on the race-course; and both swimming and fishing at Willow Beck. Much information is also available now on the various entertainments and sports in the nineteenth century.

The Theatre Royal

Samuel Butler a well-known actor and dramatic impresario staged productions in Northallerton as early as 1789 when the North Riding Quarter Sessions at North Allerton sanctioned "Tragedies, Comedies, Interludes, Operas, Plays or Farces at his theatre during the winter season of 1789 – 90". In 1800, however, he had the new "Theatre Royal" purpose-built at the bottom of "Tickle Toby" yard adjacent to the Applegarth as one of five theatres which included the famed surviving Georgian Theatre at Richmond. His plan was to rotate his theatre company around his theatre houses spending two months in each place with Northallerton's session in September and October coinciding with St Bartholomew's fair, Northallerton races and the Quarter Sessions.

Evidence of the "Theatre Royal" exists in various forms including bill posters, advertisements, share certificates and even the 'Prologue' spoken by Mr Meadows at the theatre's opening night on Monday evening 6th October 1800. Seats were priced: Boxes 3 shillings, Pit 2

The Theatre Royal (1800 to 1834)

shillings and Gallery one shilling with the exhortation – "Ladies and Gentlemen who take Places, are requested to send their Servant in time to keep them." It is believed that the famous Edmund Kean started his career on the Northallerton stage in 1806 and all the leading actors of the time played at the "Theatre Royal" including Stephen Kemble who appeared as 'Falstaff' in Henry V for which it was said he did not need make-up as he weighed thirty stone!

With falling box-offices the 'Theatre Royal' became economically unviable and on 1st February 1834 it was sold at the 'Golden Lion' by public auction to the Primitive Methodists. It became their chapel until they moved in 1891when the "Theatre Royal" was sold to a butcher and was being used as a slaughter-house in the twentieth century at the end of which it reached the present stage of its chequered career and became a public bar, the "Sportsman's Club."

Entertainments

Northallerton's fairs, races and agricultural shows attracted visiting entertainers and nationally famous shows such as Sangster's Circus (1890 and 1897) and Wombwell's Menagerie (1850 and 1891) came to

FOR FIVE NIGHTS ONLY.

Theatre-Royal, Northallerton.

On *WEDNESDAY* Evening, the 3d of October, 1810,

THEIR MAJESTIES SERVANTS

Will perform a favourite COMEDY, called THE

Inconstant;

OR, THE

WAY TO WIN HIM.

Old Mirabel,	Mr DAVIS,	Bisarre,	Mrs BUTLER,
Young Mirabel,	Mr JEFFERSON,	Constance,	Miss CRAVEN,
Captain Duretete,	Mr BUTLER,	Lamorce,	Mrs DUNNING,
Dugard,	Mr SMITHSON,	Ladies,	Mrs MURRAY,
Petit,	Mr DUNNING,		Miss JEFFERSON,
Page,	Master BUTLER,		
Bravo's, Mr BALLAM, Mr G. BUTLER,			
Mr GEORGE, Mr MARTIN,			

A Favourite Song, by Mrs. DUNNING called

THE PRIMROSE GIRL,

A Favourite Song by Mr. BENNETT, called

TOM STEADY,

To which will be added, a favourite MUSICAL PIECE, *never acted here*, called

Killing no Murder.

Sir Walter Walton,	Mr GEORGE,	Tap,	Mr G. BUTLER,
Jack Walton, as Bradford,	Mr SMITHSON,	Mrs Watch,	Mrs WILSON,
Apollo Belvi,	Mr DUNNING,	Miss Nancy,	Mrs JEFFERSON,
Buskin,	Mr DAVIS,	Fanny,	Mrs DUNNING,

BOXES, 3s.—PIT, 2s.—GALLERY, 1s.   To begin at 7 o'Clock.

TICKETS to be had of Mr BUTLER, at Mr Wood's, and at the PRINTING-OFFICE.

Ladies and Gentlemen who take Places, are requested to send Servants in time to keep them.

On THURSDAY, a new Play never acted here, called the FOUNDLING of the FOREST, with the JEW and the DOCTOR.

Theatre Bill of 1810

the town. The Wombwell visit of November 1850 was sensational not only in its array of lions, tigers and elephants but also because its owner George Wombwell died there in his caravan, his body being transported south to be buried in Highgate Cemetery.

The town had its own amateur entertainers of various types who performed mainly in the "Golden Lion" Assembly Rooms but also in the Town Hall after 1873. There was a brass band in the 1830s and by the 1880s two brass bands: the Volunteers Band under Bugle Major Arnold Barker and the Northallerton Temperance Band led by Thomas Jenkinson Junior and then from 1891 by Charles Fowler.

Northallerton Choral Society dated to at least 1854 and was a foremost organisation singing to packed houses with performances like the "Messiah" in December 1886 and "Judas Maccabeus" in January 1891. Variety shows were frequent and the most popular local group in the latter part of the century were Northallerton's "Original Darkies", who though ill-named for nowadays, were talented with well known locals such as solicitor Ernest Gardner (Grace Gardner's father), Robert Prest and SD Crawford, the Northallerton Grammar School headmaster.

For the more well-to-do dances and balls were high on the social agenda taking place principally again in the 'Golden Lion' and the Town Hall. Annual events were the "Race Balls" in the first half of the century, the "Tradesmen's Ball" which from 1849 became a most popular yearly fixture and the "County Ball" which 'under the patronage of the County Families in the Neighbourhood' became the grandest affair of the social season. Scheduled by the 1880s in January the County Ball attracted all the local North Riding gentry and their ladies who always organised the evening. It also featured: a great number of people to see the arrival of the well-known; sumptuous fare and vintage beverages; far-famed dance bands; and lavish coverage in the local and regional press with listed attendees which was inevitably a "who's who" of the northern North Riding.

Sporting Northallerton

Northallerton and the surrounding district had always had a strong sporting reputation since Tudor times – Roger Ascham's love of archery gleaned from his Kirby Wiske roots springs to mind – and this tradition was extended into the nineteenth century when sporting activities became more varied, ordered, organised and publicised.

Tradesmen's Ball Poster - 1854

Northallerton Races

In the early 1800s until the late 1850s the jewel in Northallerton's sporting crown was its race meeting which took place over three days in October and was one of the most prestigious in the north of England with not only the Silver Cup (value £50) which had been raced for since 1770 but also a Gold Cup valued at 100 guineas which was introduced in 1808 and competed for on the second day of the races until 1849. The gentry invariably had horses entered for the major cups and they also acted as stewards of the meeting which drew such a concourse of people to Broomfield that special patrols and their undivided presence was offered by the Northallerton constables.

One of the most famous names associated with the "Northallerton", as it was called in racing parlance, was John Jackson (1788 – 1859) who was born in the town, became one of the country's leading jockeys winning the 'classic' race the St Leger on no fewer than eight occasions and then settled in Northallerton owning Broomfield Farm and then the 'Black Swan' public house. Unusually for a racing man, he is commemorated on a tablet on the north wall of Northallerton Parish Church placed there in 1900 by his grandson of the same name. Like all the others, John Jackson's public house would be literally overflowing on race nights when the inns were described by J Fairfax-Blakeborough as "open all night long and the town was full, not of licentious ruffians, but men of high spirits, up to any lark."

The 'Racing Calendar' described 'a substantial stand, from which the whole of the running may be seen' and this Grand Stand was situated where the County Hall now stands, at the end of the finishing straight which ran parallel to Racecourse Lane. It seems that the railway attenuated the already cramped course when it was constructed from 1838 onwards and numbered the days of Northallerton races which were reduced to two days and finally abandoned after the meeting of 1880. After such a colourful hey-day the disappearance of the "Northallerton" was very much regretted not only in the town but more widely in racing, sporting and northern social circles.

Cricket

Cricket was the first of the now major sports to be established in Northallerton. It was certainly played in the town in the eighteenth century but the first categoric record is a brief report in the "York Herald" of 4th November 1811 which stated:

THE NORTHALLERTON MEETING WAS ESTABLISHED IN 1765.

Northallerton and North-Riding MEETING, 1879,

Will take place on THURSDAY and FRIDAY, October 16th and 17th,

UNDER THE RULES OF RACING AND GRAND NATIONAL RULES.

STEWARDS.

Viscount Castlereagh, M.P., Viscount Helmsley, M.P., His Grace the Duke of Montrose, Lord Lascelles, G. W. Elliot, Esq., M.P., F. A. Milbank, Esq., M.P., H. F. C. Vyner, Esq., R. C. Vyner, Esq., Charles Perkins, Esq., Major Dent W. H. Wilson-Todd, Esq., J. J. Maclaren, Esq.

MESSRS. DAWSON & JOHNSON, MALTON AND YORK, CLERKS OF THE COURSE AND STAKEHOLDERS.
MR. RICHARD JOHNSON, OF YORK, JUDGE, CLERK OF THE SCALES, AND HANDICAPPER. MR. J. RIDLEY, OF YORK, STARTER.

Thursday, Oct. 16th.

The Great North-Riding Handicap Plate of 155 sovs. for THREE-YEARS-OLD AND UPWARDS. A winner of any handicap after the declaration of the weights (October 8th, 7 p.m.) to carry 7lb, of two handicaps or of any race value 150 sovs 9lb, or of any race value 200 sovs 12lb extra (extreme penalty). Any number of horses the property of the same owner may run for this plate. Entrance 5 sovs.—*One mile and a half.*

st lb
6 12 Mr R. Osborne's b g Brown George, 3 yrs ...... Bell 1
6 12 Mr T. Lindsay's b c Badminton, 3 yrs .... Jones 2
6 6 Mr H. Hall's ch f Sunnybrae, 3 yrs .... Coates 3
8 3 Mr R. C. Vyner's gr m Looking Glass, 6 yrs 0
7 9 Mr C. Maurice's br f Jollification, 4 yrs (inc. 9lb ex.) 0
7 8 Mr Cardner's b f Skelgate Maid, 4 yrs 0
6 10 Mr E. Hutchinson's b f High Heels, by Macgregor, out of Vanity, by Littlecote son of Wild Dayrell, (h.b.) 3 yrs 0
8 2 Mr R. C. Vyner's b f The Rowan, 4 yrs
8 Mr R. Jardine's br h Pilchard, 6 yrs
6 10 Mr C. Perkins's ch f Glenara, 3 yrs

The Crosby Welter Selling Handicap Plate of 100 guineas for THREE-YEARS-OLD AND UPWARDS. The winner to be sold by auction for 50 sovs, and any surplus of the sale to be equally divided between the second horse and the race fund. The winner of any race after the weights are published (October 8th, 7 p.m.) to carry 9lb extra. Any number of horses the property of the same owner may run for this plate. Entrance 5 sovs each.—*Six Furlongs.*

st lb
10 4 Mr R. C. Vyner's ch f Oblivion 3 yrs ...... Griffiths 1
10 12 Mr W. I'Anson Jun.'s br f Little Bird, 3 yrs Fagan 2
11 1 Mr W. H. Shaw's ch c Heather, 4 yrs .... Snowdon 3
11 7 Mr Shiers's br h Nutboy, 4 yrs 0
11 2 Mr T. Colpitts's b g Little George, aged 0
10 9 Mr T. Green's br g Ivanhoe (late Priestcraft), 3 yrs 0
10 6 Mr T. S. Dawson's b g Maximus, 3 yrs 0
10 4 Mr R. Walker's Forfeit, 3 yrs 0
10 9 Mr G. Oates's b c C.B., 3 yrs
10 4 Mr R. Glover's Chesterfield, 5 yrs

The Selling Plate of 100 guineas for ALL AGES; two-years-old 8st, three 9st 7lb, four 10st 3lb, five and upwards 10st 5lb; mares and geldings allowed 3lb The winner to be sold by auction for 100 sovs; if for 50 sovs allowed 10lb, maiden three-years-old allowed 3lb, four and upwards 7lb (allowances accumulative). Any excess of selling price to be equally divided between the second horse and the race fund. Any number of horses the property of the same owner

The Harewood Handicap Plate of 100 guineas, for THREE-YEARS-OLD AND UPWARDS. Any number of horses the property of the same owner may run for this plate. The winner of any race after the weights are published (October 8th, 7 p.m.) to carry 5lb, of two races, or one value 150 sovs, 9lb extra (extreme penalty). Entrance 4 sovs.—*Six Furlongs.*

st lb
9 8 Mr H. Bragg's br g Grand Flaneur, aged.. R Osborne 1
6 8 Mr T. Colpitts's br m Aurelia, 5 yrs 2
6 2 Mr H. Hall's ch f Sunnybrae, 3 yrs .... Coates 3
8 0 Mr R. C. Vyner's b g Bargee, 6 yrs 0
8 0 Mr J. Trotter's b f Garterless, 4 yrs 0
8 2 Mr R. D. Shafto's br f Nellie Macgregor, 3 yrs (inc. 5lb ex)
7 12 Mr R. Jardine's Cupola, 4 yrs (inc. 9lb ex)
7 11 Mr W. H. Shaw's b f Cleopatra, 5 yrs
6 6 Mr T. P. Hope's b c Ben More, 3 yrs
6 6 Mr Shiers's b c Nutbush, 3 years
6 6 Mr C. Perkins's ch f Glenara, 3 yrs
6 0 Mr R Glover's Chesterfield, 5 yrs

The Northallerton Hunters' Selling Plate of 40 sovs, for *bona fide* hunters; four-years-old 12st, five 12st 5lb, six and aged 12st 7lb. The winner to be sold by auction for 70 sovs; if for 50 sovs allowed 9lb; the surplus if any to be divided in the usual way. Maiden five years old and upwards at starting allowed 5lb (allowances accumulative). Any number of horses the property of the same owner may run for this plate. Entrance 2 sovs each, to go the funds To be

Northallerton Races 1879

"On Saturday sennight (week) a match at Cricket the best of three innings was played at Lazenby, between the Gentlemen of Northallerton, and those of Danby Wisk, which was won by the latter by an innings and 21 notches."

By the 1820s regular scores of what was now a Northallerton club appeared and the first known full score-card of the Northallerton club was printed by the "York Herald" concerning a cricket match on 26th October 1828 "between the clubs of Northallerton and Thirsk". Thirsk scored 57 runs in one innings to defeat Northallerton who made 22 and 23 in two innings. The Northallerton team was: WB Ainsley, H Harrison, R Linton, John Best Jun, John Best Sen, R Smailes, Thomas Coverdale, William Coverdale, R Bowman, Charles Fielding and Robert Fielden.

Northallerton originally played at the Victoria ground on the Racecourse at Broomfield but in the 1860s moved to Bullamoor near

Elm House and it was here that the flourishing club staged an historic match when on 16th, 17th and 18th June 1870 a Northallerton Twenty Two played an All England XI. It was a great occasion with a crowd of over two thousand and the North Yorkshire Volunteers band present but heavy rain marred the game with only one innings each completed – Northallerton XXII 138 and All England XI 125.

In 1886 they moved to a new ground at the old racecourse adjacent to Racecourse Lane (now the County Hall inner quadrangle) playing their first game there in July 1886 against Bedale. For much of this period Captain George Gardner of Balaclava was the club President and such was Northallerton CCs status that in 1896 they became a founder member of the prestigious North Yorks and South Durham League which included Darlington, Middlesbrough, Stockton and Thirsk, and Northallerton even employed a professional cricketer, William Blenkhorn.

Such also was the popularity of local cricket by the end of the century that in 1897 the Northallerton and District Cricket League was formed with six teams: Northallerton 2nd XI, Ainderby, Brompton, Crakehall, Thirsk Victoria, and Romanby (North Eastern Railway) – a sign of the railway 'times' in the district then – with Thirsk 2nd XI joining in 1898.

Rugby Union

A form of rugby football had been played for a considerable time in Northallerton and the official formation of the Northallerton Rugby Club took place on Monday 3rd October 1881 at the "Golden Lion" Assembly Rooms as reported in the "York Herald" with George W Elliot (the last Northallerton MP) President, Arthur Gardner (the son of Captain George Gardner) captain and secretary, and John I Jefferson (Grace Gardner's grandfather) treasurer.

The first corroborated match was on 26th November 1881 when the club were defeated at Bishop Auckland and some of the earlier matches evidenced the difference in the opposition sides with for example Hartlepool Rovers and Thirsk Parish Church in 1882 and the vagaries of scoring when they beat Thirsk Parish Church by "a try, five touch downs and a protest to nil"! The match against Stokesley on Saturday 13th November 1886 was noteworthy because the fifteen Northallerton players and the formation were stipulated: Thompson (back); Storey, Gale and Wetherall (three quarter backs); Render, Wilbert (half-backs);

Nelson, Wetherall, Leach, Fowler, Watson, Storey, Reed, Oyston and G Johnson, capt (forwards).

Association Football

Football had been played at Northallerton since at least the fifteenth century and the town and district was caught up in the "football craze" which swept the country in the latter part of the nineteenth century with the English Football League being formed in 1888. It seems that locally the Richmondshire League was inaugurated around the same time which was in full swing by the 1890s with hundreds attending the games. As many as two thousand spectators turned out for the main matches for the Richmondshire League title with the Elliot Bowl the coveted trophy for the winners (presented by Sir George Elliot now the Richmondshire MP) and the Milbank Senior Cup donated by Sir Frederick Milbank and the Milbank Junior Cup given by Lady Milbank for the under sixteens at stake in cup competitions.

Between 1892 and 1897 the Richmondshire League comprised Richmond, Bedale, Leyburn, Brompton, the Green Howards (Richmond) and three Northallerton clubs: Northallerton who played on the old Racecourse at Broomfield; Northallerton Thistles whose ground was at the North End in the middle of the cycle track behind the"Railway Inn" (now the "Standard"); and Northallerton Centrals playing at the old Showfield (now the Northallerton College site).

The matches were avidly reported (the ordinary football being transported into the realms of the "oval", "globe" and "sphere"!) and fiercely competitive sometimes with "fisticuffs flying". All of which moved the "Green Howards Gazette" to comment in 1893: "It is a wonder to many folk that anyone can be induced to act as a Referee at a football match nowadays, unless he be stone-deaf and has been trained as a prize fighter."

There were great occasions at the seasons' end when winning teams were chaired around the town led by the Volunteers band with cups lavishly filled and equally drained with Henrici's Railway Hotel (now the Station Hotel) adjoining Broomfield often the scene of celebration. Ultimately Northallerton FC were so successful that they won the Elliot Bowl outright by winning the league for the third successive time in 1896 – 97 and with no trophy to play for the Richmondshire League lapsed. However, Northallerton sportingly returned the Elliot Bowl for competition in 1899 and the football

Northallerton FC. All Conquering Team 1896 – 97
Back Row: Mr J Peacock, N Smithson, A Thompson, E Render,
W Dickens, W Lee, A Henrici
Front Row: A Crow, J C Reed, F Hide, G H Rider, G Whittaker.

century ended on the high note of the re-launch of the Richmondshire
League.

In the meantime junior football had prospered with competition for
the Milbank Junior Cup and school matches were frequent with
Northallerton Grammar School often in action.   Finally a football
'sensation' was reported in a local paper in the form of a ladies match
between two teams from Teesside in April 1896 at Broomfield.   The
spectators, however, "in the form of creature-man were disposed to be
unchivalrous and indulged in facetious remarks" ('Darlington and
Stockton Times') which evidently reached their heights when one lady
in an athletic movement swung on the cross-bar and broke it!

Nevertheless, ladies football had come to Northallerton as a forerunner to what is now becoming an increasingly popular women's pastime.

Athletic Sports

Athletics flourished in various forms in the district. In the first half of the century one-to-one foot 'matches' were popular such as that on 6th July 1833 when in a challenge match on the Racecourse Mr Todd an innkeeper beat fishmonger, Joseph Blackett by half a yard watched by a very large crowd. Later on more organised athletic meetings took place attracting good fields of flat-race competitors, Jeator Houses (1881) and the Northallerton cricket field (1891) being two of the venues. The most lasting and consistent athletics activities, however, concerned Northallerton Harriers who were first noticed in 1814 and were still holding meetings at the end of the century like those at the Applegarth (1887) and the North End (1894).

The two most colourful and attractive sports meetings were the Romanby Cherry Feast and the Brompton Whitsuntide Sports. The latter were held over the weekend on Brompton Green and the field next to the railway station and apart from the sports and races there were booths, side-shows, roundabouts, with crowds flocking in particularly via the railway and it seemed especially from Hartlepool. Brompton was an atmospheric festive place and the village still holds these traditional Whitsuntide celebrations. Romanby's Cherry Feast in the Cherry Garth on the other hand has died an urbanised death but in its nineteenth century heyday it lasted for two days and apart from races and sports it had novelties like climbing the greasy pole and catching the greasy pig.

Horse Matches

Like foot-matches, horse-matches were in vogue in both the eighteenth and nineteenth centuries. Leeming Lane with its long straight stretch was a favourite venue and in Northallerton Darlington Road was the favoured galloping place. A most unusual horse match was staged on 21st May 1804 with an extremely large purse for the times of 200 guineas at stake with Mr Tennant's chestnut galloway pitted against Mr Hawman's black pony over one hundred miles with the owners riding – going round Northallerton cross each time, once to York and back and twice to Thirsk and back. The galloway beat the pony by six miles.

Greyhound Racing

Northallerton has a special place in the history of greyhound racing because of the training skills of Northallerton native and resident John Shaw and his greyhounds. The Waterloo Cup was the greyhound equivalent of horse racing's Derby and John Shaw's greyhounds won this, the most coveted prize in that sport with a £500 prize, on no less than three occasions. "Coomassie" was the winner in 1877 and 1878 and he and his trainer/owner were given hearty receptions on their return by train to Northallerton.

These paled in comparison to the acclaim received by "Wild Mint" and John Shaw when that greyhound had triumphed in the 1883 Waterloo Cup. On arrival at Northallerton railway station they were greeted by a huge crowd of hundreds and the Volunteers band which played "Here the Conquering Hero Comes" led the excited cheering crowd down South Parade with enthusiasts dragging the coach with John Shaw and 'Wild Mint' aloft to the "Golden Lion" where celebrations continued into the early hours.

The Hurworth Hunt

The Hurworth Hunt held the hunting 'country' from Darlington to Northallerton and from east to west from Dalton nearly to Stokesley and records had been kept of their activities since 1798 even though the Hurworth went farther back. It was essentially a farmer's hunt with new kennels built in the 1860s for its foxhounds at Hurworth and particularly noted for its 'characters' on whom it is believed Surtees the renowned author of sporting fiction based some of his best-known caricatures. The Hurworth was both popular and prominent throughout the nineteenth century meeting regularly at Northallerton with the Boxing Day meet in the High Street becoming traditional and its Master of the Hunt for many years "Squire Wharton" of Skelton Castle a particularly far-famed character.

Other Sports

Cycling came to the fore in the 1880s and a cycle track was built at the North End in January 1886 behind the Railway Inn for Northallerton Athletics Cycling Club. By 1898 there were two more cycling clubs

Northallerton Mutuals and Northallerton. The latter had such a membership that 131 of its cyclists attended a Richmond meeting in 1898, it had its headquarters at West House school at the Applegarth and the enthusiastic Alfred de Lande Long as President who was principal of Dorman and Long iron and steel company and lived at Crosby Court.

Shooting of a varying nature featured in Northallerton throughout the nineteenth century. A pigeon shooting club existed early on with its headquarters at the 'George and Dragon' (Lloyds Bank site now) in 1839 and by 1895 at the 'Rose and Crown' (North End) when the field next to the Gas Works was used for competitions. On 31st August 1888 Northallerton racecourse was the scene for a very different type of shooting when archery returned to the town in the form of the ancient Scorton Silver Arrow competed for since 1673, the Silver Arrow being won on this occasion by Dr Edgar of the North Ribblesdale Archers.

Rifle shooting took place at Greenhowsike target range where Northallerton's H Company became undisputed champions of the North Yorkshire Volunteers Battalion. A national success occurred in 1874 when Corporal William Atkinson won the Queen's Prize at Wimbledon to become best marksman in the country. Although shooting for Durham Rifle Volunteers he was born, educated and had served his apprenticeship as a joiner at Northallerton before moving to Stockton.

Lawn tennis became a popular sport in Northallerton in the 1880s with the first club formed at Northallerton cricket club where games were often watched by a "numerous company" and then another club was started by 1898 at the Applegarth. Angling continued to remain the sport with a very high level of participation with the Cod Beck (especially for trout) and the Swale the most popular fishing places with many competitions staged at Morton Bridge on the Swale. It was near here in April 1899 that Nichol Smithson had a remarkable catch of six large pike which his father William displayed in his stationer's shop window.

Ice skating was a favourite pastime during the severe winters, which were quite the norm. In January 1886 for example literally hundreds resorted to Jenkins' Field on Yafforth road reducing Northallerton to a "ghost-town". And this was not unusual as time and again the cavortings on the "Jenkins" were reported expressively in the local press as in January 1891 when the field was "covered with beautiful ice" as well as the adjacent Meynell's brickyard fields which were used by graceful and energetic skaters to fashion "an exquisite midnight scene."

211

Organisations and Societies

Several organisations were formed which were to play important roles in Northallerton life. A Bible Society was founded at a meeting on 7th August 1816 in the "Theatre Royal" to act as a branch of the British and Foreign Bible Society with a stated remit to involve females in its activities.

A Mechanics Institute was inaugurated in 1849 and by 1851 the annual general meeting indicated the progress made and particularly the support it was receiving not only in donations but of the local gentry concerned including the President, WB Wrightson the Northallerton MP who chaired the meeting which was held in the North Riding Court House. Two hundred and eight members had been enrolled including thirty one females and the educational essence of the organisation was evidenced by the setting up of a library with 625 volumes (3355 issues) and nineteen lectures delivered at the rooms of the Board of Guardians which housed the institute. Future annual reports continued to demonstrate the thriving nature of the Mechanics Institute which by 1885 had 2000 books and in its nineteenth century way was the germ in Northallerton of the enormous adult education programme now in place at Northallerton College.

Later in the century another philanthropic organisation aimed most particularly at the professional and artisans of the younger classes was instituted - the Young Men's Mutual Improvement Society. Held in the Zion school room the society was led by zealous adults such as the Northallerton parish church curate Rev Joseph Saywell and listened to visiting lecturers, held debates and generally aimed at moral and educational betterment of the young people.

The Anchor Lodge of Freemasons (No 1337) pledged to brotherly love, faith and charity was formed in 1873 with its headquarters soon at Durham House on the High Street. Many of its members were the leaders in the business and professions of Northallerton and the annual ceremonies of the installation of a new Worshipful Master were brilliant occasions. Its standing and influence in the town at the end of the nineteenth century was high and exemplified by the rebuilding of the Parish Church chancel, the inauguration, dedication and opening of which was accompanied by Masonic ritual and proceedings.

Major Events

As would be expected events and occasions punctuated nineteenth century Northallerton of interest and import starting at the very outset in 1800 when the "Inhabitants of the ancient Borough of North Allerton" sent a loyal address to George III whose life had just been attempted by a would be assassin. It was presented by Edward Lascelles the Northallerton MP, dated 27th May 1800 and appeared in the "London Gazette".

George IIIs Jubilee on 25th October 1809 was celebrated in Northallerton with a banquet in the "Golden Lion" followed by a ball at night at the "King's Head" obviously for the indulgence of the privileged classes and the involvement of the ordinary people was not in evidence to anything like the extent as in similar royal occasions later in the century.

Excessive feelings ran high in support of Queen Caroline in her 1818 trial and a loyal address was later sent to the Queen by twenty four notable men from the "Golden Lion" to which Queen Caroline replied on 10th January 1821: "The gentlemen, clergy, freeholders, and inhabitants of Northallerton and its vicinity will accept my unfeigned thanks for their loyal and affectionate address."

A fleeing and fleeting visitor to Northallerton in January 1829 was Johnathan Martin the York Minster arsonist who came to Northallerton immediately after he had set fire to the cathedral staying with his brother-in-law for several hours before going on to south Durham. An entirely different visit was paid by Earl Grey, the Prime Minister on 28th August 1832 at the height of his popularity as the architect of the 1832 Parliamentary Reform Act. He stayed for lunch (probably at the 'Black Bull') with an immense crowd gathered to pay tribute, the town band playing patriotic airs and the church bells pealing merrily out.

Historic Female Petition

An unusual, important but little publicised event occurred in May 1833 when the women of Brompton and Northallerton sent a petition to parliament containing seven hundred signatures praying for the immediate emancipation of the slaves. The Abolition of Slavery bill was passed soon afterwards but this local landmark in women's movement to political involvement and equality with men is not just of interest but of high significance as the first record of coherent, unified unilateral women's political intervention in the Northallerton district.

Royal Occasions

Northallerton's celebrations of royal occasions in the 1830s were all of a loyal nature but of increasing gusto and popular involvement. William IVs Coronation on 3rd September 1831 saw the church bells ringing, "demonstrations of joy" and the main event of a banquet at the "Black Bull" for the more well-to-do: "a numerous assemblage of gentlemen and tradesmen, resident in the town and neighbourhood" ('York Herald'). Queen Victoria's 21st birthday ('majority') saw a series of volleys fired by the North York Yeomanry to mark the day but the emphasis was more this time on attention to the young, aged and poor with 'treats' for the school children, old people, Workhouse inmates and "Maison Dieu" widows.

Victoria's Coronation

The Coronation Day of Queen Victoria on 28th July 1838 according to the 'York Herald' saw "rejoicings such as the oldest inhabitant never witnessed in this place" and a "day memorable in the annals of Northallerton": all of which seemed borne out by William Smithson earmarking this special day in his memoirs of fifty years later. It was a general holiday with all the shops closed marked with widespread flags and bunting, pealing bells and a Parish Church morning service followed by a repast of roast beef and plum pudding for six hundred on the Applegarth. After this came the highlight of a procession of seven hundred children led by the town band to the Vicarage where tea was served to the young concourse. The sick were given 2s. 6d. in lieu of the dinner, one hundred and thirty poor people received 1s 6d. and the "Committee" and helpers eventually sat down to an ample meal in the "Golden Lion".

Royal Passage

Another outstanding memory of old Alvertonians was the passage of the Royal train with the Queen, Prince Albert and their entourage in August 1850 en route from York to Newcastle to open Newcastle Central Station. The railway was a comparative novelty, still in its first decade and all along the route large numbers assembled to watch the royal progression. At Northallerton the vantage points were the station, bridges and Castle Hills from all of which distinct glimpses of the Queen were afforded to the throngs of excited spectators.

By the time of Queen Victoria's golden and diamond Jubilees in 1887 and 1897 such was the accumulated loyalty and affection for the sovereign and the national buoyancy of Victorian England on the crest of a wave as it were, that the celebrations were unsurpassed in Northallerton's history.

Golden Jubilee 1887

For the Golden Jubilee in June 1887 flags, bunting and banners festooned the town which exuded a general gaiety which was abroad: a spectacular procession of over a thousand led through the town by the Volunteers band at mid-day; a 'meat tea' for three thousand in the afternoon in the market place with three marquees linked together to provide one enormous unique awning; sports at Broomfield attended by four thousand in the afternoon; dancing in the main street and 'Golden Lion' until early morning; and a firework display watched by hundreds at Bullamoor. Both Brompton and Romanby had equally successful festivities with Romanby having "one of the most pleasant days it had ever known" and Brompton's lasting for three days!

A great legacy of the Jubilee to the town was the planting on the initiative of Christopher Palliser trees up Thirsk Road, South Parade (limes and purple beeches) and the North End which now adorn modern much-urbanised Northallerton. It is interesting that the idea was mooted to set aside the Applegarth as a Jubilee memorial, which though it was not implemented was prophetic for the future gifting of the Applegarth to the townspeople.

Diamond Jubilee 1897

It would seem that Diamond Jubilee celebrations in 1897 even exceeded those of 1887 with the "Darlington and Stockton Times" stating – "Altogether the day was the most memorable of general enjoyment that has been known in Northallerton." On this occasion in the procession all the children carried flowers or flags, tea this time was served in the Town Hall with continuous sittings at sixty tables and bonfires were the order of the day, seventeen cartloads of wood forming the Bullamoor bonfire which was again attended by hundreds trekking up from town with another thirty bonfires visible in the district.

Sensations

There were several sensational events in Northallerton and district during the century and the one which probably excited the most interest in the town was the fatal shooting perpetrated by Johnson Metcalfe (64) who had been in the employ of Thompson Cade for twenty seven years as a watch and clock maker. On Saturday 26th January 1862 having been drinking heavily he encountered two Brompton weavers William Parker (29) and Joseph Todd who were homeward bound after a drinking spree and after a brief altercation he entered his house in Walker's yard adjacent to the "Pack Horse Inn" procured a gun and shot Parker in the main street. Although tended by the doctor who amputated his damaged arm in the "Buck Inn", William Parker died the next day and Johnson Metcalfe was sentenced eventually at York Assizes to ten years penal servitude for manslaughter. He served seven years in gaol and before his death in 1880 expressed the wish that he be buried upright in order that he would be prepared "to run at the sound of the last trump."

Another tragic shooting took place at Leeming in September 1890 when the village policeman Sergeant Weedy was fatally shot by a local gardener Robert Kitching. This incident again aroused great excitement and indignation locally against the accused to the extent that when he was removed by railway to Northallerton it was only with extreme difficulty that the police escort was able to extricate Kitching from the angry crowd that had gathered at the Northallerton railway station subway and drive him speedily to Northallerton gaol. Robert Kitching was subsequently found guilty and hanged for his crime whilst a substantial subscription was gathered for the widow and children of Sergeant Weedy.

Customs

Some Northallerton customs were still carried on such as that at the New Year which was ushered in by the pealing of the church bells with 'waits' perambulating the streets singing festive airs and 'lucky birds' visiting houses to let the New Year in. Despite some opposition "Guy Fawkes Night" of 5th November remained a literally explosive affair until the end of the century. In 1888 for example there was the frequent roar of a large cannon, a huge bonfire just below the Town Hall and several tar-barrels all aflame were set wheeling dangerously up the street with the aid of long poles. This tar-barrel scenario was repeated in 1894 when there were three huge bonfires: at the Town Hall; north of the church on the green; and one on Romanby green. On all occasions evidently despite the dangers the surge of popular custom rendered the police powerless to take action.

The custom which created the greatest uproar in the Northallerton district was that of "Riding the Stang" which was resurrected from olden times in the 1880s. This consisted of the mob taking the law into their own hands regarding an unfaithful wife or husband who had defected with another partner and making sure that public exposure would cast a stigma on the recalcitrant couple. Effigies were made of the couple in straw and pulled around the town in a cart with bells ringing and chanting doggerel such as:

> "Tickleton! Tickleton! Tang! Tang! Tang!
> This is the night we ride the stang."

In October 1882 the "stang" was ridden on three successive nights from Northallerton to Romanby back to Brompton and finally to the North End where the delinquent couple were living. The climax came on the third night when a great mob finally assembled outside the couple's house on North End green and burned the straw representations of the couple which had been suspended from gallows! Finally in February 1896 another tumult was caused which brought an official protest by the Northallerton Urban District Council and the end to the "Riding of the Stang" in Northallerton.

Future Trends

The curtain was rung down dramatically and appropriately on the nineteenth century by direct portents of the technical and massively changed century Northallerton was moving into - the motor car and electricity suddenly appeared.

On Saturday 28th November 1896 a minor but wholly prophetic report in the "Darlington and Stockton Times" gave the first intimation of the new phenomena, the motor car, in Northallerton:

"Yesterday afternoon quite a sensation was caused at Northallerton by the appearance of two gentlemen on a motor car which went through the town street. It went smoothly and admirably, and seemed to be under complete control, turning in and out with great precision."

Just Before the Motor Car. Cobbled High St – 1890s

Northallerton was soon to have its own motor car owner in John Ernest Hutton (the son of John Hutton MP of Solberge Hall) who in 1898 was engaged by Northallerton Urban District Council to install electricity in Northallerton. For this purpose the "Northallerton Electric Light and Power Company" had been formed with 22 years old Ernest Hutton as Managing and Technical Director and CL Ringrose, the North Riding Registrar of Deeds Chairman.

To facilitate the completed electric lighting installation Hutton busied himself around the town in his motor car being described thus by the "Darlington and Stockton Times": as the "zealous young Hutton often seen sailing into town appropriately borne in by the strange electrical influence over which he has such skilled control." Almost simultaneously Hutton was involved in Northallerton's first ever motor car accident on Tuesday 27th June 1899 when driving down the main street a horse and trap appeared out of Romanby road and the horse reared with fright on encountering the car and broke the trap shaft. All was well with no injuries to the trap occupants or their horse.

The electricity fed to four arc lights on tall hollow steel poles carrying aluminium wires, was powered by a generator situated in the "Fleece Inn" yard. Apart from the Northallerton UDC the Electric Light and Power Company already had twenty five other customers including the Mount School and the town GPs Doctor Baigent and Doctor Hutchinson. Inside his contracted schedule the brilliant Hutton completed the electrification process and appropriately the modern was

Late Victorians – at Thompson the Butcher's High St East

timed to coincide with the traditional when Northallerton was suddenly and dramatically illuminated as the electric power was turned on with the town thronged on the night of the Northallerton Agricultural Show – 15th September 1899.

John Hutton MP and Chairman of the North Riding County Council performed the opening ceremony in the "Fleece" yard, wished his son the young engineer whose plans had effected the installation every future success and was proud to point out that Northallerton was "the only town of its size in England which had had the electrical installation." He felt that "Northallerton had proved itself one of the most enlightened towns in the country" which is a fitting note on which to end the nineteenth century saga.

Indisputably Northallerton had always possessed a basic constituent characteristic of an eye for both the past and the future - conservation with a forward thrust. It was a traditionally formidable combination of both an ancient and a progressive town.

8

TWENTIETH CENTURY DAWN AND THE GREAT WAR
(1900 – 1918)

Prelude to War (1900 – 1914)

Health and Sanitation

The new century did not alleviate the health hazards abroad in
Northallerton which still existed despite the new water supply especially
in the yards. In 1900 there were twenty four typhoid cases which was
followed by 17 typhoid patients in 1901 and epidemics remained
unabated for over a decade - seven cases of scarletina occurring in New
Row in September 1903. In 1911 Dr Baigent made a very telling
statement in a Medical Report on the yards observing that many houses
were clean and tidy but some were dirty, dusty and comfortless
reflecting not necessarily the poverty and numbers in the family but
rather the character of the people.

Two fundamental improvements which combined to ameliorate
Northallerton's health were the renovation of the water supply and the
installation of a new sewage system. In November 1907 a Service
Reservoir for the water supply was commenced at Bullamoor near the
"Fox and Hounds" two reservoirs being soon completed there. 1908 saw
the planning of a new water supply which would cost £12,000 adding a
new reservoir 600 yards above the old one at Oakdale which was to be
provided by the building of a great dam. On 16th August 1909 the
Northallerton Water Act received Royal Assent and the first sod cut in
the enterprise was in May 1911, Alfred Fowler A.M.I.C.E. being the
Superintendent Engineer for the works.

The water supply which had brought freedom from the polluted
wells was augmented by a new sewage works. A government loan of
£8,950 was awarded, land was purchased outside Romanby west of the
Bedale road, work commenced on the site in December 1909 and by
April 1911 the sewage works was working efficiently taking away much
of the town's effluent.

Caring Assets

There were other important changes in the health area, notably as already noticed the gift of the Cottage Hospital to the townsfolk by Henry Rutson owner of Newby Wiske Hall in October 1905. Drs Baigent and Hutchinson who were Northallerton Medical Officers gave their professional and dedicated services free to the hospital and both are remembered in Northallerton for other reasons as well: Dr Baigent was nationally famous as an expert on fly fishing being especially well known for the bait he invented called the "Baigent Brown"; Dr Hutchinson when he died left land and four bungalows to be occupied by worthy senior citizens of the locality which are situated off Grammar School Lane in Hutchinson Drive.

Another acquired asset was the new purpose-built Isolation Hospital at Sandy Bank off Crosby Road in 1906. Four acres at Crosby Road were purchased in a joint Northallerton UDC and RDC venture and the hospital isolated patients with contagious diseases thus lessening the chances of epidemics and their spread. For example with the scarlet fever outbreak in March 1914 all nine known sufferers were confined in the Isolation Hospital.

The North Riding Rural Nurses Association was formed in 1899 and became a very important organisation regarding the rural area of Northallerton. Such was the increasing prestige and success of the Association that in 1912 it moved from the Rutson Hospital to its own headquarters having at this time many of the most influential ladies on its committee led by the Marchioness of Zetland who was Chairman.

Finally the North Riding Red Cross Association which was to be closely involved with Northallerton and District's health throughout the twentieth century was particularly prominent just prior to the First World War when on 6th June 1914 a great Red Cross rally was held in a field adjacent to "Southfields" on Boroughbridge Road. There were 700 women in Red Cross uniforms, 400 men in dark blue uniforms and 1100 ambulance students with 35 marquees erected. Sir William Nussey Chairman of the North Riding Cross Association hosted the guests including Major General Sir John Cowans a member of the Army Council - the presence of the latter emphasising the importance accorded to the rally by the military with the First World War indeed only two months away.

Building Projects

The Market Cross re-erected in 1913

  The building process of private houses initiated by the development of South Parade continued into the new century and Thirsk Road especially was adorned with new villas suitable for the most prosperous Northallerton citizens commencing in 1900. Racecourse Lane which had formerly been a narrow track was widened in 1910 and a most important re-introduction to the High Street was the Market

Northallerton Carnival Fancy Dress Lady Cyclists - 1910

Cross by its owner John Ingelby Jefferson in 1913 with subscribers from throughout the community meeting the cost of its re-erection.

A very important construction was that of Romanby Bridge completed in July 1914 on the edge of the village on the road to Yafforth. Previously the road had contained a "water splash" but on numerous occasions when Romanby Beck flooded, the road became impassable. This was now negated by the new bridge which cost £417 to build.

The number of artisans' houses increased in the Ivy Cottages and Malpas Road vicinities but not to the extent to make any of the yards redundant. As it was pointed out at the time emancipation from the yards for the working classes was hardly encouraged when the respective rents were: Ivy Cottages 3s 9d and the Yards 1s 6d per week.

Bold Buildings and Modern Schools

In the public sphere striking building enterprises were achieved with the resplendent North Riding County Hall (1906), and the imposing North Riding Police Headquarters (1910), the re-organised Northallerton Grammar School (1909) and the revolutionary Applegarth Council School (1908).

North Riding County Hall

With the North Riding offices spread throughout the town (the Education Offices were accommodated in South Parade for example) the provision of a new County Headquarters had long been on the County Council agenda with the Chairman John Hutton particularly championing the cause saying that it was "a total necessity". At last on Wednesday 4th May 1902 it was agreed by the narrow margin of 31 to 28 that land at Broomfield of 9 ¾ acres should be bought for £5,300 to erect County buildings and on 29th October 1902 County Hall building plans were approved for £25,000 overall cost by 28 - 11 votes.

Walter Brierley designed the County Hall in a quiet English Renaissance style, with local bricks for the general walling, bright red Leicestershire brick for facings, Whitby and Farndale stone for dressings, roofing of Westmorland slates, and joinery of yellow pine inside, mahogany in the entrance hall and oaken doors. Messrs Joseph Howe and Co. Hartlepool obtained the tender to build and John Hutton laid the foundation stone on 29th July 1903 with the Northallerton Vicar Rev S.M. Thompson and the Bishop of Richmond Rev. Pulleine giving their blessings. A platform for spectating and a marquee for champagne refreshment and toasts were erected.

The County Hall was in use by 1905, but the first official meeting of the North Riding County Council and the opening of the new headquarters was on Wednesday 31st January 1906. £33,264. 16s. 11d was the final cost with £5,300 to be added for the land purchase. As far as Northallerton was concerned the establishment of the County Hall was crucial in its economic position and the consolidation of its role as the county town of the North Riding.

Police Headquarters

The North Riding Police Headquarters in East Road adjacent to the House of Correction, like the other county buildings was no longer large enough to cope with operational needs. Thus in October 1907 the North Riding County Council voted by 47 to 12 to have a new Police Headquarters and senior officers' residences built. Racecourse Lane was chosen as the site, Blacker Bros of Bramley, Leeds had their tender to build the Police Headquarters accepted at a cost of £9,429 and the building was completed and occupied on 1st May 1910.

Northallerton Grammar School – full complement 1909

Northallerton Grammar School

Northallerton Grammar School's illustrious history stood out in stark contrast to its decline by the start of the twentieth century. However, when the school came under the authority of the North Riding County Council plans to build a totally new school were put into operation. On 11th April 1906 the old premises opposite the Parish Church, where the school had been situated since 1322, were sold for £620 to Tom Willoughby, builder. A new site on the old "back lane" of approximately 8 ½ acres had been acquired previously by the Northallerton Grammar School governors from the Ecclesiastical Commissioners and the North Riding Education Committee in November 1907 purchased the land for £306. 19s. 6d.

Walter Brierley the County Hall architect designed the new school initially for 130 boys and girls which was opened by the Archbishop of York Gordon Cosmo Lang on 23rd September 1909 accompanied by John Hutton the Chairman of the Governors and Dr J.W. Bearder, Headmaster. The Archbishop was presented with a symbolic solid silver key by Messrs Clarksons and the total cost excluding the site of the Grammar School was £7064. 2s. 11d. In June 1911 the first of numerous alterations in the rest of the century were announced raising the school capacity to 175 and costing £5010.

Applegarth Council School

Applegarth Council School

Controversy gripped Northallerton over the new purpose designed Infants School - should it be Church of England or a religiously neutral Council School? Because of the furore the North Riding Education Committee decreed that the matter should be decided by a County Council Election - Herbert Clidero represented the Church of England interest and James Guthrie the non - sectarian Council School supporters.

Held in March 1907 the subsequent North Riding Council Election on the sole issue of the Northallerton school was deemed "such that the public feeling had never been so deeply stirred" ("Darlington and Stockton Times"). It was narrowly won by James Guthrie by 365 votes to Herbert Clidero's 354 with 11 spoiled papers out of an electorate of 860. Consequently the non-sectarian Council school was sited not at the Church of England National Schools but at Springwell adjacent to the Applegarth, and built by Paul Rhodes of Leeds at a total outlay of £4,297. 0s. 6d. with Miss H.M. Smith the first Head teacher.

National School

The National Schools also had a good reputation with several pupils doing exceptionally well in business, agriculture and academics. Yet the attendance record of the schools was very poor - typically in November 1902 out of a roll of 564, 141 were habitually absent, presumably the majority because of the utilisation of another pair of hands to add to the household economy. The efficiency and strength of the schools was greatly increased by the merging of the Boys' and Girls' schools into one mixed National School in September 1911.

County Affairs

The only County business now transacted outside the County Hall was that of the Registry of Deeds and the North Riding Quarter Sessions at the old Court House in East Road. The nearby Gaol had come under the Government as opposed to the North Riding in1880 and in February 1905 it was designated for Young Offenders in the North.

A significant event was the painting in oils of John Hutton of Solberge Hall, who had been Chairman of the NRCC for twenty years, with the resultant portrait to hang in the County Hall. This was in July 1914 when a unanimous Council members' statement cited his skill, impartiality and firmness, the universal respect in which he was held and his constant promotion of the North Riding's interests.

The North Riding Police Force made steady progress in these years particularly in the development of technical devices. By 1902 the Northallerton Headquarters had acquired photography, electricity and the telephone, all of which were improved when it entered its new buildings in 1910. Motor cars were gradually obtained predominantly used by the Senior Officers. Major Robert L. Bower KBG, CMG, Chief Constable 1898 - 1929 was very innovative and by 1913 had formed the nucleus of a Criminal Investigation Department. Amongst other things he greatly encouraged the possession and use of dogs. As early as 1900 he had possessed himself of a "Hutton" motor car manufactured in Northallerton – another example of his forward-thinking.

Political Fervour

The immediate turn of the century did not bring change in the Conservative profile of the Richmondshire constituency of which Northallerton and district constituted a major part. Indeed in late 1900 at the General Election the Conservative incumbent MP since 1895 John Hutton of Solberge Hall was re-elected, with an increased majority of 1456 polling 4573 votes to the 3117 of his Liberal opponent Hon. Geoffrey Howard of Castle Howard, Yorkshire. Though the votes were counted and the result announced at Richmond Town Hall John Hutton soon reached Northallerton via Bedale by railway train and in his "home" town where he was considered "their own" he was greeted with enormous enthusiasm his carriage being pulled by his supporters down South Parade to the "Golden Lion" from the balcony of which he addressed a vast crowd.

The January 1906 General Election in Richmondshire was an entirely different matter. John Hutton had retired and was succeeded as Conservative candidate by Lord Ronaldshay, the eldest son and heir of the Marquis of Zetland whom he later succeeded. His rival was Francis Dyke Acland for the Liberals and both men and parties waged tremendous campaigns. Acland was an unusual and popular victor in January 1906 with 4468 votes to 4360 (108 majority) - part of a national trend which brought a Liberal landslide.

Acland had a successful session in Parliament but the Conservatives were planning a powerful campaign with the adoption of Hon. W.G. Agar Orde-Powlett (later to be Lord Bolton) as candidate. Amidst great fervour the General Election of January 1910 took place and the Liberals' descent in national popularity was reflected in Richmondshire where the Conservative Orde-Powlett was elected with a 1083 majority (W.G.A. Orde-Powlett 5246 and F.D. Acland 4163). In Northallerton the day was climaxed by the arrival and appearance on the "Golden Lion" balcony of the triumphant Orde-Powlett who drew concerted roars from his animated audience.

Incidentally the growing influence of motor cars was evident in the January 1910 Election as cars touring the constituency were estimated by their different favours as 46 Conservatives and 14 Liberals. Another General Election was held in December 1910 and this time Hon. W.G. Agar Orde-Powlett was returned unopposed. Indeed the Conservatives have retained the seat until the present time.

Industry and Commerce

Agriculture in the environs and commerce with some industry in the town continued to flourish in early twentieth century Northallerton. Down the North End there was the Provident Corn Mill, Thomas Place's timber yard, Walker's Tanneries and the Railway Goods Yard all doing steady business and each employing a regular labour force. Apart from the North Riding County Council which was continuously increasing its employees the other large employers in Northallerton and Romanby

Wilford's Mill Group

The WENSLEYDALE
PURE MILK SOCIETY, Ltd.

Head Dairy & Offices,
NORTHALLERTON, YORKS.

Wensleydale Pure Milk Society established in 1905

were the Northallerton Linoleum Company, the Wensleydale Pure Milk Society and the North Eastern Railway Company (passengers and goods), whilst at Brompton Wilford's steam weaving mill was still going strong with 100 employees.

When George Elliot started the Linoleum Factory the annual turnover was £3000 in 1885 but when it was taken over by Miles Sykes in early 1912 the turnover was £100,000 per annum. The path however was not smooth for in February 1908 the workers went on strike for more pay and did not settle terms for a month. The Wensleydale Pure Milk Society Ltd was started at Northallerton in 1905 with milk being collected here and re-distributed to the large urban consumers. It proved highly successful especially with proximity of the main line and Wensleydale railway lines, with a spur line being built to a factory gantry from which the milk was received and delivered directly by rail. The factory has thrived for over ninety years in a highly competitive marketing climate.

Approximately fifty personnel worked on the passenger railway station and additionally over a hundred men were employed in the locomotive sheds below and to the immediate west of the railway station on the low line. In August 1911 the Station Passenger Staff went on strike causing a local sensation. But the strike petered out in a few days – traditionally Northallerton has had little propensity for strikes.

The shops were a major business factor and some of the main ones existed into modern times. J.W. Clapham had started his own small bow fronted draper's shop on the east of the High Street just north of the "Golden Lion" in 1885. In 1890 he took over the next door premises and expanded again in 1902, with the whole shop front being re-modelled in 1925. The shop is now Boyes' store.

This success and expansion story was emulated by William Barker, a farmer's son who was born at Wiske House near East Cowton in 1868 and came to Northallerton in 1882 as an apprentice to John Oxendale, Draper. Such was William's progress with the Oxendale firm that when the owner John Oxendale retired in 1907 he made his son C.E. (Clarence) Oxendale and William Barker partners in the business on the west of the High Street. The latter became the sole owner of the firm in August 1919 which became "William Barker's" and his industry, foresight and enterprise led to the eventual development and emergence of the multi- store "Barkers of Northallerton" created by William's descendants and staff.

George Oxendale at the turn of the century ran the successful

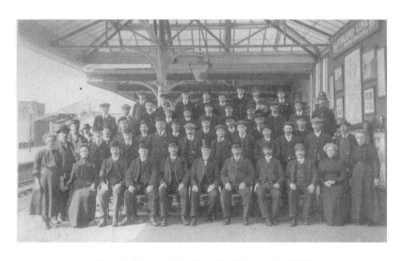

Northallerton Station Staff – April 1913

J W Clapham's 1912

"Bon Marche" draper's establishment situated on the east of the High Street. In November 1906 he announced that his business of sending goods all over the country in a 'mail order' system had grown too large for his premises. He moved it to Manchester to a six storey warehouse to expand business. He was highly successful in this, the mail order firm became internationally known and is still thriving.

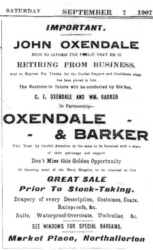

Lewis and Cooper's - now one of the finest and best known specialist grocer's in the North East was founded in 1900 and in November 1906 moved next-door from their original building to occupy the premises they are still in. Mr B.B. Cooper worked for many years in Johannesburg, South Africa before he returned to England in 1901 and met George H. Lewis who was a grocer's assistant in York wishing to set up his own business. Mr Cooper had money to invest and provided the collateral with which Mr Lewis could start the business. The lively Mr Lewis with foresight and unlimited energy developed the shop into a going concern. After successfully launching Lewis and Cooper's and consolidating the business George Lewis retired to Harrogate.

Frank Finlay Clarkson was one of the best Northallerton craftsmen his forte being in silverware and a high point in his career was when he won two gold stars at the Albert Hall Exhibition in 1903 and had the honour of selling two exhibits to Queen Alexandra, an iron casket and a hammered powder box. Mr Clarkson produced numerous articles locally including silverware for the Northallerton Parish Church and probably his last important creation at the age of eighty four was that of a gold chain for the Chairman of the UDC in 1950 which is still worn by the Mayor of Northallerton.

An indication of the progress of the town can be seen from the growth of the Post Office which in 1868 had Post-Master Mr Smithson with six staff and in 1908 comprised thirty three staff. Prosperity was also shown by the banks in Northallerton: Messrs Barclay and Co Ltd was fully established by 1914, the Northallerton Savings Bank joined forces with the York County Savings Bank in October 1913 and the

Oxendale and Barker's 1908

Yorkshire Penny Bank arrived in July 1914. The population figures explicitly chart the town's progress 1841: 3088 and 1911 : 4806.

Agriculture

Agriculture was of course still the predominate local industry and though there was no dramatic change in the new century inevitably as mechanism was introduced and transport improved, differences were clearly discernible.

The most obvious change was in the marketing of animals regarding marts, fairs and sales. Initially there were two marts - Northallerton Livestock Mart Co (the "Station Mart") and the North Yorkshire Farmers' Stock Mart Company (the "Malpas Mart"). Their fortunes prospered and on 4th October 1907 a third mart was opened by the enterprising entrepreneur John Todd adjacent to the Applegarth with fifty covered cattle stalls and pens for 1000 sheep. It too was immediately successful, and it proved the most durable of the marts being the last one to remain open.

At the same time as the marts flourished the Northallerton "Fairs" declined with modern transport methods whereby animals could be sold and bought at the convenience of all concerned. The Candlemas (February) and May Fairs were still going though in a much reduced manner. In 1901 the May Fair Horse Show attracted seventeen National and two Foreign dealers and for the Candlemas Fair of February 1905 special trains were run to Northallerton. Nevertheless, marts and sales were replacing the animal fairs. The Christmas Shows and Sales of meat and animals in December were now firmly established and other sales were regular throughout the year.

The one Fair that did survive was the May "Pleasure" Fair though it was not as rumbustious as of old. In 1911 the mechanisation of the Fair was referred to with the "big machines belching black smoke" and on 5th May 1913 the Fair was described as "a bedlam of noise". Though the Horse Fair took place it was hardly noticed in comparison with only three decades ago when the town at the May Fair was thronged with horses, horse dealers, grooms and the stables in the public houses full.

The Northallerton Agricultural Show held annually at the Showfield on Friarage Fields (where the present Friarage Hospital stands) was not only extremely popular and a highlight of the town's year but it epitomised both the essential part played by agriculture in the area and the continuing success and development of that industry. For example in 1903 over 4,000 people attended and in 1906 rail excursions attracted visitors from Newcastle, Sunderland, Leeds and York bringing in record receipts of £227. It is interesting to note that the 1911 Show had 318 horse entries.

Some agricultural items of this era were of particular interest: in November 1903 the internationally known local poultry breeder Simon Hunter exported five pens of hens to South Africa; March 1911 saw the sale of the famous Warlaby Shorthorn Herd started by Thomas Booth in 1790 and carried on by Richard Booth, the sale being "good rather than sensational".

The Boer War

The Boer War (1899 - 1902) continued to evoke tremendous national fervour with Northallerton no exception. Every success was eagerly received and celebrated with unabated joy and every local man serving in the Boer War became a hero.

When seven Volunteers returned on Monday 10th June 1901 they were accorded a Civic Reception by the Urban District Council and received a tremendous home-coming by the public. The bellman had announced their progress by train and when they arrived at the railway station, they were greeted by one of the densest crowds in living memory stretching into South Parade, including two bands – the Volunteers and the Temperance. Each man was presented with a silver watch and £2 at a memorable banquet that evening in the 'Golden Lion'.

Meanwhile great festivities had greeted British achievements with the bands playing around the town, hundreds of flags appearing and the church bells ringing merrily out. The "Relief of Ladysmith" in February 1900 resulted in "unparalleled enthusiasm", on March 1st 1900 the "Relief of Mafeking" brought a day off school for the children, and in June 1900 the "Fall of Pretoria" was marked by a public tea in the Town Hall for over 800 children, 215 sitting at each session.

On the other side of the coin several locals were fatalities of war and these included: C.F. Smith was killed at Spion Kop; Private S. Greetham of Market Row died at Paaderberg; Trooper Omroyd Jackson fell in 1901 as did Colonel J.G. Wilson CB of Cliffe Hall who was a member of the North Riding County Council. The Boer War ended in June 1902 with a negotiated peace and Services of Thanksgiving in all the Northallerton churches.

The Church of England

Although it wielded nothing like the power it had a century before in Northallerton, the Church of England was still a strong influence in the town's affairs. The Reverend S. M. Thompson was the Vicar throughout this period and some examples of the Parish Church's varied events were: in April 1901 a wall plaque was erected on the north wall to the celebrated jockey John Jackson by his grandson; the tombstones at the south of the Church were laid flat in May 1911 and in time all the tombstones were flattened; the Archbishop of York Gordon Cosmo Lang visited the town in September 1909, March 1911 and June 1913.

Organisations

Some of the main organisations in these years were: the Anchor Lodge of Freemasons No. 1337 which met at Durham House; several "Friendly Societies" two of which met at the "Rose and Crown" - the "Yorkshire Rose Lodge of the Ancient Free Gardeners" and the "Rose and Thistle Dividing Society"; the Amalgamated Society of Railway Servants (the forerunner of the National Union of Railwaymen); the Young Men's Mutual Improvement Society; and the Northallerton branch of the 'Mothers Union'.

The Licensed Trade

The famous brewery "Theakston's of Masham" was boldly advertised in 1904 as were "Baxter's Celebrated Ales" in 1908 of the Thornton-le-Moor brewery dating to 1750 which was taken over by Lord Cathcart's coachman Newsome Baxter in the 1850s who amassed a small fortune. The "pubs" were social centres of the town and several were strongly associated with sport: Henrici's "Railway Hotel" was the headquarters of Northallerton Football Club and the "Golden Lion" Romanby that of Romanby F.C.; "pub" quoits clubs abounded and the "Old Golden Lion". had forty members; and the "Nag's Head" started a thriving lawn bowls club in 1907.

General Booth, the national leader of the Salvation Army stayed at the "Golden Lion Hotel" in August 1904 and 1911 and it continued to house important people, meetings, auctions and dinners. But a sign of future times was the closure as a licensed premises of the "Unicorn and Turf" on Thirsk Road which had its hey-day when the Northallerton Race-course was in full swing (1765 to 1880).

Entertainments

There were abundant "live" entertainments in Northallerton led by the May Fairs and large passing extravaganzas such as the "Wild Bill Hickok Show", "Sangster's Circus" and "Bronco Bill's Great Wild West Expedition" in July 1913. Northallerton Amateur Theatricals staged regular productions as did the Amateur Operatic Company: "Mikado" (1906), "Iolanthe" (1908) and "Pirates of Penzance" (1909) all in the Town Hall. The Swaledale Tournament of Song took place regularly in the town and the Northallerton Male Voice Choir was launched in 1908.

A Northallerton Carnival was inaugurated in 1908 at the Showfield and was extremely popular with hundreds arriving into a town agog with an anticipation that was not disappointed. Consequently, it was held annually with an impressive Fancy Dress Procession initiating each Carnival and amidst a welter of attractions in 1913 and 1914 the appearance of famous flyers giving aeroplane 'flips' over the town gave a charged air of excitement.

Plate 1 Copy of an oil painting impression of the Bishop of Durham's Palace

Plate 2 "The Battle of the Standard" painted in 1893 by the historical painter Sir John Gilbert RA (1817-1897) in the Guildhall Collection, London

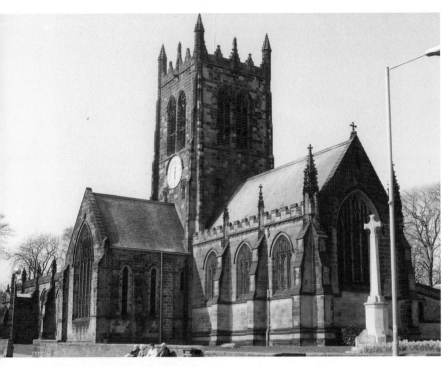

Plate 3 Northallerton - Parish Church

Plate 4 Old Northallerton - The Vicarage Wall and "Odd Fellows Arms"

Plate 5 Northallerton Grammar School - rebuilt 1776

Plate 6 Dr Townsend's Vicarage of 1828

Plate 7 The resplendent North Riding County Hall by Walter Brierley seen in 1909

Plate 8 Northallerton Market Place

Northallerton CC team v Yorkshire CCC 1904

Sporting Northallerton

Northallerton Cycling Club had its track behind the Railway Inn (now the "Standard") at the North End and in April 1900 a meeting at the "Golden Lion Hotel" established a Bowling Club which began to play on a new bowling green in the centre of the cycle track. George Lewis of "Lewis and Cooper's" was the originator and inspiration of the Club which bought land for nearly £600 in Thirsk Road where it moved to a permanent home of sequestered greenery in 1910.

Northallerton had rugby, men's hockey and golf (Bullamoor Road) clubs. However, Association Football was the most played and popularly supported sport. Northallerton drew great partisan crowds to their successive grounds - Broomfield, Vicar's Croft and the Applegarth. They competed in the Allertonshire League with Romanby, Brompton, Bedale, Thirsk, Leyburn, Masham, Green Howards, Vale of Mowbray and Kellbank Rangers.

On their new pitch at Broomfield Northallerton Cricket Club

played first in North Yorks South Durham League and then in the Thirsk Senior League. The greatest cricketing occasions were when the mighty Yorkshire County Cricket Club First Eleven played a Northallerton Eighteen in three day matches in May 1902, 1903 and 1904. All the games were rain interrupted and drawn but it was auspicious that such famous all-time great cricketers appeared such as George Hirst, Wilfred Rhodes, Lord Hawke, Hon. F.S. Jackson, Brown and Tunnicliffe on the site now occupied by the County Hall.

Hundreds watched each day of the three matches which were initiated by the close friendship between Lord Hawke the Yorkshire captain and the Hon WD Russell of Newton House, Leeming the Northallerton CC President. A feast of cricket was served up – George Hirst scored centuries in 1902 and 1903, FS Jackson 112 in 1903 and Wilfred Rhodes took 12 wickets for only 21 runs in 1904. Indeed cricket locally was at its zenith with the addition of a Thursday Cricket League for half holiday personnel, a Northallerton Ladies team and Northallerton Grammar School boys and girls elevens'.

The Railway

The Northallerton to Melmerby line was opened in February 1901 with a new southbound platform for Ripon, Harrogate and Leeds. Other main changes at Northallerton were: in 1907 a new Refreshment Room of a brick structure was erected adjoined by a W.H. Smith bookstall on the south-bound platform; a new long glass awning was provided over the north bound platform in 1911 whilst simultaneously the old iron bridge over Boroughbridge Road was replaced by a bridge double the width.

Station staff and travellers had a miraculous escape on 1st October 1909 when a train travelling southwards smashed into the eastern (south bound) platform at 9.10 a.m. The telegraph office was completely destroyed along with other damage but the three telegraph clerks along with other people in the immediate vicinity were unscathed.

Technical Advances

Electric light was extended from the High Street to Thirsk Road and South Parade by 1904 and gradually it was introduced to other streets, industrial and commercial premises, public buildings and private houses. This is illustrated by the profits of the responsible firm, the

Northallerton Electric Light and Power Company, which rose from £24 in 1902 to £317 in 1912.

Hutton Cars

Hutton Cars Newspaper Advertisement

Ernest Hutton of Solberge Hall, the town's electric light pioneer, also founded a motor car manufactory the "Ohm Electrical Works" on the north east side of Northallerton near the Methodist Church in 1900. Here Hutton constructed his "Voiturette" and "Simplex" cars which were reviewed in the "Autocar" (1900) and the "Motor Car Journal" (1901). C.S. Rolls collaborated with his friend Hutton for some time at the Ohm Works before going to work with Royce at Derby and achieve lasting fame. In 1902 Hutton closed the Ohm Works and went south, becoming manager of Wolseley Motor Car Co., and a well known motor car racing driver and designer.

The Motor Car Tour of Great Britain stopped at Northallerton in 1900 with 68 cars and by 1902 there were two garages in town - those of James Naylor and Tom Smirthwaite, which had started as cycle shops before selling cars and existing almost side by side on the south east of the High Street. Petrol was sold in two gallon tins before Naylors installed the first petrol pump. Smirthwaites became prolific car vendors

Hutton Voiturette – Manufactured in Northallerton 1900

- in 1913 they advertised cars of six different names , including Ford and Humber.

Scruton Lane Ends, Ainderby Hall and Northallerton Town Hall were accident black spots but the only fatality was Miss Emily Breckon (34) of East Harlsey who died in the Rutson Hospital from injuries sustained when she was catapulted from her trap in Quaker Lane, her horse bolting at the appearance of a motor vehicle.

A telephone was installed in the North Riding Police Headquarters at Northallerton in 1903 and in April 1904 the first telephone system was inaugurated involving seventeen shops. Animated pictures by means of a cinematograph were shown by Lewis Prest at the Town Hall basement in 1911 and then the Drill Hall. Northallerton's first "Picture Hall", the "Cinema de Luxe" was opened amidst much excitement on 14th March 1914 to show "silent" films. Situated on the south side of Romanby Road, it was built by Messrs Blackett and Co. of Darlington to hold 400 and later acquired the affectionate soubriquet of the "Bughouse"!

Royal Events

The news of Queen Victoria's death in January 1901 was greeted with sensation and awe and many bodies paraded to the Parish Church on the day of her funeral 2nd of February 1901 accompanied by the muffled drums of the Volunteers' band and the dumb peal of the church bells. The church was fuller than in living memory.

Contrastingly the Coronation of Edward VII in August 1902 was celebrated joyously on a memorable day for Northallerton. George Vth's Coronation in June 1911 was of similar mode with the highlight a great marquee in the High Street which housed innumerable children and old people for tea and then dancing until the late hours.

Those Magnificent Men in their Flying Machines

Gustav Hamel's monoplane – Friarage Fields 1913

Northallerton's strong flying links were forged in aviation's embryonic days. Aeroplanes first entered Northallerton "air space" during the "Circuit of Britain Race" on Monday 24th July 1911 when countless excited citizens had taken up vantage points by 7 a.m. to see the intrepid flyers "on" their aircraft. At 5 p.m. Gustav Hamel the popular German, who was lying fourth in the race, flew over close to Northallerton Railway Station thus becoming the first person to fly over the town.

Hamel became an even greater local hero when he came to Northallerton Carnival in 1913 to give aeroplane 'flips' around the town, taking off and landing on a small strip on the Showfield next to the workhouse. Hamel achieved eleven flights with wonderful skill and

Fatal RFC Air Crash near Lovesome Hill 15th May 1914

the first townsman to fly was Tom Smirthwaite, the garage proprietor who paid £5 for the privilege and made his historic flight in the Bleriot Monoplane at 3 p.m. on Thursday 30th July 1913. Alas, the Gustav Hamel story has a tragic ending because in 1914 he disappeared on a flight from Paris over the English Channel and was never seen again.

Rowland Ding another famous aviator came to fly at the 1914 Carnival in July but it was a difficult flying day, being attended by "air pockets" and on his second flight with his passenger Lewis Prest, he swooped down scattering the numerous crowd and the aeroplane crashed on a hawthorn hedge. Both pilot and passenger were unhurt but this episode spelled the end of flying at the "Friarage Fields".

An aviation tragedy of national moment had occurred in the vicinity just previously on the 15th May 1914 at approximately 6.50 a.m. No 2 Squadron of the Royal Flying Corps was engaged in a unique exercise of air to ground co-operation with military vehicles from Salisbury Plain to Edinburgh and back. Their progress was attended by huge crowds and there were an estimated 50,000 people to see ten biplanes take off on a bright early morning from Seaton Carew to the Knavesmire at York where a great crowd awaited them

They were approaching Northallerton when disaster struck as they flew into dense fog and planes simply fell out of the sky - six in all. The most shocking crash was that of BE Biplane 331 which hit a field's

242

National Reserve Parade July 1913

dividing hedge between Lovesome Hill and Hutton Bonville burying the
pilot Lieutenant John Empson and his passenger Air Mechanic William
Cudmore in a ploughed field - both men dying instantaneously.
Lieutenants Rodwell and Martin alighted at Walter Todd's Lazenby Hall
Farm at Danby Wiske, Captain Dawes and Lieutenant Corballis landed
at Bedale but flew off the next day and Lieutenant Harvey Kelly
collided with a hedge at Swain's farm, Darlington Road, Northallerton,
his aircraft and that of Rodwell being wrecked.

The whole affair had a tremendous local impact which seemed to
crystallise around the fatalities. Crowds flocked to see the scene of the
accident and though Lieutenant Empson's body was removed directly to
his home in the East Riding, the transfer of Air Mechanic Cudmore's
remains from Lovesome Hill to Northallerton Railway Station en route
to his Manchester home, allowed thousands to pay their respects.
Although it was only six a.m. as the cortege passed slowly through the
town led by the 4th Battalion Green Howards and their band and flanked
by a Royal Flying Corps escort, the route was deeply lined throughout.

A question was even asked in the House of Commons about the
fatalities by Robert Harcourt MP which was replied to by Howard Baker
MP on behalf of the Prime Minister H.H. Asquith who expressed the
sympathy of the House for the relatives.

Voluntary Service

The 1st Battalion Green Howards (Volunteer) continued to thrive and became a part of the Territorial Army on 1st April 1908. The new North Riding Territorial Army Association (Chairman, Lt Colonel W.H.A. Wharton, Skelton Castle) was centred at Northallerton and was divided into the 5th and 4th Battalions with their Headquarters Scarborough and Northallerton respectively. The Northallerton detachment of the 4th Battalion was named "H" Company. On 7th December 1911 a new T.A. Headquarters Drill Hall was opened at Thirsk Road, Northallerton at an overall building cost of £4958. Finally an ultra keen Northallerton National Reserve was formed of patriots who could not join the Armed Services.

Another new development which emphasised the voluntary effort of the town and district was the formation in November 1912 of the Red Cross Voluntary Aid Northallerton Detachment, with Major Bower as Commandant. It was to play a vital part in the Great War especially in the running of the Red Cross Hospital at the County Hall which dealt with hundreds of wounded soldiers.

The First World War 1914 – 1918

1914 Your King and Country Need You

The critical incident which led to the First World War was the assassination on 28th June 1914 at Sarajevo the capital of Serbia of the heir to the Austrian Empire Archduke Franz Ferdinand and his wife by a Bosnian student. In the maelstrom which followed every British hamlet, village, town and city was affected and the story of the Northallerton district and its people was typical of the nation's numerous market and various County towns.

What eventuated as one of the saddest periods of Northallerton's history commenced with an opposite atmosphere of excitement and militaristic euphoria, with the assembly of the 4th (Territorial) Battalion Alexandra Princess of Wales Own Yorkshire Regiment (The Green Howards) at Northallerton which was its headquarters. The Battalion, which was often referred to as the "Northallerton Territorials" was at annual camp near Conway, North Wales when war was imminent and it was immediately hurried home in readiness for war preparations.

The territorial soldiers first returned to their own homes before

244

Drill Hall cannon (bottom left), Thirsk Rd

mustering at Northallerton - H Company (Northallerton) and the Thirsk, Bedale and Helperby detachments on Tuesday 4th August followed on Wednesday by the other companies from Middlesbrough, Guisborough, Yarm, Redcar and Stokesley. The Drill Hall in Thirsk Road was the Battalion Headquarters, and several buildings were commandeered as soldiers' accommodation – the new Grammar School, Town Hall, old Court House, National School, and also the new Applegarth Council School.

Northallerton presented an extraordinary spectacle with great commotion and excitement and crowds of people watching the operations especially around the animated Drill Hall. The town had never been quite the same as this.

An important official event took place on the afternoon of Saturday August 8th when the 4th Battalion Colours were handed over for safe-keeping to the North Riding County Council, emphasising the strong ties between the two - indeed the special place the 4th Battalion held as the North Riding's own regiment. The proceedings were at the entrance to the North Riding County Hall with many County dignitaries present including appropriately the Lord Lieutenant Sir Hugh Bell, the father of the 4th Battalion's Commanding Officer Lieutenant Colonel Maurice Bell.

In his acceptance of the Colours the North Riding Chairman John

245

Hutton made a strong and patriotic speech ending:

"You are going away if needs be to lay down your lives for your King and Country. May I venture to offer you a motto to take with you: Courage and Truth. May God Defend the Right."

This oratory was typical of that up and down the land as a generation was called to war, over a million never to return.

An outstanding spectacle even in Northallerton's long history occurred on Sunday 9th August 1914. The 4th Battalion Territorials of nearly a thousand strong assembled to march off to war down South Parade to the railway station at 10. a.m. Led by Lieutenant Colonel Maurice Bell they were an impressive sight stretching as far as the eye could see. And as it tragically transpired the majority never returned.

Only a few months later in April 1915 the untried Battalion having only been in France for ten days were flung with the Durham Light Infantry Territorials into a breach in the British lines caused by the first German gas attack of the war. At this, the Second Battle of Ypres, the 4th Battalion acquitted themselves magnificently but lost many officers and men. This was just the start of continuing bravery and accompanying attrition, through the Somme (1916), Passchendaele (1917) and other war theatres. By 1916 one hundred and seventy seven of the 4th Battalion had been killed and six hundred and sixty nine wounded. A final war's end count on 31st October 1918 recorded that there were only nine officers and eighty nine men left in the Battalion. The honoured dead are commemorated on war memorials throughout North Yorkshire including of course Northallerton, Brompton and Romanby.

The first local soldiers to face the Germans directly were mainly in the 2nd Battalion of the Yorkshire Regiment (Green Howards) which formed part of the British Expeditionary Force in 1914. A feature of the war were "eye-witness accounts" given by returning soldiers and one of the first such reports was given by Sergeant Joyce of the Green Howards and Dudley Terrace, Northallerton to the "Darlington and Stockton Times" in December 1914 about the First Battle of Ypres. By coincidence he described the capture of Corporal Tom Riordan of the Green Howards (the author's father) who at that time had no connection with Northallerton.

Also captured in the same action was 2nd Lieutenant William Worsley of the Green Howards who later became the father of Katherine the Duchess of Kent. His father was Sir William Worsley of Hovingham Hall and Chairman of the North Riding County Council

Northallerton Grammar School – HQ 4th Battalion (1914 – 16)

Education Committee based at Northallerton. Sir William Worsley at this time lost his son-in-law Captain Pemberton killed in action with the Life Guards and this sad event epitomised a national trend whereby the families of the aristocracy and gentry suffered wholesale losses. For example Lord Bolton had lost three nephews by October 1914, and the following year on 21st May 1915 his own eldest son 2nd Lieutenant W.P. Orde-Powlett was killed serving with the 4th Battalion Green Howards. The son of Colonel Sir James Legard the Vice Chairman of the North Riding County Council Lieutenant R.J. Legard was killed in 1916. And the list went on and on.

Meanwhile at home in Northallerton the war was transforming the town especially with the recruiting drive for "Kitchener's Army" - "Your King and Country Need You" with placarded pointed finger. Hundreds of local volunteers came forward to make up the Second Line Fourth Battalion Green Howards (Territorials) 2/4th commanded by Lieutenant Colonel W.A. Wharton of Skelton Castle. With its headquarters at Northallerton several buildings were commandeered by the army and consequently the Grammar School students were educated in the new North Wing of the County Hall and those of the National School at the Town Hall. Apart from the Green Howards 4th Battalion local men were very much involved with other service units and exemplifying the strong tide of recruitment, by October 1914 twenty two of the County Hall staff and seventy nine North Riding CC employees had joined up.

The more unsavoury side of wars' effects on the civilian

County Hall Red Cross Nurses parade past the 'Harewood Arms'

population was seen in two aspects in Northallerton at the outbreak of
war in August 1914. There was a rush on food and hoarding with items
sold out and a sudden rise in prices. The other unpleasant incident was
the rounding up for interrogation at Northallerton Police Station of about
fifty Germans. They were all released on condition they report regularly
to the police but it was a humiliating experience for these people many
of whom had lived in England for decades including Father Tils the
Roman Catholic Priest for Northallerton.

The great preponderance of activities at home, however, in 1914
were of a positive nature and the first of these was the help offered to
Belgian refugees who had fled to Britain when Germany invaded
Belgium. It was Belgians who were the first patients to be cared for in
the temporary Red Cross Hospital established in the North Riding
County Hall in 1914.

This hospital became a most important military medical facility in
Northallerton and soon it was full of soldier patients with this situation
continuing throughout the war and altogether one thousand six hundred
soldiers were tended during war time. Situated in the Committee Rooms
of the County Hall there were thirty two beds with ten reserved for the
4th Battalion of the Yorkshire Regiment (Green Howards). Shot and
shrapnel wounded were catered for, Dr Baigent being Commandant.
The patients dressed in bright blue and these and the Red Cross nurses

in their attractive uniforms became a permanent and very popular feature of the Northallerton scene.

Regular collections and fund raising activities for the troops or the war effort were made. In the forefront of these activities were the local farmers: John Todd presided over a Patriotic Mart Sale which raised £106 and in September 1914 the Northallerton and District Farmers sent a telegram to Lord Kitchener offering provender to the army to which Kitchener replied "Very grateful of the patriotic offer of Northallerton and District Farmers - contact Officer i/c Supply Depot Leeds – Kitchener." An historic telegram indeed for the local farmers.

The event which had by far the greatest impact on the North Riding and its County town was the bombardment of the east coast towns Hartlepools, Scarborough and Whitby in the early morning of Wednesday 16th December 1914. At Scarborough and Whitby twenty one civilians were killed and one hundred and twenty injured. In the County seat of Northallerton a tremendous sensation was caused and the North Riding County Council on 27th January 1915 from the County Hall wrote to Scarborough Council: "the Council representing the people of the North Riding, would like to officially and solemnly to protest against this dastardly action and to express its sympathy with those who had suffered."

1915 – Trench Warfare Paramount

Of primary importance to Northallerton in 1915 was the involvement of local men in the main theatres of war especially on the western front with subsequent feats of gallantry and endurance tinged sadly with the casualities suffered of dead and wounded: a pattern which was to be repeated until the Great War's end.

The large majority of the locals serving were with the Yorkshire Regiment - Green Howards. The casualties were great and included local stalwarts: "Pal" Thompson of New Row who lost his left eye; Private Benny Langton (29) the son of the Northallerton iron monger who had been married the previous year who was wounded, and died of blood poisoning in a Ramsgate hospital; and Private Thomas E. Banks of the 4th Battalion Green Howards was killed at Ypres - the first old Northallerton Grammar School student (Old Alvertonian) to give his life in the war of an eventual death toll of twelve.

It befell the 4th Battalion Yorkshire Regiment Green Howards (Territorials) to establish a national reputation for its martial qualities.

Private Thomas E Banks killed Ypres 1915

After mustering at Northallerton it had subsequently trained at Darlington and Newcastle. In April 1915 the Battalion sailed for France but instead of a gradual introduction to active combat, within only ten days they were thrust into the gap in British defences left by the first German gas attack of the war (24th April 1915) which had decimated the Canadians.

In describing their exploits with those of their fellow Durham Light Infantry and Northumberland Fusiliers Territorials, the war correspondent of the London "Times" at this the Second Battle of Ypres accorded them praise which rang through the country. Entitled "Tribute to Dogged Fighting at Ypres" he wrote:

"The hardest task, perhaps fell to the men of North England. -------Consider what is meant by the fight of these Northern Territorials. Men only lately out of home, most of whom had never before seen a shot fired in battle, were flung suddenly into the most nerve wracking kind of engagement. They had to face one of the worst artillery bombardments of the war and the new devilry of the poison gas. The result was a soldier's battle, where we escaped the annihilation which by all rules was our due by the sheer dogged fighting quality of our men and their leaders."

The objective of the counter attack was to push the enemy back to St Julien and this they and the other Territorial Battalions achieved. The Chief of Staff General Sir John French gave huge praise to the "Heroes of St Julien", stating; "You deserve the highest praise and your actions were particularly magnificent. On coming out here you were called upon in a time of danger and emergency to take the place of trained troops in the trenches. It is the highest example of all patriotism."

Of course the losses and suffering were the high premium paid. Amongst the 4th Battalion officers who fell in the St Julien campaign in 1915 were: Captain Gilbert D.P. Eykyn the Adjutant of Northallerton; Captain R.A. Constantine the son of the shipping magnate from Harlsey Hall; and Lt Erasmus Darwin the Secretary to Messrs Bolckow, Vaughan and Co of Middlesbrough, and grandson of Charles Darwin the author of the "Origin of the Species".

Private W. Leach of New Row, Northallerton wrote home in June 1915 of the debilitating effects of the gas which was making them so ill they could hardly put one foot in front of the other. Still he ends on a typically sanguine note - "I am glad that so many of the lads of Northallerton and round about have answered the call of their country." Unfortunately many of the "local boys" were either killed or became casualties of the fray. Three who were killed from the 4th Battalion were: Sergeant W. Taylor of North End a prominent Northallerton Town footballer, Private Joseph Burn of Brompton who succumbed to the effects of gassing and Private Chapman a Northallerton footballer and Territorial bandsman.

Poignant memorial services had become the order of the day and a service at Northallerton on 4th May 1915 saw the Parish Church packed as never before as all the casualties were remembered. Several local young men were also killed during the Dardanelles invasion of 1915 and amongst these were the sons of two prominent Vicars: Harold Winch the son of the Vicar of Brompton Rev GT Winch and Lieutenant Leslie Gifford-Wood whose father was the Vicar of East Cowton.

The presence of the Second Line 4th Battalion Green Howards (Territorials) along with the County Hall Red Cross Hospital gave Northallerton a military air. Northallerton Grammar School pupils continued to be taught in the new North Wing of the County Hall which was officially opened on 26th January 1915 and any overflow of service patients were now transferred to the Rutson Hospital which increasingly accommodated military wounded as the war progressed.

Having trained intensively for several months and built up many friendships in the town, the Second Line 4th Green Howards (Number 2/4th) moved off to Northumberland to replace the First Line 4th Green Howards (1/4th) who had left for the Western Front in April 1915. Though early in the morning a large enthusiastic crowd cheered off the Battalion as it entrained for the north on 15th April 1915.

As soon as the Second Line (2/4th) Fourth Battalion departed another Reserve Battalion (Third Line 3/4th) was formed under Lt Col Lord Southampton which quickly established itself like its forerunner and trained assiduously until the Battalion moved to Redcar in Spring 1916. With the departure of the soldiers the town took on an air of almost eerie emptiness so dominating had been the military presence.

Collections and events for the war needs continued. The North Yorks Farmers Mart raised £538 by various auctions for the British Red Cross, and Mount Pleasant by courtesy of Mr and Mrs Weston Adamson was the venue of a concert with the proceeds going to the Green Howards. Caroline Hutton (John Hutton's wife) collected 2072 garments for the soldiers in France and Belgium and Cicely Gardner of "Alverton", South Parade (Grace Gardner's mother) collected similarly.

John Hutton retired in May 1915 as Chairman of the North Riding County Council a position held since 1895. One of the worst motor fatalities ever recorded in the area took place on 5th March 1915. A motor car driven from Northallerton plunged into the Tees immediately north of Croft Bridge in the early hours of the morning, with all five local occupants being drowned.

The war, however, was the main issue to be addressed. Volunteers had flooded into the Armed Services from all over the area and this war awareness was illustrated by two of Northallerton's best known shops: three men had been commissioned as officers from Oxendale and Barker's; and six employees of Lewis and Cooper's had enlisted.

1916 – War of Attrition

The welter of deaths and casualties continued in 1916 with the Western Front locked in the war of attrition of trench warfare. The 4th Battalion Green Howards had already suffered great losses when it

Wright family group – Nags Head, mid war

entered the Somme campaign at 6.30 a.m. on 14th September 1916. By 3rd October it had sustained 399 casualties killed, wounded or missing including 7 officers and 75 other ranks killed or died of wounds. The Battalion also became a part of military history when on the attack of 14th September on Flers they were accompanied into action by heavily armoured cars better known as 'tanks'. It was the first time that 'tanks' were used by the British in warfare.

Many locally connected soldiers became casualties with the 4th Battalion during 1916 including: Commanding Officer Major Lindsay Alfred Barrett who was killed at the head of the Battalion aged a mere 24 years; Mr and Mrs J. Robinson of North End had lost their son Pt T. Robinson at Gallipoli in 1915 and in September 1916 a second son Pt J.W. Robinson was killed in France with the Fourth Battalion; two Brompton brothers were killed William (23) and Fred (18) Tyreman, both being prominent Brompton footballers; and Lance Corporal Osborne of Thornton-le-Moor killed on 18th September received this accolade to his father from Lt D.P. Hirsch who the following year obtained the Victoria Cross - "He was a keen brave soldier ----- He was universally loved and buried on the field where he gave his life."

Two particularly tragic losses were Green Howards Lieutenants brothers Tom and William Swain on the Somme, the sons of Jack and Emily Swain of Darlington Road, Northallerton. The loss of highly

Lieutenant Tom Swain fatally wounded on the Somme

popular and well known North Riding County Councillors Captain 'Tiny' Rowlandson MC (ex Cambridge University goalkeeper) and Lord Feversham who was leading 'The Farmers' Battalion' which he had raised when he fell, shocked the whole county.

And all these fatalities merely represent a fraction of the dead throughout every local community.   By August 1916 the Green Howards alone had been awarded 18 MCs and 29 MMs for bravery including several decorations for local Northallerton men.   But the price paid was out of any proportion to any rewards or military gains.

At home a significant pointer to the future use of the Northallerton area by the Royal Air Force was in September 1916 when South Otterington was used as a landing ground by No. 76 Squadron Royal Flying Corps for Avro 504s and BE2s. In the same month C Flight of 76 Squadron used Catterick as a landing ground. Catterick became a permanent training station on 1st December 1917 and at the end of the

1914 -18 war it had ten hangars and a repair shed. Helperby was used as a night landing ground from March to October 1916 and Appleton Wiske also had a landing strip opened in October 1917.

War events overshadowed all else at Northallerton where civilian war efforts continued. A Northallerton Red Cross Bazaar in the Town Hall (March) made £968, and on 16th August there was a "British Prisoners of War Day". At a Broomfield Farm competition for Women on the Land there were 32 entries including 19 for ploughing. Cattle driving, milking and harrowing also took place and it was said that some came to scoff and went away to engage a women worker!

Zeppelins bombed and killed several inhabitants of North Riding villages on 1st April and even before this because of Zeppelin raids on the Midlands, the Northallerton UDC ruled that there would be no more public lights after darkness. Joseph Constantine of Harlsey Hall donated £40,000 to found Constantine College, Middlesbrough in June (now the University of Teesside); and a highlight of the year was the visit of the Archbishop of York Gordon Cosmo Lang to Northallerton on Monday 10th April when he gave an inspiring sermon to a full church including fourteen clergy.

1917 – Deadlock and Death Continued

Although it seems barely credible the annual number of war deaths increased in 1917 especially with the Allied offensive at Passchendaele – the 3rd Battle of Ypres (Oct/Nov) in which a quarter of a million British lives were lost. As with the general trend Northallerton and district casualties mounted and it was especially significant that in the major local papers - "The Darlington and Stockton Times" and "The York Herald" - there was hardly room to do justice to the deceased.

In the year four Northallerton Grammar School "Old Boys" were killed; Corporal F Cowling in France and three at Ypres – Second Lieutenant W Prince (of South Parade), Signaller G C Steel and Lieutenant A M Kirby of Thimbleby Grange. Many others were wounded and all the ex Northallerton Grammar School casualties were in their late teens or early twenties.

The mounting death toll reached a crescendo with Passchendaele. Not only the town but every village in the vicinity lost young men. Brompton for example had four killed with the 4th Battalion Green Howards alone and those who died from well known local families included Lt. Col. Laurence Godman DSO of Great Smeaton Manor and

Lieutenant A M Kirby killed Ypres 1917

both Lt. Col. J H Bowes-Wilson and his brother Captain G H Bowes-Wilson (Green Howards) of Hutton Rudby. Stories of heroism and citations of decorations for bravery crowded the local papers but above all the attrition worsened. It was illustrated by the weekly Roll of Honour to the local dead in the *York Herald* of 13th October 1917 which contained nineteen names of which ten were from the Northallerton area.

'The effects on those who lost loved ones was always profound and sometimes dramatic. For example Regimental Sergeant Major Buss of Northallerton and the Somerset Light Infantry was awarded the Distinguished Conduct Medal for bravery but was killed soon afterwards. On hearing this news his wife collapsed with a heart attack and died, leaving orphans of only seven and three years old.

The war effort of fund-raising continued at home with the "British Red Cross Farmers' Fund" at Northallerton reaching £550. There were noteworthy occurrences: a sign of the agricultural times was the revolutionary use of ten motor ploughs to till the North Riding land initiated by Richard Booth of Warlaby; the North Riding Police Force began to use motor cycles and sidecars to replace ponies and traps; and Hubert Thornley who had been appointed Clerk to the North Riding County Council and Clerk of the Peace on 1ˢᵗ April 1916 also undertook the post of Registrar of Deeds in 1917. Finally in June 1917 the Royal House abolished their German names and titles and His Royal Highness the Duke of Teck, became the Marquis of Cambridge and also had Viscount Northallerton in his titles.

1918 – Unremitting Losses and Blessed Peace

Major Dudley Gardner MC RFC

As if the former war years had not been enough in human sacrifice, in 1918 losses reached a deluge of death. Evidence of this and the local losses can be found from the incidence and length of the Rolls of Honour published in the press. In the daily "York Herald" in the week beginning Monday 18ᵗʰ April there were fifteen full columns of indigenous names in the Rolls of Honour and this was equalled in the following week. Such were the deceased numbers that by the end of June only the names of Officers appeared in the Rolls of Honour.

Private Sydney Weighell

Northallerton and area had its share of victims which made a very sombre 1918 scenario despite the ultimate Allied victory with the Armistice on the eleventh hour of the eleventh day of the eleventh month. The Northallerton high casualty rates were reflected by the Northallerton Grammar School old boys statistics: many were wounded and five paid the supreme sacrifice - the highest annual total of any war year. Three fell with the Army – Privates R Garbutt and T E Thompson and Second Lieutenant Herbert Clidero – S Cowell went down with his mined ship and Private Sydney Weighell of the Fourth Battalion the Green Howards died as a Prisoner of War.

An Old Alvertonian who miraculously survived despite being involved almost continuously in the aerial warfare was Dudley Gardner who emulated his famous grandfather Captain George Gardner of Balaclava in his heroism, ending with the rank of Major in the Royal Flying Corps and being awarded the Military Cross "for consistent and meritorious bravery", having been mentioned in dispatches three times.

Amongst other local gallantry awards were Captain H N Constantine of Harlsey Hall and the Green Howards 4th Battalion MC.; Captain J W Hunter, Sowerby Grange DSO and the Italian Croix de Guerre; Captain Thomas Flynn MC of South Parade; Sergeant Orlando Bollands, a warehouse man with N Russell and Sons grocers, DCM;

Private Thomas O'Malley a local builder MM; Alfred Key of Bridge Terrace and the Tank Corps MM; Allan Rider a member of the Northallerton pork butchers' family MM; and Private TE Coulson of South Terrace, Northallerton and the 4th Battalion Green Howards MM.

The stunning losses and their devastating effects, however, overwhelmed all else. For example on the 13th July no fewer than four Northallerton district war deaths were announced in the 'Darlington and Stockton Times'. Private Albert Walker (one of Kitchener's Army) who was from Brompton and had worked at Wilford's linen mill; Private George Tweddle of the 4th Battalion Green Howards and Oak Tree yard who had been employed at Hay's flour mill; Private R Clemmett of Romanby a peace-time Linoleum Factory worker; and Corporal JE Barker who had been a fireman on the North Eastern Railway died of wounds.

The repercussions of the war losses were immense and lasting in the community. An occasion which brought this starkly home was a moving ceremony at an Empire Day concert in the Town Hall in May when children from the National School who had lost their fathers during the war were given war bonds. Thirty two children were presented – and they were only a proportion of those in the town who had been rendered fatherless.

It was in this climate of sorrow and remembrance at the end of the war in 1918 that Mrs Hird and family along with John Todd and others bequeathed to their fellow townspeople landholdings in the Applegarth to be a play area and recreational ground as a permanent war memorial to those who had fallen.

The Churches featured strongly in maintaining civilian morale and large parades and congregations attended the Parish Church on Sunday 6th January on the "National Day of Prayer" and on National Remembrance Day – 4th August. On the hospital front the County Hall Red Cross and the Rutson hospitals were full to overflowing with wounded soldiers. Changes continued in agriculture with the North Riding War Agricultural Committee encouraging both women land workers who totalled one hundred and forty-one and the use of tractors with forty-seven in operation in the Riding.

News of the end of the war did not burst upon Northallerton – rather it crept imperceptibly in, with rumours of the Armistice circulating on the morning of 12th November. But soon the air of indecision evaporated with official Police confirmation of the end of hostilities. Great excitement and rejoicing reigned along with gladness and sheer relief.

A Thanksgiving Service in Northallerton Parish Church on Thursday 14th November was eloquently conducted by Rev A S Nesbit Vicar of Ainderby before a packed and profoundly moved congregation. All thoughts and prayers were for the casualties, especially those killed and their relatives.

The Aftermath – Colours and Memorials

Battalion "Colours" were laid up and war memorials erected to the dead throughout the area as tangible reminders of the "Great Sacrifice".

The "Colours" of six of the Green Howards "Service" Battalions – battalions formed specifically for wartime needs – were placed "in perpetuam" in the Council Chamber of the North Riding of Yorkshire County Hall at Northallerton. They were the 7th, 8th, 10th, 12th, 13th and 16th Battalions whose battle honours included Ypres, the Somme, Arras, Passchendaele, Loos, Cambria, Bourlon Wood, Poperinghe, Fricourt and North Russia. Their valour was epitomised by the distinction of having five Victoria Cross awards between them.

In an impressive ceremony of Friday 20th April 1920 their Colours were accepted for safe-keeping by Sir Henry Beresford-Peirse the Chairman of the North Riding County Council who deemed it the greatest honour to be selected as the custodians of the "Colours" of such eminent battalions from their own county. Eighty years later they still proudly hang in the Council Chamber.

Northallerton's war memorial proposals of a double venture were adopted at a public meeting of the townspeople called for that purpose on Friday 9th May 1919 and presided over by the Chairman of the Northallerton Urban District Council Thomas Woodhead. It was stated that the Applegarth had been offered to the townspeople by Mrs Hird and family, John Todd and others as a permanent war memorial to the fallen of Northallerton in the Great War to be used as a recreational ground and park. Proposed by the Chairman, seconded by R Jameson and unanimously carried, the gift of the Applegarth was gratefully received by the town.

It was decided that the Northallerton War Memorial should be of a two-fold nature: a symbolic memorial obelisk in the Northallerton churchyard to commemorate the dead and the Applegarth to be made into a memorial recreational ground and park. To bring these plans to fruition a War Memorial Committee was appointed of eighteen

All Saints' Church, Northallerton.

DAY OF REMEMBRANCE
December 29th, 1918.

Northallerton and Romanby Men who have given their lives
for their country.

Officers.

Gilbert D. Eykyn
F. J. Myers
Charles J. M. Thompson
William Swain
Thomas Swain

John Brown
Herbert Clidero
J. H. Laycock
Willie Prince
Allan Kitching

Non-Commissioned Officers and Men.

George Chapman
Arthur Hayes
Benjamin Langton
Harry Holmes
Allan Telford
John Bendelow
Alfred J. Wilson
W. G. Cockerill
William Pratt
Gordon Maude
A. W. Martin
Joseph J. Flynn
Maynard Hartley
George Wm. Brown
John Henry Robinson
Thomas W. Sunley
G. Ernest Pattinson
Peter Binks Pratt
James Prince
Tom Candler
James Muirhead
John Thomas Thompson
Richard Sturdy
Herbert Playforth
Clarence Roper
William H. Hillborne
Charles E. Peacock
William Willoughby
Tom Gains
Alfred Watson
Herbert Peacock
Oliffe Carter
John Horner
James Castle
Henry Dunnington
Elijah Wilkinson

Thomas W. Robinson
George E. Suffil
William F. Pattison
Ben Robson
C. Ford
Frank Cowling
Fred Wright
Ralph Joyce
James Fowler
John R. Ellis
Sylvester Cowell
William Pattison
F. Richard Wilbor
Joseph Wells
Lance Atkinson
Rowland Pearson
Harry Pearson
Frank Bulmer
James Thomson
Robert Thornton
George Pollard
Willie Naylor
Herbert Walburn
David Shields
John Shields
Charles Longstaffe
Robert Fawcett
J. Edward Barker
Robert Clemmitt
George Ernest Exton
Harold Senior
William Morrison
Lloyd Jones
Harry Waines
Tom Walburn
Joe Taylor
Harry Bell.

" They died the noblest death a man may die
Fighting for God, and Right and Liberty."

Service of Remembrance 1918

gentlemen and sixteen ladies along with members of the Urban District Council. It was decided that the war memorial costs should be met out of voluntary private subscriptions paid into a War Memorial Fund.

The offer by Nathaniel Russell of land at half its £40 value was later accepted to complete the parcel of Applegarth land at the north west and by the end of 1919 the Applegarth had been laid out with roads and fencing and was in use as it had been intended as a public recreational area.

The final balance sheet of the War Memorial Committee's fund was issued on 22nd September 1922 as follows:

"Receipts from voluntary subscriptions" - £ 934. 2s. 1d
"Obelisk and expenses" - £ 609. 3s. 5d
"Equipping the Applegarth as a
recreational ground and park" - £ 324. 18s. 8d.

On Saturday afternoon 6th August 1921 the Northallerton War Memorial was officially unveiled when in the words of the "Darlington and Stockton Times" – "The memory of the men of Northallerton who fell in the Great War was commemorated on Saturday afternoon in a deeply moving and impressive manner, when Sir Hugh Bell, Bart, Lord Lieutenant of the North Riding, unveiled a beautiful monument erected by the inhabitants of the town in commemoration of their fallen comrades heroic deeds."

The memorial built in Portland stone by T and J Willoughby contractors in the south east corner of the churchyard was in the form of an ancient Saxon Cross of 800 AD discovered in the Parish Church and ninety eight names of the fallen were inscribed.   The Vicar of Northallerton Rev S M Thompson dedicated the memorial "to the memory of those who responded to the call of duty, who gave their lives for freedom and honour." A momentous and nostalgic occasion in Northallerton's history was concluded by the singing of the hymn "O Valiant Hearts" and the sounding of the "Last Post" and "Reveille".

There were other War Memorial dedications in Northallerton and district. The Grammar School Memorial, consisted of an oak tablet executed by Old Alvertonian Charles Hudson bearing the names of the twelve fallen and the names of those who had served. It was unveiled significantly on Armistice Day (11th November) 1920 by Colonel W.H.A. Wharton of Skelton Castle who had commanded the 2nd Line of the 4th Battalion Green Howards which had been stationed at

Romanby War Memorial

Northallerton in 1914 with its headquarters at the Grammar School.

Dr Bearder, the Headmaster, stated that of the 137 boys who had left the school and become eligible for military service, 107 had joined up. Of these 12 had fallen, (all aged only twenty-one or under) 19 had been wounded, 5 gassed and several made Prisoners of War. Rev S.M. Thompson dedicated the memorial and the 'Last Post' was appropriately played by an ex pupil Mr Oakley.

The Memorial of the North Riding County Council to 29 staff killed in the war was unveiled on Wednesday 26th October 1921 at the County Hall, again by Colonel Wharton. It consisted of two handsome mahogany panels placed on either side of the Grand Committee Room entrance. It was the gift of the late W.C. Trevor the Clerk to the County Council and Rev Canon Garrod dedicated the memorial.

The Brompton memorial was opened on 28th May 1921 commemorating 34 of the village who had perished in the war. It comprised a lychgate entrance to the Brompton St Thomas Parish Church - surmounted with a Celtic cross and costing £550. It was unveiled by J.P.Yeoman MBE and Rev G. Bardell Vicar of Brompton, dedicated the lychgate. Colonel Maurice Bell's appearance was particularly appropriate because 16 of the dead came from the 4th Battalion Yorkshire Regiment (The Green Howards) Territorials which he had commanded when it distinguished itself at Ypres in 1915. Additionally eight more of the dead belonged to other Green Howards' Battalions making 24 Green Howards in total.

Romanby's war memorial was not completed until 1927. It was a handsome plinth of a tall clock tower and situated at the junction of Ainderby Road and Harewood Lane. The stone was fashioned and the monument built by Dan Oakley, the architect was James R. White the North Riding County Architect and the cost £500. On Saturday March 19th 1927 Major Alan Hill-Walker VC, Maunby Hall who had been born and spent his boyhood at Romanby unveiled the memorial in an impressive ceremony which honoured the fourteen who had been killed from the village.

A final memorial erected in Northallerton was that of a stained glass window in the Parish Church inscribed with the words " In memory of Lieutenant Charles John McKinnon Thompson who fell in action near St Eloi Ypres in 1916." He was the son of the Vicar S M and Mrs Thompson and the window was unveiled by the Earl of Casillis before a full church on Thursday 14th December 1922.

War Postscript

A fitting postscript to the First World War belongs to the local 'Fallen'. The Alexandra Princess of Wales Own Yorkshire Regiment, the Green Howards were prominently mentioned and representative at every memorial ceremony in the North Riding including Northallerton, Brompton, Romanby, Bedale, Osmotherley and all the other local villages. In all the Green Howards – the North Riding's own regiment – lost 464 Officers and 7036 Other Ranks.

At the end of the war the known death toll of sacrifice for Northallerton, Brompton and Romanby was a combined total of one hundred and forty six men – the equivalent of over five hundred in today's population ratio. The meaning and the awesome figures speak for themselves.

9

The Inter-War Years (1918 to 1939)

General Election 1918

After the numbness of the Great War came the often harsh realities of the peace, when life had to go on. The main event of the closing weeks of 1918 was a General Election the Richmondshire Division having two candidates, Lieutenant Colonel M. John Murrough-Wilson representing the Conservative Unionist Party and William Parlour standing as the "Farmers'" candidate. Lieutenant Colonel Hon WGA Orde-Powlett the Member of Parliament for the constituency since January 1910 had decided to relinquish his Parliamentary responsibilities making way for Murrough-Wilson of Cliffe Hall, near Darlington and the local Liberals did not field a candidate.

William Parlour, a farmer from Croft Spa, began his campaign at the "Golden Lion" Assembly Rooms Northallerton on 13th November and Lieutenant Colonel Murrough-Wilson campaigned throughout the constituency holding a successful meeting in Northallerton Town Hall on Thursday 12th December.

A sweeping Conservative Unionist victory followed the voting on Saturday 14th December:

Lieutenant Colonel MJ Wilson (Con. Un)	9857
William Parlour (Agriculturist)	4907
Conservative Majority	4950

Women had been enfranchised and Mrs Mason of the High Street was the first woman to vote. Northallerton was the electoral centre for the Richmondshire constituency, the votes being counted in the Town Hall and Ernest Gardner the Returning Officer announcing the result flanked by candidates from the Town Hall balcony. Later M.J. Murrough-Wilson addressed a large crowd from the "Golden Lion" balcony.

Armistice Day Parade 11th November 1928

Armistices and Memorials

In the years of peace there were solemn and sombre reminders in every national locality with the dedication of war memorials, and the profoundly sad and nostalgic Armistice Day commemorations in memory of the fallen annually at the eleventh hour of the eleventh day on the eleventh month.

At Northallerton the Armistice ceremony was the usual format of a parade to the War Memorial where a service was held led by the Vicar of Northallerton supported by the Ministers of other local denominations. Wreaths were then laid by the various participating organisations, followed by the nationally observed "two minutes" silence beginning at 11 a.m. A trumpeter finalised the event by sounding the "Last Post" and "Reveille". Sometimes the occasion seemed particularly special such as 1927 when every school pupil in the town from four to eighteen attended.

Apart from the Northallerton and other war memorial dedications already referred to a succession of these took place locally including: Thornton-le-Moor (9 names) in May 1920; Ainderby (9 names) November 1920; North and South Cowton (9 names) July 1921;

Langton (7 names) September 1921; and Leeming Bar (11 names) September 1923.

The Land, Shows and the Fair

There was growing mechanisation on the land but the horse still held agricultural sway immediately after the First World War as exemplified by the horse entries at the Northallerton Show which were as high as pre-war with 351 in 1921. By the end of the decade, however, technology was beginning to dominate farming, so much so that only 67 horses were shown at the 1929 Northallerton Show, which was to cease soon afterwards.

However, in the early 1920s on its permanent site at "Friarage Fields" the annual Northallerton Agricultural Show continued to be "one of the finest one day shows in the North." In 1919 after a five year war lapse the show returned to beat all attendance records with a crowd in excess of 10,000 and over 1,000 animal entries. A really big coup in 1922 was the appointment of Viscount Lascelles KG, DSO as President, just after his marriage to Her Royal Highness Princess Mary, which brought large crowds to the Show. Indeed it was a great occasion with £1000 in prizes and St Hilda's Colliery Band - "the premier band in England."

This show proved to be the zenith because although further good shows were held, notably in 1927 when Major Alan Hill-Walker V.C. was President, there was a gradual decline in entries and public interest. The last official Northallerton Agricultural Show until the end of the Second World War occurred in 1931. Horses were becoming very much fewer and with horses the traditional fulcrum of the Show it was their dwindling numbers which caused the Agricultural Show Committee to call it a day.

The three marts - Station, Malpas and Applegarth - continued to flourish with the railway and its landing dock providing a main facility for animal distribution from owners to purchasers. Drovers would drive the animals to and from the marts and the local farmers would similarly drive their flocks and herds into and out of the marts on market and sale days. The marts had weekly sales on Tuesdays and Wednesdays and periodic large sales of horses, cattle, sheep and pigs which had already made the old horse and cattle fairs totally redundant.

Market Day on the traditional Wednesday was always the main day of the week with stalls from Zetland Street to the Town Hall

A Wednesday Market Day 1925

immediately to the north of which, with their horses safely stabled, were the farmers' upturned traps. Slowly but surely the latter disappeared being replaced by motor cars and lorries. The farmers' wives produced butter and eggs in large cane baskets, dead rabbits and live hens. The "pitch" for these commodities was just to the south of the Town Hall with the market not closing until 8 pm.

Of particular importance was the foundation and growth of the Northallerton Branch of the National Farmers Union (N.F.U.). By 1923 one hundred and fifty members attended the Annual Dinner, which indicates the size and the local influence of the organisation. The NFU took over the local farming wage settlements and were often at loggerheads with the farm workers regarding wages as in 1922. With the advent of wage boards and standardised wages and hours, "Hirings" were outmoded and disappeared.

Thomas Place Timber – From Horses to Motors 1920s

Another body which made a distinctive entry on to the agricultural scene was the Northallerton and District Young Farmers Association. This began as a Calf Club around 1930 when they held their First Annual Show and Sale. In 1935 they commenced annual dances and for example in 1937 two hundred and fifty attended what was a typically robust and lively affair.

The May Fair was still the main entertainment of the year and though it had started as St George's Agricultural Fair in 1554 it was solely a 'Pleasure Fair' by the 1920s. The fair set up from Zetland Street to the Parish Church with pride of place going to Murphy's proud peacocks and Brumbie's jumping horses. The latter were replaced by Sam Crow's "Galloping Horses" and Sam also introduced the first real speedster into town - the affectionately remembered "Noah's Ark".

There were "Chair-o-planes" skimming roof levels, skittle alleys, coconut shies, roll a penny stalls, children's rides, boxing and football booths, pony rides to the church and oddities to see from all over the world. The sound of the fairground organ with bells and cymbals mingled with the smell of smoke and oil from large steam engines conjured in the senses of that generation an unforgettable fairground recollection.

Industry and Commerce

Northallerton's work force, apart from agriculture, was engaged in light industry, commerce and administration. Thomas Place operated a very successful timber merchant's yard at the North End of the town with draught horses being gradually superseded by heavy motor vehicles. Adjacent were the Union Flour mills and across the old Great North Road was the very active goods yard of the London North Eastern Railway.

At the southern end of the town the main railway station employed over two hundred: the mainline Station Staff numbered around forty and at the locomotive sheds immediately to the south dealing with local traffic were drivers, firemen, engineers, maintenance men and plate layers. Nichols pump factory was situated south of the railway on the east side of Boroughbridge Road. In 1936 the North Riding County Council opened a Depot on the west side of Boroughbridge Road for highways and other maintenance.

Next to the main railway line but on Romanby Road was the Wensleydale Pure Milk Society Factory: by fast mainline railway service fresh Wensleydale milk was whisked to the doorsteps of urban complexes the next morning including even North London. Ultimately the successful business was taken over by the Cow and Gate Company of Guildford on April 27th 1932 for £8,250.

In February 1928 a new pork and bacon factory was opened at Leeming Bar (on the site of the old Plew's Brewery) named the Vale of

Northallerton Linoleum Factory 1922

Mowbray (VOM) which could "process" up to one thousand pigs a week. It was initiated and owned by the Rider brothers from Northallerton. Two smaller but profitable businesses were the Northallerton Light and Power Company centred in the "Fleece" yard (profits 1923, £1258) and Bell and Goldsbrough mineral water factory at the end of Brompton Road.

The garages gave employment for some and the building firms (Dan Oakley, J. Stockdale and Willoughbys) to others. In such a prosperous and lively area there were ample job opportunities in shops and businesses of every description. The County Council was increasing in professional and administrative personnel. In twenty one years the Clerk's department had increased from 6 to 48 which was typical of the general growth which had necessitated extensive building additions.

The Linoleum factory between Malpas and Romanby roads was the other largest employer in town. Having been started by Sir George Elliot MP it was now owned by Miles Sykes and despite an explosion and fire in the cork section which claimed two lives - Robert Todd (65), Barker's yard and James Connor (26), New Row - in November 1923, fifteen months later the factory took on new "hands" bringing the work force to 320.

Nevertheless, such is the transience of industry - seen again and

A New Northallerton Fire Engine - 1928

again in Northallerton's history - that in May 1938 the closure of the Linoleum factory was announced with the loss of all 320 jobs. Aptly headlined "A Serious Blow to Northallerton", there was little chance of a reprieve. The incident obviously affected the whole town including the shopkeepers who had benefited by the factory's wage bill of £700 per week. By the end of the year Northallerton had a burden of 500 unemployed out of a 4,500 population.

Of great import was the gaining by the Urban District Council of the Town Hall, market rights and tolls. These had been held since 1873 by the Town Hall and Market Improvements Company who had purchased them from the Ecclesiastical Commissioners when the Town Hall was built.

Ultimately in December 1923 it was agreed that the UDC could purchase the rights of the company for £6000 and a public meeting of ratepayers in the Town Hall gave a unanimous mandate. Negotiations continued and on 1st March 1925 the Town Hall and Market Improvements Company sold all their rights and holdings to the Northallerton UDC for £6000 and went into liquidation their last

Chairman being William Barker, the founder of 'Barkers of Northallerton'.

Public Utilities

The Urban District Council was also responsible for several other innovations during these years. As early as 1922 Councillor Fred Severs advocated the provision of Public Conveniences but it was not until 1938 that these were completed for £800 to the south of the Town Hall. Refuse collection was motorised and in April 1928 a new fire engine was purchased and housed at the Fire Brigade Headquarters on Crosby Road behind the prison.

Housing

A significant UDC involvement was in housing where there was a great shortage of adequate property. In January 1922 for example there were one hundred applications to rent a vacant house and exacerbating the whole position were the "yards" where the majority of the working class of the town lived. Some of the houses were unfit and barely fit in the yards - a situation largely operative until after the Second World War. The Urban District Council did make some attempt to alleviate the system and start the process of re-housing in the 1920s and 1930s.

Vicar's Croft was bought in 1920 for housing development by the UDC from the Ecclesiastical Commissioners, consisting of six and three quarter acres at £300 per acre. The initial scheme was for 28 houses built down Lascelles Lane and along East Road, for private sale costing £480 each, the builders firms being those of A.H. Moody and C. Garnett. By the end of the building operation in 1926, all of the houses had been purchased by clients.

After this foray into the "private" housing market, the UDC moved into the Council Housing area. The UDC's Housing Committee required tenders for 24 houses in August 1931 and by June 1935 these Vicar's Croft houses had been completed   (Lawson and Boddy, Darlington contractors), the tenants being selected by the UDC. On 22nd June 1935 the houses were officially opened.

In the meantime private housing had gone on apace in most areas of Northallerton, which continued the process of the movement away from living in the High Street. Some projects were: T. Willoughby in 1921 commenced to develop the north side of Racecourse Lane with eight houses all of different design; two houses were built at Sandy

Lascelles Lane and East Road Parlour Type Houses 1926

Bank and twelve new houses were authorised for Boston Avenue in January 1932; houses were built along Thirsk, Brompton and Crosby roads; in Romanby houses were erected on Boroughbridge Road, Harewood Lane and Ainderby Road in the 1920s and 1930s, whilst earlier in February 1925 four houses on Romanby Green were built by the LNER for railway pensioners.

County Buildings

Some of the most impressive building achievements were those concerning the North Riding County Council. The new Registry of Deeds was built in Racecourse Lane opposite the County Hall in 1926 - 1927, the building tender accepted from Dan Oakley being £10,384 and the final over-all cost £12,546. Extensions to the County Hall followed in 1930 with the erection of a South Wing parallel to the North Wing and then just before the commencement of the Second World War an East Wing was started joining the South and North Wings. A new Court

New County Court House 1936

House was badly needed and this was authorised in 1935 at a cost of £31,000 which was constructed adjacent to the new Registry. The contractors for the Court House were G.W. Lazenby and Co, Ferryhill and the Architect James White NRCC County Architect. Finally a much needed purpose built County Library replaced the inadequate North Riding County Library premises in Zetland Street. Designed by J.L. Coverdale, the County Education Architect, it cost £6,960 and was opened at its premises opposite the Grammar School on 13th September 1938.

Roads and Motor Vehicles

With the coming of the "Motor Age", roads and their quality became of prime importance. Several main roads were made North Riding "county roads" and these included the High Street, Thirsk Road, South Parade, Romanby Road and Friarage Street. Dangerous corners like the bottom of Mill Hill junctioning with Thirsk Road, the Racecourse Lane meeting with Thirsk Road and Lees Lane which was widened to eighteen feet, were all improved

Reflecting the numbers of motors there were five garages on Northallerton High Street (Kellett and Pick's Central and Metropole, Naylor's, Smirthwaite's, and Greer's/Elcoates) and alarming crashes with many accident black spots within range of the town where victims

Market Row from the West

were killed and injured with great frequency. Some of these were the Wiske and Morton bridges on the Northallerton Bedale road, the A1 at Catterick and between Londonderry and the Leazes, Baldersby, Clack Lane Ends and Ellerbeck. Two decades were strewn with road victims.

A most controversial and contentious issue arose when the Ministry of Transport designated the Boroughbridge – Northallerton to Darlington road as the A1 in August 1923, as the main part of the old Great North Road - the A1 from Edinburgh to London. Immediately there was an objection from Ripon and Richmond who wanted the A1 designation given to Leeming Lane (the other Great North Road section). These towns sent a deputation which was backed by the Auto Cycle Club of England and Wales to the Ministry of Transport to plead their case which was eventually successful with the A1 road number being re-allocated to Leeming Lane.

Yards and Health

In a brief study of Northallerton's yards as dwelling places in their last phase before they became extinct we are indebted to George H.

Kelley (who was Mayor of Northallerton in 1980 – 81) in "a contribution to Local History - Northallerton 1926 - 1939." Many working class families, like Mr Kelley's, lived in the yards and they formed tight little communities getting on well together with a spirit that was prominent in times of emergency, sickness and bereavement.

Nearly all the cottages faced south, looking mainly on to the backs of the cottages in the next yard or stables with some being very narrow like Barker's Yard and others quite spacious such as Market Row. The cottages consisted of a living room (about 12 feet by 9 feet) a bedroom reached by stairs in the living room, an attic and a pantry beneath the stairs. Each yard was named after the shop at the front with a few exceptions - Flag Yard, New Row and Waterloo Yard for example. Most houses were lit by candles, paraffin or gas, with some electricity being fed in later on.

The toilets in the early days were the ash pit type and were cleaned out once a week in the evening by the Council sludgecart. Water was obtained from a standpipe in the middle of the yard usually and everyone seemed to have an enamel bucket filled with water for drinking and cooking, with several having wash-houses containing big iron mangles, rubbing boards and metal tubs. Above all great efforts were made by the majority to keep the yards tidy, whitewashing walls, cleaning sills and steps and even growing flowers in old sinks.

There was no National Health until July 1948 and by paying benefit one was entitled to unemployment benefit and the doctor's services though not hospital treatment, the latter problem being circumvented by joining and paying into a local hospital scheme. By March 1935 this Northallerton, Romanby and District Assurance Association was well developed with individuals and most firms paying contributions.

In general the health of the town and its yards was relatively good for the times though several epidemics did occur - measles (1920), scarlet fever and influenza (1924) and scarlet fever and diphtheria (1934 and 1937) - whilst Brompton had a typhoid outbreak in 1926. The worst cases were transferred to the Isolation Hospital at Sandy Bank which had twenty two beds and was filled to capacity when epidemics broke out. An important move affecting the whole County was the opening of a Tuberculosis Sanatorium at Morris Grange near Middleton Tyas in 1921 with 52 beds.

Rutson Hospital

The main hospital for Northallerton was the Rutson: 'Northallerton people have a great love for their Cottage Hospital' ('Darlington and Stockton Times' November 1931). Wonderful (at the time) was the provision of a wireless in February 1926 which gave "great pleasure and resource to the patients." Another feature was the annual 'Pound Day' which for example reached over 800 lbs (soap, groceries etc) as well as money received in November 1931 and there were also special collections such as those promoted by the farmers of the district.

Most important extensions took place at the Rutson in 1931/32 which gave it 28 more beds with marble floors in the corridors and wooden ones in the wards which had hot water radiators with each patient equipped with an electric light and wireless ear phones. T & J. Willoughby of Northallerton were the building contractors of the ward block which also included a new operating theatre the overall cost being £7803. Lord Bolton performed the opening ceremony from a platform erected in front of the old Vine House building, on 23rd July 1932. He stated that this was a red letter day for the Rutson which had been mainly incepted by his friend the late John Hutton of Solberge Hall.

Schools and Education

A change in the Grammar School took place in the headship in 1921 when Dr J.W. Bearder resigned and Hall T Palmer MA (Cantab) was appointed. On 14th October 1931 evening classes were started in the school in Mathematics, Engineering, Science, Domestic Science, Needlework and Woodwork - an historic date in view of the school's future. The prestige of the school can be gauged somewhat by those who presented the speech day prizes including Sir William Worsley (1922), Lord Bolton (1924) the Archbishop of York, Dr Temple (1930), Sir James Baille LLD, PhD Vice Chancellor of Leeds University (1933), and the Bishop of Whitby (1939).

On the latter occasion Sir Bedford Dorman opened new premises - mainly a Gymnasium and a Library - which had been recently built by Dan Oakley to the design of J.L. Coverdale North Riding Education Architect at a cost of £6600 for the buildings and £800 for equipping them. This had been necessitated by the growth of the school roll to 256 (1936) with a gradual annual increase.

Applegarth School Children - 1933

Another and much greater building undertaking planned in 1938 and commenced in 1939 was that of an 11 - 15 Modern School in Northallerton on 12 acres down Brompton Road designed for 560 pupils at a cost of £37,100. This school which was to become the Allertonshire Secondary Modern School was one of the first of its type in the country. The tender for £29,113 of Messrs William Birch and Sons Ltd of York was accepted, work started in June 1939 and the school was opened in September 1941.

Another vital project of the North Riding Education Committee was that of a Library Service which commenced in 1924 when Stanley Beagley was appointed as County Librarian at £300 per annum with one clerk as his staff operating from two rooms in Zetland Street. He worked assiduously, obtained storage space in the old Courthouse and soon sent out boxes of books in the small red charabanc the 'Sunflower' to all points of the North Riding. In 1924/25 13,074 books were in stock which had reached 109,774 in 1939 by which time the new library in Grammar School Lane was fully operative.

In Northallerton all the children of infants age (5 to 8 years) went to the Applegarth Council School headed by Miss Weighell with a roll of 260 and the vast majority then continued at the National School, (Headmaster J. Turner) until leaving school at 14. There was one important private preparatory school Wensley House (5 - 13 age group) run by Mrs H. Lord in South Parade and popularly referred to as "Lords".

The Railway Scene

There were three local railway crashes: at Brompton Station on 17th March 1924 when 14 casualties were ferried to the Rutson when the Leeds - Hartlepool express mounted the platform; in March 1930 the only injured were the train crew when the "Newspaper Train" crashed at 2 a.m. one morning; and in February 1933 a shunting train destroyed the telegraph office at the north end of the Northallerton south bound platform, the telegraphists fleeing for their lives with no injuries miraculously occurring.

Two great engineering feats took place on the railway at Northallerton. The widening of the main line to include four lines made it necessary to support the line whilst making a completely new bridge this being accomplished within the allotted 24 hours and being hailed in October 1930 by the "York Herald" as "A Great Engineering Feat at Northallerton." In March 1931 engineers and workmen built another bridge at the low level line, again succeeding in just 24 hours. Finally it was announced in October 1931 that a robot electric system of colour signalling (red, yellow and green) was to be introduced on the York to Newcastle track and in November 1935 the Stationmaster R.P. Haw announced that the new system was operating instead of hand signals from Northallerton to the south.

Politics – Parliamentary

On the parliamentary scene of the Richmondshire constituency, although affairs were keen they were never as volatile as on previous occasions. There were in fact only two contested elections in the twenty years in 1929 and 1935 and Sir Murrough -Wilson (as he became) never defended his seat, being returned unopposed in 1922, 1923 and 1924 before retiring as Conservative candidate in favour of Captain Thomas Dugdale of Crathorne Hall who contested the seat in June 1929.

"Tommy" Dugdale became a very popular representative and he overwhelmingly defeated the Liberal candidate J.B. Hinks in 1929, the election result announced by the Returning Officer Hubert Thornley from the Northallerton Town Hall balcony being:

Captain TL Dugdale (Con)	19,763
J.B. Hinks (Lib)	14,634
Majority	5,129

At the General Election of October 1931 Dugdale was unopposed and then in 1935 history was made when the Labour Party entered the Richmondshire fray with their first ever candidate A.J. Best of Darlington who was soundly beaten in a record Conservative victory:

TL Dugdale (Con)	25,088	
A.J. Best (Lab)	7,369	
Majority	17,719	

Much more was seen in the future of Thomas Dugdale but in these his early parliamentary days he was Parliamentary Private Secretary to the Prime Minister Stanley Baldwin in which post he was centrally involved in the Abdication Crisis of 1936, concerning Edward VIII and Mrs Simpson.

Public Figures

In connection with the Quarter Sessions ladies began to play some part with Lady Bell of Rounton Grange and Lillian Weston Adamson of the Mount, Northallerton becoming the first women JPs in 1921 followed by Joyce Guthrie of Northallerton (1932).

Outstanding amongst all public figures Alderman John Hutton of Solberge Hall and latterly Sowber Gate passed away in December 1921 weakened by a fall on a London station platform. He gave unprecedented public service to the North Riding in general and Northallerton in particular. There was universal local regret at his death and he was fittingly buried at North Otterington churchyard in the middle of his devoted county and countryside.

North Riding Police Force

Another tremendous character was Sir Robert Lister Bower KBE CMG who became Chief Constable of the North Riding Police Force in 1898 which he led outstandingly (being knighted in the King's Birthday Honours List of June 1925) until his death on 13th June 1929 after a short bout of pneumonia at his residence West House, Thirsk. Three years after his death a memorial window was unveiled to him in Thirsk Parish Church by the Marquis of Zetland after a Dedication Service by the Bishop of Whitby. At Ibadan, western Nigeria where he had been Resident Governor 1892-1898 a tower was erected to his memory on a hill in the centre of the town which was opened in December 1936 by his children Commander R.L. Bower RN, MP for Cleveland and Miss Constance Bower. A copper plaque inside the tower bore an inscription to Sir Robert which ended with the assertion: "THIS WAS A MAN"

Lieutenant Colonel John Clervaux Chaytor DSO MC succeeded as North Riding Chief Constable on 1st October 1929 with a distinguished twenty one years' Army record in the South Staffordshire Regiment particularly in a protracted period around Ypres in the Great War where he was decorated with the DSO, MC, French Legion of Honour and Belgian Croix de Guerre.

During the Inter - War Years in the Police Force the development of motor vehicles and the wireless were the most significant advances and some of the main innovations were: wireless apparatus was introduced into the Northallerton Police Headquarters in September 1925; speedometers were fitted to motor cycles in 1928; mobile patrols were instituted in 1931 when the force was to have three Alvis 12/50 saloon cars and eighteen motor cycles mainly garaged at the Northallerton Headquarters; later four motor cycles were replaced by four small saloon cars.

The Churches

Strongly backed by Alderman Thomas Place the Baptist Church on Friarage Street was extended and refurbished, the improved premises being opened by Mrs Thomas Place in September 1923.

After the sale of their old chapel in Malpas Road for £347-10s a new Roman Catholic Church was built and opened in 1934 along with a Presbytery and Catholic Social Hall, all on the Thirsk Road site. The church was a tribute to the work and vision of Northallerton's Catholic priest Father Tils.

The Vicar of Northallerton Canon John Thomas Brown (1925 to 1929) was responsible for the building of a social hall, the Church House, at a cost of £4,500. Viscount Lascelles (who became Lord Harewood in 1929) laid the foundation stone on 9th August 1928 and Wilson and Willoughby constructed the building which was opened by the Archbishop of York Dr William Temple in 1929. Canon Brown's widow carved a niche in local folk-lore by becoming the voluntary teacher of the travelling "Fair" children, living in a caravan, touring with the Fair and becoming affectionately known as 'Aunty Brown'.

Rev Frederick T J Baines was the Vicar of Northallerton when a new Lady Chapel was built in January 1937 being dedicated by the

Northallerton
Peace Celebrations.

⊱⊰⊱⊰⊱⊰⊱⊰

Dinner   TO

Ex-Service Men
of the Great War,

At the Town Hall, Northallerton.
September 25th, 1919, at 7 p.m.

Presided over by
John Hutton, Esq.

Bishop of Whitby. The project cost £470, embellished by R. Thompson 'The Mouse Man' of Kilburn who produced the screen and furniture and Frank Clarkson of Northallerton who crafted the altar ornaments.

Other noteworthy occasions of the period were: the Northallerton ancillary of the Bible Society was one hundred and ten years old in 1926 having been initiated in the old Northallerton Theatre Royal on August 7th 1816; and J. Vivian Thomas was ordained as a curate on 1st November 1925 by the Bishop of Whitby - the first ordination in the Parish Church for centuries.

Notable Occasions and Events

National peace celebrations took place on 19th July 1919. At Northallerton in "a general feeling of joy" the bells pealed out, children's teas were served in the Town Hall the old people being similarly entertained in the Parish Room, sports were held at 6 p.m. and a dance held on the Showfield in the evening.

Many of the notable occasions during this period were royalty orientated commencing with the betrothal of the King and Queen's only daughter Princess Mary to Viscount Lascelles DSO the eldest son of Lord Harewood. A congratulatory telegram was sent to Viscount Lascelles from the Northallerton Urban District Council in December 1921 referring to the "long and intimate connection between the Lascelles family and the town and neighbourhood".

The next local royal event on Saturday 24th July 1926 is still recalled with pleasure. There was "A Great Welcome at Northallerton" for Princess Mary who had come to inspect the North Riding Red Cross at the cricket field adjacent to the County Hall. It was a special honour because this was the Princess's first official engagement since she had

Princess Mary's Visit 24th July 1926

been gazetted as the national Commandant in Chief of the British Red Cross Society. Arriving into town she was greeted by a gaily decorated High Street and a host of people to receive an address from the Chairman of the UDC amidst great enthusiasm from the crowd. At the cricket field she inspected 764 personnel made up of 23 women's detachments and 6 men's, supported by many VIPs including Sir Hugh and Lady Bell who were presented with Golden Wedding presents by Princess Mary.

On Tuesday 21st March 1933 the Duke of York (Prince George the future King George V1) paid a fleeting visit to Northallerton. He had been to Catterick Camp to inspect the 2nd Battalion East Yorks Regiment and travelled by motor car to Northallerton arriving just before 3 p.m. to catch the "Queen of Scots" Pullman to London. A large crowd raised a hearty cheer when the Prince alighted from his car but the public were not allowed on the platform.

The Coronation of George VI in May 1937 brought a flurry of Northallerton activity commencing with a religious service in the Town Hall (because of inclement weather) led by the Vicar Rev F Baines. A successful Carnival procession was followed by parties in all the schools and the day culminated with a Ball in the Town Hall. A stone plinth to celebrate the occasion was erected in the Applegarth along with the planting of thirteen beech trees, twelve of which are still flourishing. The brass tablet attached to the plinth reads:

Floods 1931 – Opposite the Rutson Hospital

"G.R. May 12th 1937. These Purple Beech Trees Were Planted In Commemoration Of The Coronation Of His Majesty King George V1."

Flooding was a regular event when Sun Beck and Willow Beck overflowed with excessive rainfall. Normally Friarage Street was flooded with the Sun Beck waters often swirling towards the Parish Church whilst from the opposite direction came the Willow Beck waters flooding the North End. The floods of 1923, 1931 and 1933 were outstanding. The other vulnerable places in the area at these times were Springwell Lane and Brompton where the village green at Water End resembled an inland lake.

Apart from the Linoleum factory conflagration there were other major fires in the district fortunately in these instances without loss of life. In January 1922 the Co-operative Stores became ablaze but the fire was soon contained by the Fire Brigade. When the Metropole garage belonging to Clarence Oxendale caught fire in November 1924, however, it burned completely to the ground. Pasture House on Thirsk Road had a dangerous fire in November 1938 but the Northallerton Fire Brigade was soon on the scene and the occupant, authoress Mrs Clive Muir and all the valuable racehorses stabled there escaped unharmed.

The Old Order Changeth

Many of the older generation passed away and these included: Northallerton and Knayton's popular Dr Tweedy who founded the Northallerton Boy Scouts in 1908; in 1923 the shipping magnate from Harlsey Hall Joseph Constantine (67) as well as W.R. Smithson (90) who produced Smithson's Northallerton Almanack (1863 - 1914); Mrs Annie Hird widow of wool merchant James Hird in 1924 who was held in great esteem having gifted her land in the Applegarth to the town as a War Memorial; Herbert Wilford (74) Brompton's well known linen millowner in 1925; in 1926 Thomas Place (78) who started the timber yard, Sir Henry de la Pore Beresford Peirse (75) Chairman of the North Riding County Council (1915 - 26), Walter Brierley (64) the prolific architect and Gertrude Bell CBE, FRGS of Rounton Grange, traveller, writer and Arab/Iraqi expert.

John Weston Adamson of Mount Pleasant, the shipowner left £285,071 in 1928; John Ingleby Jefferson (75) the leading Northallerton solicitor and his son-in-law Coroner Ernest Gardner both died in August 1929 - a double shock for the Gardner family; the Lord Lieutenant of the North Riding Sir Hugh Bell (87) in 1931, the headlines proclaiming "Yorkshire Loses a great son"; Northallerton stalwart Dr W. Baigent (71) internationally famous in the fly fishing sphere (1935); three very North Riding men died in successive years 1936 to 1938 - Sir William Worsley (75) a great public figure, Albert E. Doxford shipping magnate of Newby Wiske aged 69 and Major R.B. Turton Chairman of the North Riding County Council 1926-38.

Entertainment and Sport

Entertainment began to take on a different ambience in these years. Of course there were still the live entertainments provided by Northallerton concert parties like the "Jolly Boys", the orchestral and musical productions - the "Messiah" in 1925, the Northallerton Amateur Operatic Company's production of the "Mikado" (1922), the Swaledale Tournament of Song in the Town Hall adjudicated in 1923 by Dr Vaughan Williams and the "Northallerton Amateurs" who produced some excellent plays.

But new forces were coming to rival the old like the wireless which gradually became established in most homes, the gramophone and the cinema. The "Cinema de Luxe" picture house was already

OPENING CEREMONY

by

MISS E. R. HALL, S.R.N., A.R.R.C.

Matron of the Rutson Hospital.

THE NATIONAL ANTHEM.

Fox Films Present

GRACIE FIELDS

in

WE'RE GOING TO BE RICH

BRITISH MOVIETONE NEWS
Also Full Supporting Programme

*Proceeds in aid of the Rutson Hospital and The Red Cross
Motor Ambulance Society, Northallerton*

Lyric Cinema Opening 1939

established down Romanby Road when Richard Hardisty its owner
embarked on the project of building a second cinema and by 1921 the
"Central" picture house had been built on the site of the demolished
Melbourne Yard next to the Trustee Savings Bank. In 1937 it was

announced that a new super cinema was to be built at Northallerton which eventually transpired to be the "Lyric" which was opened in 1939.

Occasionally live entertainment on a grand scale came to the town. In this category was Bostock and Wombwell's menagerie and several circuses including Sangster's performed at Johnson's field (now Crow's). It was a great thrill in 1930 to greet Sir Alan Cobham's Air Circus at Broomfield's Bluestone Field. Stunt men did wing walking and planes looped the loop - great exciting stuff on that or any day.

Organised sport was much the same as before the Great War. Despite all the football teams having lost players killed or wounded in the war, they all re-formed and competition continued to be very strong in the Allertonshire Football League and at junior level. Northallerton's team was pre-fixed 'Comrades' and then 'United' until Northallerton Alliance became the title. The latter was the direct forerunner of the present Northallerton Town Football Club and in the 1936/37 season it won the Allertonshire League undefeated. Northallerton had a strong cricket team in local terms and in 1926 they won the Thirsk Senior League. The Northallerton and District Cricket League still flourished.

Northallerton Rugby Club restarted in 1931, Lawn Tennis had teams associated with the Northallerton Cricket Club, the Mount and the Civil Service at the Post Office, and there was an attempt to resurrect horse racing at Northallerton's Wiske Moor track (1922-24) but this did not succeed sufficiently to be a viable long term proposition.

Rifle Shooting of a high standard regularly occurred at the Greenhowsike "Targets", the Bowling Club down Thirsk Road was flourishing, the 'Cow and Gate' had a good Social and Sports Club and the Northallerton Angling Club was reputed to be one of the most powerful in Northern England. Even the pigeons held sway on some days as in June 1928 when 30,000 pigeons were transported from King's Cross in fifteen vans to be released at Northallerton station and thence to fly home to the south.

Prelude to the Second World War

With Hitler's Nazi Germany's continuing aggression, in 1938 preparations for war swept the country Northallerton being involved even more so because it was a County town. The North Riding County Council began organising Air Raid Precaution teams (ARP) in 1938 with Hubert Thornley appointed as County Controller and in July

Friarage Hospital – an Original Wooden Hutted Ward

Northallerton was one of the places designated as an ARP headquarters. The latter was sited in the basement of the Town Hall. Other Civil Defence measures in 1938 were the digging of trenches at the County Hall and the Public Health Institution (Workhouse) in the immediate vicinity of these buildings.

The Royal Air Force was beginning to build up and had a very high profile in the area. May 1938 saw the start of Royal Air Force Topcliffe to add to Royal Air Force stations Catterick, Dishforth and Thornaby which were well established - the latter with No. 608 (North Riding) Squadron the auxiliary squadron of the area under the auspices of the North Riding Territorial Army and Auxiliary Air Force Association which had its headquarters at the Northallerton Drill Hall. A vital local development was that of Royal Air Force Leeming which became a most important entity in the Northallerton area. Work on Leeming aerodrome commenced at the beginning of 1939, and after great efforts the station was opened with the first aircraft received in 1940.

As war approached evacuees arrived from Gateshead and Sunderland, to seek rural safety from the bombs which were expected to fall on industrial areas. After much preparation children and some mothers arrived on 1ˢᵗ/2ⁿᵈ September 1939 on three trains. The new arrivals either stayed in Northallerton or were bussed out to the villages. Those who remained settled down within the schools (Applegarth, National and Grammar Schools) whilst many returned home quite quickly as the "phoney war" of little aerial activity set in.

Of great future significance was the planning of an Emergency Hospital in 1939 because of the impending war and the perceived need to provide hospital beds in the event of the bombing of the civilian population of Teesside. The site chosen was that of the old Carmelite Friary which by a remarkable coincidence had been dissolved four hundred years before in 1539.

The British government initiated an Emergency Hospitals Scheme and in conjunction with this the North Riding of Yorkshire County Council took steps to provide an emergency hospital. They purchased the site of 5 acres adjacent to the Northallerton Public Institution from a local builder James O'Malley the deed being dated 3ʳᵈ July 1939 and the cost £592.

In September the site was rented out by the North Riding County Council to the Ministry of Health at a nominal annual fee of £25 for seven years and shortly afterwards eight wooden huts of Canadian origin were erected in what had been Northallerton Showfield to form the basis of the Emergency Hospital. This eventually became the nucleus of the Friarage Hospital in 1948 which was thus born by an accident of war.

10

The Second World War (1939 – 1945)

1939 - 40   Setting the War Scene

On the morning of 3rd September 1939 the British Prime Minister, Neville Chamberlain, broadcast to the nation the momentous news that a 'state of war' existed between Great Britain and Germany. It was a fine day at Northallerton with cloudless skies so that in the tranquillity and peace of the day the very idea of war seemed incongruous. But war it was and the ongoing exigencies were rapidly forwarded whilst new plans were soon implemented.

The Siren, air raid warning, became a regular feature with the 'Alert' an up and down wailing sound which caught the breath as it started up and the welcome "All Clear" - a single noted high pitched, elongated sound. The first 'Alert' at Northallerton was on Monday 29th February 1940 at 9.30 a.m. to 10.29 a.m. and alerts followed frequently later - mainly at night. If the "alert" was in the middle of the night, school did not commence until 10 a.m. - which generated many young prayers for late "alerts"!

Sandbags were in great prominence protecting the main buildings - County Hall, Town Hall, Drill Hall and Police Station. Air-raid shelters began to appear and all the schools eventually had brick built shelters (four are still standing at the Allertonshire School). The vast majority of homes, had the Anderson out-of-doors underground shelter or the Morrison shelter in the house which resembled an oblong steel bed with a steel roof covering. In the event of gas attack all the population had gas masks by 1939 the school children being equipped via a 'test hut' in the Applegarth. Static water tanks in case of fire were placed at the Parish Church, the north of South Parade and in the County Hall grounds (now the ornamental ponds).

The biggest impact of all in the day to day routine was the

Do you remember when the headlines said—

"No potatoes for this Sunday's joint"

While thousands of housewives enjoyed another little grumble, the wiser families who had dug for victory enjoyed their Sunday joint with all the potatoes and other vegetables they wanted. Learn from experience. To be sure of the family's vegetables, you must grow them yourselves—women and older children as well as men. If you haven't a garden, ask your Local Council for an allotment. Start to

DIG FOR VICTORY **NOW!**

A Wartime Exhortation

"Blackout" after daylight aimed to eliminate all light which might attract enemy aircraft. Windows were covered with black out material and criss crossed with sticky tape as an anti-blast measure. Vehicle lights were heavily shaded to offer only a slit of light and to aid uncertain navigation kerbstones were painted black and white. On moonless or cloudy nights total darkness enveloped the town in which progress was difficult and eerie.

Everyone had to hold a National Identity Card. All food, clothes, sweets and so on were rationed and Ration Books controlled this. Production of food was of course a key factor in the local war effort and many householders responded to the Government's motto "Dig for Victory" and patriotically turned their lawns and flowerbeds over to produce vegetables. A similar movement on a massively greater scale was the policy of ploughing out the grassland and replacing it with arable land. In September 1939 the North Riding War Agricultural Committee decided to "plough out" 35,000 acres and by May 1940 40,000 acres had been ploughed. Another colourful and popular innovation was the formation of the national Women's Land Army, known as 'Land Girls', wearing distinctive green jerseys and khaki breeches to work on farms. By November 1940 the North Riding had 110 such lady workers, many in the Northallerton area.

In the event of invasion, concrete road blocks were constructed narrowing road entrances into the town at: Boroughbridge Road railway bridge; the junction of South Parade, Thirsk Road and the High Street;

at the North End; and on East Road. Blockhouse sandbagged fortifications were built around the town in various fields. These wartime additions were accompanied by great convoys of lorries, tanks and troops regularly going through the town. Many troops were now billeted in the town and their numbers were maximised after Dunkirk when exhausted troops lay cheek by jowl on the grass verges of South Parade and Thirsk Road and filled the brand new Friarage Hospital. Afterwards the South Staffordshires and Border Regiment remained in the town in tented accommodation for several weeks, Boston's field (between Thirsk Road and Boston Avenue) being a main venue.

From the outset of the war a steady stream of local recruits left the town to join the Armed Services on "call up" with the Fourth Battalion (Territorials) Green Howads being mobilised at the Drill Hall. Also formed at this time was the local Volunteer Defence Force, renamed shortly afterwards the Home Guard, who were given uniform and weapons as they became available from the Drill Hall which was an absolute hive of activity and industry.

Remarkable developments concerned hospitals in Northallerton. In September 1939 the North Riding County Council medical authorities created an emergency maternity hospital within thirty six hours. It was established at Mount Pleasant a country house on Yafforth Road which was leased for the purpose by its owner John Weston Adamson. Nine babies were born in the first year which increased to over seven hundred annually by the 1980s.

The eight wooden huts which were the initial Northallerton Emergency Hospital were of Canadian Oregon pine with cedarwood cladding and they were erected in December 1939. In July 1940 eight brick built wards and other buildings were added to complete the wartime hospital complex. On 4th June 1940 the emergency hospital had received its first occupants but these were largely not patients but troops returning from the evacuation of Dunkirk. There were some wounded and casualties, however, and these were cared for in Ward 5 by Voluntary Aid Detachment Red Cross nurses.

Fortunately the hospital was never used in its incepted role for civilian bombing casualties but as soon as the Dunkirk situation resolved the hospital assumed its now intended function as an Emergency Medical Services Hospital for personnel of all the Armed Services. The Medical Superintendent was Dr Alexander Curtis with Major Pym the Medical Registrar and Michael Wallace the North Riding County Council Administrator. The nurses were largely dedicated locals.

Despite the material drawbacks the hospital had a happy atmosphere from the very outset - a situation repetitive throughout its history - and already a strong rapport was growing up with the town and surrounding area where the patients in their bright blue uniforms and red ties were soon a familiar and welcome sight. The Emergency or 'Base' Hospital was firmly established and running well when the second chapter of the Friarage story opened on 1st January 1943 the hospital being totally taken over by the Air Ministry to become Royal Air Force Hospital, Northallerton for the rest of the war and in fact until November 1947.

Northallerton at war was a different scene with the "blackout," sandbags, soldiers, blockades, static tanks and the sheer austerity of the times. How the mothers for example fed and clothed their often large families with rationing restrictions was a minor miracle. Every war event - good and bad - was eagerly or stoically received. Overwhelmingly, however, camaraderie and communal spirit pervaded - a true case of "all for one and one for all".

Non-militaristic happenings of course punctuated the time. Simon Hunter (79) the internationally famous entrepreneur of poultry breeding of Sowerby-under-Cotliffe who had had Queen Victoria, other Royalty and the Rothchilds amongst his clients died, as did Father Tils the well loved Roman Catholic priest who had pioneered the new Roman Catholic Church. Weather took an icy hand as the 1940 winter was the worst in living memory with snow-blocked main roads, stranded cars becoming ice covered hummocks and the River Wiske frozen for miles except at the bridges.

A most auspicious addition to the entertainment of the town was that of the Lyric Cinema opened 28th October 1939 on the east side of the North End by the demolition of old properties including Bowman's yard. It was the epitome of cinema luxury at the time. Miss E R Hall, Matron of the Rutson performed the opening ceremony, the main film was Gracie Fields in "We're Going To Be Rich" and there was a full supporting programme which included the British Movietone News. The Lyric which held 700 people was built by Walter Thompson and Son. Finally the Northallerton Music Society produced no fewer than five oratorios in eighteen months - the last Handel's "Messiah" - under its vastly talented Conductor A. Mattinson Wilson (affectionately known to all as "Gerry") which did much to elevate spirits in those dark days.

But really all things were subordinated to the war. The adoption of "HMS Hood", Britain's premier battleship by the Council (Applegarth)

NORTHALLERTON AND DISTRICT
SPITFIRE FUND

EXHIBITION OF

Messerschmitt

109

IN THE ENCLOSURE BEHIND THE

URBAN DISTRICT COUNCIL OFFICES

The Friarage, 72 High Street

DAILY FROM THE

14th to the 21st December, 1940

1 P.M. TO 4 P.M.

(WEDNESDAY, THE 18TH DECEMBER, 11 A.M. TO 4 P.M.)

ADMISSION:

ADULTS 6D.   H.M. FORCES 3D.

CHILDREN 3D.

Spitfire Fund Attractions 1940

School brought much pleasure to both parties. By August 1940 four chests of letters and 'comforts' had been sent by the school and a 'pen-pal' system had been evolved. After the Battle of Britain a "Spitfire Fund" was inaugurated on the 24th September 1940. Collections, entertainments and events (Crow's roundabout for Fund rides) took place. Highlights were the exhibition for a week in December of a shot down German Messerschmitt 109 fighter in the Northallerton UDC garden linked to a Spitfire display over the town on 14th December 1940.

At the operative end of the war Captain Thomas Prince (ex Northallerton Grammar School) fought off an enemy plane attacking his ship "Otterpool" with a rifle but unfortunately his citation for this action in the "London Gazette" was posthumous as he was lost at sea when the "Otterpool" was torpedoed and sunk. Captain Arthur Peter Godman (31) of the Bucks Light Infantry was killed in action - the only son of Air Commodore and Mrs A L Godman. Private Arthur Brown of Crosby Road was killed with the 4th Battalion Green Howards. The latter's Commanding Officer Lieutenant Colonel C N Littleboy MC, TD was awarded the DSO and Captain Alan Watts of Harewood House, Northallerton obtained the MC for operations in the evacuation of Dunkirk.

The Vale of York resembled one "large landing strip" such was the profusion of bomber airfields and aeroplanes became a salient part of Northallerton's wartime life. A great rapport was set up from the outset between the town and Royal Air Force Leeming which exists until this day. Royal Air Force Leeming was bought by the Crown in 1938 consisting of parts of Clapham Lodge and Wilson's Farm which along with the adjacent Newton House had housed one of the first flying clubs in the country named the Yorkshire Air Services. A decoy airfield was built at Burneston four miles away.

Blenheim IF nightfighters of 219 Squadron were the first planes into Leeming detached from Royal Air Force Catterick in June 1940. In July 1940 the first bombers arrived in the form of No. 10 Squadron's Whitley Vs and they carried out the first of innumerable raids from Leeming on 20th July 1940 when nine Whitleys attacked a German aircraft factory at Wenzedorf. No 10 Squadron carried out several more brave raids including Hamburg, Milan, Turin, and Berlin in their two engined Whitleys.

Notably historic was the arrival at Leeming on August 1st 1940 of No 7 Squadron with Stirlings because these were the first four engined bombers in Squadron service in the Royal Air Force. When it had become operational No 7 Squadron moved to Royal Air Force Oakington. No 35 Squadron significantly with four engined Handley Page Halifax bombers came to Leeming in November 1940. Although this Squadron only remained a few weeks its appearance was portentous because of the momentous part the Halifax was to play in Leeming's illustrious wartime record.

1941 - In Adversity

In 1941 Britain stood alone in the depths of danger. Total food rationing was now in force and the Northallerton Urban Food Control Committee monitored all food matters. Good cheap meals could be obtained at the popular British Restaurant at the Northallerton railway station where a good meal cost 11d (soup 2d, main dish 6d, sweet 2d and mug of tea 1d). During early 1941 the "Spitfire Fund" continued and reached £4000 with high hopes of achieving the £5000 needed to buy a complete Spitfire. A congratulatory telegram was received from the Government Minister involved Lord Beaverbrook:

"I rejoice with you in the swift progress of the Northallerton Spitfire Fund. Northallerton's own fighter will take its place among the defenders of our homes and liberties."

Hard on the heels of the "Spitfire" fund came a "War Weapons Week" (17th- 24th May) whereby people were encouraged to invest in War Bonds or National Savings Certificates thus in effect loaning money to the Government to buy weapons. This advertisement appeared in the local papers issued by the Northallerton War Savings Committee:

Girl Guides Collect Aluminium

"LEND YOUR MONEY FOR VICTORY
OUR AIM £60,000 FOR THREE BOMBERS
£END AND SAVE TO DEFEND."

An "Indicator" on the Town Hall showed the progress of the appeal (it was altered each evening amidst great enthusiasm) and after four days the target of £60,000 had been reached.

On Saturday 17th May the Green Howards' Band appeared at the opening of War Weapons Week by Lord Bolton and on Sunday it led the parade of over five hundred made up of all manner of contingents centred on a "Drum Head Service". Various "Days" followed:

"Children's" (Tuesday), "Farmers" (Wednesday), "Civil Defence" (Thursday) and "Empire" (Saturday 24th). The final total was a magnificent £151,600 which exemplifies the spirit and determination of the local people in adversity.

A matter of some controversy was the removal of most of the iron railings in Northallerton late in 1941 for salvage and use in the making of munitions by order of the Ministry of Supply, only a few sites being spared such as the National School, Applegarth School and Drill Hall. Thus ornamental railings disappeared throughout Northallerton - a great environmental loss of lasting effect. Incessant troop movements continued through Northallerton – shades of the medieval armies.

Enemy action took place on the night of 11th/12th May 1941 when Northallerton was bombed for the only time in the war. Around 1 a.m. a lone German bomber approaching from the north dropped four High Explosive bombs across the town and several incendiary bombs in the vicinity of the County Hall. The latter set fire to the offices of the County Architect in the main building but this was soon extinguished and the damage minimal. The HE bombs dropped successively on the auction ring of the Applegarth Mart, in a garden at Ashlea Road, on a house called the "White House" on South Parade and the last one in a garden of Hatfield Road behind Thirsk Road. The most damage was done by the South Parade bomb which sliced through the "White House" (now rebuilt as Stanley Court) damaged nearby houses, riddled several lamp posts with shrapnel holes and killed an unfortunate soldier who was the only fatality of the raid. He was Private Joe Bolton of the RASC and Darlington.

May 1941 also saw an outstanding and traumatic event, the sinking of the elite British battleship "HMS Hood". Shocked disbelief greeted this in the town and in particular amongst the young Applegarth children (aged 5 to 9 years) whose school had adopted the ship and whose older pupils were "penpals" of sailors on the ship. It was learned that the "Hood" had received a direct hit to its magazine from the German battleship the "Bismarck" and had gone down with all its crew of 1418 except for three survivors on 24th May. The "Bismarck" was hunted down and sunk on 27th May but really this was scant consolation for the Applegarth schoolchildren.

A new feature of Northallerton was the reactivation of the Northallerton Gaol which had been closed during the "Inter War Years", into an Army Gaol or "Glasshouse" for military offenders. The field next to (now part of) the Northallerton Grammar School (College) was used for training and became popularly known as the "Prison Field".

The war continued to take its local toll which included the Leeming Vicar's son Reginald Kent who was killed in the Middle East with the Royal Signals, a County Hall clerk Sergeant Pilot John Dunning (20) whose plane crashed in the North Sea and Sgt Brian Kirk an Old Alvertonian and Spitfire pilot who died from wounds sustained in the Battle of Britain.

Major T L Dugdale MP whose illness had forced him to leave the Army was appointed Government Deputy Chief Whip and later in the year he was bereaved when his father Lionel Dugdale the "Squire of Crathorne" died. The worst snowstorm apparently since 1888 occurred at Northallerton in March.

Significant in 1941 was the opening of the Allertonshire Secondary Modern School which received its first intake of students in September, Clifford Snook becoming the first Headmaster. The Allertonshire was one of the first three 'Modern' schools in the country, and as such had its own niche in the national educational history and was the flagship of the North Riding Education Committee's ambitious and enlightened school building programme which took place over the next twenty years initiated by the Secretary to the Education Committee, Frank Barraclough of Thirsk Road Northallerton.

Meanwhile carrying the fight to the enemy in those dark days of war were the Leeming bomber squadrons - most importantly not only from an operational viewpoint but also as a civilian morale booster. No. 10 Squadron bombed enemy targets with Whitley Vs and later in the year started to convert to four engined Halifaxes. In September 1941 No.77 Squadron came to Leeming with Whitley Vs having just sunk a U Boat (U705) in the Bay of Biscay.

Spitfires of No. 122 Squadron were located at Royal Air Force Scorton and Royal Air Force Catterick had at different times five squadrons of Spitfires, three squadrons of Hurricanes, Beaufighters (No 256 Squadron) and Blenheims (No. 313 Squadron) based there during the year. A Spitfire of 141 Squadron based at Catterick crashed on the stroke of midday on Sunday 29th July 1941 at Stone Cross, Northallerton, killing the pilot Sergeant Durrell who was buried at Catterick village churchyard with military honours.

1942 The Gloom Lightens

Important in the exposition of Second World War history was the lack of direct contemporary information available. This particularly appertained to local newspapers with all details of naval, military and air force activities under a strict security blanket. "Careless talk costs lives" was a universal maxim practised.

"Warship Week" (21st - 28th March) proved to be a highlight of 1942 at Northallerton when the aim was to attract £62,000 in Government savings to buy a minesweeper/trawler. The week was opened outside the Town Hall by the Lord Lieutenant of the North Riding Lord Bolton supported by the Chairman of the Fund the former Bishop of Norwich Rt Rev Bernard Heywood of Lees Lane, Northallerton, and accompanied by the Liverpool Scottish pipes band. Farmer's Day scheduled for Wednesday market day was most successful as too was a realistic "mock battle" to capture Northallerton staged in the High Street on Tuesday. The final total was £132,449, making £284,049 invested in Government Savings in Northallerton over a period of a year.

Local indignation was aroused by the German "Baedeker" bombing raid on the cultural centre of nearby York on the night of 28th/29th April. On the other hand morale was greatly raised by 'The First Thousand Bomber Raid on Cologne', "Operation Millennium" on 30th May followed in rapid succession by similar raids on Essen and Bremen, No 10 Squadron with Halifaxes from Royal Air Force Leeming taking part in all three raids.

Arnold Pearson of the Northallerton district and an ex Northallerton Grammar School pupil, flew as a Wireless Operator/Air Gunner in a Lancaster of No. 50 Squadron on the Cologne raid, the city being a mass of flames when his aeroplane arrived to drop its bombs after being the last aircraft of the Squadron to take off at 23.45 hours. After Cologne he continued to fly in Lancasters latterly with the elite 'Pathfinder' Force which led the bombing raids and marked the targets. In all he completed sixty seven missions, reached the rank of Squadron Leader and was awarded the DFC and DSO for gallantry.

In November the Eighth Army of "Desert Rats" under General Montgomery defeated Rommel's Africa Corps in the crucial battle of El Alamein and in Northallerton as throughout the nation, the long silenced Church bells were rung in celebration of this victory on Sunday 21st November by Government direction.

In taking the fight to the enemy No. 10 Squadron at Leeming until August 1942 were in the midst of things under their Commanding Officer Wing Commander Donald C.T. Bennett from Queensland,

**Squadron Leader Arnold Pearson DSO, DFC
with his wife Gladys at Buckingham Palace**

Australia. They supplied Halifaxes for each of the Thousand Bomber Raids - 22 for Cologne and 20 each for Essen and Bremen. The Squadron were detached to Royal Air Force Lossiemouth to attack the battleship "Tirpitz" at Trondheim, Norway, and during the action Wing Commander Bennett's aircraft was shot down but within five weeks having escaped from Norway he was back at Leeming. He obtained the DSO for this episode and went on to become one of the Royal Air Force's most decorated pilots leading the 'Pathfinder' Force.

Royal Air Force Leeming had its station crest authorised by the King during the year consisting of a shield depicting a sword with the point uppermost underlaid with the motto "Straight and True". In

Halifax Bomber of No 10 Squadron

August the Canadian No. 419 (Moose) Squadron arrived at Leeming for a short time before being replaced in September by RCAF No.408 (Goose) Squadron. Finally on 1st January 1943 Leeming was transferred to the new No. 6 Group Royal Canadian Air Force and became No. 63 (RCAF) Base which was part of Royal Air Force Bomber Command.

However before Leeming was Canadianised a series of VIP visitors came to the station as if in tribute to the great bravery shown by the aircrew in consistently bombing far flung enemy targets. Over three hundred men lost their lives as 75 planes "failed to return" from August 1940 to May 1942.

On 25th March 1942 King George VI arrived to decorate several aircrew accompanied by Queen Elizabeth and Princess Elizabeth. On 10th May Marshal of the Royal Air Force, Lord Trenchard visited and five days later on 15th May the Prime Minister Winston. S. Churchill with his deputy Prime Minister Clement Attlee came to Leeming leaving via Northallerton Railway Station. The "bush telegraph" had imparted the news of the latter visit and the many people who surrounded the railway station including numerous schoolchildren were thrilled when the great war leader arrived by car from Leeming en route to London via

Northallerton Army Cadets

Northallerton Air Force Cadets

rail. Hearty cheers rang out for him to which he responded in his Royal Air Force, Air Officer's uniform with his famous V for victory hand sign.

Meanwhile on the civilian front youth was being trained in No 3 Cadet Force of the Green Howards at the Drill Hall and No 1026 Squadron Air Training Corps based at Northallerton Grammar School both of which were very well supported. Thomas Dugdale MP was made Chairman of the national Conservative Party - the youngest ever - a most onerous post but one which it was felt he would cope well with. As the national "Daily Telegraph" reported: "He is qualified for it by tact, charm of manner and over four years experience in the Whip's office."

1943 Hail Canada

Farming continued to take a most prominent place in the local war effort and the North Riding dairy farmers topped the National League For Milk Production. A great drive was made to obtain the necessary farm labour with advertising such as "LABOUR FOR HAYTIME NEEDED", women and children over twelve being particularly targeted and encouraged. An added labour dimension was that of Prisoners of War and in Northallerton Italian and German prisoners were based and used locally mainly on farms. They lived in two small encampments at Malpas Road in wooden huts and at Stone Cross in a group of Nissen huts. North Riding members of the Women's Land Army held a rally at Northallerton on 22nd May with 315 marching from the "Golden Lion" to the Allertonshire School, where the Yorkshire Chairman Lady Graham presented diamond brooches for good service.

"Wings for Victory" week was opened by Group Captain J.L. Plant the Commanding Officer of RCAF Leeming outside the Town Hall on Saturday 8th May with a target of £80,000. Wednesday was the now traditional "Farmer's Day" and by the end of "Young People's Day" on Friday the "Target" on the Town Hall indicator had been exceeded with £96,483 saved. £152,000 was the final grand "Wings Week" total of the Northallerton and district which was a reflection of the esteem felt in the area for the RAF and RCAF and their dangerous missions.

Cyril Garbutt the Archbishop of York embarked on a pilgrimage walking through the villages which on the second day included Thimbleby, Osmotherley and Mount Grace. Finally the "Allertonshire Players" with their production at the Allertonshire School of "Juno and the Paycock" raised £72 for the Green Howards Prisoner of War Fund.

Several local servicemen were decorated: Pilot Officer Peter Stead of Brompton obtained the DFC having been involved in raids on the Rhur Valley and the Cologne "Thousand Bomber Raid". Lieutenant Charles Bedford Dorman, the son of the Chairman of the North Riding Education and War Agricultural Committee, gained the MC for tank action with the Eighth Army; Pilot Officer Arthur Stafford of Northallerton who had flown forty sorties including Italy and four daylight raids as a Wireless Operator/Air Gunner was awarded the DFM; and Flight Lieutenant Maurice Morley of Thirsk Road, Northallerton who was a pilot in Coastal Command earned the DFC.

By this time the vast majority of the young men of Northallerton and many young women who had volunteered were in the Armed Services where sad losses on active service continued.

With the coming of No.6 (Bomber) Group Royal Canadian Air Force to the County the strongest Yorkshire/Canadian links were forged - none more so than at Northallerton with Royal Canadian Air Force Leeming nearby and Royal Air Force Hospital Northallerton on the Friarage site the recipient of all the Canadian casualties in the vicinity. When away from flying duties the Canadians were regulars in the town and its accommodating pubs and cafes which they treated like home.

No. 408 (Goose) Squadron RCAF remained at Leeming until 26th August when they moved to RCAF Linton. On 5th May Leeming's first permanent Squadron No. 427 (Lion) RCAF was posted in, re-equipped with Halifaxes and remained until after the war ended. Metro Goldwyn Meyer (MGM) the Hollywood film studio which also had a lion emblem adopted the Squadron in May 1943 and consequently several Halifaxes had film stars names such as DK140 - Lana Turner. No. 429 (Bison) Squadron RCAF arrived on August 13th, re-equipped with Halifaxes and remained as No. 427s partner at Leeming throughout the rest of the war.

No 429 ("Bison") Squadron had previously flown in Wellington bombers since their formation in Yorkshire on 7th November 1942 their first raid being on Lorient on 26th January 1943. Their Squadron motto was "Fortunae Nihil" – "Nothing to Chance" – and in January 1944 they were presented at Leeming with a magnificent Bison's head by the Canadian National Railways. "Lion" Squadron probably because of their 'movie' connections were constantly in the news media and one graphic account of a raid on Hamburg on the night of 27th/28th July 1943 by James Stuart of the 'Evening Standard' was memory etching – "Hamburg was lit up like a prairie sunset."

The Duchess of Gloucester greeted by Group Captain J L Plant

"Lion" and "Bison" Squadrons joined the main Bomber Command Force on continuous operations: for example four raids on Hanover in September and October and two on the industrial centre of Kassel in October. Losses at Leeming were consistently heavy - illustrated by this anecdote of a surviving flyer. With his crew he arrived at Leeming on 3rd December to be informed that they would have to stay in the Airmen's Mess overnight as the Sergeants' Mess was full. However, they were told that there was an Operation that night and in consequence there would be room in the Sergeants' Mess tomorrow. Sure enough this proved to be tragically correct as during the raid of 527 aircraft on Leipzig, 23 planes were lost and Leeming was one of the heaviest sufferers. The lost crew that the new crew replaced had been on its seventeenth mission.

Illustrative of the vicissitudes of war were two entirely disparate events in 1943 at Leeming. On 12th July a German aircraft infiltrated and bombed the station fortunately to minimal effect as the bombs fell on the perimeter of the airfield. The station, however, was honoured on

Canadian Fatality Telegram – Springwell Lane Crash

14th October by a royal visit from HRH the Duchess of Gloucester, Chief Commandant of the Women's Auxiliary Air Force (WAAF) who was escorted by the Station Commander, Group Captain J L Plant and Flight Officer Helen Scott, the Senior WAAF Officer. The memorable occasion gave much pleasure and was a strong morale booster in those hazardous times.

On the 2nd December 1943 at 14.30 hours Halifax V DJ 932 K-King from RCAF 1664 Conversion Unit Croft piloted by Flying Officer William J. Taylor of St. Thomas, Ontario took off from RCAF Croft on a routine training flight. Half an hour later K-King was a crumpled mass of burning debris in Springwell Lane, Northallerton with all the crew of four Canadians, two Welshmen and an Ulsterman dead in the wreckage. The sensation was even greater because the stricken aircraft had narrowly missed crashing on the Northallerton Applegarth Council School where all the children aged five to nine in Northallerton were in mid-afternoon lessons. But for a few short yards the tragedy would have been horrendous.

The aircraft was on an Air Affiliation Exercise with a Spitfire doing quick movements for fighter evasion and the most likely cause of

The Canadian Aircrew Graves – Stonefall Cemetery

the crash was a technical fault which jammed the rudder. "Evidence would suggest the Pilot lost control due to rudder imbalance" stated the Aircraft Investigation Report and this accorded with the record of the Halifaxes which were beset with technical difficulties. In the event K-King turned on to its back, was temporarily righted but then went into a slow spiral from 6,700 feet with the crew having no chance of baling out, before plunging into the ground. It hit Foster's bungalow just behind the Applegarth School setting it on fire but fortunately the occupants were out at the time. The RCAF Leeming and National Fire Service Northallerton fire tenders speedily extinguished the fires and the bodies of the seven aircrew were removed by ambulance.

Every person present in Northallerton has indelible memories of that day – particularly those in the Applegarth School. The average age of the crew was only twenty one. The two Welshmen were buried at Mountain Ash and the Ulsterman in Belfast. The four Canadians were interred in the Stonefall cemetery, Harrogate where 661 Canadians lie who were killed in this country flying with No 6 RCAF Bomber Group. RCAF Croft had a dreadful and tragic day because on the evening of 2nd December another Halifax missed the main runway and crashed killing five of the crew. The three Canadians involved were buried alongside their colleagues who had lost their lives earlier in the day at Northallerton.

1944 - The Great Offensive

By 1944 the tide of the war had turned and the Allied offensive against Nazi Germany was in full spate with notably the invasion of Italy, the all out bomber attacks and most significantly the D Day landings at Normandy on the 6th June which signalled the Allied invasion of Europe.

The sky over Northallerton on the night of the 5th/6th June was continuously filled with an armada of aircraft bringing a throbbing drone of engines as stream after stream of planes overflew the town in support of D Day. No 6 Bomber Group (RCAF) including of course Leeming took part in this great bomber offensive which preceded "Operation Overlord" and prayers for the success of the invasion were said in Northallerton Parish Church on Sunday 10th June and at the County Hall meeting in the town of the North Riding County Council on Wednesday 13th June.

Local men on active service were involved in all the theatres of war and the hard won successes of the Allies were received at Northallerton with a mixture of relief and thanksgiving for the victories and regret and sadness at the local losses of many young servicemen. The fighting in Italy was fierce and here the casualties included Sergeant Stanley Forth of the Coldstream Guards and Harry Kilding of the Green Howards both of Brompton and both dying of wounds as well as Lieutenant Ernest Place and Albert Norris who were killed outright. At the ferocious battle of Cassino Sergeant Tom Riordan (the author's eldest brother) of the Royal Engineers was awarded an 'on the field' MM for bravery in bridging the river Rapido.

The bombing operations over Germany and occupied Europe carried a very heavy toll and local volunteers flying in the Royal Air Force Volunteer Reserve of Bomber Command who lost their lives on missions included Sergeants George Law, Derrick Roper and Harry Playforth and Flight Sergeant Louis Windress. In the advance into Europe several local young men were killed and amongst these were Reginald Cariss of Northallerton and Arthur Dunn of Brompton in July at Caen in France, Albert DiPalma of the Green Howards on detachment with the Durham Light Infantry fell on the Somme and early in 1945 Rifleman Harry Megginson died serving with the Cameronians just after his nineteenth birthday on the Dutch – German border.

Like so many other local Northallerton men in the two World Wars the fallen were mainly laid to rest in "foreign fields" in extraordinarily ordered military cemeteries immaculately kept by the Commonwealth War Graves Commission. For example Harry Kilding is buried in Italy in the Beach Head Cemetery, Anzio and Albert DiPalma in France in the London Cemetery near High Wood on the Somme along with thousands of others from both World Wars. Harry Megginson lies in the

Riechwald Forest Cemetery in Germany just over the Dutch border between the villages of Kleve and Coch and away in the Far East Able Seaman Douglas Shields is interred in Maccasar Cemetery having died as a Japanese Prisoner of War in Moena Island Camp.

At home "Salute the Soldier" week in May exceeded its Savings Target in Northallerton when a highlight was an Open Day at the Royal Air Force Hospital with over 500 visitors. The North Riding Women's Land Army held a large rally at the Allertonshire School and another auspicious visit was again to the Allertonshire on 21st October when Lady Baden Powell, the Chief Guide addressed fourteen local Girl Guide groups.

Three great North Riding stalwarts, all strongly connected with Northallerton in their lifetimes, died during the year. Britain's oldest VC Major Alan Hill-Walker of Maunby Hall passed away aged 84 on 21st April. Six trumpeters of his Northamptonshire Regiment sounded the "Last Post" and "Reveille" at his Maunby funeral. Sir Maurice Bell (73) "Industrial Chief and Soldier" died on 17th November. Many attended his funeral at East Rounton when appropriately buglers of the Green Howards played the "Last Post" recalling his major role as Commanding Officer of their Fourth Battalion in the heroic action at St Julien in 1915. Lord Bolton (75) who died at Bolton Hall, Wensley on 11th December as the Hon. W.G.A. Orde-Powlett had become MP for Richmondshire in January 1910 for the Conservatives until 1918 and fought in the First World War with the Yorkshire Regiment (Green Howards) reaching the rank of Lieutenant Colonel. In 1935 he was appointed by the King as Lord Lieutenant of the North Riding.

Unceasingly the Canadian Leeming bomber squadrons 427 (Lion) and 429 (Bison) attacked enemy targets with the main Bomber Command Force with a tremendous bravery but at a high price. For example in a raid on Magdeburg 21st/22nd January 1944, of the 55 bombers lost four were from "Lion" Squadron. There were many remarkable experiences and stories such as that of Sergeant E.J. Steere the Flight Engineer in a Halifax which raided Acheres on D Day night 6th/7th June. The pilot was fatally wounded and Sergeant Steere had taken over the controls of the Halifax, and though with no previous flying experience, flew the plane home and landed it safely, for which amazing feat he was awarded the Conspicuous Gallantry Medal.

Several Halifaxes crashed locally and one of these was piloted by Flying Officer R. K. Laut of 427 Squadron. On take off from Leeming just after midnight on 20/21st February on a bombing raid to Stuttgart it simply gained height and then nose dived into the ground on what is now Romanby golf course with the ignition of its entire bomb load of 834 incendiary bombs. The seven crew died instantly and the three Canadian members were buried at Stonefall, Harrogate.

An outstanding occasion of 1944 at RCAF Leeming and Northallerton was the visit of King George VI accompanied by Queen Elizabeth and Princess Elizabeth on Friday 11th August to decorate 'Lion' and 'Bison' Squadrons aircrew. E.J. Steere (now commissioned as a Pilot Officer) was one of these being awarded the CGM and "Lion" Squadron was especially mentioned because of the number of decorations achieved. After leaving Leeming the Royal Party, joined by Princess Margaret who had spent the day locally elsewhere, entrained for the North at Northallerton. With the news spreading like wildfire of the Royal presence, the town turned out in force at Northallerton railway station where the Royal Party were greeted with great acclaim and affection.

Royal Air Force Hospital Northallerton (1 January 1943 to November 1947) was crucial to No 6 Bomber Group Royal Canadian Air Force with its geographically central location to eight RCAF bomber stations - Leeming, Skipton-on-Swale, Topcliffe, Dishforth, Dalton, Linton, Croft and Middleton St George. Aerial activity within the area was intense and because of the speed involved and frequently explosion, fire or gunshot, severe injuries and burns were commonplace. There was an increasing number of casualties with Canadians comprising by far the majority of patients:

"155 RCAF personnel were hospitalised at Northallerton in one month: in addition there were many more attending as out-patients and a great number of surgical operations were performed on Canadians." (Official History of the Canadian Medical Services).

The dedicated Staff initially were British: 14 Medical Officers, 6 other Officers, 51 Nursing Officers, 219 Other Ranks (147 WAAF and 72 RAF) and 36 civilians. Group Captain W.A.S. Duck OBE was the Commanding Officer throughout the war and in 1944 most important additions to the Staff were Canadian Medical Officers and Nursing Sisters who developed a reputation for "work hard play hard" and like the Staff generally were admired and respected. Casualties had to be wheeled from the wards into the open air to and from the Operating Theatre and it was their proud boast that they'd never lost a patient because of this.

Waycot Café

Medical equipment and facilities in the hospital were greatly improved and of particular importance and innovation was a Mobile Surgical Unit to go out to crash and accident scenes. It was the brain child of Squadron Leader John Howkins (later Wing Commander and then Professor of Anatomy at St Bartholomews Hospital, London). By May 1944 it was fully developed with a Humber Shooting Brake and a medical team of a Surgeon, Anaesthetist, Resuscitation Officer, Theatre Sister and Operating Room Assistant.

The Mobile Surgical Unit made twenty five operational runs in two years of a vital nature which included: Black Hambleton 28th September 1943 to a midnight Halifax crash to resuscitate two aircrew survivors; Skipton-on-Swale 5th August 1944 where a Halifax had hit a house and the MSU arrived within 20 minutes to aid the badly injured crew; 21st November 1944 to a Leeming Halifax crash at Thrintoft to treat six air crew; Topcliffe 28th November 1944 to attend seven badly burned in a flares explosion when six were saved; Felixkirk 15th January 1945 across snow on foot for ½ mile but the Halifax crew were dead; Driffield 27th July 1945 to aid an officer which was the last operational run of the MSU.

As with RCAF Leeming strong links were forged between the hospital and town. Entertainments were given by local organisations such as the Allertonshire Players and Northallerton Grammar School, dances were regularly held at the Town Hall, hospital collections were held especially in the places mainly frequented by the Staff and patients - the "Fleece," "Black Bull," "Golden Lion," Russell's Café and Waycot Café.

Well-known visitors came to the hospital such as ENSA celebrities Robert Donat and Bernard Miles and two events were very auspicious. On 19th April 1943 a royal visit took place when HRH Princess Royal, sister of King George V1 and wife of Lord Harewood came to the hospital with the Director General of RAF Medical Services Air Marshal Sir H.E. Whittingham and the Matron in Chief of the Princess Mary's RAF Nursing Services. After inspecting the premises and speaking to the patients in all the wards, the Princess and her party were entertained to lunch in the Sister's Mess.

Finally after an absence of just over four hundred years official religion returned to the Friarage site when the hospital Chapel was dedicated on Sunday 8th April 1945 by the Bishop of Whitby aided by the Assistant Chaplain-in-Chief of the RAF, Reverend Wright.

Of particular local interest, excitement and involvement was the making in the district of the epic film *The Way to the Stars* concerning the colourful life of a wartime flying station which starred Michael Redgrave, John Mills and Rosamund John with Stanley Holloway, David Tomlinson, Trevor Howard and others. The serving members of the cast were billeted at RAF Catterick and the film locations included Leeming, Catterick, Bedale and memorably the 'Golden Lion Hotel' Northallerton. The film produced by Anthony Asquith (who became enamoured with the rural North Riding, visiting many times subsequently) as time progressed took on a 'cult status' being re-shown for example time and again on television.

1945 – Victory and Peace

Victory and peace were the watchwords of 1945 with the unconditional surrender of the Germans in May and the Japanese in August. VE Day (8th May) and VJ Day (15th August) were marked in Northallerton by military parades, street parties, dancing and general rejoicing. The pervading feelings, however, were of profound relief and thankfulness as epitomised by the Thanksgiving Service at Northallerton Parish Church conducted by the Vicar Rev F.T. Baines on Tuesday 13th May when the church was filled to overflowing.

Before the war ended Northallerton experienced a minor air attack when on the night of 3rd/4th March at 2200 hours a German intruder cannon-shelled a goods train in the North End Goods Yard. Only slight damage was inflicted and no casualties occurred in the raid which was one of several simultaneous enemy intrusions in the North East that evening.

Nos. 427 (Lion) and 429 (Bison) Squadrons continued the bomber offensive receiving Lancasters in March at Leeming. The station's last operation was on 25th April when ten Lancasters from each of "Bison" and "Lion" squadrons attacked gun positions on the Island of Wangerooge. The record of two squadrons was quite remarkable summing up the endurance, bravery, achievement and tragic sacrifice over only two years:

	Sorties	Aircraft Lost	Aircrew Lost	Decorations
Lion	3328	90	501	176
Bison	3221	71	402	56

The announcement of the unconditional surrender of Germany on 8th May 1945 (VE Day) broadcast at 3 pm by Winston Churchill the victorious Prime Minister was heard by the entire station personnel over the tannoy system. Jubilation was great and a Victory Dance was held in the evening in the Airmen's NAAFI with free beer served to over eight hundred attending the historic occasion. On the 8th, 9th, and 10th May Nos 427 and 429 Squadron Lancasters flying at 3000 feet ferried one thousand, eight hundred and ninety three Prisoners of War back from Brussels and Juvencourt to Britain – easily their happiest mission of the war.

The Canadians in No 6 Group began to return home in June 1945 and Air Marshal Arthur "Bomber" Harris personally attended Middleton St George to bid farewell to the first Canadian Lancasters to thunder off home to Canada via Cornwall and the Azores. The strongest links had been formed with North Yorkshire, in the case of Northallerton by several marriages which included two in one family: the daughters of Mrs Walton Fairless, 2 Bridge Terrace, Northallerton, Peggy and Moira married Flying Officer Rae Butchart, Toronto and Flying Officer Conley

DFC, Saskatchewan respectively and followed their husbands to Canada.

A memorable day occurred on Saturday 16th June when the local civilian population came in their thousands to be entertained at Leeming's "Open Day" with films, a football match, a softball game and other functions accompanied by a buffet in the hangers followed by a dance. As the "Darlington and Stockton Times" accurately stated:

"The occasion will be remembered by the visitors who were only too glad to acknowledge their gratitude to the Royal Canadian Air Force."

Northallerton despite continued austerity, soon returned to peacetime events including: the publication of the first list of fifty pupils who had passed the new 11+ examination to enter Northallerton Grammar School of which sixteen were from, the Northallerton National School; the Northallerton Show and Gymkhana was held at Broomfield on Saturday 14th July with 350 entries, the Green Howards band in attendance and the proceeds going to the Rutson Hospital.

The highlight of these months was the first General Election in the Richmondshire Division for a decade in July. Sir Thomas Dugdale the incumbent MP had been knighted in the New Year's Honours List of 1945. He was firm favourite to retain the seat against his opponents: Maurice W. Darwin the Liberal candidate a very popular local auctioneer and valuer from Northallerton; G.H. Metcalfe, Labour, hoping to open up the constituency for his party; and Corporal Roy N. Chesterton of the new Commonwealth party.

The electioneering was determined and forceful with all four candidates appearing at Northallerton often supported by nationally familiar figures. Maurice Darwin the Liberal representative was particularly indefatigable once speaking at six meetings in a day and holding a record late meeting for the Richmondshire constituency speaking until midnight under the famed old oak tree at Redmire. Hubert Thornley the North Riding Clerk of the Peace and Returning Officer finally announced the election result from the Northallerton Town Hall balcony as follows:

Major Sir T.L. Dugdale (Conservative) 18,332
M.W. Darwin (Liberal) 9427
G.H. Metcalfe (Labour) 6104
Corporal R.N. Chesterton (Commonwealth) 813
Majority: 8905

Decisive as this victory was the Conservative majority was halved compared with the 1935 election despite Sir Thomas Dugdale's stature and popularity in the constituency, which probably reflected the overall swing in the country against Winston Churchill's Conservatives which led to a landslide Labour victory. Maurice Darwin was the most successful Liberal candidate since Francis Dyke Acland won the Richmondshire seat in 1906.

Local men and women from every branch of the Services were "demobbed" and returned home, as did Prisoners of War. Accompanying the joy of peace was of course the tragedy of lost loved ones amongst the prime young men of the district. Forty one Northallerton servicemen failed to return along with others from Romanby and Brompton. The losses from Northallerton Grammar School were twenty old boys - almost double those of the 1914-18 war. The Northallerton dead were commemorated on the Northallerton War Memorial in the Parish churchyard, alongside those killed in the First Great World War. No 6 Bomber Group Royal Canadian Air Force's sacrifice was also remembered on the Northallerton War Memorial: thousands of Canadian aircrew were killed in the all out bomber offensive waged by No. 6 Group.

The Roll of Honour of those killed from Northallerton took the form of a wooden tablet worked by Robert Thompson of Kilburn ("The Mouseman") which was placed on the western wall inside Northallerton Parish Church and it was dedicated on 13th November 1949. Just previously on 31st October 1949 Northallerton Grammar School's memorial to its twenty fallen Old Alvertonians was unveiled and dedicated by the Archbishop of York Dr Cyril Garbutt. It consisted of wrought-iron gates set into rustic brick pillars at each end of the north and south drives with a bronze plaque inscribed with the twenty names of the dead.

11

The Post War Revolution – (1945 to 1974)

Social Revolution

Such was the magnitude of change in Northallerton and its environs in the period from the end of the Second World War to that of the twentieth century that contemporary historical judgement and qualitative analysis of advances, trends, aspects and values is difficult. The least to say is that there was an urban revolution and agricultural revolution, a doubling of population which is even more remarkable in an essentially rural community and a technological advance of overwhelming and even bewildering magnitude with an enormous rise in the standard of health and living and a commensurate amelioration and amendment of social and working habits as the computer replaced the quill.

Peace-time Austerity

The first half of the twentieth century had already encompassed two cataclysmic World Wars and it is little wonder that the nation recovered only gradually after 1945 with austerity and bleakness the order of the day despite the undeniable and priceless luxury of peace after total war. Signifying the slow pick-up of living conditions "Rationing" did not end until 1954 but before this there had been a significant uplifting of spirits with the Festival of Britain in 1951.

In Northallerton the latter was celebrated mainly by a production of the "History of Northallerton" over three nights (18th, 20th and 23rd June – Monday, Wednesday and Saturday) staged outside on the Church Green with the ancient Northallerton Parish Church an appropriate backcloth. Edwin Bush the Northallerton Grammar School history master produced this "Pageant" which had scores of locals in the cast.

NORTHALLERTON FESTIVAL

LIST OF EVENTS.

Date.		Place.	Particulars in brief.
1951 APRIL	29th	PARISH CHURCH	**A United Service of Dedication at 3 p.m.** Preacher : The REV. TOM SYKES.
MAY	3rd 4th 5th	ALLERTONSHIRE COUNTY MODERN SCHOOL	ALLERTONSHIRE PLAYERS present "**Wives and Daughters**" by Margaret Mannerers. A three act comedy of the 1900's.
	10th	TOWN HALL	CHORAL SOCIETY present "**Merrie England**" at 7-30 p.m.
	18th	TOWN HALL	**Chamber Music—Recital** at 7-30 p.m. by CLIFFORD J. WALKER (Violin), A. MATTINSON WILSON (Piano).
JUNE (Entire month)		MOUNT GRACE PRIORY	**Collection of Manuscripts and things of interest will be shown within the Priory.**
	3rd	PARISH CHURCH	**Choral Society—Concert of Music** at 2-30 p.m. 15th Century—20th Century.
	16th	HIGH STREET	**Parade of Veteran and Vintage Cars** Organised by the Local Road Safety Committee.
	18th 20th 23rd	NORTH SIDE OF PARISH CHURCH and CHURCH GREEN	The Citizens of the Town and District present **THE HISTORY OF NORTHALLERTON.** **A Pageant in Six Scenes** at 7-30 p.m. By the Rev. I. N. Jury, Rector of Spennithorne. (If wet the Pageant will be given on the following week-day.)
June to June	18th 23rd	BAPTIST SCHOOLROOM	**Replica of the Upper Room of Talbot House, Poperinghe** (known as Toc. H.) Open at 6-0 p.m. each evening. THE BISHOP OF WHITBY will give an address on June 20th, at 9 p.m.
June to June	19th 23rd	NORTH END METHODIST SCHOOLROOM	**AN EXHIBITION** by the British and Foreign Bible Society, showing various phases in the history of the Society.
June	28th 29th 30th	PARISH CHURCH	The Mothers' Union Branches in the Northallerton Deanery will present at 7-0 p.m. **Tableaux Vivants.**
July	28th	SPORTS GROUND of Dried Milk Products, Ltd.	**Open Contest for Brass Bands.**
September 1st to September 8th		MARKET HALL	Northallerton and District Model Engineers an **Exhibition of Models and Handicrafts.**
September 29th		CHURCH HOUSE	**Orchestral Concert By the Salon Orchestra.**

Festival of Britain – Northallerton Events 1951

318

Crowds of six hundred watched each evening's performance and musical highlights included the appearance of the RAF Leeming Pipe Band and the 'Te Deum' set to a Gregorian chant by A Mattinson ("Gerry") Wilson. Percy Hartley the Northallerton Town Clerk said that "the success exceeded all expectations."

Housing and Water

By this time too outstanding processes were afoot in Northallerton's 'real' world. Firstly determined and ambitious plans were implemented to ameliorate the lot of a large section of the population by re-housing them from the age-old and often dilapidated housing in the sunless and sometimes insanitary housing in the 'yards' to newly designed and built Council Houses on the eastern Bullamoor Road area of the town. Northallerton Urban District Council initiated the scheme by building the first Council Houses to form Prospect View off Crosby Road in 1947 and at the same time Northallerton Rural District Council started building Council Houses in the surrounding villages including Romanby (Neile Close) and Brompton (Hilton Green).

As an adjunct to the new housing a 'water scheme' had been devised by Northallerton UDC in May 1949 to improve the water supply to the town by the construction of a new reservoir at Sheep Wash valley near Osmotherley which was approved by the Ministry of Health and upon which work was started by November 1951. The initial estimate of £120,000 rose to £276,180 by November 1953 and finally to £564,070 with the Ministry of Housing and Local Government contributing £145,000. Sir Thomas Dugdale MP for Richmondshire officially opened the Cod Beck Reservoir in November 1954 attended by the full Urban District Council, its officials and Chairman William Wake.

The Friarage Hospital

Contemporaneously, another development absolutely vital to the town, district and entire population had quietly taken place. In November 1947 the Royal Air Force had vacated the hospital at Northallerton which had served an essential and highly professional wartime service but one in peace-time which was no longer required. For several months a hiatus prevailed when the future of the hospital

319

Black Bull Yard (left) Waterloo Terrace (right) 1954

Priory Close Old Peoples' Bungalows 1961

was in doubt and "squatters" – civilian residents without homes – had occupied some of the now disused outer buildings.

However, in the summer of 1948 in the face of a poliomyelitis epidemic the Adela Shaw Children's Orthopaedic Hospital at Kirbymoorside was so overwhelmed with victims of the outbreak that two wards were re-opened at the Northallerton hospital to cope with the emergency. Children from Teesside and North Yorkshire were admitted, Dr Gilbert Parker a Middlesbrough orthopaedic consultant overseered the situation and the hospital was functioning so well that by "the appointed day" 5th July 1948 of the launching of the National Health Service the hospital was designated a general hospital in its own right in the NHS area of the Newcastle Regional Hospital Board.

The Management Committee of the Rutson Hospital with its Chairman John Westwood Adamson became the Management Committee of the Northallerton Group of Hospitals and in September 1948 they named the Northallerton former wartime emergency hospital 'The Friarage Hospital Northallerton' after the Carmelite Friary that had existed on the site from 1356 to 1539. The Northallerton Group consisted of the Rutson, Mount (maternity) and Friarage hospitals and remained as such until 1974.

As the major hospital unit the Friarage developed consistently professionally but it also became fundamentally essential because of its sheer 'geographical necessity' centred as it was in a vast rural area, adjacent to the arterial roads the A1, A19 and A167, with their ever mounting traffic and accident incidence and next to the main east coast railway line almost equi-distant between London and Edinburgh.

The strong rapport between the hospital and town so evident during the war continued and indeed the Friarage Hospital was the latest phase of the strong Northallerton hospital tradition that reached back to 1200 and the medieval St James Hospital. Of primary importance in the Friarage's progress was the commencement of nurse training with first an Orthopaedic Training School in 1948 and then in January 1949 the establishment of a general training school for State Registered Nurses which ensured a cadre of home-grown and dedicated nursing staff for the next four decades. In 1954 the Matron (1952 to 1963) Cassie Harker said of the nurses:

"They are our first ambassadors and to a very great extent our reputation lies in their hands."

Always significant was the atmosphere and ambience of the Friarage which Cassie Harker referred to in her book "Call Me Matron" when she wrote:

"Above all it was a happy place, not only for the staff but also as far as possible for the patients. The surroundings were not exactly beautiful but the spirit of the place impressed everyone."

Such a spirit in adversity was certainly vital in the hospital of thick brown lino floors flanked by dismal cream or green walls with big black coke stoves in the middle of the mainly wooden wards which had to be replenished night and day by porters. But as the later Clinical Nurse Manager JR ("Bobby") Cooper who came to the hospital as a student nurse in 1955 recalled there was much development:

"As well as orthopaedic wards, surgical, medical, elderly care, tuberculosis and plastic surgery wards were opened. There were Out-Patients, accident and emergency facilitities, physiotherapy and x-ray departments. The hospital received patients from Darlington and Teesside as well as our own vast area. Originally there were four children's wards, almost 100 beds."

New Houses for Old

The obvious and acute post-war housing shortage in Northallerton had been highlighted by the "squatters" encroachment into any available buildings. Essentially too, however, there was an underlying emphatic local urge and drive to get rid of the out-dated accommodation of the "yards" branching off the High Street and North End. Additionally in the housing quest there was a strong movement by the Northallerton Urban District Council spear-headed by its forward-looking, energetic and persuasive Town Clerk, Percy Hartley, appointed from Boston, Lincolnshire in 1946, to attract new industries to the town which in turn would require adequate housing facilities for the anticipated incoming work force.

By May 1953 two hundred and ninety Council Houses had been built to the west of Bullamoor Road (including Pinfold Drive, Bullamoor Road itself, Central Drive, Valley Road, Greenhowskye Lane and the Crescent) which had increased to four hundred and forty two by December 1954. Old Age Pensioners bungalows were also built initially at Priory Close in 1954 next to the Friarage Hospital, followed by Byland Avenue in 1958, Hutchinson Drive in 1962 and the Castle Close complex in 1966. The Northallerton Rural District Council also built seven OAP bungalows in Borrowby (RBA Moody Bros £9,540) and fourteen in Romanby (Walter Thompson Ltd £19,039).

August 1963 saw the Urban District Council with six hundred and fifteen houses and the Rural District Council with three hundred and seventy four houses spread through its villages including Brompton and those such as the Fairway at Romanby. Parallel to the rapid Council housing revolution had been the 'clearance' of the yards which still contained such well known housing places as Waterloo, Flag, Clapham's, and Lewis and Cooper's yards and Market and New Rows. However, the UDC had announced a 'slum clearance' plan in September 1955 to displace the yard housing be it good or bad. By another decade the housing had been cleared in these yards and in November 1965 the then Chairman of the UDC Councillor Charles Sawdon was able to announce that "all unfit property had been destroyed" calling it "a remarkable achievement."

Contemporaries would be quick to point out that many of the cottages in the yards were neat, well-kept and very adequate and in addition speculate darkly about the haphazard reallocation and redevelopment as well as of the vacuum left by the disappearance of the yards. Probably much more in an ascetic building connection could have been achieved in the replacement of the yards and such an example as the pleasant aspect of Romanby Court bears this out. However, the yard clearance was achieved in half the time envisaged in 1955, 434 people in 168 families were rehoused and in 1961 there were 2377 inhabited properties in Northallerton which was double the number in 1931. The 'Darlington and Stockton Times' echoed Councillor Sawdon by calling it "a truly noble achievement."

Further developments mushroomed up Bullamoor Road and by July 1971 when Percy Hartley the Town Clerk retired (having been at the thrust of the urban change since 1946) there were one thousand five hundred Council Houses. Side by side had been an enormous surge in building the private area for example at Broomfield Avenue (Almond Grove 1964 and Ormesby Crescent 1966), Turker Lane and Winton Road (1968), and off Crosby Road and Mill Hill by 1968. The latter houses are technically in Romanby and therefore RDC, though inter-locked with Northallerton, and relevantly the really extensive private housing drive has been to the south and west towards and in Romanby: for example Pennine View and Newsham Way in 1964. Between 1966 and 1971 3300 people moved into new council and private properties.

A new Bullamoor Council Housing plan in 1968 saw over five hundred and fifty houses erected by the Council and in 1978 significantly an equal number of eighty Council and eighty private houses were authorised at Knottabottom signalling an important policy change of an admixture on the newly developed estates of private and council housing under the new authority of Hambleton District Council.

High Street and Shops

Simultaneously with the housing development changes were taking place in the High Street and town centre which would gradually transform Northallerton as it moved through the gears – an apt description considering the enormous impact and domination by the motor car – into the twenty first century.

In 1952 sodium discharge lighting was installed for £2,200 which the local paper declared "added an atmosphere of warmth and friendliness to the town centre." Signs of shopping things to come and the supercedence of large stores in place of the multiplicity of small shops appeared on 23rd July 1954 when Woolworths opened a store on the High Street, Broughs became the first self-service grocery shop in 1960, Claphams opened a café within their multi-store in May 1958 and Barkers followed suit in 1960. The latter had increased in size five times from 1950 until 1962 taking advantage of new space available from demolished yards and with a length of 300 feet from front to back by 1963 was the largest store in the United Kingdom of a similar sized town to Northallerton.

A vital development which was to be crucial to Northallerton's viability as a shopping centre was the creation of the Applegarth Car Park which was opened by 1963 access having been gained from the High Street by the demolition of the "Central" cinema which had outlived its hey-day mainly with the arrival of television to the town in 1953.

Public Houses

Other old centres of sociability and refreshment which disappeared were some of the time-honoured public houses – the 'Oak Tree in 1958, the 'Three Tuns' in December 1964 and at the North End the 'Railway Hotel' 1946 and the 'Rose and Crown' in January 1965. It should be added, however, that a public house had been opened on the new Council estate in January 1956 called 'The Jolly Minister' after the Minister for Housing Derek Heathcote-Amory MP. Northallerton, the Ale Town of yore, was a-changing.

The Richest Town?

The town image was one of progress and prosperity and the latter had been emphasised and publicised in 1953 when Northallerton was tagged "The Richest Town in the Country" by a Report issued by the Inland Revenue based on income tax returns per head of population. Obviously this led to much press comment and comparison but the Inland Revenue reiterated their findings in November 1954. The wealth of the town was substantiated by reference to a 1950 census of distribution which gave Northallerton an impressive turnover of £1,332,000 for 167 trading concerns and a population increase from 1931 to 1961 (6,726 total) of 27% which incidentally did not include Romanby which had soared from less than a thousand to 3,962 which was approaching Northallerton's population of 4,786 in 1931! A final interesting statistic of April 1955 given by the North East Independent Development Association was that Northallerton led the way in the entire North East of England with the highest proportion of working women who constituted 35% of the work force.

War Memorial Swimming Baths

A matter of some importance and unfortunate controversy to its very end was the Northallerton War Memorial to the fallen of the town in the Second World War. A War Memorial Committee was set up and funds raised from 1945 in various ways – Saturday night dances in the Town Hall being both a major source of revenue and of endearing memory to that generation of young people. After much procrastination as to the form of the memorial, at a public referendum in 1956 it was opted to build a War Memorial Swimming Bath – Northallerton's first ever such facility – which was designed by RS Mortimer, architect and built by Walter Thompson Ltd at a cost of £27,746. Lady Masham, supported by the Chairman of Northallerton UDC Kenneth Hird opened the baths in June 1961 which were immediately popular and well used especially by the local schools and Royal Air Force Leeming.

The Hill Report

In 1964 Northallerton Urban District Council commissioned architects Peter B Hill (Leeds) to examine the High Street and the subsequent Hill Report of November 1964 recommended a need for unity of decoration and the ridding of festooning overhead wires. One hundred and ten properties entered into this High Street Improvement Plan which was put into effect and opened by T Dan Smith Chairman of the Northern Region Economic Council on 10th October 1966. It greatly improved the aspect, uniformity and appearance of the High Street which never looked back in this respect.

Town Planning

The North Riding County Council Town Plan of August 1965 allowed for a population of 13,700 by 1981, the Northallerton UDC wanted an increase of 30,000 which was refused and on the basis of the evidence of the industries with their economic vicissitudes who came to Northallerton, the North Riding planners were vindicated in their judgement. In September 1979 Hambleton District Council wanted a town growth of 20,000 but again the North Yorkshire planners stuck to the Draft Plan of growth to 18,500 by 1991. The Northallerton plan incidentally included both Brompton and Romanby in its deliberations and the prognoses were for these villages and Northallerton as a whole.

New Water Supply

To cope with the increased water demand of a rising population and incoming new industries such as Kossett Carpets in July 1967, the "Dales and Northallerton Water Board" which had been formed by the Ministry of Housing and Local Government in 1962, activated a new scheme at the Thornton Steward Reservoir (near Ripon) to extract water from the river Ure at a cost of £2,000,000. The Chairman, who was appropriately William Wake of Northallerton, cut the first sod on the 26th November 1972 and the reservoir containing 215 million gallons of water and supplying 3.3 million gallons daily was in operation by 1975.

Traffic Growth

The multiplicity of traffic was an advancing and urgent problem for in the mid 1960s over four thousand cars were travelling daily through Northallerton via Thirsk or Darlington and in May 1979 a "pedestrian check" revealed that over 7,000 people crossed the High Street on weekdays with a Wednesday peak of 13,448. Siting of zebra crossings and traffic lights in the middle of the High Street and the

Romanby junction alleviated the pedestrian safety problem but car parking and traffic congestion remained a major difficulty. Despite being opposed at a Public Meeting at the Town Hall in January 1972, disc parking and regulatory yellow lines were introduced in May 1973.

High Street Bypass

The greatest controversy, however, centred around the plan of the North Riding County Council introduced in 1972 to by-pass the High Street with a western approach road which would necessarily incorporate part of the Applegarth. In May 1972 Northallerton UDC supported Phase One of this Town Plan which provided a link road between South Parade and East Road cutting through the eastern High Street just north of the "Nag's Head". However, the UDC unanimously rejected Phase Three which mainly included the Applegarth approach road, their decision endorsing an active and well-supported movement which had held a public meeting in the Applegarth School in April 1972 from which the "Save the Applegarth Campaign" emerged.

Over a thousand letters of protest were sent to Peter Walker the Minister for the Environment and when in April 1973 the North Riding County Council had not withdrawn the Applegarth Road Scheme the outcry reached new heights against what was termed "an attack on our heritage". The essence of the objection was that the Applegarth had been gifted to the townspeople of Northallerton as a war memorial to the town's fallen in the First World War by Mrs Hird and family and others in 1918. As such it was said to be sacrosanct and it was believed that the County Council did not have the legal entitlement to implement the plan. Ultimately the North Riding County Council did not go ahead with the Applegarth Road Scheme but the link road outlined in Phase One was completed and opened in 1977 taking traffic, especially heavy vehicles, around the rear of the High Street thus greatly improving Northallerton's traffic flow.

Lost Buildings

In the sometimes seemingly frenetic process of demolition and rebuilding through the 1950s and 1960s into the 1970s much old High Street property disappeared and though development was essential the loss of some buildings and their replacement with oblongesque modern structures was much regretted especially then by the older town generation, and retrospectively by many more. Particular examples were the High Street tree clad entry to Registry House and Zetland Street's northern corner, the old 'King's Head' building replaced by the Central Arcade and "Willie Green's" tobacconist shop with a unique gabled end facing the High Street north west with the Waycot Café next door which were demolished in 1959 with a modern shop 'Babyland' their replacement.

Trade and Industry

Attraction and encouragement of industry was a major objective of post-war Northallerton's Urban District Council and though the town was essentially an administrative and agricultural centre, industry played an important part centred at the North End and Romanby Road/Springwell Lane areas. One precept had remained constant throughout the town's long history – older industries died out but were replaced by contemporary ones.

For example the linoleum factory at Malpas Road which had closed in 1938 was never re-activated but new industries used and sprang up in its buildings. Helix Springs, set up here in 1947 by VGK Walters to manufacture mattress springs thrived until the 1970s; Allerton Industries opened in 1947 by Michael Wilson, a member of the Northallerton Operatic Society Wilson family, with an outlay of £150 and flourished sufficiently to move to a new factory on Darlington Road in 1968 and had a £6 million order book by 1974; Kellett and Pick's motor vehicle repairs element 'Alverton' had commenced here during the Second World War recovering Army vehicles.

Earnshaws

The most progressive and successful firm on the site was Earnshaws Ltd, which produced dyes and pigment finishes for the leather trade. It was brought here from Huddersfield in 1947 by Bill Earnshaw with seven workers, built up an extensive international order book trading especially with India and Pakistan and by the time it opened a new five acre factory on Darlington Road in September 1979 (having moved to this industrial estate in August 1976) had 75 workers and £3 million sales orders. Bill Earnshaw was awarded the MBE in 1966 and the firm has flourished into the new Millenium.

Closures

The transitory nature of Northallerton's industry was also seen, however, with the demise of several formerly well-known and prosperous firms and organisations. Thomas Hay's flour mills stopped milling, and engaged in warehousing until final closure in the early 1970s. Northallerton's oldest industry tanning from time immemorial was phased out with Walker's Tannery at North Arch off the Church Green being closed in July 1963 by its owners for the past twenty years Fleming and Woodall of Halifax. It was one of the last oak-bark tanneries in the country, had once supplied the red and gold saddlery of Grand Duke Nicholas of Russia and its retiring manager Harold Brown was of the fifth family generation to work at the tannery.

Another reminder of changing craft and times was the death in 1960 aged ninety five of Frank Finlay Clarkson the peerless gold and silversmith who from his High Street shop (now the site of "Safeway") had supplied Queen Mary with his hand wrought masterpieces, had worked assiduously into his nineties and notably in 1950 had fashioned the gold ornamental chain for the Chairman of Northallerton UDC – now adorning the Mayor of Northallerton on official occasions. Place's timber yard which had employed an ample number over several decades closed down in the 1960s as did the North End railway Goods Yard opposite on 31st March 1968 when fourteen drivers were made redundant.

Earlier Bell and Goldsbrough's mineral water factory on Brompton Road had ceased trading in the later 1950s and the Northallerton Gas Company on Crosby Road behind the Northallerton gaol had gradually reduced its staff and had finally closed with the coming of the North Sea Gas supply to the town in July 1970.

New Firms

However, new firms were being constantly wooed to the town by the UDC with its available industrial land which it had had the foresight to purchase on Darlington Road. The two major firms which came to Northallerton and provided over four hundred jobs between them were 'Kossett Carpets' and 'York Trailers'. 'Kossett Carpets' of Brighouse, West Yorkshire opened the first phase of their operation, a £300,000 new factory on the Darlington Road industrial estate, on 14th July 1967 and were eventually to employ two hundred and ten workers. 'York

Cow and Gate Factory - 1956

Trailers' who had originated in Northamptonshire in 1958 manufacturing vehicle containers re-located a branch to Northallerton and had a fully automated factory operating off Yafforth Road by May 1968 with promise of expansion by millionaire Canadian owner Fred Davies to a work force of two hundred and fifty.

Flourishing Firms

Several other firms were thriving at the same time. John Teesdale, structural engineers, located off Romanby Road in 1946 from Wetherby were still going strongly. The 'Sashless Windows' company initiated by Redvers Chown set up in 1966 in Tannery Lane and later moved to Darlington Road. "JSW and Son" coach builders opened in 1963 and by 1966 had moved to permanent premises adjacent to the Lyric Cinema. Spark Print (Directors Geoff and Jim Spark) who produced electronic labels were given a UDC loan of £15,000 moved into a new factory at the North End in 1969 and became one of the country's largest producer of electronic labels.

By 1969 John Willis of Newby Wiske was one of the country's leading frozen turkey producers and another agricultural enterprise Farm

Feed Formulators opened an animal feeds plant on the Darlington Road estate in May 1972. Meanwhile the main agricultural providers in the area were Sam Turners who after the Second World War moved from Boroughbridge Road to Quaker Lane as they expanded.

Amongst the leading Northallerton firms were some which had been established locally for some time. The milk factory down Romanby Road changed from "Cow and Gate" to "Dried Milk Products" and by 1972 had been taken over by "Unigate" but throughout sustained a regular work force turning out quality milk products maintaining the reputation the factory had had since its inception at the start of the twentieth century. The Vale of Mowbray (VOM) bacon factory at Leeming Bar, was taken over in 1962 by CT Harris Ltd of Calne, Wiltshire and fore-shadowing future large firm rationalisation to come, in June 1968 fifty workers (including forty women) were made redundant when the sausage roll and pie making process was moved to Calne.

Sunters

Another prominent local firm which became part of a national conglomerate "United Transport" in the mid 1960s was "Sunters" heavy haulage experts which had been started in the Yorkshire Dales by the Sunter brothers Leonard, Thomas and Joseph in 1932 with wood haulage and moved to Boroughbridge Road, Northallerton in 1941 since when it had prospered to become by 1959 the third largest company of its kind in the country under the General Managership of Len Sunter. Large loads were a speciality and for example in January 1960 a fifty five tons 120 feet steel tower was taken from Stockton to Manchester which was one of the largest loads ever moved on a UK road. The firm was still thriving in 1974 when it possessed a vehicle that could move a load of four hundred and twenty tons and the firm's General Manager Peter Sunter who had succeeded his father Len in 1966, was elected Chairman of the National Road Haulage Association.

Building Firms

With so much building activity in Northallerton and district it followed that the local building firms would benefit and three that prospered were DM Willoughbys, RBA Moody Bros Ltd and Walter Thompson Ltd. The latter particularly were not only involved locally with houses, schools and other projects but also on a regional basis to the extent that by 1970 they were the largest employer of local labour (apart of course from the North Riding County Council) with two hundred and fifty workers. They were essentially a family firm headed by Stanley Thompson, who had succeeded his father Walter the founder and in common with Barkers another successful local business, they periodically selected members of their work force as Directors to sit on the controlling Board of Directors. Expertise and loyalty were thus reciprocal and rewarded.

Sir Ellis Hunter

Finally a local resident was literally a giant of national industry. Sir Ellis Hunter (born in 1882) the son of a Great Ayton village school head teacher attended Middlesbrough High School, trained as an accountant and rose to become the Managing Director of Dorman Long steel company. He moved to the Northallerton area in 1941 to live at Howden Gate, Ainderby Road and was knighted in 1947 having been elected President of the British Iron and Steel Federation in 1946. Intransigent in his opposition to the nationalisation of the Iron and Steel industry he lived at Howden Gate until his death in 1961.

Agricultural Transformation

Despite the post-war industrial upsurge the staple local economic sustenance and environmental influence was agriculture as befitted a nodal market town. However, enormous changes took place in the agrarian sphere largely due to mechanisation and advancing science and technology. Indeed another virtual "Agricultural Revolution" occurred.

Some brief facts illustrate the transformation: at the Northallerton Candlemas (February) horse sale in 1947 there were 80 entries, at that of 1951 there were only 20 horses and this time-honoured annual event ceased thenceforward; in 1938 the North Riding of Yorkshire had 393 tractors and by 1959 the tractor numbers had soared to 10,374; and within a year in 1950/51 five hundred farm workers left the land in the North Riding.

Simultaneously because of mechanisation and modern scientific advances which had made for greatly intensified farming the North Riding experienced great increases in productivity. From 1939 to December 1954 in the North Riding: wheat yield increased by five hundredweight per acre; milk production went up by eighty four per cent; and potatoes yielded an extra ton per acre.

Essentially farming needed fewer and fewer hands, agriculture became intensive and the whole agrarian culture altered. For example farming peaks such as hay, harvest and potato-picking "times" which had called for extra labour from the town to the farms and were a series of social concourses as well as joint working were no more. Obviously the numbers of farm workers living on the farms or in nearby villages decimated and Northallerton Wednesday market days gradually but perceptibly changed atmosphere and character with a lessening of farming numbers, participation and animation. Market days in Northallerton were just different – epitomised probably as much as anything by the absence of the horse and the overwhelming preponderance of the motor car.

Agricultural Administration

Northallerton remained the centre of the area's agricultural administration with the Ministry of Agriculture siting in 1952 new "Government Buildings" on the north side of Crosby Road as the Divisional headquarters with the Regional centre located at Leeds. Farm improvements were greatly encouraged by a government scheme strongly advocated by the North Riding's agricultural administrators to the extent that between September 1957 and 1962 two thousand "improvement" applications were processed and £3 million paid out in grants. Additionally new and experimental methods in farming were implemented – for example in 1954 'Land Tests' were carried out on strips of land at the Cinnamire Farm of Mr George Corner on Darlington Road.

Marts

In the early post-war years animals were still often driven to mart on Tuesday or Wednesdays and rail transport was still operative. However, as motorised animal transport rapidly and remarkably improved, this method completely took over and the economics and the face of the marts altered. Of the three Northallerton marts the Malpas Mart, which had amalgamated with that of the Applegarth in 1935, closed for the sale of animals in March 1951 and from thenceforth only held sales of agricultural machinery and implements.

The Station Mart carried on steadfastly sharing alternate Tuesday 'mart days' with the Applegarth Mart but the latter had double the business year in year out until the Station Mart closed in January 1981. As early as 1946 the Applegarth Mart with Maurice Darwin and Henry Metcalfe as auctioneers and John Todd before them, was acknowledged as "one of the best centres in the country for the Sales of sheep, store cattle and cows". The 1950s saw great improvements in the animal pens and auction ring and by 1964/65 it had a turnover of £2 million which had doubled to £4 million in 1973/74 and then continued to increase.

Agricultural Shows

Northallerton Agricultural Show officially reappeared in July 1948 at Broomfield Farm with a large crowd in attendance although it had appeared in muted form as Northallerton Gymkhana each year since 1944 on the same site by permission of Mr Almond. It ultimately became the North Yorkshire County Show in 1979.

Farming Unions

Both the union of employers – the National Farmers' Union (NFU) – and that of the farm workers – the National Union of Agricultural Workers (NUAgW) – were very strong in the Northallerton area as typified by respective high profile occasions. On 10th January 1953 the Ministry of Agriculture, Sir Thomas Dugdale the popular local MP addressed at length a packed NFU membership in the Northallerton Town Hall, a meeting that was widely and nationally reported upon. In July 1956 the NUAgW held a Jubilee Rally in Northallerton which featured a magnificent parade of "dressed" horses and in a convivial atmosphere of goodwill the Archbishop of York Dr Michael Ramsey dedicated the Union banner, the ceremony being attended by NUAgW President EG Gooch and Tom Williams the former Minister of Agriculture. Previously on Saturday 1st October 1955 Hugh Gaitskell (the future Labour Party leader) was the guest of honour at the NUAgW annual dinner at Northallerton.

Young Farmers

The Young Farmers Club movement was particularly virile and inventive in Northallerton and district. A highlight of each year was the 'Darlington and Stockton Times' North Riding Young Farmers' Clubs

Speaking Contest and in February 1950 at the Allertonshire School the Northallerton YF Club won the trophy for the first of several times. Overseas visits such as those by Dick Willis to New Zealand (1950) and Don Farndale to Finland (1962) emphasised the inter-change of ideas and the North Riding YFCs community spirit and great sociability were typified by the Annual Rally (26 clubs took part in 1964) and the Annual County Ball held at Northallerton Town Hall, the film producer Anthony Asquith being the guest of honour in 1952.

In November 1963 speaking at the North Riding Young Farmers Clubs Federation annual prize giving ceremony at Northallerton Professor TL Baywater, Head of Leeds University Agricultural Department, summed up the YFCs achievements when maintaining that the Young Farmers Clubs had been a major force and influence in farming during the last thirty years. Northallerton YFC proved it was in continuing good heart and spirit when it won the national YFC trophy for "Our Club Entertains" in 1971 and received a civic reception by Northallerton Urban District Council for this outstanding feat.

Television Coverage

With television in its comparative infancy in the Northallerton district any local TV exposure was greeted with great interest. This was the case when ABC/TV's outside broadcast on Sunday 27th December 1959 as part of a series "The Other Man's Farm" featured Pasture House farm, Thirsk Road the home of Mr Leslie and Mrs Dorothy Barker. The 'live' programme lasted an hour and a quarter giving much local and regional pleasure. In May 1960 the work of Northallerton Young Farmer's Club was seen in a BBC documentary 'A Country Wedding' which was filmed partly in the Zion schoolroom, Northallerton.

Vehicles, Roads, Accidents

Crucial to Northallerton in all its aspects were its communications of road and rail and here again enormous changes were effected in the post-war period.

The sheer added volume of traffic on the roads was the most obvious and consequential factor. Illustrative of this was that in Northallerton in the pre-war period five garages with petrol pumps had sprung up on the High Street. And by the mid 1970s all the petrol pumps had gone – whisked away by the very thing that had brought

First Local TV Outside Broadcast – Pasture House 1959

them there – the motor car and its multiplicity but bringing congestion in its wake.

Other petrol stations were available on the periphery of the town – Neasham's, South Parade; Smirthwaite's East Road; Motor Delivery, Brompton Road; Archibald, North End; and Stone Cross – but traffic congestion had brought the demise of those on the High Street. Although the major town roads were as before, numerous new roads were built around Northallerton and in Romanby to accommodate the new council and private housing estates as well as the industrial and commercial developments as 'greater' Northallerton mushroomed outwards.

Of course the utility of the motor vehicle goes without saying but its consequence in the way of accidents especially deaths was staggering. In the North Riding the accident death toll on the roads was 63 in 1951, 90 in 1960, 120 in 1969 and in 1970 an almost unbelievable 163. No wonder that in December 1959 Miss Bridget Talbot of Kiplin Hall near Scorton called a meeting in the local public house to "stop murder on the roads".

Accident 'black-spots' abounded around Northallerton and much was done to alleviate these – on the Northallerton to Leeming Bar road alone the road was radically improved at Howden Bridge (the by-pass was opened in 1957 when the now picturesque cherry trees were planted), Ainderby and Scruton lane ends. The same could be applied to all the main roads converging on the town. The North Riding Highways Department at Northallerton that was responsible for the improvements was quietly but indefatigably led by the County Surveyor, Ronald Sawtell of Racecourse Lane, Northallerton.

By far the most dangerous road was the A1 between Dishforth and Catterick particularly at Leeming Lane where accident mayhem and often carnage were commonplace. For example in 1961 before the Leeming by-pass was opened in November, seventeen people were killed on the A1 in the Leeming area and it was stated in May 1961 that the Friarage Hospital had dealt with two hundred and fifty road accidents casualties a month, the majority from the A1. The other local North Riding by-passes opened were the Catterick by-pass in December 1959 and the Boroughbridge by-pass in May 1964.

Obviously the Friarage Hospital was central to the road accident situation and it continually had to rise to emergency situations acquitting itself admirably. Two such crises from which the hospital and its staff emerged with great credit were coach crashes: in June 1964 at Birdforth involving twenty nine women, fourteen of whom were treated in the Friarage; and in August 1971 when a bus carrying elderly women ran away and hit a cottage at Helmsley with ten killed – eight in the coach and two in a car – and all the casualties were attended to at the Friarage.

Railways

The hospital also has an emergency procedure in the event of an accident on the adjacent main London to Edinburgh railway line and this had to swing into operation on 31st July 1967 when a concrete carrying freight train encroached in the path of a Kings Cross to Scotland express causing a crash ten miles south of Northallerton in which seven were killed and forty three were injured and ferried to the Friarage, which was highly praised for its efficiency, professionalism, treatment and after care of the casualties. The doctors and nurses were particularly commended in an official statement:

"The hospital staff were magnificent."

By this time of course the expresses were slashing the times of the London to Edinburgh journey by employing faster and more efficient locomotives. In 1961 the 3300 HP Delta diesel started to run cutting the east road main line Edinburgh to London journey to six hours. And in 1977 the much vaunted 125 High Speed trains began to run (accomplishing the London to Edinburgh journey in 4 ½ hours) which

Northallerton Station 1956 – original 1841 gable ends

had been mainly tried and tested on the long straight stretch of main line going through Northallerton Station. The Northallerton to London journey was reduced to two and a half hours on the direct running trains and less than three hours changing at York. Shades of the "Stage-Coach" era of two days at best only a hundred and thirty years before!

The railways had been nationalised in 1948 and came under British Rail in 1965. Before the mid-seventies there had been a great retraction in passenger lines and services and facilities at Northallerton's Victorian railway station which were precursors to its complete demolition in 1986. The picturesque Wensleydale passenger service with twelve stops between Northallerton and Hawes – an excellent Dales facility but one which was losing £14,000 a year – was closed for stated economic reasons for passenger travel on Saturday 24th April 1954. Now historic, the last passenger train left Garsdale for Northallerton at 6.40 pm carrying forty two First Class passengers and around one hundred and forty others. In 1964 the line closed for goods traffic beyond Redmire and from then until 1992 one goods train made a daily weekday return run from Redmire to Teesside with thirty six trucks carrying limestone for the steelworks.

After the "Beeching Plan" review of the railways, amidst much protest Brompton passenger station on the Teesside line was closed in November 1964 and then in September 1966 the closure of the Northallerton-Ripon-Harrogate line was announced by British Rail. The latter brought immediate protest by Northallerton Urban District

The Last Dales Passenger Run 1954

Council to Barbara Castle the Minister of Transport on the grounds of the strong and important links with the West Riding, the size and growing importance of Northallerton with its County town status and the advancing growth of the tourist industry. But all of this fell on deaf ears, the direct Northallerton-Ripon-Harrogate line closed and Northallerton station was reduced to two platforms for the main line trains north and south.

Great concern locally arose concerning Northallerton station's future and on 3rd February 1968 the Richmondshire MP Tim Kitson tabled a parliamentary question expressing this anxiety to which he received a non-commital reply from the Ministry of Transport's representative. In March 1969 Sidney Weighell from Northallerton who had become the Assistant General Secretary to the National Union of Railwaymen received a "categoric assurance" of Northallerton's on-going role as a main line active railway station from British Railways Eastern Region serving an expanding and a County town.

However, local pessimism remained as the station's run-down appearance was accentuated with some rooms being boarded up, the closure of the well-known refreshment room in 1969 and then the WH Smith station bookstall on 31st January 1970. When in July 1970 the glass awning was removed from the south-bound platform the desolation increased and though the station never closed the days of its structure and buildings were numbered.

Telephone

Finally, in the sphere of communications the automatic telephone system STD came to Northallerton on the 14th December 1964 in a purpose built new Telephone Exchange erected by Walter Thompsons in 1962 on Alverton Lane directly behind the main Northallerton Post Office. Equipped by Standard Telephone and Cables Ltd over the past year it had 1900 lines. The first exchange had opened in January 1932 with three operating positions to plug in calls and four staff who did work of a crucial nature during the Second World War from the Post Office building. By 1964 there were eighty staff with twenty three positions. In September 1973 Northallerton along with the nation went on to the completely automated STD system with manual operators no longer required – a particularly nostalgic and sad wrench for many.

Northallerton Parish Church

Although the Church of England did not wield the supreme power that it had done in olden days, nevertheless it was still vitally important spiritually, ethically and in influence. Side by side with the other Northallerton religious denominations, in increasingly ecumenical mode, it formed an essential mainstay in the structure and life of the post-war town.

The Reverend Frederick John Talbot Baines having been a stalwart in his wartime Parish moved to Essex to be Vicar of Tendring in 1951 believing that he should make way for a younger man as Vicar of Northallerton where the Reverend Stephen S Thistlewood from St Mary's Church, Monkseaton took his place. Reverend Thistlewood's major legacy in just over a decade as Vicar of Northallerton was the restoration of the Central Tower at an overall cost of £10,000 and included the re-casting and re-hanging of the eight church bells.

In August 1961 the Vicar made an appeal on BBC TV for funds for the restoration and the refurbished Central Tower was re-dedicated by the Bishop of Whitby on the 9th October 1962 and almost immediately afterwards Rev Thistlewood left Northallerton to become Vicar of Myton on Swale. Modernity was the keynote in Reverend Thistlewood's incumbency as he was the first Vicar to dwell in a new Vicarage built adjacent to the previous building which had been taken over by the Northallerton Rural District Council in 1952 and also conducted the first service ever broadcast on TV from Northallerton

Parish Church when the BBC televised the Matins service on 3rd December 1961.

Reverend John Castledine who had been Vicar of Kirkbymoorside was appointed Vicar of Northallerton by the Dean and Chapter of Durham Cathedral in December 1962. In October 1964 the Parish Church was completely redecorated internally, in Christmas 1970 the Church was floodlit for the first time and in May 1971 the organ which had been rebuilt was re-opened. A sad passing at an early age in April 1968 was that of A Mattinson 'Gerry' Wilson who had been the inspirational Choir Master at the Parish Church for many years and the virtuoso of numerous musical performances and productions in Northallerton such as Handel's 'Messiah' which remain in the memory of the generation favoured by his gifts enriched by both character and humanity.

Other Churches

The Wensleyan Methodist Church led by Reverend Lawrence Larter was an active and numerous force at this time and on 11th April 1965 celebrated their centenary on their chapel site with Ada Alsop the famous soprano performing and the President of the Methodist Conference, Rev A Kingsley Lloyd visiting – the first time a President had visited during his year of office. With the population shift more and more towards the eastern side of the town the Council estate and to the west and south with private housing into Romanby two churches made decisions to move their chapels of worship.

In 1953 the Baptists submitted a plan for a new church to the UDC, sold their Friarage Street church (the original Wesleyan chapel) to the Anchor Lodge of Freemasons in 1955 and had raised most of the £7000 needed when the stone laying ceremony by local Baptist elders Tom and Arnold Parry took place on 29th September 1955 on the chosen site on Valley Road. On 27th April 1957 the new chapel designed by architect Cecil Leckenby was opened by Hubert Thornley, the Clerk to the North Riding County Council and the Justices of the Peace and on Monday 29th April soprano Ada Alsop performed there in an inaugural concert. The motto of the church was "Look forward in faith" which was entirely appropriate in relation to their future progress as New Life Baptists.

The South End Methodist Church, built by the Primitive Methodists in the 1890s was sold in March 1964, a site having been earmarked for a new church as early as October 1958 when a fund raising barbeque was held on the designated land at Romanby just off Ainderby Road towards the £13,000 cost. A sod cutting ceremony by Northallerton Methodist Minister Reverend Lawrence Larter took place in March 1964 and in what the Vicar of Northallerton Rev John Castledine termed "a great act of faith" Romanby Methodist Church was opened in 1965.

Other churches flourishing in Northallerton in the post-war era were the Roman Catholic Church under Father Francis Connolly, the United Reform Church at the Zion and of course St James Church Romanby which was very active and well supported in the west of the Parish of Northallerton. At Brompton the Vicar Rev WB Seaton left in February 1957 after thirteen years to take up the urban challenge of St Cuthbert's Middlesbrough. His place was taken by Rev Gordon Robert Cooper who was inducted by the Archbishop of York Dr Michael Ramsey.

Politics and MPs

From 1910 onwards the Richmondshire parliamentary constituency, of which Northallerton became both the nomination and returning centre, was a Conservative Party bastion of marked political stability – in fact for over half the century from 1929 to 1983 the seat was held by only two incumbents Thomas Dugdale and Timothy Kitson both of whom were knighted whilst serving as MPs in 1945 and 1974 respectively.

Sir Thomas Dugdale – Lord Crathorne

In the General Election of February 1950 Sir Thomas Dugdale was returned with a majority of 14,305 which was an increase of 5,400 from his 1945 election success setting a numerical pattern of majorities which was to remain similar for almost four decades for the Conservatives. As was customary the election result was announced from Northallerton Town Hall balcony by the Returning Officer Hubert G Thornley: Sir Thomas Dugdale (Con) 22,999; T W Beaton (Lab) 8694 (his agent being Sidney Weighell of Northallerton and the NUR); D E Moore (Lib) 7157.

Richard Hoyle of Fir Tree Farm near Yarm representing Labour was Sir Thomas' sole opponent in the General Election of 26th October 1951 with the following result: Sir Thomas Dugdale (Con) 26,231;

Richard Hoyle (Lab) 10,915; Conservative majority – 15,316.

Following the election Sir Thomas Dugdale was appointed Minister of Agriculture and Fisheries in the Conservative government – the first Richmondshire MP ever to reach ministerial office. In April 1952 he and Lady Nancy Dugdale (who was a tower of strength to him throughout his political career) were guests of the new Queen at Windsor Castle. In September 1953 Sir Thomas entered the Cabinet but in July 1954 he was forced to resign over the "Crichel Down Affair" receiving much sympathetic Press coverage and praise for his successes as Minister from the Prime Minister Sir Anthony Eden.

In the General Election on 27th May 1955 Sir Thomas again defeated Richard Hoyle (who incidentally had just entertained Clement Attlee at his home) with an increased majority of 16,005: Sir Thomas Dugdale (Con) 24,979: Richard Hoyle (Lab) 8,974. In June 1958 Sir Thomas announced his retirement as a Member of Parliament and in the following year in the Queen's Birthday Honours List of July 1959 he was made Lord Crathorne.

As Lord Crathorne he continued to pursue a very active and successful public life which included membership of the Central African Commission (1959) and the Monkton Commission on Rhodesia and Nyasaland (1960), President of the "Yorkshire Society" in London (1962) and President of the Conservative College at Swinton. When he died in 1977 public accolades were recorded from all quarters but as much as anything he had earned and never lost the respect and affection of North Yorkshire remaining their own "Tommy" Dugdale.

Sir Timothy Kitson

Timothy Kitson who was the North Riding County Council member for Topcliffe was chosen at a constituency meeting at Northallerton in August 1958 to succeed Sir Thomas Dugdale as the Conservative candidate for Richmondshire at the next election. He had attended Charterhouse and the Royal College of Agriculture at Cirencester before farming very successfully at Pickhill for ten years. Immediately before the General Election on 8th October 1959 he had moved to the Leazes at Leeming Bar and married Miss Diana (Sally) Fattorini of Harrogate.

In the election he increased the Conservative majority in winning Richmondshire in a straight fight with Mrs Mabel McMillan the Labour candidate: Timothy Kitson (Con) 28,270 Mrs Mabel McMillan (Lab)

9,203. Noteworthy too was that this was the last time that Sir Hubert G Thornley (he had been knighted in 1958) was the Returning Officer after many years of officiating in this position and announcing the General Election results.

Timothy Kitson made his maiden speech in Parliament in May 1960 on the "farm price review" and successfully defended his seat in the General Election of October 1964: Timothy P G Kitson (Con) 25,345; Gordon Knott (Lab) 8908; Keith Schellenberg (Lib) 8787. Robert Wotherspoon who had succeeded Sir Hubert Thornley as Clerk to the North Riding County Council was the Returning Officer as he was in the next General Election which quickly followed in April 1966.

On this occasion Timothy Kitson's majority was reduced somewhat to 13,331 partly because opposing him were individually popular local candidates in the lively and colourful Labour candidate Pat Lisle (of Brompton) and the Great Britain bob-sleigh captain Keith Schellenberg for the Liberals. The election details were: Timothy Kitson (Con) 23,541; Pat Lisle (Lab) 10,210; Keith Schellenberg (Lib) 7824.

The next General Election in Richmondshire in June 1970 reflected the Conservatives' popularity with their votes increasing and the majority to 17,769: Timothy Kitson (Con) 30,471; M L Aldrich (Lab) 12,702; J R Smithson (Lib) 5354. After the election Tim Kitson was appointed Parliamentary Private Secretary to the Prime Minister Edward Heath who in the ensuing years stayed several times at the Kitson's Leazes home.

In the February 1974 General Election Timothy Kitson with 26,994 votes secured a 15,267 majority and was followed home for the first time since 1945 by the Liberals with their candidate Beth Graham polling 11,727 votes though in fact the Labour Party led by Harold Wilson were returned to power. E.R. Pearce the Labour candidate obtained 7,659 votes. Timothy Kitson was knighted before the second General Election of 1974 which took place on 10th October with the following result: Sir Timothy Kitson (Con) 23,156; Mrs P Waunby (Lib) 9528 and I A Wilkie (Lab) 8025.

Education and Schools

Just as in the rest of Northallerton great changes were wrought both in schools and education in the post-war regeneration not only with the rise in population but also in tune with modern educational concepts and their implementation. At the leading edge of this in the North Riding was its Chief Education Officer the mercurial and brilliant educationalist Frank Barraclough of Thirsk Road, Northallerton who by the time he retired in 1965 had seen a hundred new schools built with 36,000 of the North Riding's 62,000 pupils in the new buildings in the county as well as great acquisitions of land as school playing fields and sports fields.

Allertonshire School

In Northallerton (and indeed the North Riding) educational reform and change had been spear-headed by the building and operation of the Allertonshire Secondary Modern School which when it opened in September 1941 began to take into its new functional buildings with their excellent facilities and sports fields the whole cadre of the town and district's 11 to 15 year old students who had hitherto been confined to elementary schools and thus denied the broad educational spectrum of secondary education now offered to them.

Under the stable and judicious headship of Norman Bryning from 1945 – 1964, as one of the first three secondary modern schools in the country, the Allertonshire became a 'show' school with visitors from not only this country but Europe, Africa and beyond. In 1959 the school was divided into two single sex 11 – 15 secondary schools with a new building having been erected opposite the original school to the east of Brompton Road. The Boys School under the headship of Norman Bryning and then Basil Terry occupied the new school, whilst the Allertonshire Girls School headed by Mrs E S P Allen took over the older western school buildings (later the Allertonshire 'West Block').

Northallerton Grammar School

In the meantime in 1945 Northallerton Grammar School had become a selective non-fee paying grammar school under Butler's Education Act of 1944 with entry dependant upon the 11+ examination. In September 1945 the first such entrants came to Northallerton Grammar School from the town and surrounding villages including the town of Bedale and consisted of forty-nine pupils (19 boys and 30 girls) who were divided into two forms. This was the pattern of the 11+ system until 1973 at Northallerton Grammar School but with the critical difference of advancing numbers as the area's 11 plus age group increased and multiplied.

The Headmaster for much of the school's selective grammar school period was Arthur T Richardson OBE, MA (1947 to 1969) and a remarkable feature was the length of service of so many members of Staff who became household names in Northallerton and its environs: 'Peggy' O'Neill, Art (1923 – 53); Robert Robson, English (1931 – 67); 'Jimmy' Addison, Woodwork (1932 – 67); JW Clark, Maths (1932 – 66); Arthur Arrand, French (1932-67); 'Bill' Lowther, Geography (1935 – 64); Laura Webster, Senior Mistress and French (1938 – 75); and 'Reg' Welburn, Sciences (1947 – 78).

Simple statistics indicate the grammar school's growth: 1945 – 265; 1952 – 274 (Sixth Form 30); 1957 – 296; 1961 – 406; 1969 – 534; and in the last year as a selective grammar school 1972 – 73, 626 with a Sixth Form of 149. Substantial building extensions to accommodate the pupil increase took place: in 1962 costing £68,270 and effected by R B A Moody and Son Ltd (Northallerton) and including a new Assembly Hall; and in 1972 consisting of a multi-purpose building to the east of the school undertaken by Walter Thompson Ltd (Northallerton) at a cost of £351,140.

Comprehensive Transition

In December 1968 the North Riding Education Committee had made the decision to embrace the comprehensive school system and so the die was cast for Northallerton Grammar School which became comprehensive in 1973 having taken in its final 11+ selective entry in September 1972 and then accepting the whole 14+ cohort (14-18 age group) of the Northallerton area in September 1973 with the Allertonshire taking in all the 11+ age group (11-14 pupils).

In anticipation of the comprehensive system the Allertonshire single sex schools had been reunited in 1970 under the headship of Basil Terry into one merged Allertonshire Secondary School consisting of East Block and West Block separated by Brompton Road. To facilitate safer access between the sites a "walk over" bridge was installed in 1972 over Brompton Road. By the 1975-76 academic year the comprehensive system was fully operating in Northallerton, with just over 800 students at the Allertonshire and nearly a thousand at Northallerton Grammar School.

Broomfield Primary School – 1970

Primary Education

Since the war too the Primary School (5 to 11 age group) sphere had changed rapidly with new schools being built throughout the town to cope with the rapidly advancing school numbers. A new primary school was opened at Romanby on 22nd May 1953 by Lady Nancy Dugdale with Stella Lawson Headmistress who later became Chairman of the Headteachers of Yorkshire Schools Association. By 1964 extensions had had to be made to the new school at a cost of £23,743 by Walter Thompson Ltd.

Northallerton itself was served initially at primary level only by the Applegarth School and the National School (now renamed East Road) but these were joined by a new school, Mill Hill Primary School overlooking Crosby Road and backing on to Northallerton Grammar School. It was officially opened on Thursday 28th June 1956 by Ald W R Burrill-Robinson the Vice Chairman of the North Riding County Council, Walter Thompson Ltd were the builders, the architect was J H Napper of Newcastle, it had seven class-rooms and Mrs F Hunter was the first Headteacher.

Bullamoor School was the next primary school to be erected this time off Bullamoor Road on the new council housing estate for £74,000 by Walter Thompson Ltd. Mr C Craig was the first headmaster of the school which was opened on Thursday 4th September 1969 with a roll of 280. East Road School was now purely an infants school (5 – 8 years).

Finally Broomfield Primary School was built at the southern end of Broomfield Avenue at a cost of £66,000 by R B A Moody and designed by Architect Brian Jackson. It was officially opened by Romanby County Councillor Arnold Pearson DSO, DFC on 29th March 1973 with Mrs B Everington the first headmistress and though it was situated in Romanby Parish Council's area it also received children from Northallerton.

The Police Force

Law and order continued to play a time-honoured role in Northallerton's affairs. With its headquarters at Northallerton, the North Riding Police Force was of both importance and high profile in the county town. A most important acquisition as a Police Training Centre soon after the war at the end of 1948 was Solberge Hall two miles south of Northallerton, formerly the home of John Hutton and latterly that of Benjamin Talbot the steel magnate. Of note too was the building in 1949 of six police houses in Broomfield Avenue for police officers, which was the beginning of the post-war housing development to the south and west of Northallerton.

The most significant development, however, was the creation of the North Riding Road Traffic Headquarters and control centre adjacent to the Police Headquarters behind Racecourse Lane. It was the first such self-contained venture of its kind in the country, was built by the Northallerton firm of Dan Oakley Ltd., and it opened in May 1952 with the wireless information room and the North Riding's police cars in situ.

Another important departure was the purchase of Newby Wiske Hall and part of its estate as No 2 District Police Training School serving twelve counties, with twelve instructors and over one hundred student policemen. Built originally in the seventeenth century by William Reveley (grandfather of Hugh Smithson Duke of Northumberland) and altered considerably by William Rutson in the nineteenth century, the adaptations for the police training purposes cost £120,000 and Newby Wiske was opened in its new role by the Home Secretary Sir David Maxwell Fife on the 21st May 1954.

Northallerton South West Aerial View 1963

Newby Wiske had a succession of important visitors including the Archbishop of York Donald Coggan in August 1965 and the Home Secretary Roy Jenkins who carried out an inspection in July 1966. For a time in the 1960s No 2 District Training School had a detachment of entrant policemen who were trained at Royal Air Force Leeming and although training had ceased at Newby Wiske by 1974 it had already been mooted as a new regional Police Headquarters to replace the 1910 Northallerton Headquarters which was by that time too diminutive.

After a distinguished period of twenty nine years as Chief Constable of the North Riding Constabulary Lieutenant Colonel John Clervaux Chaytor DSO MC who had been awarded the CBE in 1953 retired in October 1958 to be succeeded by James Robert Archer-Burton who had a distinguished Second World War record having been wounded at the battle of El Alamein.

Around this time several policemen ('characters' of Northallerton!)

retired including Superintendent "Nobby" Clark who was awarded the Police Medal in 1955 and the MBE later for services as Chairman of the Friarage Hospital League of Friends; Sergeant George W Martin whose photographs of Northallerton especially his panoramic set of the High Street in 1956 are of intrinsic historical value; and Sergeant 'Bob' Johnson who was of the North Riding's early motor patrol and latterly the ubiquitous helpful figure on point duty at Romanby Road's High Street junction, the epitome of the old-fashioned local friendly 'Bobby'.

Major police innovations in the 1960s were a police helicopter and then in 1968 the purchase by the North Riding of nineteen "panda" cars to largely take over from the 'beat' policemen. The same year, 1968, saw the amalgamation of three Police Forces - the East Riding, York and the North Riding under the Chief Constable of the North Riding H H Salisbury who had succeeded Robert Archer-Burton in 1965. In 1972 H H Salisbury took up another Chief Constable responsibility in Australia and he was replaced by Robert Paul Boyes who headed what had become the York and North East Yorkshire Police Force which became in 1973 the North Yorkshire Police Force in anticipation of the creation of North Yorkshire County Council in 1974. Throughout the amalgamations the Police Force's headquarters remained at Northallerton's Racecourse Lane.

North Riding Quarter Sessions

Northallerton had been a venue of the North Riding Quarter Sessions since the sixteenth century which were held continuously at the old Court House adjacent to Northallerton Gaol on East Road from 1785 and then the new North Riding Court House opened opposite the County Hall in 1936.

Sir Hubert Thornley

A remarkable feature was the longevity of the Clerk of the Peace Hubert G Thornley who from April 1916 to January 1956 made 162 consecutive appearances as Clerk to the Justices and was presented with an illuminated scroll and a George II silver tea strainer by the North Riding JPs to mark the record occasion. He had already been awarded the OBE and the CBE and when he was knighted on 1st April 1958 for his services to local government the Lord Lieutenant Sir William Worsley stated: "I cannot think of anyone in the North Riding who has more thoroughly earned this honour, and it is going to give a great amount of satisfaction to very many people." This was emphatically the case in Northallerton where "The Governor" as he was affectionately alluded to had also headed the County Hall as Clerk to the North Riding County Council and had lived in the Register House, Zetland Street for forty four years when he retired in 1960.

Major changes were afoot regarding the Quarter Sessions where because of the pressure of the legal business to be transacted from January 1962 eight court sessions were held yearly doubling the customary four annual meetings. This foreshadowed the abolition of the Quarter Sessions and their replacement by County Courts for each region in the North Riding's case the York and Teesside County Courts being created to transact the former legal work of the Quarter Sessions and Assizes.

Thus the last Quarter Sessions at Northallerton was held on Thursday 7th October 1971 with Robert Wotherspoon the Clerk of the Peace and Judge Angus Stroyan QC the incumbent Chairman. The latter exclaimed "This is a sad day" and indeed it was for Northallerton which had seen the gathering there of the North Riding court and magistrates for nearly four centuries, the 'Golden Lion' for example having to close an age-old "Judges Cellar" of vintage wines reserved for Quarter Sessions officials.

Northallerton Gaol

Northallerton Prison which had been re-opened in 1939 as a military "Glass House" gaol to receive Services prisoners suddenly erupted into the headlines throughout the national press when a group of particularly recalcitrant and resolutely iconoclastic Army prisoners staged a riot on Friday 1st March 1946. Starting around 11 a.m. in no time massive damage had been done inside the prison, fires started and windows and frames smashed out.

Eventually seven ringleaders held the roof-top hurling dismantled slates at anything that moved beneath. For their own safety a numerous crowd that had gathered to watch the besieged rioters was moved out of East Road and hastily assembled fire engines played heavy jets of water on the defiant roof-top prisoners. As darkness fell searchlights dramatically lit up the prison and the watery attrition on the prisoners continued until they finally surrendered at 7.40 pm.

Northallerton woke up on Saturday morning to find itself featured

Gaol Riot Scene

on every national papers' front page with some remarkable photographs and evocative descriptions of the riot, the ringleaders of which later received long extra sentences of imprisonment. The vestiges of their action can still be seen in the "bricked-up" south facing main prison window.

The post-war history and usage of the prison was in total contrast to its wartime role with young offenders with short prison sentences being confined there. In 1959 for example it had one hundred inmates aged 16 to 21 serving six months imprisonment before going on to "Open" Borstal. By May 1964 it was "Northallerton Young Prisoners Centre" in which discipline and treatment was more relaxed and there was an increasing and conscious aim to try to fit the young men better to re-establish themselves in normal life on their release. Direct evidence of this could be seen in the educational and vocational classes which became regular features and the internal modernisation in living conditions seemed to be symbolised by the disappearance of a familiar Northallerton landmark - the sixty foot high obsolete prison chimney.

Armed Services Links

Peace-time Northallerton still retained strong links with the Armed Services in particular with the Green Howards regiment and Royal Air Force Leeming which culminated later in both of these being granted the "Freedom" of the town.

The Green Howards

With National Service of two years compulsory service for all young men of eighteen in operation until 1961 many Northallerton and district's conscripts were drafted into the local regiment, the Green Howards and saw active service in such post-war trouble spots such as Malaya, Hong Kong and Cyprus.

The county town's connections with the Green Howards were often exemplified such as in November 1952 when the 1st Battalion arrived back in England after four years of dangerous active service in the Malayan jungle in which they had lost over twenty men. They detrained at Northallerton railway station and paraded at the County Hall, led by their Commanding Officer Lieutenant Colonel Aubrey Miller DSO and headed by the Regimental Band with the Lord Lieutenant of the North Riding Sir William Worsley (himself a Green Howards veteran of the First World War) taking the salute. The Battalion then attended a civic reception to welcome them home given by the North Riding County Council.

The Green Howards Association of ex-comrades had a thriving branch in Northallerton and when they were presented with a new standard on the 8th September 1957 one hundred and fifty members of the Association paraded with Sir William Worsley taking the salute.

Remembrance Sunday

Both the British Legion and the Royal Air Force Association branches were also so thriving in Northallerton that each had new club premises opened, the former in Wheldon's yard near the Town Hall and the latter at the North End in September 1968 incidentally on the site of the "George" public house of a century before. All the ex-Servicemen's Associations joined with other local groups such as the St John's Ambulance Brigade, Girl Guides and Boy Scouts in the annual Remembrance Sunday service and parade in November at the

Northallerton War Memorial with the unfailing moving two minutes silence at 11 am in memory of the fallen.

The parade was normally led by the Northallerton Town Band conducted by Mr "Pop" Lewis and always contained an immaculate detachment from Royal Air Force Leeming whose Station Commander traditionally took the salute on the dias along with the Chairman of the Northallerton Urban District and other civic dignitaries near to the Market Cross.

Royal Air Force Leeming

After the war Leeming had become a Fighter Command Station at first with the Meteor jet aircraft – the dangers of even peacetime flying being emphasised by the number of fatal crashes – two for example in both 1952 and 1954, all four involving Meteors with their pilots being killed.

A previous crash on August 25th 1951 saw six killed in a mid-air collision between a Wellington from Leeming and a Martinet. Air cadets were involved as passengers in the Wellington and Flight Lieutenant Alan Quinton was subsequently awarded the George Cross (the highest peace-time award for bravery) for his unselfish act in putting a parachute on Cadet Derek Coates whose life was thus saved whilst Alan Quinton died in the crash. Forty years later in October 1991 a new VIP lounge was opened in Leeming named the "Alan Quinton Memorial Room" thus finally commemorating this unique act of bravery.

In April 1958 No 33 Squadron received its Standard at Leeming with many VIP's present including Air Marshal Sir Thomas Pike of Battle of Britain fame. By this time Javelin two seater fighters had replaced Meteors and then in July 1961 Leeming's role changed out of Fighter into Flying Training Command when it became No 3 Flying Training School (No 3 FTS) for the initial jet plane flying training of pilots using Jet Provosts which became a part of the area's skies for the next thirteen years.

The hazards of initial pilot training were underlined by fatal crashes in which the students under-training were killed: in a Jet Provost crash between Scruton and Great Fencote in February 1963; and a mid-air collision between Jet Provosts over Oaktree Farm, Bullamoor in April 1965. In both cases the flying instructors were fortunately able to operate their ejection seats and parachute to safety. Altogether nearly one thousand pilots obtained their 'Wings' at 3FTS between 1961 and 1974 and though they were primarily Royal Air Force pilots, twenty two other nations' trainees qualified as pilots including those from China, Iraq, Estonia, Poland, Burma, Yugoslavia, Singapore, Saudi Arabia, Sudan and Jordan.

Royal Air Force Leeming – Northallerton connections were felicitous and solidified as exampled by the annual presentation commencing in 1962 by Leeming to Northallerton of a Scandinavian Christmas tree. Important to the local area had been the closure of Middleton St George in 1962 as a Royal Air Force aerodrome and its reactivation in 1964 as a civil airport thus giving the region an air-communications link. Another Royal Air Force departure after over thirty years was from Topcliffe which in 1973 was assigned to the Army No 24 Air Portable Brigade.

In April 1971 Leeming was honoured by the Royal Visit of the Air Chief Commandant of the Women's Royal Air Force the Duchess of Gloucester who flew in by helicopter and remained for four hours being escorted by the Director of the WRAF Air Commodore PF Marshall. When the Queen Mother visited St John of God, Hospital, Scorton on 16th April 1971 she flew into and out of Leeming. No 3 FTS disbanded in October 1974 and the Archbishop of York Dr Donald Coggan gave a final address. Leeming's historic stature and prestige had been substantiated in December 1973 when the Central Flying School (CFS) of the Royal Air Force became permanently based at the station.

Social Amelioration

There was a very evident and determined mood and movement in the post-war years to help the less advantaged members of the community which was displayed not only in the official policies of the various local Councils but also in voluntary groups and organisations. The social consciousness and cumulative time and effort of many individuals was reflected in the positive results achieved.

At each end of the age spectrum the North Riding of Yorkshire's intentions were made clear when they bought and opened: the "Close" at Brompton in 1948 which was converted into a children's home housing in 1957 twenty children with a staff of twenty one; and Oak Mount on Thirsk Road was changed from a nurses' residence into an old people's home in March 1954 and has been a model of its kind from thence forward into the new Millenium. The local handicapped were greatly helped by the setting up at Northallerton's North End of a Workshop for the Adult Handicapped opened by the Lord Lieutenant of North Yorkshire, Lord Normanby in October 1966.

Voluntary Organisations

In the charitable and voluntary spheres numerous organisations took healthy and productive root. TOC H started in Northallerton in 1943 and in 1954 their legendary founder Rev 'Tubby' Clayton (with his dog "Chippie") gave his support at a Town Hall talk. The Rotary Club in Northallerton representative of every business and professional element in the town commenced in 1947, meeting weekly in the "Golden Lion" and especially aided young people and the sick at the Friarage Hospital. The Round Table with similar aims but of a younger ilk (members had to leave at forty) began in 1951 and became an energetic, enterprising and progressive contributor to local good causes with their wives joining in by forming a Ladies Circle in 1960.

Both the RSPCA and the RSPCC were prominent in Northallerton with their county headquarters centred there – for example the Archbishop of York Donald Coggan addressed the North Riding RSPCC Annual General Meeting in Northallerton Town Hall on 8th May 1973. Flag Days of these and other societies on Market Days were well supported – RSPCA June 1964 £113.

A notable voluntary organisation formed in 1957 was the "Guide Dogs for the Blind" as was 'PROBUS' which was an organisation of retired professional and business people commenced in 1970 with charitable aims. The Anchor Lodge of Freemasons met regularly in the Masonic Hall which was the former Baptist Chapel.

Another major appearance in the town was that of the charity shop which was to proliferate as time went on. Oxfam was the first such shop of the modern genre to open in early 1971 at 188 High Street with the Vicar's wife Mrs Castledine the local Oxfam Chairman.

League of Friends

The quest and need for a Nurses' Recreation Room for the nursing staff at the Friarage Hospital germinated one of the most fruitful, enduring and caring Northallerton voluntary groups. "The Northallerton Hospitals Nurses' Recreation Room Fund Committee" first met on 2nd December 1953 and on 12th January 1957 had worthily and speedily fulfilled its purpose by raising the £8,500 needed when the Nurses' Recreation Hall was opened. So cohesive and successful had the Nurses' Recreation Room Committee become that it was decided to keep it in operation as the League of Friends of the Northallerton Hospitals under the continued Chairmanship of A E 'Nobby' Clark. The League of Friends went on from strength to strength in its stated aim "to mobilise, encourage, foster and maintain the interest of the public" in the hospital raising prodigious sums of money to supply extra necessities which were outside the means provided by the National Health Service. For example the next major League of Friends contribution was a Library and Post Graduate Centre costing £5000 opened in October 1970.

Red Cross

Allied to the League of Friends at the Friarage Hospital was the Red Cross which provided a trolley service in 1952 which had developed into a full canteen service by 1970. The Red Cross also established a reception service for the busy out-patients department and was very active in the town too where it had its headquarters on the High Street just north of Zetland Street, the elderly and the blind being two particular recipients of great Red Cross support. In December 1966 the Red Cross opened a new headquarters for both the North Riding and Northallerton on the west side of Thirsk Road by re-building on the site which had been occupied by Pratts Trailer Company and two farm cottages at a cost of £12,500.

The Samaritans

Another organisation crucial to as it turned out more and more individuals, was the Northallerton and district branch of the Samaritans which opened on 1st January 1965. This was prefaced by a talk on 4th December 1964 in the Town Hall about the Samaritans by their founder Chad Varah. Forty professional people formed the first group of Samaritans which quickly established a 'help line' and was soon receiving fifty telephone calls per month. Percy Hartley, the Town Clerk of Northallerton UDC became the local Samaritans Director whose number included Thirsk Veterinary Surgeons Donald Sinclair and Alf Wight, the latter to become more or less immortalised in his novelist pseudonym, James Herriot.

Grace Gardner Trust

Of the socially conscientious local people Grace Gardner was of particular note. As a young woman she worked indefatigably at the County Hall Red Cross Hospital in the 1914 – 18 war, became local area organiser before the Second World War for the Red Cross and held a similar position later for the Women's Voluntary Service (WVS). She had a special interest in the welfare of the elderly and was the Chairman of the Old People's Welfare Committee in Northallerton until 1962 and when she died in 1966 her will translated her beliefs into realistic practicality and benefice when after small bequests she left the bulk of her legacy £21,877 in trust for the welfare of Northallerton's Senior Citizens. Since then the Grace Gardner Trust with invested interest has been a major boon to the Northallerton OAPs in a variety of ways.

Arts and Entertainments

In the Arts and entertainment field Northallerton thrived with a variety of organisations, societies, clubs and talented and enthusiastic individuals. As in the rest of the country a great change in social and entertainment habits occurred with the advent of television which basically arrived in the town in 1953 and was into almost every household within two years. The impact was most clearly seen in the Northallerton cinema-going scene where the Cinema-de-Luxe in Romanby Road had already become Foreman and Renders second hand furniture salesroom by March 1951.

Even then, however, in 1951 the "Central" and the "Lyric" cinemas were fully supported to the extent that each had a change of main film in mid-week, each night there were two showings (or "houses") of the programme and the "Lyric" had a Saturday children's "Matinee Club" and a separate Sunday main film show. A typical advertisement which appeared for the week ahead in the Saturday 1st September 1951 local newspapers:

  "Central Cinema - two houses 6 pm and 8.15 pm
  3 Sept Mon. Tues. Wed. – "The Forest Ranger" (A) Paulette Goddard, Susan Hayward
  6 Sep Thur. Fri. Sat - "Hollywood Story" (A) and "Assassin for Hire" (A)
  Lyric
  Sun 2 Sep "OSS" - Alan Ladd

The Lyric Cinema

3 Sep Mon. Tues. Wed. "Where the Sidewalk Ends" (A) Dana Andrews

6 Sep Thurs. Fri. Sat "The Browning Version" (A) Michael Redgrave"

Within a decade and only a handful of years after television's arrival the "Central" with dwindling audiences was demolished in 1961 to make way for the access road to the new Applegarth Car Park. And though the "Lyric" soldiered manfully on by 1968 its size was no longer economically viable compared with its clientele. In December 1968 having closed for five weeks for internal reconstruction it opened again with a total division and a dual role: upstairs - Cinema, and ground-floor - Bingo. How the mighty cinema of 1939 had nearly fallen! But the "Lyric" did manage to continue for over a quarter of a century after this.

During its heyday the "Lyric" had played weekly host twice a year to the production of Northallerton Amateur Operatic Society in the Autumn and the Northallerton Variety Company's pantomime in January. These two bodies embodied the spirit, enjoyment and quality in the local 'live' theatre and entertainment. From the "Mikado" (1955) onwards annually to the "Belle of New York" (1968) the operatic offerings at the "Lyric" were of an exceptionally high standard and continued as such in other venues into the 1970s. The Variety Company's pantomimes regularly brought a January week of consistent juvenile and reflected adult happiness and laughter to the extent that the cognoscenti firmly held the view that the pantomimes were better than some of those in large provincial centres.

The majority of the local actors, singers and entertainers had excellent grounding and great encouragement in the local schools first at primary level and then at the Allertonshire or Northallerton Grammar Schools which both had particularly active Choral and Dramatic Societies which staged fine concerts and plays every year without exception.

The Northallerton Choral Society's aria performances in the Town Hall under 'Gerry' Wilson's enigmatic baton and with Clifford Walker's celebrated violin lead were too of a memorable nature. The thespian torch of the town was carried by the Allertonshire Players who mainly in the Allertonshire School staged two or more plays annually and indeed nurtured young talents like Judy Bailey and Susan (Elizabeth) Bennett who went on to repertory, radio and television appearances and success as indeed had Catherine Wilson the Northallerton Operatic Society's soprano who reached the heights of a main 'lead' singer with Scottish Opera and the Glyndebourne Opera.

Perhaps the best known locally connected performer was Dorothy Tutin who became a West End, Royal Shakespearean Company, film and television household name from "The Importance of Being Earnest" filmed in 1952 to decades of success. Her grandparents who Dorothy regularly visited in the 1950s, farmed at Sigston Castle Farm and retired into very old age to Ainderby where they celebrated their Diamond Wedding in April 1958 whilst her father Dr John Tutin who was educated at Northallerton Grammar School became a naval architect settling in Putney, London.

Northallerton had flourishing Camera and Art clubs started in the 1950s and which held popular and highly credible annual and occasionally individual exhibitions, the Russell sisters of Hatfield Road being particularly gifted and well-exhibited artists.

Arthur Bell Foster

The artist from Northallerton who received the highest national accolades was Arthur Bell Foster who was born in the town in 1902 and educated at Northallerton Grammar School from where he won a scholarship to study at Sheffield College of Art after which he settled in the Midlands teaching in schools and colleges there. He came to work particularly in water colours which mainly depicted and were dominated by his North Yorkshire origins with such paintings as "Swaledale Village" (1952), "North Yorkshire Farm" (exhibited at the Royal Academy in 1953) and "Wensleydale Farm" (1961). The latter was hung at the 1961 Federation of British Artists Gallery, Water Colours Exhibition Pall Mall, London when it was stated that he "is one of the most vital and sensitive interpreters of the Northern scene."

His paintings were hung in exhibitions all over the country including: the Royal Academy (he had a Spanish water colour scene near Gerona exhibited there in 1960); regularly in the exhibitions of the Royal Society of Painters in Water Colours Gallery, Conduit Street, London where he showed "outstanding" works; and especially in Birmingham near to his Midlands base.

Arthur Bell Foster is undoubtedly Northallerton's most recognised artist and it is interesting that he took his first step to recognition actually in the town where aged 13 in April 1915 he was awarded the 2 guineas (£2. 2s) first prize for an "excellent painting" in a competition in aid of the 'Belgian Relief Fund'. He died aged 76 peacefully after a short illness in his native town Northallerton in February 1978 having just retired to live there.

Sporting Northallerton

Sport, in true Yorkshire tradition, continued to play an essential and continually active part in the life of Northallerton and district. Again the secondary schools, Allertonshire and Grammar, were the seed-beds of youthful talent which in extremely sports-orientated environments produced a regular flow into senior sport.

Northallerton Cricket Club

This was seen particularly in cricket where Northallerton CC won the York Senior League in 1952 essentially by allying younger school talent with sage experience and then later on saw both Douglas Burnett and then Arthur 'Rocker' Robinson play for Yorkshire County Cricket Club Second X1 with the latter finally playing for Yorkshire County's First team in 1971 onwards – the first time that a Northallerton C C player had ever achieved that honour.

Northallerton Cricket Club also started a local trend towards the main sports clubs owing their own grounds and facilities when they moved from the rented County Hall pitch to their own ground off Farndale Avenue, Boroughbridge Road on 23rd April 1949 where they quickly established themselves. On 24th April 1965 a brick built pavilion with dressing rooms, a licensed bar and social facilities was opened by Sir William Worsley the avid cricket loving Lord Lieutenant of the North Riding. A memorable day was rounded off by a Northallerton X1 playing a Yorkshire County side which contained most of its international players including Geoffrey Boycott, John Hampshire and Tony Nicholson.

Yorkshire County Cricket Club played at Northallerton in similar "friendly" matches preceding their County Championship programme on several occasions in convivial affairs which gave great pleasure and superlative cricket. On 21st April 1956 Vic Wilson captained a Yorkshire team which scored 218 for 7 declared against Northallerton 64 – 8 with Willie Watson, Dickie Bird and 'Fiery' Fred Trueman (3 for 16!) in the Yorkshire side. In 1959 the captain Ronnie Burnett brought a Yorkshire side which included Brian Close, Ray Illingworth, Jimmy Binks, Frank Lowson, Ron Appleyard, Doug Padgett and Brian Stott. The umpire incidentally in both the 1956 and 1959 matches was the redoubtable Albert Gaskell of Northallerton – the only local man to have ever been a First Class Umpire in the County Championship.

After winning the York Senior League three times in four seasons from 1966 onwards Northallerton CC 1st X1 returned to play in the North Yorks South Durham 'A' Division after an absence of seventy years in 1971 finishing fourth in their first season with Northallerton 2nd X1 faring well also in the NYSD 'B' Division where they had played since 1962. Northallerton Evening Cricket League flourished from the 1950s onwards with Northallerton stalwarts Albert Gaskell and WD "Bill" Hodgson being particularly associated with its success. The Northallerton "Knock-out" Granindon Cup which involved all the local village teams was a constant source of annual interest and intense competition. Just as keenly contested was the Northallerton Ladies Evening Cricket League which commenced in the 1960s and by 1970 had ten teams eagerly playing.

Northallerton Tennis Club was a section of the Northallerton Cricket Club where hard tennis courts were laid adjacent to the south of the cricket field in 1949 and Northallerton Ladies Hockey Club also played on the cricket field during the winter.

Northallerton Rugby Club

A winter sport which absolutely boomed in Northallerton was rugby which had been very slow to gain popular support when Northallerton Rugby Club was re-activated after the war. Gradually, however, the Rugby Club consolidated in the 1960s with a pitch on the Yafforth Road and a headquarters at Samuel Jackson's old school at the southern entrance to the Applegarth. By 1969 it had three senior fifteens and a colts' team and in 1971 it moved to its own ground between Stone Cross and Brompton, the first match being played on Saturday 9th October when the 1st XV defeated Huddersfield YMCA and the ground was officially opened on 20th November by the Chairman of Northallerton Rural District Council Mr C R S Tate. Finally in 1974 much hard work and fund raising came to fruition when it opened a purpose-built club house with changing rooms, a bar and other social facilities.

Football

The most popular local game remained Association Football with the main club Northallerton Alliance changing its name to Northallerton Town in 1952. In 1956 it assured its future by buying the Bluestone ground of four acres at Broomfield for £1000 which in turn was purchased by North Yorkshire County Council for possible building/parking extension facilities at the end of 1974. This sale enabled Northallerton Town to buy and develop its present ground and club house at Ainderby Road where it was 'in situ' by May 1976.

The immediate post-war years saw titanic local football battles watched by large partisan crowds between Northallerton and Brompton FC with honours often even between teams of a standard seldom seen in the district. Both of these clubs diversified away from the local Allertonshire League to meet stronger opposition but the Allertonshire League still boasted twelve teams playing traditionally on Saturday afternoons when it changed its name to the North Yorkshire League in 1970 with six of the clubs from within Northallerton itself; Northallerton Town, Spartans, Rangers and Police, York Trailers and North Riding NALGO.

Northallerton Bowling Club

There was a multiplicity of other sports clubs in Northallerton. Pride of age and continuity must be taken by Northallerton Bowling Club which in August 1950 celebrated its Jubilee and has since spanned the century. Commenced in 1900 with George Lewis (of Lewis and Cooper's) the driving force it moved to its present green swarded Thirsk Road sequestration in 1910 and bought the adjoining 'Lodge' on South Parade for £1,000 in 1930. In modern idiom it started a Ladies Bowls Club which soon had a Yorkshire County player in Edith Stone, and Northallerton Bowling Club has never stood still continuing to look to its present and future as the years have unfolded.

Other Sports

In 1953 Northallerton Quoits League was thriving with thirteen teams but with the change in buildings and social habits this essentially public house based pastime had died away by 1963 with its league defunct. On the other hand the public house enjoined Darts League in 1974 had thirty four teams comprising three Divisions. Another little heralded club of great active membership propensity was Northallerton Angling Club which fished the River Swale around Morton with competition cups such as the 'Rutson Hospital' and the 'Smithson', and in 1967 had no fewer than three hundred and forty members.

Another rising club of the 1950s to 1970s era was Northallerton Motor Club, which from small beginnings in town went on to stage National Championships at Carlton Bank for Scrambling motor cycles in 1962 and 1963 the latter attracting 5,000 people. Table Tennis had the Northallerton Table Tennis League of four divisions by the mid 1950s and under its indefatigable Secretary CK 'Ken' Palmer not only staged a County match in October 1956 in the Town Hall when Yorkshire beat Durham 9-1 but also honoured Northallerton with a table-tennis international match on 4th June 1967, England defeating West Germany by 6 games to 4.

Golf increased in popularity in the district to the extent that the Thirsk – Northallerton Club between Northallerton and Thirsk planned to extend its nine holes course to a full eighteen holes. Additionally with the Darwin brothers John and George two of the main motivators Bedale Golf Club was laid out initially as a nine hole course on the Leyburn Road (later to increase to eighteen holes) which was opened on

9. John Hutton MP of Solberge and Sowber Gate

10. Northallerton Station 1841

11.Lieutenant Alan Hill VC

Northallerton : South End

12. Conservative Headquarters - the famed Golden Lion balcony

13. 4th Battalion Church Parade 1908

14. Dedication of Northallerton War Memorial - 6th August 1921

15. Fortress Northallerton - High Street Road Block 1940

16. The Proclamation of Queen Elizabeth II - February 1952

Saturday October 14th 1967.

Finally, there were other smaller but vibrant organisations active in their own sporting hobbies which included the Miniature Rifle Club (President Richie Pick), the Northallerton Snooker League of sixteen teams in 1972, the Northallerton Badminton Club which played at the Church House and the ultra keen Pigeon Homing Society. A new sporting representative area was the Northallerton Swimming Club, new because Swimming Baths had not come to Northallerton until 1961 in the shape of the War Memorial Baths. The baths soon made their mark with an annual Swimming Gala commencing in 1961 and in 1966/67 140,000 used the baths in a year.

Equine Successes

The last sporting word rests with horses – the really traditional remnants of Northallerton's sporting existence. The Hurworth Hunt by its unfailing arrival in Northallerton for its Boxing Day Meet was a colourful and animated reminder of Northallerton's agriculture and equine heritage. The Barker family trained by their father C Leslie Barker jumped their way to the forefront of the International Show Jumping sphere led by sister Anne who at seventeen years old jumped 'Lucky Sam' to victory at the Harringay Arena on 7th October 1957 to win the "Daily Express" Foxhunter Championship.

Brothers David (21) and William (18) Barker then competed in the Olympic Games at Tokyo in 1964 riding for the Great Britain Show Jumping team and becoming the first Northallerton born sportsmen to represent their country. They both continued at the top of their sport winning many more international show jumping honours and at sixteen their younger brother Charles became Young Rider of the Year at Wembley in 1967.

In a sporting finality an equine exploit caused much excitement in Northallerton and district when Teal won the Grand National on 5th April 1952. Coming from Ireland he had been passed around the district in local ownership three times. No one imagined then that he was destined for fame as he was set about comparatively menial tasks. Thus his great National success when trained by Neville Crump was greeted all the more ecstatically in the Northallerton area especially as numerous people had backed him at long odds just for sentimental reasons!

Northallerton Grammar School Class 1951

Occasions and Events

Other events were of great local moment for different reasons. The death of King George VI on 6th February 1952 cast a shadow over Northallerton, as it did the nation, and telegrams of commiseration were sent to the bereaved Queen from Northallerton UDC and RDC. On Friday 8th February came the Proclamation of Queen Elizabeth II from the Market Cross by the Chairman of the UDC AE Skelton supported by his fellow Councillors before a large crowd which included many of the town's school children assembled for the occasion.

Great plans were made for the Coronation of Queen Elizabeth II in the following year with £350 expended on the decoration of the County Hall and £727 by Northallerton's Coronation Committee which was chaired by locally born Alastair Carter. When the great Coronation Day – 2nd June 1953 – came, however, the weather was so continually and intensively inclement that the only activities which could go ahead successfully were those held indoors – although a brave attempt was made to mount a Coronation Procession in the High Street. The abiding memory of many of the day was of clustering around the few television sets at the time to see the wonders of the outside broadcast of the Coronation 'live'!

During the post-war years Northallerton had no Royal visits but it had some 'near misses' as it were! On 15th November 1955 when the Duke of Edinburgh visited Darlington to open the Girls High School the royal train remained overnight in a siding on the Wensleydale line near to Castle Hills with a local steam engine attached to its regal equivalent to provide heating! When the Queen and the Duke of Edinburgh visited Teesside in June 1956 the North Riding County Hall was directly involved as the headquarters from which the county officials arranged the itinerary the Queen later sending a letter of thanks to the Lord Lieutenant, Sir William Worsley at the County Hall. Finally Katherine Worsley came to the Friarage Hospital to open its Garden Party on 20th June 1959 only twenty one months before she became a 'Royal' Duchess by marrying the Duke of Kent!

Two murders in the Northallerton district caused sensations. At York Assizes on 21st June 1950 James Walker (48) of Station Road, Brompton was sentenced to death for the murder of Francis Henry Wilson of the same address on 29th April 1950. Walker who lodged with the Wilson's was proven to have bludgeoned Wilson to death with an axe the Jury taking just half an hour to reach their unanimous verdict, Walker being hanged soon afterwards for the crime. The diminutive nature of Walker who was only five feet tall added to the drama of the case.

Much controversy surrounded the murder of Elizabeth Louise Strauss at their home The Garths, North Otterington by Timothy John Franklin (43) on the 26th January 1970, Franklin being found guilty of the crime and sentenced to life imprisonment at York Assizes in March 1971. A critical factor involved was that Mrs Strauss' body was hidden in the house garden and not discovered for seven months, with Franklin, who was an International Sales Director leading people to believe that she had gone abroad.

Key Civic Changes

1974 was a water-shed and a crucial year in the history of Northallerton because of the new local government legislation and division of responsibilities. After eighty five years of great local endeavour and achievement with marked urban, economic and social progress Northallerton Urban District Council disappeared and

Northallerton Town Council was instituted in its place with massively reduced powers. A second tier of local administration was created in the form of Hambleton District Council which took over most of the services and responsibilities in Northallerton district formerly held by Northallerton Urban and Rural District Councils.

Finally the old North Riding of Yorkshire County Council was superseded by North Yorkshire County Council with much extended boundaries, size and population. Critically for the town, Northallerton remained the new North Yorkshire county seat with its administration centred at the County Hall.

North Riding – North Yorkshire

In the post-war era of the North Riding County Council, extensions on the County Hall site and new buildings elsewhere in Northallerton had been essential. Motor Taxation offices had been erected at the northern end of the Northallerton Grammar School playing field in December 1956 (incidentally replacing old agricultural buildings going back to the 'Golden Lion' field coaching days) built by RBA Moody and Son for £17,495. A decade later on 4th August 1967 a flat-topped brick extension housing the Education and Archivist departments built by Walter Thompson Ltd at a cost of £165,000 was opened. It was situated to the south and east of the main County Hall building partly sited on what had been the former Northallerton CC cricket pitch.

Costing £143,000 North Riding County Fire Service headquarters with an underground control system was opened by Lord Normanby the county's Lord Lieutenant in October 1969 to the immediate east of Northallerton Gaol at the northern end of Crosby Road. In July 1971 a new building for the Highways Department was erected at the eastern flank of the main County Hall which excited much local controversy and comment as it was of a white texture in total contrast to its entire red-bricked surroundings – the County Hall, Police and Broomfield housing estate buildings. Lastly a North Riding Ambulance Station was erected on the northern side of Bullamoor Road and completed by June 1972.

When the government's re-organisation plans for the county were unfolded an exceptionally strong campaign was waged to have the new county headquarters situated near to York which was to be part of North Yorkshire and central to the new county. An influential pressure group for York's cause included the Archbishop of York Dr Donald Coggan and the propaganda was substantial. The counter argument to retain Northallerton as the county headquarters cited the effect its removal would have on the 'in situ' officers and local population in general and most persuasively the economic disadvantage of creating an entirely new county building complex. The County Architect Vernon Short reported in February 1974 that a new relocated county hall would cost £8 million as opposed to £1 million extensions at the present Northallerton site.

As it was at a crucial meeting on Thursday 7th March 1974 of a full North Yorkshire County Council of ninety three members after a full debate in which thirty seven members spoke, the motion to centre the new headquarters at Northallerton was substantially carried by 61 votes to 16. At 650,000 the new county population was almost double that of the old North Riding's 342,000. North Yorkshire's first Chairman was James Fletcher and the county was sub-divided into six second-tier administrative Districts of which Hambleton was No 2 District.

Hambleton District Council

The outgoing North Riding County Council in January 1973 gave its support to Northallerton becoming the headquarters of Hambleton District Council which had a population of 61,000 and the other market towns of Stokesley, Thirsk and Easingwold. However, the subject of where the new District Council headquarters should be was strenuously argued and the issue waged between Thirsk and Northallerton. In June 1973 Hambleton District Council's first local elections took place and Alan Herbert was elected to represent Northallerton and Matthew Cook returned for Romanby.

In July 1974 the full Hambleton District Council voted between Thirsk and Northallerton as their centre. The voting was equal 21 – 21 and the Chairman, Alan Herbert of Northallerton used his casting vote to make Northallerton the new headquarters of Hambleton District Council which was to be located at Northallerton's old Vicarage. It had been "a close run thing" and for the record this historic Hambleton District Council meeting was held in the Council Chamber of the North Yorkshire County Council at the County Hall, Northallerton.

Northallerton Town Council

As for Northallerton itself in December 1973 Alwyn Cockerill became the first Mayor designate of the newly formed Northallerton Town Council which though it had now mainly nominal responsibilities still had jurisdiction over the Applegarth. One of the main issues that was resolved concerned the Northallerton Community Centre which the Northallerton UDC had budgeted for and accepted an architect's design for a building on Bullamoor Road. Hambleton District Council accepted the responsibility for the new Community Centre in June 1974 passing a proposal for building to be started and completed by 1975.

12

The Last Millennium Lap   (1975 to 2000)

Continuing Transformation

The post-war urban and rural revolution in and around Northallerton continued unabated in the final quarter of the twentieth century – the last hectic lap as it were to the new Millennium. A summary of the findings of the joint Planning Departments of the North Yorkshire and Hambleton District Councils issued in 1977 for the Town Plan of Northallerton (jointly Northallerton, Romanby and Brompton) indicated the degree of change already: between 1951 and 1971 Northallerton had grown proportionately three times more than Hambleton District and five times more than the North Riding; the 'Private Housing' population had leapt from 8,500 in 1946 to 15,900 by 1977 with a projection of 16,500 in 1981; from 1946 to 1977 7,340 jobs had been created with 5,300 in the Service area.

A perceived fine balance between industrial expansion and progress with preservation of rich agricultural land and inherent local stability with the maintenance of comfort was a stated imperative. And in 1981 Hambleton District Planning Department termed Northallerton "a special type of town". Such bare statistics and words were visibly evidenced by the changes apparent in the structure, expansion and commerce of the town.

High Street Relief Road

Northallerton which from time immemorial had remained Leland's 1538 description of one street south to north was impinged in 1977 by a new road at the southern entry to the town linking South Parade with East Road to take the increasing weight of traffic around the eastern side of the town. Several houses including "Southlands" gave way to the new road exposing a vivid landmark approach in the form of a "cruck

371

house" of the sixteenth century. Flanking the relief road to the south a new North Yorkshire County Library Headquarters was constructed in angular style which was officially opened on 21st October 1977 by the Lord Lieutenant of North Yorkshire the Marquis of Normanby and on 1st December 1977 Katherine Worsley, now the Duchess of Kent visited the library having been unable to be present at the official opening.

The Traffic Problem

Traffic movement remained a major problem – for example in 1976 17,000 vehicles travelled daily down the High Street and East Road which had increased to 24,000 in 1984 – and the North Yorkshire County Council had re-introduced the possibility of an Applegarth western approach road again in 1983. This was again vigorously opposed by the townspeople and their Councillors culminating in a public meeting in Northallerton Town Hall in April 1983. Once more the Applegarth was cited as a war memorial gift and therefore sacrosanct as well as being termed "a green lung" in an urban sprawl. The North Yorkshire County Council withdrew this plan in 1984 but the use of the Applegarth in future road developments was not completely discarded and remained as a future planning option.

High Street Alterations

With the relief road opened in 1977 various traffic experimentations were carried out including pedestrianising the High Street from Zetland Street to Friarage Street for a period of time. Eventually, however, in May 1979 a new system was finalised with a weight restriction on traffic in the High Street which was equipped with Belisha beacon pedestrian crossings mainly controlled with traffic lights. Indeed in two decades the High Street underwent much change with extensive structural alterations.

On the east side below Lloyds Bank to the south, seventy yards of older property made way for modern shop/office buildings in the late 1960s and 1970s and in the early 1980s a similar development took place with the demolition and replacement of all the old property to the south of the Post Office on the west side. Adjacent to this a cul de sac of seated repose was made available at South Parade corner which in 1981 was named Gardner Court in memory of the town's benefactress Grace Gardner and her illustrious family. In 1989 the re-building at the

Old Romanby Road Corner

South End was climaxed by the removal of seventeenth and eighteenth century buildings comprising the northern corner of Romanby Road, which was re-developed as a modern rectangular office complex by Radco Developments.

Barkers of Northallerton

Meanwhile farther down the west High Street "Barkers of Northallerton" after organised opposition and a Government Inquiry on 14th January 1981 were given permission to replace Market Row and Hudson's Yard with a substantial shopping precinct. Barkers' Arcade which now occupied Market Row blended Barkers' store with twelve fashionable shopping units (all taken up by 1986) fronted by a café (on the site of the old "Waggon and Horses") and reaching back to the Applegarth at a cost of £1.2 million with Walter Thompsons the main contractors. This, the largest single shopping project in the town's history, was opened by the then current TV star of "Emmerdale" Ian Shorrocks on 20th November 1985.

Barkers originated from John Oxendale's drapers shop opened in

High Street Face-Lift 1987

the 1870s and taken over by his former apprentice William Barker who assumed sole ownership in August 1919. William's sons Leslie and Wilfred developed the shop until 1948 when they appointed loyal and experienced employees Don Raper and Mike Scales to the Board as Directors. Leslie Barker remained as Managing Director until the late 1970s when his youngest son Charles Barker succeeded him in this role.

The firm expanded further in April 1994 by opening a furniture store at Finkill Way, Yafforth Road which had a café incorporated. In 1998 Barkers acquired a new warehouse on the Standard Way industrial estate and the Central Arcade shopping precinct, which had been built in 1966 on the site of the former "King's Head" stage-coaching hotel. Finally, later in 1998, the firm adorned the High Street with a handsome but utilitarian and publicly well-received clock at the head of Barkers' Arcade - Market Row.

High Street Face-Lift

In November 1986 North Yorkshire County Council's planned 'beautification' of Northallerton High Street was endorsed by Hambleton District Council and this operation of re-paving and re-styling the High Street by Colash Roads Ltd, York (which had previously 'uplifted' main thoroughfares in York and Scarborough) was completed in three phases between March and August 1987 at a total cost of £350,000. As a finale in October 1987 the Market Cross was removed fifty yards to the south in the High Street thus continuing on its journey southwards undoubtedly begun by an ancient predecessor from close to the Parish Church in medieval times.

Tesco 2002

Supermarket Explosion

As these sweeping High Street developments were taking place simultaneously a shopping revolution was occurring – away from the small traditional shops to self-service shops of an increasing number and size. It could be termed the super-market explosion - in common with the national trend. By the late 1970s Dees, the Co-op, Hintons and Fine-Fare grocery self-service outlets were operating and gradually the main super-markets and large self-service stores settled into a more static situation up to the century's end.

Dees became Gateway which moved to the North End in August 1986 before becoming Somerfields in the 1990s. Fine-Fare closed and the site to the south of Zetland Street was occupied by Iceland in July 1986. Hintons had opened in 1979 on the former site of the Old Golden Lion and Clarkson's Silversmiths to the west of the Town Hall and after changing hands this super-market eventually became Safeway on 5th December 1989. A full-scale re-development at the South End of the town saw William Low build a super-market adjacent to the new link-road between South Parade and East Road at a cost of £3.3 million, which employed over a hundred people and opened on 24th October 1989. This was taken over by TESCO in 1996 and in 1998 plans were submitted for a major re-development which was completed in 2002.

Claphams to the north of the "Golden Lion" had become Uptons in 1963 and this became a multi-store in the Boyes chain in 1977 but still retains the frontage acquired by Claphams in 1925. B and Q "Do It Yourself" store located at the head of Yafforth Road on 14th June 1990 and another popular large outlet specialising in agricultural requisites Sam Turners ("The Farmers' Friend") opened a new store on Darlington Road in 1984 having moved from Quaker Lane and having formerly been at Boroughbridge Road. 'Klondyke – Strikes' were the latest local firm to re-locate moving their gardening speciality range to Darlington Road in 2000 from Boroughbridge Road into a multi-store of some proportions with café facilities.

Woolworth's, the first large store post-war comers had remained on the same site since 1954 but after the Co-operative Society ceased trading and closed in 2000, Woolworth's had the Co-op's building demolished and rebuilt moving there, just to the south of their former premises, in May 2001.

Amongst this jostling activity of multi-stores some Northallerton shops have retained their role and identity but these are few and far between and apart from Barkers of Northallerton the only shops as identifiable by name and function throughout the twentieth century are Cleminsons, Thompsons (the Butchers) and Lewis and Cooper's.

Lewis and Cooper's

The latter's reputation goes far and wide with customers from the town, district, region and beyond. The "Good Food Guide" of March 1985 described them – "One of the best food shops outside London." With a staff of ninety two whilst retaining their delicatessen and food and wine specialisms the shop has moved on with the times and had the priceless assets of enterprise, professionalism and continuity in the form of their only three Managers since 1925 – Messrs Fred Bell, Maurice Fairburn, and Tony Howard.

High Street Changes

Important permanent additions to the High Street scene were Boots (which took over Timothy Whites and Taylors) the Chemists, Clinkards shoe specialists (1970), the bakers shops Thomas' of York (1983) and Bakers Oven (1986) and Betty's tea-rooms (1978) which was amongst Egon Ronay's Guide national awards in 1986 and 1992. It was also given the prestigious "Top Tea Place of the Year Gold Award" by the Tea Council in 1987.

But the transience of the Northallerton shopping scene was amply illustrated in the new Millennium which not only saw the disappearance of the century old Co-operative Society in May 2000 but soon afterwards the closure of the "family" firms of Murray's the bakers (August 2000) and their adjacent neighbours just north of the Town Hall, Trueman's butchers (October 2000) whose original connections with the business stemmed way back into the town's past. These were followed immediately in the New Year of 2001 by the removal of another two established and popular shopping "faces" Stockdales' butchers in February and Dressers' stationers and booksellers in March.

However, the economic viability and sheer shopping magnetism of the High Street were immediately substantiated by several well-known quality outlets taking up vacant places later in 2001 which notably included the nationally renowned firms of W H Smith and Ottakers booksellers on the west and east side of the High Street respectively.

Other noteworthy features of the High Street's changing appearance and salient characteristics were the increasing number of 'charity' shops of which there were seven by 2000 and the added contingent of estate agents and building society premises. The latter were a direct result of the private housing boom in the Northallerton district with new housing property developments continuously around Northallerton and Romanby as well as "in-filling" available areas within the town with flats and town-houses. From the two estate agents in 1948 of MW Darwin and Sons Ltd., and WL Prest the number had grown to nine by the end of the century along with five building societies.

Hambleton Community Centre

In the local government administration and amenities spheres vitally important matters were afoot and outstanding projects completed in Northallerton. The Community Centre authorised by Hambleton District Council ongoing from Northallerton UDC was officially opened by the Countess of Swinton on Friday 28th November 1975.

The Hambleton Community Centre became immediately popular

hosting most of Northallerton's major entertainments and shows, becoming the Richmondshire general election returning centre initially and an election polling station as well as being used by a variety of the town's groups and organisations. It was substantially altered internally in 1994-95 but as it was costing £100,000 to run annually, in the late 1990s Hambleton Council were considering further extensive changes.

Northallerton Town Hall

The Northallerton Town Hall issue had been left in abeyance at the local government restructuring of 1974 and there was a section within the Hambleton District Council favouring its demolition. Led by the Mayor of Northallerton Councillor Bob Tennant and others there was an expressive campaign to "Save the Town Hall" in that it was "an asset and not a liability".

Ultimately it was decided at a meeting of Hambleton District Council on 20th December 1978 to offer the Town Hall to Northallerton Town Council for £1 and if this was not accepted by 30th January 1979 to demolish it. Northallerton Town Council duly accepted the offer, the "One pound Town Hall" phrase was coined and the building continued as a vital part of Northallerton's civic and social fabric becoming the headquarters of Northallerton Town Council.

North Yorkshire County Council

The county scene too had changed considerably in 1974 with the greatly increased size of North Yorkshire compared with the former North Riding and the staffing within the County Hall multiplied accordingly to 907 full-time and 470 part-time personnel on site in 1977, the North Yorkshire total employees in 1981 being 12,681 full-time and 10,913 part-time.

To cope with the additional numbers extensions were completed at the County Hall in 1976 adjoining the 1967 red brick rectangular building and the 1930 southern wing. The County Treasurer's department occupied the new 1976 building which also contained a staff restaurant. In 1988 further office space was gained by the move of the North Yorkshire County Records Office to a former factory site on the western side of nearby Malpas Road and the vexatious car parking situation was alleviated somewhat by a new car park being constructed in 1989 at the eastern end of the adjacent Bluestone football pitch which had been acquired from Northallerton Town football club.

North Yorkshire CC Re-organisation

In 1995-96 North Yorkshire was again re-organized and restructured being reduced considerably mainly by the city of York becoming a local authority in its own right and the North Yorkshire Police Force, the North Yorkshire Fire and Rescue Services and the two National Parks devolved into independent authorities directly responsible to central government. Nevertheless, the new North Yorkshire still had a net expenditure of £403.3m in 2000/2001 with Education and Libraries the main recipient accounting for £243.4m to service 393 schools with 88,000 children, 150,000 in adult education and 44 libraries. The other bulk expenditures were Social Services £77.2m and Environmental Services £34.9m. Around 19,000 people were working for North Yorkshire at the end of 2000 with approximately one thousand of these at the County Hall, Northallerton.

Brierley Building

The latter Grade II listed Brierley building received in 2000 a £200,000 refurbishment of the front entrance primarily to facilitate disabled access with an external ramp and internal lift. Much care was taken to match the stonework and retain the building's elegance and a tasteful result was achieved. A time capsule was buried with thirty cameos reflecting contemporary North Yorkshire life. Finally the ponds fronting the building were repaired and renovated with the assistance of a £12,000 grant from environmentally conscious Yorventure – a fine ornamental metamorphosis for waters hastily assembled and contained in 1939 in case of enemy bombing!

Some North Yorkshire departments were situated in well-known Northallerton buildings. The Social Services occupied the National School (1843), the Trading Standards (with a quirk of name) were at Standard House where Grace Gardner was born and the Probation Service moved from Registry House (1736) to Essex Lodge, South Parade in 1998.

Three notable North Yorkshire County Council events which specifically involved Northallerton were significant church services at All Saints Parish Church when all the civic dignitaries of the county swelled large congregations of: the Service of Thanksgiving and Re-dedication on Sunday 8th July 1989 which commemorated the centenary of the County Councils; the Service in April 1999 to mark the twenty fifth anniversary of the formation of the North Yorkshire County Council and Hambleton and the other North Yorkshire divisional councils; and the Millennium Civic Service on Sunday 9th January 2000. The affairs of the county and its county town are very inter-mingled.

North Yorkshire Police Force

Major changes in the buildings and accommodation of the North Yorkshire Police Force took place in the Northallerton area before they were transferred from county to direct government Home Office control in 1996/97. The most important movement concerned the Police Headquarters where the Northallerton 1910 building in Racecourse Lane had become patently too small to cope with the greatly increased and modernised Force. As a result a new headquarters was sought and by a unanimous decision of the Police Committee, Newby Wiske Hall was earmarked and substantially altered to become the North Yorkshire Police Headquarters in 1977.

The Racecourse Lane building became the centre of the Police Force's Northallerton Division until it was decided to move the headquarters to the Grade II Listed Friarage House immediately to the south of Porch House on the High Street. This was converted at a cost of £592,000 by Walter Thompsons into a suitable Northallerton Divisional Headquarters and occupied by the Police as such in December 1987, the Racecourse Lane building being then used by North Yorkshire County Council. A final act in the story of Northallerton Police Headquarters was one of demolition when the bulldozers moved in and the original nineteenth century North Riding Police Headquarters on East Road was literally removed in January 1991 to make way for the future development of Northallerton Gaol.

In December 1974 a one hundred and fifty feet radio mast had been erected at the Police Control Room in Racecourse Lane to become a Northallerton landmark and policing methods changed during the next two decades with advancing technology. This was exampled by intensive computerisation; a new Control Room in 1989 which was visited at the time by William Hague MP for Richmondshire; and the introduction of Closed Circuit Television in 1994 which was installed in nineteen places in Northallerton at a cost of £460,000 by April 1995.

The successive Chief Constables of the North Yorkshire force during this period were: John Woodcock who succeeded Robert Boyes in 1978 but left in April 1979 to become Chief Constable of South Wales; Kenneth Henshaw 1979 until his retirement in 1984; Peter Nobes 1985 to 1989; David Burke April 1989 until January 1998 who had started his career in 1967 as a North Riding policeman; and David Kenworthy who was deputy Chief Constable of the Avon and Somerset police force from 1994 until coming to North Yorkshire in 1998.

Chief Constable Kenworthy backed by the North Yorkshire Police Authority chaired by Baroness Harris (Angela Harris of Richmond) set about the modernisation of his force, which had the largest 'beat in the country'. In March 1999 a new control room was authorised at Newby Wiske with the necessary planning permission and repeated requests to bring the manning up to more acceptable levels were answered by an increase in the force's allowable recruitment in July 2000 by sixty-eight officers over three years. In 2000/2001 the force had a net expenditure of £83.75m.

North Yorkshire Fire Services

The North Yorkshire Fire and Rescue Services left the county council's jurisdiction in 1996 but its headquarters remained in Northallerton at Crosby Road which was equipped with a new command and control room costing £1.6m which was opened in the presence of the Chairman of the Fire and Rescue's controlling authority Caroline Seymour in April 1998 accompanied by the North Yorkshire Chief Fire officer Eric Clark. The purpose built system was faster, more accurate and efficient than its predecessor and a new radio system was planned to be installed in the early 2000s. In 1996/97 the Fire and Rescue Services dealt with 9887 emergency calls.

Highways Department

A final aspect of re-organisation by North Yorkshire County Council was the delegation of the Highways and Bridges departmental responsibilities to Mouchel, North Yorkshire in April 1999. Mouchel was located in the old North Riding Registry of Deeds building Racecourse Lane with a staff of 75 (63 of these being retained from the County Council). North Yorkshire was one of Mouchel's five county council hostings which was contracted for five years and brought quality registration with Lloyds as well as an Investor in People classification.

Regional MAFF Centre

In the agricultural administrative area Northallerton's divisional centre assumed an added importance, size and architecturally endowed appearance. 1992 saw it become the North East Regional Service Centre for the Ministry of Agriculture, Fisheries and Food (MAFF) with its staff increasing over the next few years from one hundred to three hundred. To effect the changed role the 1952 Government Buildings were knocked down and replaced in two phases between 1998 and March 1999 with a resplendent successor of pleasing architectural design built by PS Turner Constructions Limited. Named Alverton Court the new building was opened officially in November 1999 by Eric Morley MP under Secretary of State for Agriculture

The Regional Service Centre deals with Yorkshire, County Durham, Humberside and Cleveland under its Regional Director Peter Watson and is one of nine Regional Centres nationally. Of these it is one of only three Centres which will not be "down-sized" or reduced in new Government plans with it becoming re-titled the Common Agricultural Policy Paying Agency in April 2001. In keeping with this role in July 2001 the Centre was named the Rural Payments Agency (RPA) which was now associated with the Department of Environment Food and Rural Affairs (DEFRA) which had replaced MAAF.

Northallerton Prison

Adjacent to the west of the MAFF building HM Prison also underwent much structural alteration both internally and externally on the western side where the prison wall was extended past Zetland Street. The gaol, which reached its two hundredth birthday in 1985, was the second oldest in operation in the country and was used for the younger male offenders primarily from the north. In May 1983 it was made "Northallerton Youth Custody Centre" and in 1987 had a Governor and forty three Prison Officers responsible for two hundred and fifteen youths with a strong emphasis on training, education and the facilitation of re-settlement into society at the end of their custodial sentences. Fears were expressed, however, about overcrowding by the Home Office and in 1994 the role of the prison was changed to that of a Remand Centre for younger prisoners aged 16 to 21 awaiting trial and sentence.

In 1995 a £7m scheme to enhance the prison over a period of five years was announced including the replacement of the outer walls which were unsafe. The latter process was indeed being effected in early 2001 but the problems of apparent overcrowding still appeared a matter of concern with the Howard League in May 1998 reporting that the Victorian prison built for 152 now housed 260.

Hambleton District Major Developments

Hambleton District Council was concerned in major building projects in Northallerton in the 1980s and 1990s which patently added to the county town's importance as an administrative centre and also to the leisure amenities locally. On its inception in 1974 Hambleton District Council had taken over the old Northallerton Vicarage from the defunct Northallerton Rural District Council as its headquarters. After a feasibility study by consultants who gave the Vicarage building a limited future the Council voted 25 to 16 in December 1976 for the building of a new council headquarters to be sited in Northallerton.

Hambleton District Headquarters

Eventually in April 1984 the site was ratified as three acres at Stone Cross, Northallerton on an area of twenty acres the rest of which would be used for recreational purposes. Hambleton District Council headquarters building (named the Civic Centre) was duly completed at an accumulating cost of over £2 million and was occupied by September 1986 and officially opened on 4th March 1988 by Wing Commander DE Davies DFC, AFC (Retired). The old Vicarage was sold to developers who demolished the building and erected in its stead a private housing complex – Applegarth Court.

Leisure Pool and Centre

Hambleton District Council went on to build two leisure amenities buildings on the Stone Cross site which have since proved great and considerable public assets. A Leisure Pool costing £2.3 million and built by Walter Thompsons was officially opened on 29th March 1990 by Duncan Goodhew, the 1980 Olympic breaststroke gold medallist at the Moscow Games. Hambleton Leisure Centre, with excellent amenities for a variety of indoor sports and activities, which cost £1.2 million, was opened on 5th September 1991 by Robert Atkins MP Minister for Sport. Within five months of opening the Leisure Pool had registered 100,000 users and has continued this popularity from thenceforth with the Leisure Centre also being substantially used. Additionally they have hosted national attractions including the Royal Shakespearean Company annually since 1996 and the BBC TV Antiques Roadshow in October 1998, broadcast in 1999.

Applegarth Amenities

Hambleton Council provided essential services in the Applegarth car park area: public toilets had been built by June 1978 and plans are afoot for a modern replacement in the early 2000s; a Hambleton District Tourist Information Centre of octagonal design was erected at a cost of £69,000 and opened by Lady Masham in October 1990; and "environmentally friendly" container bins were provided for the re-cycling of paper, bottles and clothing which have proved of great public utility. The latter applies equally to the "waste tip" site which Hambleton Council constructed at the north western edge of Northallerton on Yafforth Road in 1981.

Citizens Advice Bureau

The Hambleton Citizens Advice Bureau centred at South Parade Northallerton from 1976 with an annual budget of £53,000 (1997) of which North Yorkshire CC provided half and Hambleton DC £18,000 per annum proved so popular that funding became a problem especially in maintaining links with other towns. However, in December 1999 the organisation was awarded a National lottery grant of £443,000 with which to buy and re-equip Mowbray House – Grade II listed – at North Arch, North End, Northallerton which was vacated as a doctors' surgery in January 2001. A net-worked computer system and disabled-access will be features and £40,000 has been earmarked to establish an employment advice service.

Staff and Industrial Development

Hambleton Council's expenditure in 2000/2001 was £21.366m with a staff of 4,300, - 260 of whom were based in Hambleton Civic

Centre at Stone Cross- an important element in Northallerton's economy. Industrial estate development was high on Hambleton's list of priorities and in Northallerton the Standard Way industrial estate's progress was so successful that more land was needed. Consequently in March 2000 Hambleton District Council purchased nineteen acres of land immediately north of Earnshaw's factory on the east of Darlington Road to provide further industrial estate property and by May 2001 design works for this £1.6 million scheme were well advanced.

National Cycle Way

In a totally different sphere Northallerton was a central feature in Hambleton Council's input in 1999 to the setting up of a National Cycle Way network costing £172 million, the council contributing £150,000 to the scheme which would take the cycle path from Humberside to Teesside. By June 2000 the Brompton to Stone Cross stage had been completed with work continuing to produce a continuation link to Northallerton.

The World of James Herriot

The exciting and highly successful Hambleton Millennium project in setting up 'The World of James Herriot' museum at Kirkgate, Thirsk at a £1.4 million cost at the former veterinary surgery of Alf Wight, the James Herriot creator, was universally acclaimed. Although essentially a part of the Thirsk scenario Alf Wight had some strong Northallerton links. For example, as already noticed, he and his partner Donald Sinclair were amongst the first volunteers to act as 'listeners' when the Northallerton Samaritans began to operate in 1965 and when Alf Wight's grandchildren were born at the Mount Maternity Hospital, Northallerton he and his wife Joan presented a painting to the hospital.

Council Housing

A crucial responsibility inherited by Hambleton District Council was that of council housing and this was delegated in 1992 to the Hambleton Housing Association which was formally established as Broadacres Housing Association in April 1993 when it took over the ownership and management of the entire housing stock of Hambleton District Council. Broadacres located their headquarters in the multi-storey block on East Road previously occupied by the North Yorkshire Architects Department. The building was refurbished for Broadacres by FT Construction for £39,950 and officially re-opened by William Hague MP in February 1994. Broadacres Housing Association holds over 4500 properties in North Yorkshire with 1082 of these in Northallerton itself excluding Romanby and Brompton.

As early as October 1978 Hambleton Council had drawn up plans for a combination of both eighty Council and eighty Private houses at Knottabottom which were constructed by the mid 1980s when in 1984 twenty flats for single people were authorised and built by Walter Thompsons at an overall cost of £347,193. In November 1985 the refurbishment of twenty-eight older Council Houses in Valley Road was begun with £5000 being outlayed on each house. Broadacres Housing Association in March 1995 announced the building of twenty houses for £950,000 near to the Ashlands Training Centre and a thirty-six flats complex of sheltered homes off Lascelles Lane which was duly completed by 1998 at a cost of £1.8 million.

Private Housing Boom

In the meantime in the century's last quarter the building of private houses in Northallerton and Romanby continued unabated with new estates around the town and the "in-filling" of flats and houses within the town. A sensation was caused in the building of Swain Court near to Quaker Lane in July 1978 by the unearthing of human bones which had been interred in the eighteenth century, this being the site of a Quaker burial ground. One of the largest developments of the early 1980s was that of the extension to the south of Broomfield of what became known as the "St James Estate" built by Waddingtons.

Flats were erected in the late 1970s on the site of the "White House" at 15 South Parade which had been bombed in 1941 and were named Stanley Court after the Principal of Walter Thompsons their builders – Stanley Thompson. Of all the local firms involved in the re-development of the town Walter Thompsons played the foremost part. In August 1988 Walter Thompsons amalgamated with George Fordy Ltd, the firms having previously been brought together as it were by the marriage of respective Directors Pauline Thompson and Malcolm Fordy. The new organisation was entitled FT Construction with a work force of three hundred and sixty. Its Managing Director Malcolm Fordy was awarded the OBE in the 1997 New Year's Honours List for Services to the Construction Industry.

Within the town retired people were increasingly catered for with developments such as: Fir Lodge in South Parade turned into flats by the support of the Abbeyfield Society in 1988; the building of the Ardens Court complex of 'Retired Accommodation' in 1989 by McCarthy Stone; the alterations to "Southwoods", Thirsk Road to convert it into an elderly peoples residential home in 1989; and Beechwood residential home on the site of the Romanby Road coal depot in 2000.

An outstanding embodiment of the building scene at the time and the premium put on suitable land availability around the town was the purchase in October 1988 by Persimmon Homes of 4.3 acres on the western edge of Romanby for £1.7 million - £325,000 per acre – on which to build forty houses. As the Principal of the estate agents involved MW Darwins, George Darwin succinctly put it – "it was simply a case of supply and demand."

Throughout the 1990s the building process proceeded mainly to the south and west of the town – indeed the population of Romanby Parish topped the five thousand mark having been around a thousand before the Second World War. True too that by a quirk of ancient boundaries and with a cavalier poetic licence of nomenclature, the County Hall Northallerton, Northallerton railway station, Northallerton Cricket Club and Northallerton Football Club – were all in Romanby Parish!

Small housing estates appeared at Sandy Bank, off Mill Hill, Helmsley Way, Harewood Lane and at Bourne's old field below CD Bramall Ford. The largest development was to the south, to the east of Boroughbridge Road in what constituted 'Romanby Park' which necessitated an additional roundabout on the main Boroughbridge Road. In the general changes both Northallerton's doctors surgeries were re-located to purpose- built medical complexes: the East Road practice to the old site of Strike's garden amenities on Boroughbridge Road in 2000 and the Mowbray House North End surgery was moved in January 2001 to the Weavers Green housing development situated on the former Linoleum Factory area, the factory having been demolished in 1999.

Traffic Congestion

A negative consequence of the housing boom was the increasing traffic volume in the town which was exacerbated by the continuous hold ups at the three railway level crossings – Low Gates at the North

End and Boroughbridge Road and Romanby to the south. Frequent traffic congestion occurred in the High Street with an occasional gridlock of motionless vehicles. All the local councils showed their concern and urgent talks were held with Railtrack. In a survey conducted by North Yorkshire County Council on two consecutive November 1999 days Boroughbridge Road level crossing was closed 25 times with an average queue of two hundred yards and Low Gates 45 times for periods up to 4 minutes. Ultimately in December 2000 Hambleton District Council echoed by various other organisations including the 'Darlington and Stockton Times' called for the urgent implementation of the Northallerton outer by-pass plan drawn up in 1990 by North Yorkshire County Council but put on 'hold' since 1993.

Industry and Trade

The pattern of industry was similar in Northallerton under the auspices of Hambleton District Council after 1st April 1974 to that of before with the Northallerton Town Council. However, closures and recessions which came hand in hand with booms and industrial successes spelled out the need for caution and judicious expansion in the encouragement of new concerns.

Closures

Industrial vicissitudes were very apparent and exemplified from the mid 1970s onwards. Helix Springs, hitherto buoyant, had closed by 1975 and in September of that year AEI Hotpoint which had located at the old Brompton Wilford's linen mill closed with eighty job losses. An even more critical closure was that of Kossett Carpets on 10th December 1980 when the Board of Carpets International (Northern) Ltd announced their withdrawal from the Darlington Road factory and redundancy notices for the 210 work force. The newspaper headline "Carpet Factory Closure Decision Shatters Town" summed up the situation and again under-lined the tenuous nature of large factory-based concerns at Northallerton.

A local consolation was the purchase in August 1981 and the subsequent occupation of the ex Kossett site by British Telecom as an important storage and distribution centre employing a hundred people. Another industrial disappearance, however, occurred in 1983 when John Teasdale's steel fabrication firm which had come from Wetherby in

1946 closed in the face of the trade recession biting into the country. The stories of three of Northallerton's best known companies at the time, Allerton Industries, York Trailers and Sunters told differing tales of the vagaries of industrial fortunes in the face of the national economic climate and commercial trends.

Allerton Industries

Allerton Industries after thriving for over three decades ran into difficulties but was re-formed as Allerton Engineering Ltd on 1st March 1983 moving to a 4.5 acres site on Romanby Road with four workshops. It has since prospered with a dedicated work force of 60 people specialising in the high classification of steel fabrications with a client base of leading firms. In 1990 it had a turnover exceeding £2.5 million and had a prestigious quality assurance accreditation by Lloyds.

York Trailers

York Trailers, despite some intermittent strikes of a very short duration (but significant locally because of the rarity of "industrial action"), in 1983 employed over three hundred workers and had a £23,416,469 turnover. In June 1985, however, its owner Fred Davies sold the company to United Parcels for £5 million and in October 1991 it went into "Receivership" with the entire work force of 240 being made redundant in November. It was immediately taken over by Aveling Barford of Grantham who re-employed 70 workers and despite heavy debts of £30 million in January 1992, turned the company around. With £3.5 million in orders by September 1993 and 150 workers the factory had stabilised when it was taken over by Utility International in 1998, an American firm who were impressed by the quality of the work-force and developed a curtain sided trailer that immediately attracted encouraging sales.

Sunters

Sunters the Northallerton road haulage firm had prospered to the extent that it expanded at its Boroughbridge Road site to the tune of £156,000 in July 1974. However, in the early 1980s it became amalgamated within the Econofreight Group and as a result of the wider economic strategy of its new owners it was closed in June 1986 with its

Sunters transport London tram 1979

workers made redundant and the town dismayed at the loss of such a familiar and local firm of national note.

Flourishing Survivors

Several stalwart local concerns survived the upheavals of recessions and intenseness of competition into the new Millennium. Examples from disparate functional spheres were: Langtons of Northallerton steel fabricators at Yafforth Road; Joanna Marco specialists in curtains and furniture upholstery on Anchorage Lane, North End; Archers Removals Ltd and J Wallace steel fabricators at Springwell Lane; and JSW and Son coachbuilders at the North End.

Other larger established firms survived and prospered. Earnshaws on their £1 million 1979 Darlington Road site continued to have a £3 million sales generation annually with fifty percent of their customers overseas, in fifty countries. The locally called "Milk Factory" on Romanby Road moved through the ownership of Dried Milk Products, to Unigate and the Milk Marketing Board before becoming Express

Dairies with a work force of 160. Sam Turners the "Agricultural and Horticultural Specialists" employed 55 at their new Darlington Road site.

Electricity

Northallerton's famous Electric Light and Power Company of 1899 had become part of the North Eastern Electricity Supply Company of Newcastle in 1930 and then the North Eastern Electricity Board in 1948. The latter made a notable addition to the High Street in 1963 by opening a Show-room on the east side which soon had 11,000 customers and the NEEB had fourteen sub-stations in the old Northallerton UDC and eight in Northallerton RDC before it became part of Northern Electric in the 1980s. Permission was given for the latter to erect a 120 foot radio communications mast at its Tannery Lane site in June 1990 by a Hambleton Council vote of 11 – 9 and finally, North Sea Gas having been installed in Northallerton at the end of 1970, the organisation extended its operations to gas to become Northern Electric and Gas in 1997.

Electronics

Two modern electronics firms had mixed fortunes based at the North End. Mowden Controls Limited designers and manufacturers of electronic control equipment, formed in 1965 by Lewis Williams and Vince Ellington and still a family firm, continued to be very successful and employed 30 people. Sparkprint, pre-fixed SE Sparkprint when taken over by SE Labels the largest self adhesive label producer in Europe, had gone from strength to strength and by 2000 were producing 500 million labels per annum with a work force of over fifty and national clients such as Railtrack. However, the unprecedented and damaging floods of the night of $2^{nd}/3^{rd}$ November 2000 engulfed Sparkprint's factory adjacent to Willow Beck to such an extent that in fear of a flood recurrence the firm reluctantly and regrettably left Northallerton to re-locate at Newton Aycliffe in 2001.

Newcomers

On the Standard Way Industrial estate several new firms including British Telecom prospered. One of these was Micromized Food

Products, originally owned by Farm Feed Formulators and then by Sydney C Banks of Bedfordshire since 1996, who process cereals, peas, beans and soya for use in the agricultural, brewing and pet food industries. Another immediately successful firm was E Wood Ltd who were formed in London in 1982 and moved to Northallerton in 1987 to produce "High Performance Industrial Paint Coatings" exporting 70% of its output to 80 countries and employing 125 personnel. They had royal visitors on 2nd August 1989 when the Duke and Duchess of York came that afternoon. Elsewhere in the town notable newcomers to Springwell Lane were Bayford Oil in 1990 and North Yorkshire Timber in 1992.

Alastair Carter

From this part of Northallerton hailed Alastair Carter from Castle Hills Farm who was one of the town's most eminent and inventive industrialists in its history. After leaving East Road School at fourteen he worked in the family farm business and led a popular local dance-band the "Swingtimers" before becoming a bomber-pilot in the Second World War and then a vigorous Northallerton town councillor and Chairman of the Urban District Council.

In the late 1950s he moved to the Midlands to open his own firm – "Carter Engineering" at Tamworth which he developed into a highly successful business making truck bodies and leading the field in the production of double-decker car transporters. He also invented an electric car – the "Carter Coaster" – which was displayed at the 1967 Motor Show in London and though it was never mass-produced it was adapted in the USA as a golf-caddy car which brought Alastair a Presidential invitation to the White House. He even piloted his own aeroplane with a private airstrip at Stone Cross. He died on 3rd October 1993 and at his Northallerton funeral oration the legendary Norman Bryning aptly referred to him as "a man ahead of his times".

Nearby Industry

In the closely related Dales area there were several examples of great enterprise and business acumen which spelled commercial success. Wensleydale Creamery at Hawes was born out of the closure of the Wensleydale cheese factory by Dairy Crest when the local management team and business man John Gibson (a Northallerton Grammar School old boy) the new Chairman took the factory over in 1992. Fifty-nine jobs were saved and an attendant local catastrophe averted. A turnover in 1992 of £2.8m was multiplied to £9m in 1999 with 130 work force and the production of 1550 tonnes of cheese.

On the Leeming Bar industrial estate: the residue of the former Vale of Mowbray Factory business producing pork pies and sausages was bought out by its general managers John Gatenby and Doug Graham in 1995 with a resultant work force of 120, stability and success; from small beginnings at Aiskew in 1976 Dalepak sped to the employment of 300 workers in 1998 and attendant big business; and Richmond Ice Cream from four employees in 1985 and a £250,000 turnover moved by 1997 to a work force of 240 a turnover of £25m and a merger with the Leeds firm 'Treats'. By 1999 Leeming Bar industrial estate contained twenty-four companies employing a thousand workers and was landscaped by Hambleton District Council at a cost of £40,000.

Motor Scenario

Motor cars played a central and increasing part in Northallerton affairs with the old order changing from small privately owned High Street garages with sales, repair and servicing areas to large nationally owned dealerships and allied units on the periphery of the town and "off the High Street".

Garages

Kellett and Pick opened spacious show-rooms in August 1963 at Durham House but these had closed by the 1980s and a new-comer Motor Delivery had opened, expanded and closed between the High Street and Brompton Road from 1958 to 1984. The two oldest concerns Naylors and Smirthwaites also disappeared. Naylors, which had started as "James Henry Naylor" at the turn of the century closed in June 1982 and Smirthwaites (opened in 1903) having moved its petrol pumps from the High Street to its rear at East Road in May 1975 finally closed at the end of 1998.

Dutton-Forshaw took over the dealership of Saab and Honda from Smirthwaites and absorbed most of their staff in showrooms and servicing and repair shops at Yafforth Road opened in January 1999. In September 2001 Dutton-Forshaw themselves were replaced by the Hull based firm of De Vries. Before this, Massingberd Ltd had opened on a three and a half acre site on Darlington Road in May 1982 for

Volkswagens and Audis employing twenty-five and winning a national award for "excellence" in August 1989.

In 1979 Mr Simon Bailes had obtained a Peugeot franchise and set up in Tannery Lane and was so successful that Simon Bailes Ltd from 1989 for eleven years in succession were awarded the prestigious Peugeot Gold Lion Award. Completing the vehicle consortium scene by the end of the century were: Lookers who had located on Darlington Road as Toyota agents; and CD Bramall Ford who had established themselves as Ford dealers at the south western end of South Parade on the former John Neasham garage site.

Road Accidents

As the numbers of vehicles on the road multiplied so too came increased performance and speed of the machines and the combination led to an inevitable rise in the road-accident rates, despite the emphasis on road safety and the introduction of safe-guards such as the breathalyser. Road accidents occurred in the Northallerton area continuously on every road with the arterial A1 and A19 leading the way with the Friarage Hospital of very high profile and necessity because of its central geographical position and its major accident and emergency unit.

There were innumerable examples of dire accidents: in July 1982 three lorry drivers were killed instantaneously in a heavy vehicle horrific multiple "pile-up" on the A1 two miles north of the Leeming Motel; in August 1983 a stubble fire emitting dense smoke caused an accident involving nine vehicles on the A19 with two persons killed; and in 1988 in a single December weekend eight people were killed in various accidents in the Northallerton area. And all these descriptions represent only a fragment of the accident strewn scene of the last quarter of the twentieth century with the town periodically stunned by local road tragedies. In 1998 the North Yorkshire road death toll was 88, in 1999 this had decreased to 68 but by December 2000 that year's total had steeped to 90.

Road Improvements

Numerous and regular improvements were made to the main roads particularly serving Northallerton and a major innovation was that of the

Gatenby fly-over approach road to Royal Air Force Leeming which had become one of the front-line operational flying stations in the country. Costing £2.6 million this was opened by the Earl of Arran, the Under Secretary of State for Defence accompanied by William Hague the Richmondshire MP in December 1991.

Bus Depot Closure

In the Northallerton public transport sphere a sign of the times was the closure of the United bus depot on the south-eastern end of Brompton Road in April 1989 precipitated by the decline of local passenger numbers. Thenceforward the local buses "pick up" area was to the south of the Parish Church adjacent to the "Buck" public house.

The Railways

Of great import were the changes that were effected regarding the railways which were really a culmination of a Northallerton railway modern metamorphosis which commenced in April 1954 with the closure of the Wensleydale line passenger service. July 1979 saw two completely unrelated events which nevertheless characterised the contemporary railway scene – enormous technological advances but attendant with possible danger. Early in the month a very familiar landmark disappeared with the removal of the wooden signal cabin at Boroughbridge Road low level crossing, its utility over, with manually worked signals giving way to automatic electronic control.

Then on Tuesday 28th July the Inter City 125 10.40 am. London to Edinburgh train derailed at 80 mph just south of Northallerton station uprooting the line and ploughing through the station but remaining upright. Quite miraculously only one of the four hundred passengers was slightly injured although all the Emergency Services – hospital, ambulance, fire and police – were immediately operated. At the subsequent British Rail enquiry the cause of the accident was announced as the gear-box seizing-up and locking the front wheels.

Northallerton Station

One of the biggest controversies regarding a building in Northallerton's recent history occurred with the demolition of Northallerton railway station building – originated at the very start of the national rail net-work in 1841 – and its replacement with a small squat building on each platform. The writing had been on the wall for its demise for some time with its gradual loss of facilities and its increasing neglect and dilapidation into the 1980s. Considerable local concern about the station was voiced particularly by local County Councillors Arnold Pearson and Tom Umpleby.

In December 1984 British Rail stated that because of financial constraints only a limited amount could be expended on the station with money not being provided by the local authorities. Eventually in 1986 the old station was gradually pulled down by Walter Thompsons contracted for £135,000 by British Rail and its modern replacement opened by Viscount Ingleby in October 1986. Contemporaneously British Rail were claiming a new speed record on this main line route where the HST 125 left Northallerton for example at 07.21 and reached London at 09.54.

Ironically the "Darlington and Stockton Times" noted British Rail's speed claims in November 1987 adding that at the same time Northallerton station had been reduced to "a bricked-up viaduct - a hideous farce" and commenting that:

"It is extraordinary that British Rail should have been allowed to destroy the character of the station in a redevelopment apparently based on cheapness rather than passenger comfort."

This forthright opinion has not been dulled by time and local older memories of a station redounding with Victorian character and a centre of modern activity and community are continuously contrasted with the cheerless ill equipped substitute. Locally it is still regretted that the Victorian main line station was not renovated or even partially preserved.

Electrification

By far the most important technological development was that of the electrification of the London to Edinburgh east coast main line with Northallerton almost mid-distant which was announced in 1985 at a cost of £306 million with the European Economic Community footing a major part of the finance. Amongst other things this involved: the raising of bridges over the main line which in the Northallerton area included Zetland and other bridges; and the closure in April 1990 of the Northallerton main line signal box which had become redundant whereas when it was installed just to the north of Northallerton station in

396

September 1939 possessed the most advanced signalling system in the country. It had then served an admirable, immediate and continual usefulness with the intensive war-time main line traffic.

Electrification on the main east coast line was completed in June 1991 with a new 225 Class 91 locomotive leaving London at 2.30 pm on 10th June to run to Newcastle. The full 225 electric service began on 4th July 1991 with journeys from Kings Cross to York taking 1 hour 43 minutes and to Northallerton 2 hours 20 minutes. In 1844 the London to Gateshead rail journey took 9 hours 15 minutes!

Wensleydale Railway

Whilst advanced technology was speeding trains onwards on the main line, the Northallerton-Wensleydale branch line was gradually grinding almost to a halt. After the cessation of passenger trains in 1954 the goods line was closed west of Redmire in 1964 with the track from Redmire to Garsdale removed in 1965. The last regular goods user on the Wensleydale line was the daily six times weekly run of a train of thirty six wagons carrying limestone from the Dales quarries from Redmire to British Steel at Lackenby, Redcar. Nicknamed 'Dusty Bin' this service ceased in December 1992, which effectively closed the Wensleydale goods line.

There had been strong advocates of the resumption of the railway on social and economic grounds which resulted in the formation of the positively minded Wensleydale Railway Association. Hope of the lines reprieve were bolstered in 1993 when the Ministry of Defence injected a £750,000 upgrade in conjunction with Railtrack and Railfreight Distribution with the aim of transferring heavy Army armoured vehicles more easily between Salisbury Plain and Catterick Camp. The first successful trial occurred in November 1993 when nineteen "Warrior" armoured personnel carriers were transported from Salisbury Plain to Redmire and this was repeated in June 1997 when twenty-one 28 tonne "Warriors" were railed from Redmire to Ludgershall, Salisbury Plain.

The new lease of life with irregular army traffic was accompanied by further passenger excursions such as that organised by the Wensleydale Railway Association on Saturday October 18th 1997 – the "Wensleydale Delight" – from Bradford to Redmire (618 seats). Pressing ahead for first the re-opening of the twenty-two miles Northallerton to Redmire line and then the stretch to Aysgarth with an integrated transport system the WRA instituted a Dales bus service in July 1998 which received a £95,000 North Yorkshire subsidy in December 1998. Finally after negotiations with Railtrack to take a ninety nine year lease on the railway the WRA formed the Wensleydale Railway PLC which on 23rd November 2000 went public by offering 2.5m ordinary shares at £1 per share with the aim of reactivating the twenty two mile railway line from Northallerton to Redmire.

Ripon Railway

In the 1990s another railway restoration group were gathering strength bent on the revival of another local railway. The Ripon Railway Reinstatement Association were aiming to restore the Harrogate – Ripon – Northallerton railway line which had been axed in the Dr Beeching cuts of the 1960s. Having obtained support from organisations such as the Harrogate branch of the Council for the Protection of Rural England, in December 2000 the association announced a £90,000 feasibility study into the railway's reactivation would take place in 2001.

Sidney Weighell

A final Northallerton-railway connection was that of Sidney Weighell who was born in the town and educated at the Applegarth and East Road (National) schools. He left school at fourteen to become a 'local' engine driver, a trade union official at Northallerton when he was only twenty and to rise to the very pinnacle of the national Trades Union tree as General Secretary and leader of the National Union of Railwaymen (NUR) from August 1974 to October 1982. This was an unprecedented achievement by a local person in the trade unions' sphere.

William Weighell his grandfather and his father Tom Weighell MBE were both staunch railway trade unionists and Sidney followed in their footsteps putting aside professional football with Sunderland FC (where he played for Sunderland reserves for two seasons) to attend fully to trade union duties. He had two books published about his life and career "On the Rails" and "One Hundred Years of Railway Weighells" and despite his success and national eminence he always remained "a man of the people" proud of his Northallerton and Yorkshire roots. His portrait appears in the National Portrait Gallery, London.

Post and Telecommunications

Communications of a different sort to road and rail but of vital importance concerned mail and telecommunications which were both under the auspices of the Post Office at the start of the last quarter of the century. This situation changed almost immediately with the telephone services being assumed by British Telecommunications which coincided with an enormous increase in the installation of private telephones which at the end of the Second World War in Northallerton had been almost confined to businesses and the well-to-do. By the 1980s almost every householder had a telephone and the telecommunications engineering services for the Northallerton area had been moved from the General Post Office on the High Street to Darlington under the new management of BT.

Royal Mail now dealt with the postal services at Northallerton Post Office which previously had taken over the site behind the High Street off Romanby Road occupied by Foreman and Render's salesroom (formerly the Cinema de Luxe) with the building being demolished to create a car park for Royal Mail vehicles. The Post Office (built in 1931) was modernised twice providing improved customer and service facilities but the greatest change was the removal of the sorting process in July 1982 to a new central Royal Mail sorting centre in Darlington costing £750,000 which had been opened by the Duke of Gloucester in May 1982. The Northallerton postal delivery and collection remained at and operated from the Post Office with this service being increasingly motorised.

IT Communication

The 1990s saw the revolution of communication by information technology with not only businesses and organisations fully equipped with e mail and internet facilities but more and more families and individuals 'on-line' and participating with their own computers. Northallerton library had been offering microfilm and microfiche services for two decades when they were able to give an internet access service to the public in 1999. Their next aim is to be electronically connected to the projected government's "People's Network".

A sign of the times with the younger generation becoming almost automatically computer literate was the successful "Technology Bid" by Northallerton College/Allertonshire School which in July 1998 brought Technology College status to the College – one of only twenty-eight schools nationally to achieve this. This put them into an 'IT enabling' position where they could bring communication learning facilities to the Northallerton district with schemes such as 'ADAPT' set up in 1998 to aid small businesses and Learndirect in 2000 whereby the public could seek learning via IT from basic numeracy and literacy through to advanced information technology.

Agriculture and Land Changes

Agriculture remained central to Northallerton's character and economy and the tremendous changes afoot since the Second World War continued until the end of the century. Complete mechanisation was achieved on the farms, major characteristics being: exceptionally intensive farming; a massive reduction in the work force with a comparative handful of personnel remaining of the agricultural worker mode; and the creation of widespread huge fields with hedgerows ploughed out and fields combined to facilitate the operation of agricultural machinery of an increasingly sophisticated nature.

A fundamental change came too in land ownership. Whereas immediately after the Second World War the farmers were mostly tenants, by the 1900s the vast majority of farms were owned by those who farmed them with a basic shift from tenant to owner farming with the large estates landowners such as British Rail selling off their holdings. A prime example of this was North Yorkshire County Council who in January 1998 despite opposition from the NFU and the Tenant Farmers Association voted overwhelmingly by 57 to 5 to sell off their 126 tenanted farms of 11,000 acres with an estimated value of £60m.

Scientifically induced crops became the order of the day with tremendous increases in yields but by the 1990s serious objections were being raised against this inorganic farming and there was a strong movement towards the growth of purely organic products.

Farming Crises

Indeed much controversy and difficulties faced the farming community latterly on a national scale with major issues. The most serious of these was the crisis in the beef industry with the onset in 1988 of BSE (bovine spongiform encephalopathy) commonly called 'Mad Cow Disease' (in humans CJD Crevtzfeldt-Jakob Disease). This caused the complete ban of British beef which led to chaos in that industry, bankruptcies and eventually the total regeneration of the country's herds to render them free from the damaging contamination and disease.

Other principle crises occurred such as a salmonella scare in the poultry area and in the later 1990s the decimation of the pig industry caused by over-production, foreign competition and the pre-dominance and control of the markets by the major supermarket retailers. Finally in March 2001 the outbreak of Foot and Mouth Disease caused another enormous problem in the harassed farming industry.

Indicative of the mood and uncertainty in the industry, a National Farmers Union (NFU) rally took place at Northallerton Applegarth mart on Friday 23rd September 1999 with four hundred farmers bringing the plight of the industry to the attention of the public with slogans and banners proclaiming 'Buy British' and similar exhortations. The demonstration received TV media coverage as the farmers marched to the Town Hall and back.

Hurworth Heyday – North End 1936

Hunting Controversy

Previously, on Sunday 28th February 1998, there had been a wholesale exodus from the district to assemble at Hyde Park in London for a "March for the Countryside" which reportedly attracted 284,000 of country folk the main thrust here being against the government threatened ban on fox hunting. The latter aroused high feelings in the countryside and even though parliament voted emphatically to ban hunting in a "free vote" at the end of 2000 the local Hurworth Hunt took place with as much animation as usual on Boxing Day 2000 traditionally in Northallerton High Street.

Farming Innovation

With farming in such doldrums survival became the watch-word by the end of the century with many farmers diversifying into other enterprises and roles for income-generation – bed and breakfast accommodation, specialised cheese manufacture, ice-cream making, pipe-laying expertise and dog boarding kennels are just some local examples. Certainly on many farms the traditional agricultural pursuance was insufficient to balance the farming economy.

In an effort to do this some progressive local farmers had for some time adopted and implemented technical and electronic methods in stock raising and production. This was seen for example in dairy farming where Bert Langthorne of Crawford Grange, Brompton introduced an electronic computer feeding method for his pedigree herd of 190 in 1986 in which year he held a farm "Open Day" which attracted 10,000 visitors. George Barker held a similar "Open Day" at his Thornborough Farm, Thirsk Road in 1994, the chief attraction being his scientifically bred and upkept dairy herd of 125 Folly Holsteins for which he had been awarded national Manager of the Year in 1993.

Another innovation to aid the ailing industry was that of Farmer's Markets where farmers were able to sell their own produce. A trial market was held at Sam Turner's, Darlington Road, Northallerton on Easter Monday 24th April 2000 which was so successful that others followed at the same venue.

Agricultural Shows

The North Yorkshire County Show, re-designated thus in 1979 to supplant the old Northallerton Show dating to 1867, consistently saw outstanding classes especially in horses and cattle which upheld the ancient traditions in these local standards. From Brawith Hall in 1979 and 1980, the "North Yorkshire" (organised by Secretary Peter Pybus until 1999) moved to Pasture House, Thirsk Road (Mr and Mrs Leslie Barker) in 1981 where it was held for a highly successful nine years until 1989 with a record crowd of nearly 18,000 and 170 trade stands on

4th August 1983. It was then held at various venues until settling permanently at Otterington Hall in 1996.

Of the smaller but intimately and familiarly attractive shows the "Osmotherley" (reputed as "the best little show in the North"), "Borrowby" and "Kirkby Fleetham" were continually popular and successively staged year by year.

Marts

The major agricultural sales were of course at the weekly marts of cattle and sheep on Tuesdays and Wednesday market days which were reduced to one venue – the Applegarth Mart – with the closure of the Station Mart in January 1981. By this time the Applegarth Mart (officially named Northallerton Auctions Ltd since 1921) had been continuously improved (a café had been added to its amenities for example) for it to remain as one of the major stock sales venues in the north of England. In 1986/87 it had an annual turnover of £20,130,506 which regularly increased and the sort of normal monthly animal average was for example: January 1989 – 578 cattle (including 202 young bulls), 2019 sheep and 403 pigs. Malpas Mart's former site was owned and run in conjunction with the Applegarth Mart as a car park and for periodic sales of agricultural machinery and implements. A sale for example in February 1993 contained over one thousand 'lots'.

Young Farmers

Also associated was the Northallerton Young Farmers Club which held its meetings at the Applegarth Mart, had celebrated its fiftieth anniversary in 1979 and remained an important entity in the local farming community. An outstanding reminder of its social force and ready talents was its appearance in the National Young Farmers Clubs Drama Finals at the Winter Gardens, Blackpool in April 1991 when a cast of seventeen performed "Dial A Dream".

Markets

By the end of the twentieth century two of Northallerton's ancient and traditional agricultural and economic centre-pieces – markets and fairs – had been either irrevocably transformed or had quite simply disappeared. By 1975 Northallerton markets had settled into a weekly pattern of the traditional Wednesdays and the Saturday market instituted in the 1950s. As opposed to the olden day markets the agricultural aspects were continually marginalized until finally the market stalls set up between Zetland Street and the Town Hall were selling every type of commercial goods ranging from groceries, vegetables and fish to hardware, toilet requisites and toys.

These markets attracted visitors from all over the region – Teesside, county Durham and west Yorkshire – to enhance Northallerton's commercial prosperity and reputation as a shopping centre with "free" parking an additional bonus. However, the market lost its farming orientated ambience the absence of which was seen both in the High Street and in the public houses which once filled with jostling farmers enjoying the bucolic Wednesday's conviviality and companionship were now sparsely occupied and utterly devoid of the Yorkshire farming fraternity atmosphere of yesteryear.

May Fair

The traditional four annual 'Royal' fairs had also long gone with the modern economic practices in agricultural and trade. There was one locally deemed precious remnant, however – the Northallerton May Fair with its roots dating over four hundred years. By now all vestiges of agricultural and trade had evaporated and the event was purely a "Pleasure Fair" in the first week in May from Thursday until Monday in the High Street from the Parish Church to Zetland Street which by the 1960s was sealed to traffic.

The Crows and Murphys were still the leading 'Fair' families and the traditional shooting galleries, fun of the fair stalls and activities such as children's bell-ringing roundabouts along with the timeless "Dodgem" or "Bumper" Cars were inter-mingled with speedster machines of increasing velocity, bewildering movement and spectacular flashing technicolour. Succeeding generations derived equal enjoyment from the yearly event and there was much opposition when Hambleton District Council mooted the need to remove the May Fair from the High Street in the late 1980s.

A great "Fair Debate" ensued with the fair being moved experimentally from the High Street to the Applegarth Car Park in May 1990. A public meeting in March 1991 in Northallerton Town Hall was of united opinion led by the Vicar Canon Ian Fox and the Mayor John Coulson and unanimously supported by Northallerton Town Council that the historic town tradition should be upheld of staging the May Fair annually in the High Street. In the following month an agreement was reached between Hambleton District Council and the Fair's representatives that the May Fair would continue on the High Street.

Friarage Hospital

A major factor and prime example of the progress, growing economy and general burgeoning of Northallerton was the development and extensive structural modernisation of the Friarage Hospital. Indeed

First Friarage Babies – February 1987

it was fortunate for a town of such size to possess such medical facilities and assets as Northallerton by the end of the century which along with its county, central and local government concerns and buildings made it unique in the north east of England.

Re-organisation

The fundamental basis and groundwork during and after the Second World War at the hospital led to it being ear-marked for re-building as early as 1962. Its cause was helped by its subsequent transfer into the new Yorkshire Regional Health Authority with the re-organisation of the National Health Service in 1974 which decreed that all districts should be largely self-sufficient with the consequent considerable extension of clinical services in the Friarage.

The hospital had become a unit in the Northallerton Health District and on 1st April 1982 Northallerton Health Authority was established as one of the seventeen health districts in the Yorkshire Regional Health Authority headquartered at Harrogate. Northallerton Health Authority was centred at the Friarage Hospital and was chaired initially by the Reverend Benet Ormerod until April 1988 when Caroline Thornton-Berry of Swinithwaite Hall became Chairman, followed by Brigadier Johnny Wardle in 1994.

Re-development – Phase One

Redevelopment of the Friarage Hospital became a reality with the first swing of the demolition ball to remove the hutted brick wartime wards in November 1982 to commence the re-building programme. This was planned to take place in three "Phases" at an overall cost of £19 million and to be completed by the mid 1990s.

The building of "Phase" I of the new hospital commenced early in 1984, the main contractor being Taylor Woodrow Construction (Northern) Ltd and such was the progress that the "topping out" (completion of the main structure and roof) ceremony was performed ahead of the contractual time on 27th September 1985 by Leon Brittan QC (soon to be knighted) the MP for Richmondshire, Secretary of State for Trade and Industry and a member of Margaret Thatcher's Conservative party's Cabinet.

The comparatively resplendent "Phase" I building was designed recognisably on the architectural lines of the oldest edifice on the Friarage site – the 1858 "Sunbeck House" old Northallerton Workhouse at the entrance to the Friarage Hospital. "Phase" I was a three storied complex constructed on the Department of Health's nucleus principle which facilitated future possible expansion and comprised five wards with 140 beds for acute cases, a maternity unit of 31 beds and 10 special care cots and accident, emergency and X-ray departments.

In December 1986 all the new units were opened except the maternity unit which was activated on the weekend of 31st January/1st February 1987. The latter meant the rather nostalgic closure in many local minds and families of the historic Mount Pleasant maternity

Duke and Duchess of York – Friarage Visit

hospital which since its emergency opening in September 1939 had been the birth-place of thousands of local children. Taylor, Young and Partners were the "Phase" I Architects and the official opening of the £8 million building was carried out by the Under Secretary of State for Health Edwina Currie MP on Friday 13th November 1987.

Phase Two and Royal Visits

The building process of the hospital continued with the erection of the £3.6 million "Phase Two" complex which provided a much needed essential medical facility for the Northallerton area of a Mental Health Unit as well as a ward for needy elderly patients. "Phase Two" was topped out by Sir Bryan Askew Chairman of the Yorkshire Health Authority on 13 November 1990 having been constructed by Wiltshire Northern Limited. The first psychiatric patients were received into the Mental Health Unit in March 1991 and "Phase Two" had an official Royal opening on 4th June 1992 which was undertaken by Her Royal Highness Princess Alexandra who was received and accompanied by the Chairman of the Northallerton District Health Authority Caroline Thornton-Berry.

Previously to this, on 2nd August 1989, the Friarage Hospital had been honoured by another Royal Visit by the Duke and Duchess of York who planted a tree and showed an animated interest in the hospital and its proceedings. Shortly afterwards the hospital's administrative and financial procedures were taken over by the Northallerton Health Services Trust which became a self-accounting unit.

Military Addition

A major change came in 1998 when the Army Medical Services for the northern region became based at the Friarage Hospital. This came about with a cost-cutting and financial rationalisation by the Ministry of Defence (Army) in its medical services which saw the closure of the Duchess of Kent's Military Hospital at Catterick Garrison and the removal of its medical responsibilities and staff to the Friarage Hospital.

The hospital had had to compete with the Darlington Memorial Hospital for the military multi-million contract and partnership. William Hague the leader of the Conservative Party and local Richmondshire MP welcomed the merger observing that "it will maintain the geographical integrity of our local services". The civilian and military hospital entities quickly dovetailed into good working arrangements and procedures despite the initial problem of a lack of accommodation.

Scott Suite

On 5th December 1997 a new breast cancer assessment centre had been opened by Lady Masham of Ilton which was described by consultant Mr Robert Bryan as a magnificent acquisition which would act as a focal point for immediate GP access and diagnosis. The unit was called the Scott Suite after Mrs Elsie Scott whose generous bequest had initiated the quest for the £400,000 necessary for the project, with the League of Friends the public and hospital staff making tremendous efforts to complete the amount.

League of Friends

Indeed this was the latest in a series of contributions to the Friarage Hospital organised by the League of Friends which of course owed its success to the drive, commitment and attitude of the entire district: towns, villages, individuals, organisations, churches, businesses both near and far. Innumerable gifts and voluntary efforts were achieved by the League of Friends – community alliance and some were substantial. A Relatives Overnight Stay Accommodation costing nearly £8,000 which consisted of two flatlets for patients relatives who lived at a distance was opened on 21st August 1975 and was named Clark House after the Chairman of the League of Friends "Nobby" Clark who was awarded the MBE for his services to the hospital as was his successor 'Brenny' Archer, their Chairmanships spanning thirty six years.

A new minibus was purchased for £15,000 in the summer of 1987 and 1990 saw the completion of a £45,000 project which produced a Postgraduate and Nursing Education Library. Nearly two years of vigorous campaigning and multi-source fund raising eventuated in the installation of a £1.2 million CAT Scanner in 1992. Finally in October 1998 a Friarage Millennium Appeal was launched by the League of Friends and backed by the 'Darlington and Stockton Times' to raise £500,000 by which to replace the old wooden wards 11 and 12 which housed the high dependency unit for elderly patients – around 1000 annually. The Northallerton NHS Trust would match this amount which would then serve to replace Phase III of the original hospital reorganisation and rebuilding plan which had been shelved for fourteen years because of NHS financial short falls.

Ministry of Defence Hospital Unit

The local response to the Friarage Millennium Appeal was as typical as it was remarkable and with the total standing at £463,000 on 31st March 2000 demolition work started on Wards 11 and 12. The League and the Trust's joint effort was merged with the Ministry of Defence Hospital Unit's (MDHU) need for accommodation and the resources were pooled to produce a £2.5m three storied building which was added to by a ready made unit which arrived for the MOD in May 2000 from Yokon of York consisting of forty six steel framed modules and costing £500,000.

Adjoining the north side of the hospital the new complex consisted of a 27 bed orthopaedic ward, a 29 bed surgical ward and offices and meeting rooms for MDHU use. Officially termed "Ministry of Defence Hospital Unit (Northallerton)" the building was opened on Friday 8th December 2000 by Dr L Moonie MP Parliamentary Under Secretary of State for Defence in the appropriate presence of 'Lol' Bailey Chairman of the League of Friends, Alastair Shepherd Commanding Officer MDHU, Johnny Wardle Chairman Northallerton NHS Trust and Councillor Jack Dobson, Mayor of Northallerton.

By the end of 2000 the only hospital units remaining in old buildings were pharmacy, pathology, laboratories, some children's beds, and a kitchen. The redevelopment programme was finalised in August 2001 when Ian Botham, famous cricketer and leukaemia treatment fund raiser 'extraordinaire' who lived locally near Richmond, officially opened the Millennium Building which combined the latest building projects.

Rutson Hospital

A fitting footnote on Northallerton's quite remarkable hospital heritage of eight hundred years falls to the Rutson Hospital, itself an integral factor in the local hospitals' saga. In 1977 it was made an acute hospital unit for General Practitioners and surgical cases with twenty seven beds and in the early 1990s a proposal to close the Rutson by the Regional Health Authority was strongly and successfully opposed by the local GPs led by Dr Boersma of Northallerton to the extent that rebuilding and reconstructure at the rear of the hospital was completed by FT Construction Ltd in 1998. The Rutson presently houses GP beds for acutely ill patients, the Rehabilitation Unit and accommodation for staff of the mental health department.

The Church of England

Religion and the churches continued to play a central role in the life of Northallerton with the support and commitment of congregations reflected in a variety of ways including several successful building programmes.

Northallerton All Saints Parish Church was led into what would be its third millennium of presence by successive Vicars, John Castledine and Ian Fox who were both made Canons whilst in office. During Reverend Castledine's incumbency the only external structural addition of the twentieth century to the Parish Church took place with the construction of a new parlour at the north east corner in 1977. Of a flat-topped style from the outset it seemed out of kilter with the ancient building's architectural lines and this was remedied in 1995 when a pitched slate roof was added giving a more blended appearance.

Renovations and Fund Generation

The Parish Church indeed was almost continuously renovated and refurbished. In 1986 the Tower pinnacles were repaired, the floor under the Tower was replaced in 1988 and in 1995 the Church clock – a static yet ubiquitous chiming town friend – was repainted a refreshing blue and gold. These improvements cost £11,000 and in July 1999 an appeal was launched for £75,000 for major renovations – replacing stonework, re-leading the north aisle roof, fitting new fall-pipes and re-flooring the south aisle.

Within thirteen months the requisite amount had virtually been raised in what the Vicar Ian Fox termed 'a magnificent effort' by the town and in particular by the "Friends of Northallerton Parish Church" group of all denominations which had spearheaded the fund raising to the extent of £30,000 with the local councils, businesses, trusts and individuals from near and far supporting the cause. The planned work on the church was completed early in 2001. Income generation of an on-going basis of course was essential and apart from the continual backing of the "Friends" such things as the annual Church Bazaar and the perennial collection of newspapers for re-cycling proved key financial sources.

Choir and Bell Ringers

Constant contributors to the ethos and atmosphere of the church were the choir and the bell-ringers. Both of these latterly had been augmented and embellished by the fairer sex and several girls were recipients of the coveted annual Gerry Wilson Chorister Award – Mary Lawson (1979), Helen Murdoch (1986) and Alison Christon (1988). In January 1992 two bells were added to the bell tower and the bell chamber ceiling was replaced in April 1993 largely through the enterprise of the Captain of the bell-ringers for over twenty years, David Town.

Church Events

The Archbishop of York Rt Rev John Hapgood visited the church twice: in June 1985 in celebration of the centenary of the 1885 restoration and building of a new Chancel; and on 22nd November 1992 to conduct a Confirmation Service. His predecessor Archbishop Stuart Blanche visited St Helens Church, Ainderby on 7th January 1979 on the commemoration of that church's eight hundredth anniversary; and later in 1979 he preached the sermon at St Thomas' Church, Brompton on Remembrance Sunday 11th November.

The Vicar of Brompton, Reverend Gordon Cooper, after serving the parish for twenty three years was succeeded by Reverend Harry Lee in 1982 who remained in post until 1991 when he was followed in 1992 by Reverend Michael Snowball MA DipTh.

Musical events of a high standard took place in the Northallerton Parish Church such as: Christ's College Cambridge choir on 14th March 1992, King's College Cambridge choir on 31st March 1993 and local groups like the North Yorkshire Chorus who performed the 'Messiah' in 1989. The Bishop of Whitby Rt Rev Gordon Bates conducted Canon John Castledine's Retirement Service in September 1985 and inducted Ian Fox as Vicar and Rural Dean of Northallerton on 1st December 1985. The latter hailing locally from Redcar brought his strong belief in a "living church" from Bury in Lancashire to Northallerton.

Ecumenical Movement

Reverend Ian Fox, who was made a Canon in 1996 and all the Northallerton clergy of different denominations were committed to a strong ecumenical movement which was abroad in the town and evidenced by a yearly 'March for Jesus' organised by the Northallerton Christian Council of Churches which started at Romanby processed through the High Street and ended with an inter-denominational service in the Northallerton Parish Church. The first of these was held in September 1990 and another example of the movement to Christian unity was the establishment of the 'Churches Together Bookshop' opened at the United Reformed Church by the Mayor of Northallerton Jane Harvey on 7th October 1995.

The culmination of this ecumenical co-operation was a history-making event which was said in a way to reverse the Reformation when in December 1999 twelve churches signed a covenant expressing their willingness to work together. Signatories of this historic document included all the leaders of the main Northallerton churches – Church of England, Methodist, New Life Baptist, Roman Catholic and United Reformed.

Lady Curate

Another sign of the religious times was the ordination of the first woman priest in Northallerton's All Saint's Parish Church history. On what was described as a 'momentous occasion' Reverend Karen Gorham from Essex was ordained at Northallerton by the Bishop of Selby Rt Rev Humphrey Taylor attended by Rt Rev Gordon Bates the Bishop of Whitby on Monday 24th June 1996. Immediately previously Rev Gorham had been deaconess where she found 'the people warm and friendly' and she now became curate and as such able to conduct all religious services including Holy Communion.

United Reformed Church

In June 1978 Northallerton had received its first woman cleric when Rev Christine Collin had become Minister of the United Reformed Church – formerly the Zion Congregational Church until the Congregational and English Presbyterian churches were unified nationally in 1972 to become the United Reformed Church. The Northallerton United Reformed Church was extensively renovated and re-opened in June 1979. Reverend John Parker's Ministry in the last years of the century was characterised by great support of the needy and the ecumenical concept and practical promotion of this in Northallerton.

Methodists

The oldest established non-conformist church in Northallerton, the Methodist with a strong congregation and an exceptionally gifted choir which produced several popular cassettes of hymns and religious music, was flourishing and it too completed major re-building and renovation programmes. In March 1997 the first phase of this costing £375,000 was accomplished which saw the re-vamping of the area between the hall and the main body of the church which was itself completely refurbished.

The second phase of over £200,000 consisting of a front re-structure with a new terrace, ramp and landscaped forecourt was attractively completed before a Service of Celebration on 26th March 1999. This was led by the Superintendent Minister Rev Keith Phipps who praised the tremendous efforts which led to the church restoration and the sermon to a packed congregation was delivered by the President Designate of the national Methodist Conference Rev Stuart Burgess Chairman of the York and Hull Methodist District.

New Life Baptists

In Romanby the Methodist Church had completely established itself and the New Life Baptist Church had so outgrown its Valley Road church that in January 1993 the church temporarily took over the Hambleton Community Centre on Sundays such was the size of its congregations. The New Life Baptist buoyancy was expressed annually from 1994 onwards by their 'New Life for Romania' pre Christmas appeal when they secured wholesale local support for the cause of supplying aid to the town of Timisoara in Romania including two hospitals and two orphanages. Each year a team of New Life Baptists led by Pastor Rev Rodney Breckon ran a truckload of medical supplies and other equipment to Romania.

The problem of a sufficiently capacious church was resolved for the New Life Baptists by their purchase of the former "Lyric" cinema from owner Robert Harris in September 1997. £160,000 was raised for the project which also necessitated the complete gutting and re-establishment of the building into a church and premises which included

Youth Centre facilities that contained a 'dry-bar' – the 'Ravens'. The New Life Baptist Church at the Lyric was opened with celebratory worship, music and drama on Sunday 10th April 1998 with the Mayor of Northallerton Councillor Jim Stafford present. Six hundred packed the church on a day described by Rev Rodney Breckon as a "momentous day for us and a wonderful day for Northallerton."

Jehovah's Witnesses and Evangelicals

"The Jehovah's Witnesses" had developed from small beginnings in 1948 meeting in the Scout hut, Malpas Road to be vibrant enough to build their own Kingdom Hall in Romanby Road in 1995. Another new church was the Evangelical Church which opened on 30th June 1979. This church was a converted house purchased for £14,000 on the east side of North End and Reverend John Legg was the first Evangelical Minister.

Roman Catholics

Finally from the modern to the longest established religious faith of much more than a thousand years at Northallerton – the Roman Catholic Church continued to be very well supported and prospered at their Sacred Heart Church, Thirsk Road. Father Francis Connolly came to Northallerton as parish priest in 1938 was canonised in 1972 and served the parish until 1978 when he was succeeded by Father Damian Noonan. The latter was followed by Father Patrick 'Joe' Brennan in 1984 just after a concelebratory Mass by fifteen Diocesan priests to mark the fiftieth anniversary of the Sacred Heart Church opened in 1934. After a most popular incumbency Father Brennan retired in 2001 to be succeeded by Father Norman Jacobson.

Politics and MPs

On the parliamentary political scene Timothy Kitson twice retained his Richmondshire seat and received a knighthood in 1974 and in the following year the former Prime Minister Edward Heath stayed at Sir Timothy's Leazes, Leeming Bar home after speaking at Northallerton Town Hall on 29th May regarding the coming Referendum on Britain's joining the European Economic Union and giving his strongest recommendation to vote "YES!" In the ensuing June 1975 EEC Referendum North Yorkshire voted conclusively in favour of joining the Common Market by 234,040 (76.3%) votes to 72,805 (23.7%).

415

Sir Timothy Kitson – General Election May 1979

Sir Timothy Kitson again won Richmondshire for the Conservatives in the General Election of 10th May 1979 which saw a Margaret Thatcher Conservative Government returned for the first time. The Richmondshire result was declared at Northallerton Community Centre, and was as follows: Sir Timothy Kitson (Con) 28,958; GS Hodgson (Lib) 9964; KR Bratton (Lab) 8,173 - Majority 18,994.

In 1982 having served on the House of Commons Select Committee on the Falkland Crisis of 1981, Sir Timothy announced his retirement as an MP at the end of that Parliament. To mark his distinguished and locally caring parliamentary career from 1959 to 1983 his Richmondshire constituents presented him with a 1911 painting "View of the Thames".

Leon Brittan – General Election May 1983

From a list of two hundred and thirty candidates, Leon Brittan, the MP for Cleveland and Whitby constituency which was to be phased out, was chosen as the next Conservative candidate to contest the Richmondshire constituency. Leon Brittan justified the Tory confidence in him with a comfortable majority of 18,066 in the General Election of May 1983 the full result with a 68.7% "turn out" of electors being Leon Brittan (Con) 32,373; David Raw (Lib) 14,307; Barbara Hawkins (Lab/Co-op) 4997.

A former President of the Cambridge University Union in 1960 who was called to the Bar in 1962 and became a Queen's Counsel in 1978, Leon Brittan was immediately made Home Secretary and a member of Mrs Thatcher's Cabinet after the May 1983 Election and thus became the holder of the most important Government post of any of Richmondshire's MPs so far in its century of existence. As Home Secretary he had a very high mass-media profile but spent much time in his constituency at weekends and holidays residing at Spennithorne in Wensleydale.

June 1987 General Election

Leon Brittan launched his campaign for the General Election of June 11th 1987 in Northallerton and gained the regulation and expected decisive Conservative victory: Leon Brittan (Conservative) 34,995;

David Lloyd Williams (Lib/Alliance) 15,419 and Frank Robson (Labour) 6,737: Majority 19,576 in a 72.1% poll. By this time Leon Brittan had become Minister for Trade and Industry in a 1985 Cabinet re-shuffle and in July 1988 as a result of the controversial 'Westland Affair' which concerned a 'leaked' confidential document he resigned his ministerial and allied cabinet posts.

Shortly afterwards he announced his intention of leaving parliament upon his selection as the British European Commissioner of the European Economic Community. He took up this post on 1st January 1989, received a knighthood on the same day and for several years bent his considerable talents to the EEC cause becoming Vice President of the European Commission in July 1991 and finally being elevated to the peerage as Lord Brittan in January 2000. He continued to retain his North Yorkshire links with his home in Wensleydale and reciprocally his wife Diana was awarded the CBE in 1995 for her work on the European scene.

William Hague

In November 1988 William Hague aged twenty seven had been chosen to succeed Leon Brittan as Richmondshire's Conservative candidate with his adoption ceremony taking place at Northallerton. A Yorkshire man from Wath-on-Dearne where his family had a soft drinks firm of a hundred years standing he had first come to political notice with a Tory and Thatcher captivating speech when aged only sixteen at the 1977 Conservative Party Conference. At Oxford University he had obtained a First Class Honours degree in Philosophy, Politics and Economics (PPE), before unsuccessfully contesting his home area Wentworth seat in 1987.

By Election 1989

The Richmondshire by-election resulting from Leon Brittan's resignation was nothing short of sensational in terms of an acknowledged Conservative stronghold and eminently 'safe' seat. "Tories scrape home" exclaimed the headline as the Conservative majority was slashed from 19,576 to 2,634 with Frank Robson the Labour candidate losing his deposit. What with the youthfulness of William Hague and the "additional" unorthodox candidates it was an Election with a difference in Richmondshire's colourful history. The full election result announced at the Hambleton Community Centre, Northallerton was: William Hague (Con) 19,543; Mike Potter (Social Democrat Party) 16,909; B Pearce (Liberal Democrats) 11,589; Frank Robson (Lab) 2591; Dr R Upsall (Green Party) 1473; Lord Sutch (Monster Raving Loony Party) 167; A Mills (University Information Officer) 113; L St Claire (Corrective Party) 106 and N Watkins (Official Liberal) 70.

General Election April 1992

Unruffled by his narrow victory put down to "by-electionitis" William Hague flung himself indefatigably into parliamentary and constituency affairs attending innumerable local functions and holding one hundred and twenty eight constituency 'surgeries' in a year. He was rewarded by a landslide victory at the General Election on 9th April 1992 – William Hague (Con) 40,202; George Irwin (Liberal/Democrat) 16,698; RF Cranston (Lab) 7,523; AM Barr (Independent) 570. The Conservative majority was 23,504 (36.2%).

William Hague continued his strong Richmondshire constituency commitment and involvement throughout the 1990s as well as making a meteoric and unprecedented rise through the ranks of the Parliamentary Conservative Party. In July 1995 he was appointed as the Secretary of State for Wales and elevated to the Cabinet and then in the re-formation of the Conservatives Party after the heavy defeat by the Labour Party in the 1997 General Election he was selected as the Leader of the Conservatives in Parliament and per se the Leader of the Opposition at the age of thirty six.

1997 General Election

With the political weakening of the Conservatives throughout the country the Richmondshire result in the 1997 General Election was a closer run affair than in 1992 with William Hague's majority more than halved to 10,051. Steve Merritt of Northallerton polled more Labour votes than anyone in the constituency's history with 13,275 and Jane Harvey who was also a prominent Northallerton local politician obtained 8,773 votes for the Liberal Democrats.

The full 1997 result was: William Hague (Con) 23,326 (48.9%), Steve Merritt (Lab) 13,275 (27.8%), Jane Harvey (Lib Dem) 8,773 (18.5%), A Bentley (Referendum Party) 2,367 (5%). Conservative Majority 10,051 (21.05%). Electorate 65,058. Total Vote 47,741. Poll 73.4%.

Political Bulletin

There were local political happenings a-plenty in the last quarter of the century. Two noteworthy deaths were those of stalwart and popular North Yorkshire parliamentarians Lord Crathorne in April 1977 and in January 1994 Lord Tranmire of Upsall, formerly Robin Turton MP for Thirsk-Malton from 1929 for forty five years. In January 1986 Joseph Barnard of Harlsey Hall was knighted for political and public services having been Chairman of the Richmondshire Conservative Party, a survivor of the Grand Hotel, Brighton bombing in 1984 and Chairman of the Northallerton Magistrates Court for several years. The Conservative Prime Minister John Major stayed at Crathorne Hall Hotel (Thomas Dugdale's former home) in September 1995 on his "Round Britain Meet the People" tour.

Dr Marjorie "Mo" Mowlam who was then "Shadow" Minister for Northern Ireland on 4th November 1995 gave a keynote lecture in Northallerton's Hambleton Community Centre on "Labour and the Peace Process" which presaged her crucial contribution in this critical area after she became Minister to Northern Ireland in 1997. Of local interest too was the verbal cut and thrust of the rival party leaders particularly at the now televised Prime Minister's Question Time – Premier Tony Blair and William Hague, whose constituencies bordered each other only a few miles from Northallerton.

General Election June 2001

The General Election of Thursday 6th June 2001 held unexpected drama. Richmondshire's result announced at Northallerton in the Hambleton Leisure Centre which was the constituency Returning Centre was predictably a comfortable victory for Conservative leader William Hague with a majority of 16,319 and a swing of 8% from Labour to the Conservatives. With the national electorate turn out at 59% the lowest since 1918 the Richmondshire response of 67.4% voting was comparatively satisfactory. Richmondshire's full result was:

William Hague (Con) 25,951 (58.9%):
Fay Tinnion (Lab) 9632 (21.9%):
Edward Forth (Lib Dem) 7,890 (17.9%):
Melodie Staniforth (Loony Party) 561 (1.3%)
Conservative Majority – 16,319.

William Hague accompanied by his wife Ffion received the Richmondshire result at 4.10 am at the Leisure Centre and then left Northallerton immediately for Conservative Central Office, Smith's Square, London. Here just four hours later around 8 am he announced his resignation as leader of the Conservative Party to an assembled battery of the mass media because of the repeated landslide majority of Tony Blair's Labour Party. His sensational resignation was marked both by its dignity and the regret engendered particularly in his own constituency where the election result had reflected his local conscientious attentions and popularity.

Education and Schools

East Road School

In the educational sphere an occurrence of some moment was the closure of the East Road Infants School in July 1980 which as the National Schools since 1843 had pioneered the education of all classes of children in Northallerton. Innumerable success stories of humble back-grounded children who had reached professional, business, industrial and civic heights redounded to its credit but time had eroded its educational effectiveness and it was taken over by North Yorkshire Social Services Department as their headquarters.

Primary Education

Alverton Infants School was built off Crossbeck Road by RBA Moody and Son at a cost of £219,343 (the National School cost £917. 2s. 2d. in 1843!) to accommodate the children aged 5 to 8 with 160 moving there in 1980 which soon rose to a roll of 240. Alverton soon became the first school in Northallerton to be equipped with a nursery unit by North Yorkshire education authority which was opened by the Mayor of Northallerton Jennifer Davies on 1st April 1988.

A Royal Visit

In July 1995 the charity ICAN offered to set up a specialised unit attached to Alverton School for children with speech and language difficulties at a cost of £120,000 over two years after which North Yorkshire education authority principally would take over. There was added anticipation and auspiciousness when it was announced that Her Royal Highness Princess Margaret who was a patron of ICAN would perform the opening ceremony.

Princess Margaret arrived by Rolls Royce to a warm welcome by a large crowd to officially open the ICAN unit on 7th October 1996. She was conducted around the school by the Alverton headteacher Mrs Anne Condon who commented that "she was charming, put people at their ease and had a great sense of humour." It was an historic occasion as the first royal visit to a school in Northallerton since James I's to Northallerton Grammar School in 1617!

Nursery provision was a strong educational feature with all the primary school catchment areas in Northallerton having this facility by 1992. The primary schools including Brompton and Romanby all achieved good standards in the government statutory tests (SATS) but a perennial problem was that of large class numbers and some accommodation shortages. The latter was offset to some degree with a major extension of four classrooms at Mill Hill primary school at a cost of £280,000 opened by William Hague MP in October 1990 who became a regular visitor and supporter of Northallerton schools throughout the next decade.

Plans to extend the Applegarth primary school were welcomed by its long serving head teacher Al Proctor and these went ahead in the summer of 2001 authorised by North Yorkshire County Council. The extensions were effected at a cost of £368,000 by RBA Moody Bros, the Northallerton building contractors which seemed appropriate because this firm like Walter Thompsons had been central to the tremendous building surge in Northallerton and district since the Second World War.

In surrounding village schools there were contrasting fortunes. At South Otterington a new primary school was opened for seventy children in July 1993; in the same month Ainderby primary school celebrated its twenty fifth anniversary on its 1968 site at Morton-on-Swale; but an inclement calamity overtook Brompton primary school when the floods of $2^{nd}/3^{rd}$ November 2000 made the school uninhabitable for months with the children bussed out daily to various temporary teaching venues.

Sacred Heart RC School

Finally after strong controversy centred mainly around the siting, a new school, Sacred Heart Roman Catholic primary school, was opened at Broomfield, Northallerton in September 2000. The traditional first sod cut to commence the building was turned by the Roman Catholic Bishop of Middlesbrough Rt Rev John Crowley on 11th February 2000. The building costing around £800,000 was erected by SGK Construction and the first headteacher was Peter Griffin who would eventually have ninety pupils aged 5 – 11 in the school.

Secondary Education

"Progressive" would aptly describe the primary education situation in Northallerton during the last quarter of the twentieth century but only "Revolutionary" would do for the secondary sphere which was literally transformed. The ancient Northallerton Grammar School has seen many vicissitudes in its colourful six hundred and eighty years history but no change as great as the fundamental alteration of its educational function from a grammar to a comprehensive school in 1973.

Necessary accommodation extensions had been provided at Northallerton Grammar School with a rectangular multi-purpose block running eastwards to Colstan Road in 1972 and extra classrooms, science laboratories and other facilities were built at a cost of £332,610 to the north towards Crosby Road. These were opened by Lady Bell, Chairman of the Governors, on 23rd January 1980.

Obviously the buildings were only a part of the problems of change from a selective system based on academic prowess to an open-ended all-ability combined educational school entry and programme. Great adjustments had to be made and difficulties encountered until the Grammar and Allertonshire Schools emerged as genuine comprehensive educational entities and by the 1990s were fully settled into their new roles with commensurate stability, positive progress and achievements.

A telling indication of both the effectiveness and nature of the new Grammar School scenario was seen simply in the sixth form statistics – between 1984 and 1994 the annual sixth form numbered around 250 which approximated to the entire school roll between 1945 to 1955.

Northallerton College

Another strong movement during the fruitful headship of John Bell (1984 to 1997) was that towards the provision for and the encouragement of part-time adult "Continuing Education" – later termed "Life-long Learning" to which there was a ready and continuing response from the district's community to the extent of 2000 adult part-time students by 1992.

An ultimate eventuality of the absolute change of the grammar school into a comprehensive community school was the re-naming of Northallerton Grammar School in 1994, after six hundred and seventy two years of that nomenclature, to become Northallerton College. Succinctly described officially "to reflect more accurately the true nature of the school", the change though justified was nostalgically regretted by many in the town and particularly ex-scholars – Old Alvertonians.

However, in its modern role and ethos Northallerton College forged ahead, from September 1997 under its first female head-teacher (now termed Principal retitled with the school in 1994) Jennifer Slater. In October 1997 in partnership with the Allertonshire Northallerton College launched a "Technology Bid" which was successful after the achievement of raising £100,000 from the supportive local businesses and public. £700,000 over six years was unlocked from government sources to develop information technology, Northallerton College was designated a 'Technology College' and William Hague MP, the leader of the Opposition who had launched the bid, officially opened the Northallerton College/Allertonshire technology college in July 1998.

Northallerton College also remained observant of and true to its ancient traditions as exampled in 1999 by the presentation of an oaken 1939-45 War Memorial Roll of Honour of the twenty fallen ex-pupils by the Durham University foundation Governors of 1322 connection.

The buoyancy of one of the oldest schools in the North of England as it embarked on yet another century can again be gleaned by sheer statistics. In 2000 the Northallerton College roll was 1029 full-time students and of these 452 were in the Sixth Form (30 in 1952!) of voluntary attendance. Additionally there were 3500 part-time adult students in 'Life-Long Learning' courses. Four thousand students had voted with their feet!

William Hague celebrates Northallerton Schools Technology Status

Northallerton College – Girls Rugby 1998

Services Links

The links between the Service units most closely associated with Northallerton, the Green Howards and Royal Air Force Leeming, were strengthened "in perpetuam" with both being accorded the "Freedom of Northallerton" and the right to march through the town "with bayonets fixed, drums beating and colours flying."

Green Howards Freedom

The county town county regiment connection which had been especially close with the headquarters of the 4th Battalion (Territorials) Green Howards being centred in the town since 1911 was given official recognition on 2nd August 1980. In an emotive ceremony the entire 1st Battalion Green Howards paraded through the route-crowded town led by the stirring Regimental Band of the Green Howards and joined fittingly by the veterans of the local Green Howards Association and the youthful Green Howards Northallerton Cadet Force. Lieutenant Colonel John Byrne the Commanding Officer of the 1st Battalion was then presented with a scrolled "Illuminated Address" granting the town's freedom to the Green Howards from the Mayor of Northallerton Councillor George Kelley himself appropriately a former Green Howards 4th Battalion soldier with a distinguished Second World War record of active service.

Band Farewell

Another historic Green Howards event fell to Northallerton on Thursday 14th July 1994. The 1st Battalion Green Howards exercised their right that afternoon to march through Northallerton but the significance of the occasion was that this was the very last appearance of the Green Howards Regimental Band which had been an inspiration to the regiment since 1750. As its very last movement it headed the Green Howards northwards through the High Street playing the stridently evocative Green Howards regimental march "The Bonny English Rose". And then as it neared All Saints Parish Church it took up "Auld Land Syne" wheeling left at the church out of High Street sight, its last fading echoing strains signalling the silence of the disbandment of an awesome tradition.

Royal Air Force Leeming - Northallerton Connection

Royal Air Force Leeming too was the author of much latter millennium interest. The ceremony of the presentation of an "Illuminated Scroll" for the freedom of Northallerton effect took place on 21st April 1978 by the Mayor of Northallerton Councillor Doug Walkland to the Commanding Officer of Leeming Group Captain Peter Vangucci with Air Marshal Sir Alex Roe the Air Officer Commanding Support Command and James Wellbeloved MP the under Secretary of State for Air in attendance. A large and enthusiastic crowd watched the "freedom" parade of a three hundred Royal Air Force contingent led by the Royal Air Force Regiment band and the famed Queen's Colour Squadron, both from nearby Royal Air Force Catterick, overflown by four "Bulldog" aircraft.

Throughout the next two decades Leeming paraded the "Illuminated Address" exercising their freedom of Northallerton on an annual basis with an associated service at the Parish Church and a fly past. The civic and service bonds were also complemented by: the presentation of a flag-pole in 1981 by Leeming to Northallerton for ceremonial purposes at the Town Hall; the continued annual gifting of a Christmas tree to the town from Leeming; and the appearance every year of a Royal Air Force Leeming contingent as the main Services representatives at the Remembrance Day service and parade through Northallerton at which the station's Commanding Officer always took the salute accompanied by the Mayor of Northallerton.

Royal Connection – Prince Andrew

With the Central Flying School (CFS) present and frequent VIP flights Leeming was seldom out of the public eye in the early 1980s. Both the Queen Mother twice and Princess Anne thrice flew in and out and the royal connection and media concentration was heightened when Prince Andrew was posted to Leeming in 1980 to undergo initial pilot training with the Royal Naval Elemental Flying Training School stationed there. Prince Andrew successfully gained his "wings" after his four months course during which he lived in the Leeming Officers' Mess and was often present locally in social mode – including the "Fleece Inn" at Northallerton. The Duke of Edinburgh visited Leeming when his son was there in June 1980 being met on arrival at Northallerton railway station by the Lord Lieutenant of North Yorkshire the Marquis of Normanby.

Pope John Paul II at Leeming

A fleeting but highly historic and auspicious visit to Leeming occurred on 31st May 1981 when during his momentous tour of Great Britain the Pope John Paul II flew into Leeming in the morning. He was whisked by helicopter to and from York on his memorable visit to that city, before being flown in the afternoon from Leeming to Edinburgh in a British Caledonian BAC III. Crowds gathered in a solid mass from Leeming village to Londonderry and on every bridge and vantage point to catch even a glimpse of the papal visitor – who had in fact, with Leeming bordering the Swale, been in the very vicinity of the river where around 630 the baptism of thousands by Paulinus had been the subject of a Papal encyclical by Pope Gregory the Great.

Front Line Defence

In September 1984 Leeming's future into the twenty first century was assured when the Ministry of Defence announced that it was to become a keystone of the nation's defence and to receive Tornado fighter squadrons to fulfil this commitment of the Air Defence of two hundred and twenty five miles of coastline running eastwards over the North Sea. Over the next three years Leeming was re-developed, including twenty-one especially hardened aircraft shelters, at a cost of £170 million. No11 Squadron of Tornado F3s had arrived on 1st July 1988 and were followed by Nos 23 and 25 Squadrons of Tornados in 1989 which operated from Leeming into the next century with the exception of No 23 Squadron which was disbanded in 1993 as a result of government defence cuts.

Leeming Summation

Apart from their basic United Kingdom defensive role the Leeming squadrons were involved in crucial operations in the Gulf War of January 1991 and the Bosnian crisis of 1993. No 11 Squadron had sixteen Tornados engaged in 'Operation Desert Shield' to protect Saudi Arabia during the Gulf crisis and five hundred Leeming aircrew and groundcrew received Gulf War active service medals. The Leeming Tornados were again prominent in air defence during the Bosnian crisis flying from the Italian base Gioia del Colle to enforce a 'no fly zone' over Bosnia.

427

Leeming was honoured by a four hour official visit by HRH Princess Margaret on 26th June 1991 when she inspected four hundred 'Gulf War' veterans and both the Queen and Princess Anne flew in and out of Leeming in 1992.

Leeming was extremely supportive of local good causes in particular old aged pensioners in the nearby villages and the Friarage Hospital at Northallerton where children of station personnel were born at the hospital's maternity unit. With the redevelopment of Leeming over three hundred new married quarters had been built at the station and in 2000 there were sixteen hundred Royal Air Force and two hundred and fifty civilian personnel at Leeming, which made it a very important economic factor in its surrounding district including Northallerton.

It was very important therefore to the whole area when the operational future of Leeming was confirmed by the Ministry of Defence in December 1999. The Tornados were to be phased out it was announced but these would be replaced at Leeming by two squadrons of the multi-role Eurofighter, which had been developed jointly by Britain, Germany, Italy and Spain. The Eurofighter would be officially called the "Typhoon" and Leeming would receive thirty of the aeroplanes.

Social and Charitable Organisations

The post-war momentum to help the disadvantaged, needy and less able continued through the auspices of the North Yorkshire County Social Services and other official bodies and by means of a large number of caring societies, organisations and individuals.

The Mentally Disabled

Foremost acquisitions in Northallerton for the mentally disabled were the Ashlands Centre provided at Bankhead Road by the Local Health Authority at a cost of £69,000 and a Mencap Centre at the North End which was opened in October 1982 by the famous actor Brian Rix, the Secretary General of the Royal Society for the Mentally Handicapped. Funds for this enterprise had been raised over a period of twenty four years and an annual event had been a Mencap Gala since 1976 which for example in 1979 attracted three thousand people and raised over £2,000.

Year of the Disabled – Round Table

Some events were illustrative of the charitable endeavours of different organisations and one of these was the International Year of the Disabled in 1981 which saw numerous efforts in aid of the handicapped which included a concert at the Community Centre given jointly by the Allerton Players, Northallerton Young Farmers Club and the Amateur Operatic Society which raised £500 and a sponsored walk by the Round Table around the boundaries of North Yorkshire which brought in £2000. Indeed the Round Table were consistently energetic and successful in their charity work and in March 1992 celebrated their fortieth anniversary with guests William Hague MP and the Mayor of Northallerton John Coulson. A singular honour was the appointment of Tim Grover as National President of the Round Table movement in 1982.

Rotary Club

Northallerton Rotary Club were exceptionally and continuously active in charitable work. In 1977 they celebrated the 25th anniversary of their charter on 25th March with a convivial evening under the chairmanship of Dr David Smith and with many guests including Sir Timothy Kitson MP. Taking a typical year, in 1994 they raised over £8,000 which included £5120 from their annual charity swim involving thirty seven teams. Rotoract, the young arm of the Rotary Club, was prominent in the 1990s by which time a second Northallerton club had been formed – the Mowbray Rotary Club – which was indicative of the strength of the movement locally.

Additionally, the Inner Wheel, a ladies' organisation consisting of Rotarians wives and relatives since their formation in 1951 had given consistent and sterling support to the Rotarian movement and were particularly notable for their charitable and caring efforts within the community.

Women's Organisations

Other women's organisations also played a prominent role in Northallerton's charitable activities and these included the Women's Royal Voluntary Association, Ladies Circle, Northallerton Lionesses (who raised £2,000 in 1996/97 for the Scott Suite and Bosnian Relief) and the Ladies Lifeboat League which collected over £3,000 in 1991. The North Mowbray group of Women's Institutes met at Romanby Women's Institute and had been in existence since 1946. It is still flourishing with thirteen enthusiastic member institutes with twelve to thirty plus members in each of the various groups.

Other Organisations

The Northallerton branches of the NSPCC and NSPCA continued to thrive with a strong nucleus of dedicated volunteers which applied equally to the British Red Cross. The latter were especially in evidence in various volunteer capacities at the Friarage Hospital and their North Yorkshire headquarters were the subject of an important move in 1998 from Thirsk Road to a new building named Red Cross House at the junction of Zetland Street with East Road. Another important organisation was the Northallerton Voluntary Service Association established in November 1980 with a Volunteer Bureau housed at No 10 South Parade.

Health and Disabilities

Organisations concerned with health and disabilities abounded. The various cancer relief bodies saw thousands of pounds donated and collected in the 1980s and 1990s; leukaemia research saw the appearance of the famous cricketer Ian Botham in 1991 at Solberge Hall to receive a cheque for £350,000 resulting from his charity walk of twenty eight days and at Hambleton Community Centre in October he was presented with £1,391 raised by local youngsters in a multi-sports marathon; diabetic, heart and stroke clubs were set up; and the Alzheimer's disease society of Hambleton based at Northallerton by 1996 had received £52,000 in three years for a befriending scheme. The Guide Dogs for the Blind Association regularly raised annual sums of up to £1,000 and by the time the Northallerton 'Talking Newspaper for the Blind' reached its twenty first anniversary in October 1999 it was supplying one hundred cassettes at any one time and had built up an imposing taped source of social anecdote and history.

Young Support

The young people of Northallerton and district were constantly bent on fund-raising for good causes with every school participating. This was exemplified in the case of the senior schools by the Allertonshire School contributing £7,100 to Martin House Hospice for Children, Boston on Spa in July 1986 and Northallerton Grammar School pupils gathering £16,000 for the Friarage Hospital's Neuro Surgical Unit's research programme in 1987 in memory of their school colleague Sarah Hukin who tragically died of a brain tumour in 1986.

The Elderly

The elderly were especially charitably supported by a variety of organisations, carers and individuals. Oak Mount old people's home had £15,000 raised for a mini-bus for example and the Grace Gardner Trust continued to contribute very actively to the social welfare of Northallerton's senior citizens organising dances and social events in the Town Hall and regular trips away from the town – Scarborough 1987, Whitby 1989 and so on.

New Projects

The ongoing, determined and diversified nature of the various movements and voluntary efforts was illustrated by some developments at the very end of the millennium. In June 1997 a Pavement Project was launched in Northallerton with the aim of broadening the outlook and supporting young people aged up to twenty five, helping them to make informed choices on education, training, health and leisure. £110,000 was obtained by way of a national lottery grant over three years to facilitate the project with four part-time detached youth workers appointed to the scheme.

Also in 1997 a Northallerton branch of Friends of Chernobyl was set up to assist orphan children from the area of Belarus affected by the nuclear disaster of 1986. Funds were raised and commencing in August 1998 groups of young Belarussian children were brought over to the Northallerton district for a holiday each year staying with local families and being entertained by a whole programme of events and diversions.

Northdale Horticulture

A remarkable story concerned 'Northdale Horticulture' which provided training and work for adults with learning disabilities. After spending almost ten successful years at the 'Mount' grounds with their lease running out, in 1997 they launched the 'Northdale Appeal' to obtain independent premises. Backed by the "Darlington and Stockton Times" the Appeal aroused tremendous support from businesses and a multiplicity of local sources to the extent that by 2000 £277,000 had been raised which supplemented by a National Lottery grant of £130,975 enabled the opening of an attractive purpose-built Northdale Horticultural Centre. Situated adjacent to Jenkins' field on Yafforth Road the centre was officially opened by William Hague MP accompanied by his wife Ffion on 16th September 2000 it being rightly deemed by him as "a huge achievement."

The Samaritans

Playing an unheard, unsung but vital role were the Northallerton and Dales Samaritans founded in 1965 as the first rural group nationally in the movement who had proved a solid, permanent and dependable addition to the caring town scene. In 1985-86 they received 2280 calls and by 1991 this had risen to 7161 calls of which 4005 were asking for help. By 1991 there were seventy 'volunteer listeners' operating from their headquarters at 7 Crosby Road. A constant need for funding was answered locally – for example £900 from Wensleydale Farmers in September 1992 and £1530 from Redmire in June 1994.

The Arts, Leisure and Entertainments

Within the leisure and social fabric of Northallerton societies and groups continued to flourish such as: the Camera Club founded in 1933 and still earning wide acclaim; the Flower Club dating to 1962; the Horticultural Society with its roots in the nineteenth century hey-day of its President John Hutton of Solberge Hall; the Caledonian Society who had come into their canny Scottish own every Burns night of fervour, song and poetry since 1945; and the Probus Society which marked its thirtieth anniversary in 2000 by presenting its Presidential Scroll to Northallerton Town Council.

Local Heritage and History

The emergent and avid interest in local heritage and history was strongly manifest in many ways. In 1979 Northallerton Civic Society was inaugurated and thenceforth was a vigorous voice in the preservation of the town's ancient environment. It was joined in October 1990 by a Family History Society and then in 1994 by Northallerton and District Local History Society which was soon promoting local history projects of note.

The Northallerton Branch of the University of the Third Age (U3A) began its encouragement of cultural and arts pursuits for people of retirement age in 1992 and by 1994 had over one hundred members. Finally in 1997 after an initiative by local historian Michael Riordan acted upon by the Mayor of Northallerton Jane Harvey and the Town Council and effected by the Clerk to Northallerton Town Council Dr David Severs, Northallerton was adorned with thirteen handsome wall plaques on appropriate buildings depicting their historic pedigree.

Dr Severs was also the author of an impressively researched and valuable contribution to Northallerton's history and indeed national clock-making lore – "Northallerton Clockmakers – Hugh Pannell and His Successors" published in 1998. Dr Christine Newman of the Durham University staff also produced a most erudite and revealing book on a period of Northallerton history "Late Medieval Northallerton – A Small Market Town and Its Hinterland 1470-1540" published in 2000.

Literature

In the literary field a native of Northallerton of the well-known Willoughby family of builders Mrs Louise Cecilia Craven writing under her maiden name of Cecilia Willoughby had two popular novels published 'Friday's Moon' (1932) and 'Mallory's Yard' (1934) by Johnathan Cape which had a local setting. Her achievement was all the more creditable because she was totally deaf and after her death aged 79 in 1985 a 'Yorkshire Fiction Memorial Bookcase' in her memory was opened in Northallerton Library on 20th September 1986.

Two other successful local novelists were North Riding / Yorkshire Police officers Jack Mason who had five fiction books published commencing with "The Saboteurs" and Peter Simpson who wrote under the pseudonym of Nicholas Rhea. The latter was a permanent feature writer with the "Darlington and Stockton Times" and his popular novels concerning a policeman's life in a rural North Yorkshire setting commenced with 'Constable on the Hill'. The books became the basis for the famous long-running Yorkshire Television series "Heartbeat"

which had an enormous national and international success and following.

Finally a former Head Girl of Northallerton Grammar School in 1921, Mary Northgrave of Rounton writing as Anne Tibble has left an evocative description of life and school in North Yorkshire of her day. She had several successful novels published and it was in "Greenhorn – A Twentieth Century Childhood" published in 1973 that her atmospheric portrayal of the rural Northallerton area of her youth appears. Her father was groom and coach driver to Sir Hugh Bell of Rounton Grange where she was brought up and toed and froed to Northallerton Grammar School by bicycle and train for seven years.

Northallerton Schooldays -'Greenhorn

Cinema Demise

Television had come to dominate leisure time habits by the latter quarter of the twentieth century which in Northallerton entertainment terms spelled the the final demise of the cinema which had been such a phenomena in the film boom-time 1940s and early 1950s. With the 'Cinema de Luxe' and the 'Central' long gone, the 'Lyric' battled on alone as the only cinema venue until it finally showed its last reel on the evening of Thursday 15th June 1995 and though Bingo continued for a while it finally closed as an entertainments centre in 1996 when bought and converted into the 'New Life Baptist Church' by 1998.

The Stage

The two centuries' tradition of live on stage entertainment at Northallerton still continued principally in the Town Hall and the Hambleton Community Centre. 'Northallerton Amateur Operatic Society' annually staged musicals of a uniformly high standard and 'sell-out' popularity for a week each autumn from "Brigadoon" in 1975 to "Oklahoma!" in 1999. These were performed in the Community Centre as were the Northallerton Variety Company's yearly pantomimes in January for a week which were a 'must' for young and old alike and raised much money for charity. Their final pantomime of the twentieth century was 'Sleeping Beauty' in 1999 which attracted packed audiences like its predecessors.

The 'Allerton Players' too trod the boards to good and popular effect staging major plays at least once a year, winning several area drama festivals (Sedgefield 1980 for example) and playing constantly to full houses.

Music

Choral music still held a strong place in Northallerton with Northallerton Male Voice Choir, Northallerton Methodist Church Choir and the North Yorkshire Chorus giving regular concerts of a high calibre and the time-honoured Northallerton Parish Church Choir continuing the fine choral tradition which undoubtedly had medieval roots with the 'grammar and song school' being attached to the Parish Church in 1322. Northallerton Silver Band, now under the baton of David Lewis who had succeeded his father 'Pop' Lewis as conductor in both expertise and enthusiasm, fulfilled an essential role in Northallerton's civic functions such as the Remembrance Sunday service and parade as well as giving concerts and making frequent public appearances.

Young Arts

The district's musical youth too found great expression and invaluable training in the various bands of the combined music department of the Allertonshire and Northallerton Grammar School/College. Drama and dance also flourished in the schools with talented youngsters appearing in dance performances in the Millennium Dome in 2000. Art and Design too had a very fine record with an increasing emergence of gifted young people which would have been much to the satisfaction of old pupil Arthur Bell Foster.

Hotels and Public Houses

A five centuries old and key feature of Northallerton's leisure and business scenario were the public houses and hotels and significant changes took place here. The 'Old Golden Lion' closed in June 1978 and the "North Riding Hotel" on South Parade and the "King's Arms" on the west side of the High Street followed in 1985. Finally came the closure of the "Black Swan" on the east side of the High Street on 1st January 1987, the latter being one of the oldest recorded hostelries in Northallerton with a history rich in characters and interest.

New Premises

However, a century of public house closures was reversed in the 1980s and 1990s. In 1985 a new public house the "County Arms" was opened by the Wetherill brothers on the north eastern approach road to the Applegarth car park. A "night club" had been located shortly before this behind the east side of the High Street and in 1989 this was taken over by George and Greta Crow, substantially altered and re-named the 'Amadeus' club with an adjoining public bar – "Maestros", these being officially opened in April 1990.

In 1988 the "Sportsman's Club" public bar was opened in the old "Theatre Royal" premises on the eastern edge of the Applegarth and in October 1991 "Elders" public house was established by the Cochrane family in the former British Legion building at the eastern end of Tweddle's Yard off the High Street. Two elaborate public house renovations and alterations had also occurred in 1991 by the Beckwith family to the "Fleece" and the "Harewood Arms" which was re-opened as the "Tickle Toby Inn" (its former name before 1851) on 10th September of that year.

The "Tanner Hop" public house was opened in 1994 in Friarage Street and in 2001 was altered and renamed the "Tithe Barn" recalling the former role of the building in 'old Northallerton'. Finally in 2001 DiPalma's café on the east side of the High Street was redeveloped by its new owners the Crows as a licensed premises and called "Bar One Hundred".

436

Sports and Social Clubs

A feature which mirrored the changing Northallerton social scene was the increasing number of clubs with licensed premises which included the Cricket Club (Farndale Avenue), Rugby Club (Stone Cross), Football Club (Ainderby Road), Bowling Club (South Parade), Royal Air Forces Association Club (North End), Thirsk – Northallerton Golf Club (Thirsk Road), Romanby Golf Club (Yafforth Road) and the Working Men's Club (Tweddles Yard). The latter had a particularly interesting history having started in a plumber's hut before the Second World War, graduated to Jackson's old school at the south of the Applegarth and then built its own premises at the rear of the High Street for £18,000 in 1966. In June 1972 it opened new extensions which had created excellent facilities for £42,000 and thenceforth had continued to prosper.

Hotels

The local hotel sphere also saw major change firstly with the addition of the first purpose-built residential hotel since 1901 when the Station Hotel (then the "Railway Hotel") was altered. Named the "Sun Dial Hotel" this was constructed by Walter Thompsons/George Fordy Ltd at the North End at a cost of £1.4m for its initiator and owner, Fred Davies (who had brought York Trailers to Northallerton) and opened by Sir Leon Brittan on 17th June 1989.

The "Golden Lion Hotel" was also involved in a major change when it was bought from a national consortium in November 1998 by George and Greta Crow. They effected timely, telling and congenial alterations which included the restoration of an ancient well which became a novel feature of the bar/lounge area. This imperative face-lift befitted the "Golden Lion" as the premier hotel of North Yorkshire's county town and its restitution in local ownership after eighty years was regarded very favourably in Northallerton.

Four hotels in Northallerton's hinterland underwent important changes. The Tontine on the A19 below Osmotherley established in 1804 was taken over by the McCoy brothers Tom and Eugene of Middlesbrough in 1979 and soon became renowned for its restaurant's cuisine for which it won prestigious Egon Ronay awards. Just to the north of the Tontine, Crathorne Hall, the Dugdale's seat built in 1906, was converted into an hotel in 1979 and bought by Richard Branson's

Virgin Group in November 1987 for £3.5 million to become of national reputation.

Solberge Hall just south of Northallerton (the former home of the Huttons) was converted into a twenty-five bedroom hotel in 1986 and purchased by twin brothers John and Michael Hollins in 1993 who then ran it in conjunction with the "Golden Fleece", Thirsk as the Mowbray Hotels Company. Finally the Motel on the A1 at Leeming was refurbished by Carl Les in the late 1990s and re-named The Lodge.

Local Sport

Cricket

Sport maintained its essential place in local leisure activities. Northallerton Cricket Club consolidated both on and off the field with pavilion extensions costing £12,000 in 1977. In 2000 the first eleven performed creditably in the high standing North Yorkshire South Durham Premier Division with the second eleven in Division Two and the third eleven in Division Four. The Granindon Knockout cup named after the Places and a reminder of four generations of support and play by that family was still strongly contested after seventy years. A sign of the club's finances and progress was the appointment of a 'professional' in 1975 who appropriately was local player Arthur 'Rocker' Robinson from Brompton who had gone on from Northallerton CC to play regularly for Yorkshire CCC and was awarded his Yorkshire county 'cap' – a feat unique in Northallerton's cricketing history since 1811.

The Northallerton Evening Cricket League was still 'in situ' in 2000 as was the Northallerton Ladies Evening League which was exceptionally keen and afforded an honour when Gill Smith who played for Ingleby Arncliffe as a fast bowler was chosen not only to play for Yorkshire Ladies but also for England against India at Grace Road, Leicester in 1986. She continued to regularly represent her country including selection as vice-captain of England in 1993.

Northallerton Ladies team had moved gradually from their rustic-type pitch at Hutton Bonville to the comparative playing grandeur of Northallerton cricket club's ground and two of their players Sheila Minto and Fay Lacy had been selected for Yorkshire. The strength of the Northallerton Ladies Evening League was further evidenced by Karen Jobling of Middleham playing for Yorkshire and England.

Football

Northallerton Town FC playing at their new Ainderby Road ground equipped with a clubhouse and floodlights entered the regionally prestigious Northern League in 1981. They were promoted to its First Division in 1989 but having been relegated in 1997 narrowly missed promotion back to the First Division in 2000.

On the broader local football front a decisive and distinct change occurred which seemed to reflect changed times and social habits. The Northallerton based North Yorkshire League playing on Saturday afternoons from having nine clubs in 1989 had ceased to function by 1996. Paradoxically the Hambleton Football Combination played on Sunday mornings for clubs within a twelve mile radius of Northallerton formed in 1977 and adeptly organised for twenty years by its Secretary Mark Jarvis prospered. By 1999-2000 the Hambleton Combination had forty two teams in three divisions with five hundred young men involved. Century old Saturday afternoon local football had been completely superseded by that of Sunday morning.

Rugby

The other main Northallerton winter sport of Rugby Union became consolidated with Northallerton RUFC on its new ground at Crawford Grange in the narrow green belt gap between urban Northallerton and Brompton. Now with excellent social and playing facilities the club fielded three XVs and a Colts team every Saturday and in 1981 celebrated its centenary. Northallerton Rugby Club continued to thrive until the end of the century when in 1999-2000 the First Fifteen was playing well in the Yorkshire League Division Two.

Hockey and Tennis

Northallerton Ladies Hockey XI were going strong in Fox's Yorkshire League Division Two at the end of the 1990s having had two decades of competitive endeavour which had seen much success including highlights such as winning the Rotterdam Hockey Rally of 1988. Jackie Holden after winning the Yorkshire under 12s tennis title in 1979 had become the most formidable woman's tennis player ever in the local area, captaining the Mississippi University USA team and winning a succession of North of England and Yorkshire singles and doubles titles including those of 1990. Northallerton Tennis Club was in the Thirsk Sunday League in the 1990s.

Memorial Baths

Swimming in Northallerton received a major blow when the Northallerton Memorial Baths were declared unsafe for use and closed in December 1989. Subsequently the baths building was bull-dozed into oblivion in January 1995 and shortly afterwards the Vicar of Northallerton Canon Ian Fox dedicated a commemorative plaque on the site where the swimming baths had stood as a memorial to the Northallerton "fallen" of the Second World War. The popular Hambleton Leisure Pool opened at Stone Cross in 1990 compensated much for the loss of the Memorial Baths but were not suitable for competitive swimming.

Other Sports and Games

Northallerton Bowling Club continued to thrive with a strong membership of over two hundred, both the men's and women's teams being successful in the Yorkshire leagues and a new pavilion erected in 1988 at its South Parade sward. It reached a memorable milestone in 2000 when it celebrated its centenary – a hundred years of continual bowling existence since George Lewis and friends launched the first jack at the North End bowling green. Other sporting activities prospered including: Northallerton and District Motor Club with popular meetings at Bilsdale; Northallerton and District Darts League with thirty four teams in three divisions; Northallerton Billiards League; and Northallerton Homing Pigeons Society which regularly raced three hundred pigeons released in the Midlands and further afield to wing their way home.

Golfing Expansion

Golf literally boomed in the area with more and more adherents of both sexes. Bedale golf club increased its course to eighteen holes as did the Thirsk-Northallerton golf club. The latter expended £215,000 including a £43,000 lottery grant on its nine extra holes and a new clubhouse extension opened in March 2000 for its four hundred and fifty members – a far cry from the casual days when Alf Wight (alias James Herriot) played there, when sheep gently grazed and dogs accompanied their golfing owners on the course! Evidence of the game's soaring popularity was the creation of the completely new Romanby Golf Club of eighteen holes between Romanby and Yafforth on Craven's Crowtree Farm in 1992 followed by an adjacent golf driving range. Its instant success enabled it to add a palatial new clubhouse and social facilities at a £500,000 cost opened by top European and Ryder Cup golfer Colin Montgomerie on 28th July 2000.

Equine Activities

In the time honoured equine tradition of the district the Hurworth Hunt met regularly although its ancient existence was threatened by the pending government legislation to abolish hunting with hounds. Show jumping saw another Barker emerging into the front ranks when Paul, the son of 1964 Tokyo Olympian David Barker and his wife Lynne of Pasture House, Thirsk Road in 1994 when aged sixteen became the Leading Junior Show Jumper of the Year at Wembley and also the Young Show Jumper of the Year at Olympia (he was the only person ever to achieve this in one year). In 1998 he was also Young Show Jumper of the Year for the second time – this too was a unique achievement.

Flat horse-racing contained a touch of the old and new in the district. In October 1981 a Northallerton Races Silver Cup of 1772 then worth £50 presented by the Stewards Sir James Pennyman and Sir Thomas Peirse surfaced at a Bath auction and in 1999 a Northallerton Races Gold Cup of 1818 of 100 Guineas value then, was notified as having laid unclaimed in a bank vault since 1916.

Assurance that local horse-racing pedigree was by no means all in the past came in the shape of lady jockey Alex Greaves who hailed from Rounton and was educated at the Allertonshire and Northallerton Grammar schools. After competing as a flat-race jockey for some time as an Apprentice from 1986 for trainer David Nicholl's stable near York she was so successful that she forfeited her Apprentice weight allowance and became a fully fledged senior jockey. She was the first lady rider ever to achieve this feat in racing history and continues to set new records including the first woman ever to win a Group One horse race.

Alan Hinkes – Mountaineer

Final place in Northallerton sporting and outdoor pursuits achievement must be appropriately reserved for Northallerton born and educated Alan Hinkes who became Britain's top high altitude

Alan Hinkes

mountaineer. He took his first climbing steps on the North Yorkshire moors whilst at Northallerton Grammar School where his love of climbing was born. Having climbed and trained to great levels of expertise and physical fitness he began to come to national notice in the 1980s when for example in April 1988 he was in Chris Bonnington's team seeking the "Abominable Snowman".

By this time he had set himself the goal of being the first Briton to climb the fourteen mountains in the world over 8000 metres. Surviving avalanches, injuries and other hazards by 1999 he had conquered eleven of the 8000 plus peaks including the highest, Everest, and the treacherous K2, Nanga Parbat and Makalu. In 1999 he was made a 'Sporting Ambassador' by Sport England. Sponsored by Berghaus and other organisations in early 2001 he was preparing to leave for Katmandu and then to acclimatise at base camp for his assault on Kangchenjunga the twelfth mountain in his "Challenge 8000". He had already climbed himself into history as the most successful British mountaineer of all time.

Visits and Events

As North Yorkshire's county town Northallerton was regularly in the eye of the media in the last quarter of the twentieth century with frequent important visitors – royalty amongst them as indeed had been the case throughout the second millennium since William the Conqueror in 1069!

Visits by the Duchess of Kent (1977), the Duke of Edinburgh and Prince Andrew (1980), the Duke and Duchess of York (1989), Princess Alexandra (1992) and Princess Margaret (1996) have already been noticed. In November 1981 the royal train sojourned overnight near the town on the Wensleydale line with the Queen and the Duke of Edinburgh aboard before the Queen officially opened the Tyneside 'Metro' the following morning.

In common with the nation two royal events had the maximum of diametrically opposed effects of pleasure and sadness. The royal wedding in August 1981 at St Paul's Cathedral of Prince Charles and Lady Diana Spencer brought to the town quite simply "a day of joy" with a holiday, parties, official events and celebrations being marked by the Town Council by the distribution of one thousand commemorative 'crowns' to the town's school children. Stark and sombre emotive contrast followed the news of the tragic death on 31st August 1997 of Princess Diana. A stunned week in which a book of condolence was opened in the Town Hall and flowers of remembrance were variously and fully laid was followed by the funeral Saturday of a marketless shop closed town paying its last respects.

Visitors of importance were of differing modes and included: the Archbishop of York David Hope to Northallerton College on 25th June 1996; Johnathan Dimbleby chairing a live BBC Radio 4 'Any Questions' programme from the Town Hall on Friday 22nd July 1988;

Archbishop David Hope (right) – 1996
Visiting Northallerton College

the Lord Chancellor Lord Elwyn Jones in April 1977 to address four hundred legal brethren in the Community Centre; Peter Pillay the Speaker of the African National Congress to speak at the Town Hall in March 1994; and Alan Hinkes back on the terra firma of his native heath in November 1999 to graphically describe to a packed Community Centre his self effacing but epic exploits in the Himalayas in his "Challenge 8000".

In January 2000 the honouring of the actress Dorothy Tutin as a Dame gave much satisfaction in Northallerton with her strong local connections.   The passing of town centenarians held high in local affection and esteem, Mrs Annie Pratt who died on 14th October 1994 aged 106 years and Norman Bryning in June 2000 a few months after his hundredth birthday were causes of regret tinged with nostalgia and admiration.

The two events of tremendous herald and media-focus the "Eclipse" of the sun at 11 am on Wednesday 11th August 1999 and the arrival of the third Millennium on 1st January 2000, if not anti-climatic were certainly low key affairs in Northallerton.   In 1927 on the last occasion of the sun's eclipse Northallerton was in the band of the total eclipse whilst in 1999 the effect was not as spectacular with the full effect being seen in Cornwall. For the dawning of the third Millennium although numerous private parties were held nothing of a public nature was staged in Northallerton as opposed to Brompton which marooned itself with inward road access barred so that the village could unitedly share the birth of the new Millennium with appropriate festivities.

Viscount Northallerton

A noteworthy death of Northallerton royal connection was that of the Marquis of Cambridge whose funeral on 23rd April 1981 at St George's chapel Windsor was attended by the Queen as he was her great uncle. He had been Prince George of Teck until 1917 when all the royal Germanic titles were relinquished as a result of the Anglo-German conflict and dissension of the First World War. One of the British titles he then assumed was Viscount Northallerton which had last been held by George II before his accession in 1727. Thus when he died in 1981 without an heir the title of Viscount Northallerton became extinct.

The Modern March

The Northallerton of George II of course was that described in Roger Gale's brief "History of the Borough of North Allerton" in 1739 which had utterly and irrevocably changed by the end of the twentieth century, a truism which applied almost equally to Saywell's Northallerton of 1885 when he wrote the last history of the town.

Fundamentally the population of the town would have been around 1700 in Gale's time, it was 3692 in Saywell's and by 1991 it was 9628 which had in fact doubled since its 1931 total of 4786. The true picture was even more dramatic with Romanby included which had surged from 414 in 1881 to 5333 in 1991 making the real contrast with Romanby inextricably woven into Northallerton of 4106 in 1881 to 14,961 in 1991. This was a remarkable increase of almost four times and in 1991 the population of 'Greater Northallerton' – Northallerton and Romanby with Brompton added – was 17,025.

The population factor, however, was only part of a massive modern revolution and transformation with only the fundamental fulcrum of the High Street remaining – though in essence it too was vastly different as now the hub of motorised mayhem at peak traffic times! Commensurate with the population dwellings had multiplied – Northallerton 3920, Romanby 2151 and Brompton 921 in 1991. But it was not only in the numbers but in their nature that the houses had changed from less than a century before when the High Street area contained the bulk of the Northallerton people with over a third living in the yards off the main street.

The vast majority of the population now lived in the estates flanking the town and the comparatively congenial living conditions were emphasised by the type of 1991 houses: in Northallerton 18.4% lived in detached houses, with 37.7% in Romanby and 20.7% in Brompton; and the semi-detached numbers were Northallerton 30.5%, Romanby 48.1% and Brompton 25.3%.

It will be recalled that in the Georgian days the Northallerton properties were in the hands of the few led by the Peirse and the Lascelles/Harewood families. Now home ownership reflected the vast difference in the social fabric of society even in this sense since the end of the Second World War. In Northallerton in 1991 63.7%, in Romanby 84.9% and in Brompton 64.4% were home owners or mortgagees of their own property.

Another sign of the affluent and essentially more personally independent society was seen in motorcar ownership which before the Second World War was confined to a handful of families. Households in 1991 with one or more cars amounted to 67.6% in Northallerton, Romanby 83.5% and Brompton 74.9%.

And all of this hardly does justice to the immensity of the transition – in Saywell's time to say nothing of cars, no-one had electricity, running water, and sanitary facilities, many (and all females) were deprived of a parliamentary vote, there were just six beds in the local hospital (which had just obtained its first tin bath!), there was no such thing as a typewriter let alone a personal computer and radio, television and telephones were unheard of. Neither was there the multitude of modern houses and the array of public buildings – expansive county, central and local government – extensive schools and a resplendent hospital – nearly all of which the twentieth century saw birth.

None of this could be envisaged by Northallerton's earlier historians and yet they were all proud of the progress that the town had made, imbued in common by the overwhelming sense of Northallerton's ancient and historic past, aware of its contemporary ebullience and with a strong sense of the town's solid permanence and its fundamental place in the future scheme of north Yorkshire and even national things.

Today's historians would adhere to all of that but perhaps with an added sensitivity to the enormity, speed and almost bewildering kaleidoscope of advancing technology and modernity with their sweeping changes. Automatically and categorically this factors an instinctive and inherent determination to preserve and promote Northallerton's intrinsic heritage and to nurture its unique history – ancient and modern.

"We are not content to pass away entirely from the scene of our delights, we would leave, if but in gratitude, a pillar and a legend."
Robert Louis Stevenson.

Bibliography

General (1)

"An Historical Account of the Borough of NORTHALLERTON in the North Riding of the County of York" by Roger Gale Esq. 1739 printed Nichol's Bibliotheca Topographica Brittanica No 2 Part 2 1781

"The History and Antiquities of NORTHALLERTON In the County of York" 1792 (2nd Edit 1813 – 'Considerably Enlarged') Printed and Sold by J Langdale, Northallerton

"The History and Antiquities of Northallerton" CJD Ingledew Bell and Dalby 1858

"The History and Annals of Northallerton" Reverend JL Saywell J Vasey Northallerton 1885

"The Victoria History of the County of York North Riding" Edited William Page FSA London 1914 (Northallerton by Marion Weston)

General (2)

"History, Directory and Gazetteer of the County of York" Volume II Edward Baines (1823)

"A Topographical Dictionary of Yorkshire" Thomas Langdale 1822 Printed J Langdale, Northallerton and T Langdale, Ripon

"The Universal British Directory of Trade Commerce and Manufacturing" Second Edition 1793

"Yorkshire Gazetteer" Stephen Reynolds Clarke 1828

"New Commercial Dictionary" Pigot 1828/29

"Brittania" William Camden circa 1590 Translation Fourth Edition Dr Edmund Gibson 1772

"Barnabees Journal" attributed Richard Braithwait (1588 – 1673) 3rd Edit 1723

"A Topographical, Ecclesiastical and Natural History of Yorkshire"

Rev Thomas Cox 1731. Printed E & R Nutt London (Royal
      Exchange)
"History of York and the North Riding of Yorkshire" Volume II
      T Whellan 1859
"A New and Complete History of the County of York" Thomas Allen
1831
"The Annals of Yorkshire" John Mayhall FRHS 1878
"Topographical and Statistical Description of the County of York"
      George Alexander Cooke 1810
"History Gazetteer and Directory of the East and the North Ridings of
Yorkshire" White 1840
"Slater's Commercial Directory of Yorkshire and Lincolnshire" 1849
"Post Office Directory of the North and East Ridings of Yorkshire"
      1872 (2nd Edit) 1879 (3rd Edit)
"Kelly's Directories of the North and East Ridings of Yorkshire"
      1889 1893 1905 1913 1921 1925 1929 1933 1938
"Bulmer's North Yorkshire – Cleveland and Richmond Divisions"
      T Bulmer 1890
"Yorkshire Geneologist and Yorkshire Bibliographer"
      J Horsfall-Taylor 1888
"A Picturesque History of Yorkshire" JS Fletcher
      Volume IV London 1898 Caxton Publishing Co.
"The North Riding of Yorkshire" Captain WJ Weston
      Cambridge County Geographies 1919 Cambridge
"Companion into the North Riding" JH Ingram 1952 Methuen
"Fair North Riding" AJ Brown 1952 Country Life Limited
"Yorkshire – North Riding" Arthur Mee 1941 New Edition 1970
"Yorkshire From AD 1000" David Hey Longman 1986
"Old Yorkshire – The Story of the Yorkshire Landscape and People"
      Richard Muir pub Michael Joseph 1987
"The Historic Towns of Yorkshire" John Burgess 1990
"Yorkshire North Riding" Malcolm Barker 1977 BT Batsford
"Northern England" Regions of the British Isles series
      3rd Edition. Smailes 1960
"A History of Yorkshire" FB Singleton and S Rawnsley 1986
"Vernacular Houses in North Yorkshire and Cleveland" Barry Harrison
      and Barbara Hutton 1984

"The Buildings of England – Yorkshire the North Riding" 1966
      Nicholas Pevsner

"The Yorkshire Anthology of poems and songs" collected by
    James Halliwell FRS pub London 1851
"Holroyd's Collection of Yorkshire Ballads" edit Charles F Forshaw
    1974
"Ballads and Songs of Yorkshire" CJ Davison Ingledew 1860
"Lost Villages of Yorkshire" MW Beresford 1955
"Yorkshire Through Place Names" RW Morris 1982
"A History of North Durham" Canon Raine
"A History of Darlington" N Sunderland 1967
"Cleveland Ancient and Modern" Rev JC Atkinson 1881
"Hird's Annals of Bedale" edit Lesley Lewis NYCRO
"Lost Houses of York and the North Riding" Edward Waterson, Peter
    Meadows pub Jill Raines Thornton le Clay, York 1990

Maps:
Camden "Hole North Riding 1607"
John Bill "The Abridgement of Camden's Brittania" 1626
John Speede "The North and East Ridings of Yorkshire" 1610
John Ogilby "Brittania" London 1675 Plate 8 – "The Continuation of
    the Road from London to Barwick beginning at York and
    extending to Chester in ye Street"
Emmanuel Bowen's Map of 1720 "Brittania Depicta"
Thomas Jeffrey's "The County of Yorkshire" 1775

"Oxford Companion to Sports and Games" edit John Arlott
    Oxford University Press 1975
"Ancient Bridges of the North of England" E Jervoise 1931
"Yorkshire Legends and Traditions" Rev Thomas Parkinson
"Cleveland and Teesside Local History Society Bulletins" 1 – 37
"Northern History – Leeds University School of History" Volumes
    1 – 22
"Allertonshire Wills" – Peculiar of the Dean and Chapter of Durham
(1446 – 1826) Durham Cathedral College Library
"Northallerton Affairs" Records Collection – Northallerton
    North Yorkshire County Record Office (NYCRO)

Chapter One to 1100 AD

"Roman Roads of Great Britain" Ivan D Margary Volume II 1957
"Roman Yorkshire" FR Pearson 1936

"Anglo Saxon Chronicle" edit Dorothy Whitelock
"The Domesday Geography of Northern England" HC Darby & IS
Maxwell
"Domesday Book – 30 Yorkshire" - General Editor John Morris
    Phillimore, Chichester 1986
"The Significance of 'Waste' in the Yorkshire Domesday Book" WE
    Wightman London 1975. Northern History Volume 10
"Roman Britain" Peter Salway 1981 Oxford University Press
"Anglo Saxon England" Sir Frank Stenton, Third Edit 1971
"The Romans in Yorkshire" Arthur Raistrick, Dalesman Publications
    1970
"Vikings, Angles and Danes in Yorkshire" Arthur Raistrick, Dalesman
    Publications 1965
"Place Names of the North Riding of Yorkshire" AH Smith 1928
    (revised 1969)
"The Norman Conquest of the North William E Kapelle 1979: The
    Region and its Transformation 1000 – 1135"
"Opera Historica" Symeon of Durham Rolls Series (i 99)
"The Norman Conquest of Yorkshire" J Le Patourel (1971) Northern
    History Volume 6 Leeds University School of History
"North East England in the First Century" Keith Branagan
"North East England in the Second Century" Julian Bennett
"Ordnance Survey Map of Roman Britain" (Third Edition) pub 1956
"The Concise Oxford Dictionary of English Place Names" 4th Edit.
    Eilert Ekwall   Clarendon Press Oxford 1960
"Registrum Honoris de Richmond" Roger Gale 1722

Chapters Two and Three
Medieval Northallerton (1100 to 1485)

"Changes in the Pattern of Ecclesiastical Jurisdictions in and connected
with the diocese of Durham during the nineteenth century"
    Margaret McCollum 1982
"Transactions of the Architectural and Archaeological Society of
Durham and Northumberland" Volume 6
"Cartulary of the Medieval Archives of Christ Church College Oxford
University" N Denholm-Young 1931
"Gray's Register" – St James Hospital Ordinance 1244
"Oxford University Calendar" 1893
"Calendar of Estate Papers" Christ Church College, Oxford

"Allan Tracts" Volume I George Allan FAS "Collectanea ad Statum
     Civilem et Ecclestiasticum Comitatus Dunelmensis"
"Yorkshire Fines" Durham Cathedral Library 1247 to 1330
"Yorkshire's Ruined Castles" JL Illingworth 1938
"From Domesday Book to Magna Carta (1087 – 1216)" Austin J Poole
     1955 Oxford Clarendon Press
"The Thirteenth Century (1216 – 1307)" Sir Maurice Powicke 1962
     Oxford Clarendon Press
"The Fourteenth Century (1307 – 1399) May McKisack 1959
     Oxford Clarendon Press
"Notitia Monastica" Thomas Tanner pub 1744 by John Tanner
     Reprinted Cambridge University Press
"Medieval Religious Houses" David Knowles and R Neville Hadock
     1953
"The Medieval Monasteries of Yorkshire" Joan and Bill Spence
"English Medieval Monasteries 1066 – 1540" Roy Midner
"A History of Christianity in Yorkshire" FS Popham
     The Religious Education Press 1954
"Early Yorkshire Charters" Volume II William Farrer MSS
     (YAJ Record Series)
"Durham Priory 1400 – 1450" RB Dobson
"Monastican Eboracense and the Ecclesiastical History of Yorkshire"
     John Burton MD York, Coffee Yard 1758
"A Concise History of the Endowed Grammar Schools in England and
     Wales" Nicholas Carlisle 1818
"Yorkshire's Fairs and Markets" KL McCutcheon 1940
Thoresby Society Publications
"Owen's Book of Fairs" 6th Edit 1770 William Owen, Fleet Street,
     London
"Manuscript Map of Britain" Matthew Paris circa 1250

Battle of the Standard:
"British Battlefields (North)" Phillip Warner
     Osprey 1972
"Anglo Saxon Chronicle" Volume II Rolls Series Ed Dorothy Whitelock
"Ivanhoe" Sir Walter Scott
"The Battles and the Battlefields of Yorkshire" William Grainge
"Yorkshire Battles" William Hebden. Dalesman Publications 1971
"Complete Ordnance Survey Guide to the Battlefields of Britain" David
     Smurthwaite Michael Joseph 1984

"The Battle of the Standard" PM Turner 1984 unpub
"Darlington and Stockton Times" Series October 1909
"Surtees Society" Documents 1863 Volume 1 Canon Raine
"Yorkshire Archaeological Journal" Volume 10 1889 Alex DH
        Leadman

"Yorkshire Archaeological Society":
        Vol 3 1875 "Jewish Documents Relating to Northallerton" JT
        Fowler
        Vol 9 1886 "Northallerton Church" JL Saywell
        Vol 21 1896 "Yorkshire Lay Subsidy 1301" W Brown
"Northern History – School of History Leeds University":
        Vol 4 "Pattern of Trade in North East England 1265 – 1350
        Constance Fraser
        Vol 11 "Farming in Northern England" Edward Miller
        Vol 18 "Survey of Secular Education in Northern England" 1350 –
        1550 Helen J Jewell
        Vol 22 "The Emergence of the Northern Nobility" 1250 – 1400
        JA Tuck
"Cleveland and Teesside Local History Society":
        Bulletin No 10 "1377 Poll Tax Return North Riding" BJD
        Harrison 1970
"The Ryedale Historian":
        "Medieval Fairs and Markets in North East Yorkshire" Brian
        Waites 1982
"Surtees Society Documents":
        Vol 4 Northallerton Church 1322, Vol 10 Sir John Gower Speech
        1315
        Vols 23, 24, 40 St James Hospital 1228, 1237, 1272
        Vol 40 Lazenby Hospital 1315
"Bishop of Durham Langley's Register" 1406 to 1437 Durham
        Cathedral Library
"Victoria History – North Riding" Northallerton refs – Marion Weston
        1914
"Late Medieval Northallerton – A Small Market Town and its
        Hinterland c. 1470 to 1540" Dr Christine Newman. Paul Watkins
        Publishing 2000

Chapter Four
The Tudors 1485 – 1603

"Late Medieval Northallerton – A Small Market Town and its
    Hinterland c. 1470 to 1540" Dr Christine Newman. Paul Watkins
    Publishing 2000
"Patent Roll 33 Henry VIII Part 9, m. 30 (15)" 1541
"Listed Buildings of Special Architectural or Historical Interest –
    District of Hambleton North Yorkshire – Northallerton" 1988
"England under the Tudors" GR Elton. Courier Printers. Halifax 1970
"The Itinerary of John Leiland That Famous Antiquary Begunne about
    1538" pub Thomas Hearne in 1710 for the Bodelian Library,
    Oxford
"John Leyland – The Itinerary" edit LT Smith (1964)
"Brittania, or a Geographical Description of Great Britain and Ireland
    (Yorkshire,North Riding) Volume II" 2nd Ed 1722 William
    Camden (1551 – 1623) circa 1595
"The Tudors in Yorkshire" Michael Pocock 1970 Dalesman
    Publications
"The Earlier Tudors" (1485 – 1558)" JD Mackie 1952 Oxford
    Clarendon Press
"The Reign of Elizabeth (1558 – 1603) JB Black 1959
    Oxford Clarendon Press
"The Pilgrimage of Grace 1536 – 37 and the Exeter Conspiracy 1538"
    Volumes 1 & 2 Madeline Hope Dodds and Ruth Dodds 1971
"The Crown and the North of England 1559 – 70 – a study in the
    rebellion of the Northern Earls, 1569 – 70" Susan C Taylor
    Thesis Dr of Philosophy University of Manchester
"Cartulary of the Medieval Archives of Christ Church College, Oxford"
    N Denholm-Young 1931
"Oxford University Calendar 1893"
"Notitia Monastica" Thomas Tanner pub 1744 by John Tanner
    Reprinted Cambridge University Press
"Masterless Men: The Vagrancy Problem in England 1560 – 1640"
    AL Beier. London 1985
"The Tudor Age" Jasper Ridley. Constable and Co 1988
"Political History of England" Volume V (1485 – 1547) HAL Fisher
"Yorkshire's Fairs and Markets" KL McCutcheon 1940
Surtees Society Publications:
    Vol 12   Pilgrimage of Grace 1536 Northallerton Friary 1540

454

Vol 15 Thos Gale 1581 Will
Vol 59 Northallerton Church 1535
"North York Militia" – Robert Bell Turton (1907)

Chapter Five
The Stuarts (1603 – 1714)

"The Hearth Tax List for the North Riding of Yorkshire Michaelmas
    1673" Pub 1991 Ripon Historical Society, Ripon. Harrogate
    District Family History Group
North Yorkshire County Records Office:
"Affairs of Northallerton" series
    Baptisms, Burials, Marriages 1603 –1714 Church Registers
    Churchwardens Accounts   1687 – 1714
    Charities Records: Francis Kaye John Elshall John Kettlewell
"Memorandum Book of Richard Cholmeley of Brandsby 1602 – 23
    pub NYCRO 1988

"The Early Stuarts 1603 – 1660" Godfrey Davies 1959 Oxford
    Clarendon Press
"The Later Stuarts 1660 – 1714" Sir George Clark 1956 Oxford
    Clarendon Press
"Yorkshire County Magazine" 1892 edit J Horsfall Taylor
"Samuel Pepys Diary" edit Henry B Wheatley FSA 1904
"Life of Marmaduke Rawdon of York" Camden Society Volume 85
    (1863 – 4)
"Yorkshire Fairs and Markets" KL McCutcheon 1940
"Correspondence of John Cosin DD Lord Bishop of Durham"
    Surtees Society Volume 55 1872
"North Riding Quarter Sessions Records – 1605 – 1712
    Edit Rev JC Atkinson 1882
"House of Commons Journal 1st January 1646/47: 1640"
"North Durham" Canon Raine
Northern History Leeds University School of History:
    Vol 5 "Land Sales and Repurchases in Yorkshire After the Civil
    Wars"
    Vol 10 "North Riding Justices and Sessions 1603–25"CS Forster
    PG Holiday
    Vol 15 "The Northern Gentry and the Great Rebellion 1640 – 60
    JS Morrill

"Seventeenth Century Life in the Country Parish" Eleanor Trotter 1919
Yorkshire Archaeological Journal:
>Vol 5 "Colonel D'Arcy's Regiment North Riding 1688"
>Vol 43 (1971) "Yorkshire Commissioners Appointed for the Trial of Charles I – 1647" WLF Nuttall
>"Yorkshire and the Restoration 1660"
>"Glebe Terriers and Open Fields 1685" MW Beresford
>Vol 52 (1980) "Civil War in Yorkshire Jan – Apr 1644" PR Newman
>Vol 26 (1922) "Henry Jenkins Longevity" Major RB Turton

"John Kettlewell (1653 – 1695) Canon TT Carter 1895
"Memoires of the Life of John Kettlewell" compiled Francis Lee 1718
"Northern Memoires" Richard Franck 1658
"Barnabees Journal" Richard Braithwait. London

Chapter Six
Eighteenth Century (1700 – 1800)

"An Historical Account of the Borough of Northallerton"
>Roger Gale 1739
"The History and Antiquities of Northallerton"
>James Langdale 1792
Newspapers:
"York Courant" 17th December 1728 onwards weekly
"York Chronicle and Weekly Advertiser" 18th December 1772 onwards
"York Herald" 1793 onwards
"Quarter Sessions Records – North Riding County of York"
>edit Rev JC Atkinson (1883 to 1892 – Seven Volumes)
>via the North Riding Record Society for Publication of Original Documents relating to the North Riding of the County of York
Maps:
Emmanuel Bowen 1720 'Britannia Depicta'
Thomas Jeffreys 1775 'The County of Yorkshire'
Plan:
"Northallerton – This Plan Taken in 1793" (North Yorkshire County Record Office) WT Jefferson and Son Solicitors
North Yorkshire County Record Office (Northallerton References):
"Births, Burials and Marriages – Northallerton Parish Church Registers
"Select Vestry Order Books" (1775 – 1806)
"Church Wardens Accounts" (1687 – 1729)

"Constables Accounts Books" (1738 – 1766: 1797 – 1826)
"Manor of Northallerton Court Book" (1774 – 1779)
Vicarage Lands 1781: Elizabeth Raine's Charity Accounts (1780 – 83)
Schedule Northallerton Parish Church Pews 1788:
Vicarage Schedule – Details 1777: Certificates of Settlement:
Turnpike Trust Loan £100: Overseers of the Poor Records:
Northallerton Grammar School Rebuilding Subscription List 1776

Cleveland and Teesside Local History Society Bulletins including:
    No 3 Duties of Constables in Yorkshire 1788 – EW Pargeter Nos
    36 and 37 (up to 1800)
    "The Royal Mail in North Yorkshire & South Durham"
    DW Pattenden
Yorkshire Archaeological Journal
    Vol 37 1949 "Northallerton Parish Register 1782" LG Horton
    Smith
    Vol 41 1965 "North Riding Justices 1690 – 1750" JS Cockburn
"The Works in Architecture of John Carr" York Georgian Society
    (1973)
"Lists of Buildings of Special Architectural or Historical Interest –
    Northallerton" 1988 Hambleton District Council
"The Whig Supremacy 1714 – 1760" Basil Williams 2nd Edition 1962
    Oxford Clarendon Press   (revised by CH Stuart)
"The Reign of George III 1760 – 1815" J Steven Watson 1960
    Oxford Clarendon Press
"A Six Month Tour Through the North of England" Arthur Young
    (1770)
"The Drovers – an Epic of the English Countryside" K J Bonser (1970)
"Old Coaching Days in Yorkshire" Thomas Bradley (1889) Leeds
"Owen's Book of Fairs" 6th Edit. William Owen 1770 11 Fleet Street,
    London
"Yorkshire Fairs and Markets" KL McCutcheon (1940) Thoresby
    Society
"A Tour Through the Whole Island of Britain" Daniel Defoe 1725/26
"A Journal of the Rev John Wesley" edit Nehemiah Curnock (1909)
"Northern Turf History" J Fairfax-Blakeborough (1944) Vol II
"The Work of the North Riding Quarter Sessions in the Early Eighteenth
    Century"
    JS Cockburn Thesis for LLM Leeds University 1961
"Harewood– The Life and Times of an English Country House" Carol

Kennedy 1982

"Poverty and the Treatment of Poverty in the North Riding of Yorkshire 1780 – 1847" RP Hastings PhD Thesis 1982 Borthwick Papers York

"Unreformed Workhouses in the North Riding of Yorkshire 1730–1834" RP Hastings

"An XVIII Century Diary – William Metcalfe – His Book Diary of a North Yorkshire Farmer and Banker 1786 – 99" edit Arthur W Dyson

"Oxford Companion to Sports and Games" Ed John Arlott Oxford University Press 1975

"Northallerton's Clockmakers: Hugh Pannell and His Successors" Dr David F Severs 1998

Chapter Seven
Nineteenth Century (1800 to 1900)

"History and Antiquities of Northallerton" CJD Ingledew 1858

"History and Annals of Northallerton" JL Saywell 1885

"The Age of Reform 1815 – 1870" Sir Llewellyn Woodward 1962 Oxford Clarendon Press

"England 1870 – 1914 Sir Robert Ensor 1936 Oxford Clarendon Press

"History of York and the North Riding of Yorkshire" T Whellan 1859

Newspapers:

"York Courant" 1800 to 27th April 1848 (incorporated into "York Herald")

"York Herald" 1800 onwards

"York Chronicle" 1800 to 29th April 1840

"Darlington and Stockton Times" 2nd October 1847 onwards

Maps:

Ordnance Survey Map 1856

Tithe Apportionment Maps: Northallerton 1844; Romanby 1839 Brompton 1939 (North Yorkshire County Record Office)

Northallerton Borough Map 1831 (drawn by Rbt K Dawson Lt RE)

North Yorkshire County Records Office (Northallerton references):
Baptisms, Burials and Marriages – Northallerton Parish Church Registers
Vestry Orders Books 1806-1824, 1824-36, 1836-71, 1871-1922
Constables Accounts 1797 – 1826

Collections: at Communions 1826-1884; on Briefs 1816-1883
Highway Books 1813 – 1830
Church Rate Book 1857 to 1868
North Riding County Council Meeting Minutes – 1889   onwards
Reports:
"Parliamentary report on the Borough of Northallerton"
HW Tancred (London 1831)
"Report to the General Board of Health on a Preliminary Inquiry into the
Sewage, Drainage and Supply of Water and Sanitary Condition of
the Inhabitants of Northallerton" W Ranger (London) 1849
Superintending Inspector
"List of Buildings of Special Architectural or Historical Interest
Department of Environment – Town of Northallerton" (15th
November 1988)
Census Records Northallerton, Romanby and Brompton –
1841, 1851, 1861, 1871, 1881 and 1891

"North Riding Registership Election May 1829 – Freeholders List"
"North Riding Quarter Sessions Records" 1800 onwards
"Calendar of Felons and Gaol Delivery" Castle of York (1820 – 1851)
"Smithsons Almanack" (annual Northallerton Digest 1863 onwards)
"Rutson Hospital 1877 – 1977 pub Hospital Management Board
"Poverty and the Treatment of Poverty in the North Riding of Yorkshire
1780 – 1847" RP Hastings 1982 Borthwick Papers York
"A General View of the Agriculture in the North Riding of Yorkshire" J
Tuke, London 1800
"A Trip to Coatham" William Hutton 1810
"Yorkshire Notes and Queries Volume II" ed J Horsfall Taylor
Idle Bradford 1888
"By Highway and By way" edit TJ Wilkinson ("Falcon")
1889 Leeds
"Industrial Revolution in Yorkshire" Fred Singleton 1970
"The Railways of Britain" J Simmons London (1961)
"A Regional History of the Railways of Great Britain – North East
England" Volume IV K Hoole 1965
"North Eastern Locomotive Sheds" K Hoole 1972
"The North Eastern Railway" Cecil J Allen 1964
"The Coming of the Railways Social and Economic Change in
Nineteenth Century Northallerton" HL Fairburn 1998 (NYCRO)
"North Yorkshire Essays 1780-1850" RP Hastings (NYCRO) 1981

"The Making of Modern Yorkshire" (1750 – 1914) JS Fletcher
    Allen and Unwin 1918
"Old Coaching Days in Yorkshire" Thomas Bradley 1889 Leeds
"The Swale" Thomas Bradley 1891 Leeds
"A History of the Yorkshire Agricultural Society" Vance Hall 1997
"Once A Howard Twice A Citizen" Col WJ Tovey Major AJ Podmore
    1997
"The First Hundred Years of the North Riding of Yorkshire
    Constabulary"
"Townsend's Tour in Italy in 1850" Dr George Townsend Canon of
    Durham pub Rivingtons, St Paul's Yard, London
Yorkshire Archaeological Journal Volume 9 (1886)
    Northallerton Parish Church Rev JL Saywell
Cleveland and Teesside Local History Society Bulletins
    No 35 "The Royal Mail in North Yorkshire and South Durham" D
    Pattenden
    No 37 "Private Law Enforcement Organisations Nineteenth
    Century North Riding" RP Hastings
    No 8 "The Linen Industry in the Northallerton District"
"North Country Ghosts and Legends" Terence W Whitaker 1983
"Northern Turf History" J Fairfax-Blakeborough Volume II 1944

The Twentieth Century
Chapters Eight to Twelve (1900 to 2000)

Newspapers
"Darlington and Stockton Times" January 1900 – December 2000
"North Riding and Northallerton News" 2 July 1904 – 21 January 1927
"York Herald" (New Series) 12 February 1902 – 18 June 1954
"Yorkshire Gazette" to 18 June 1954
"Yorkshire Gazette and Herald" 25 June 1954 onwards

Record Sources
    North Yorkshire County Library Headquarters, Northallerton
    North Yorkshire County Record Office, Northallerton
    Public Record Office, Kew
    British Newspaper Library, Colindale, London
    York City Reference Library
    Air Historical Branch, Ministry of Defence, London
    Darlington Central Library

National
"England 1870 – 1914" Sir Robert Ensor 1936
    Oxford Clarendon Press
"English History 1914 to 1945" AJP Taylor 1965
    Oxford Clarendon Press
"Who Was Who" 1929 – 1950
"Dictionary of British Art and Artists 1880 – 1940"

Local Government
"A Guide to Services – North Yorkshire County Council" 1988
"Hambleton CC – Official Guide" 1984
"North Riding Quarter Sessions Records"
"North Riding County Council Minutes and Records"
"The First Hundred Years of the North Riding Constabulary (1856 –
    1956)"
"Festival of Britain Handbook 1951"
"Northallerton UDC Handbook" 1922. 1933. 1968
"Northallerton Chamber of Trade Handbook" 1982
"Northallerton Carnival Handbook" 1909
"Northallerton High Street – UDC Report" 1966

Railways
"A History of the LNER 1939 to 1948" Michael Bonavia. Allen &
    Unwin
"North Eastern Branch Lines Since 1925" K Hoole 1978 Ian Allen

Religion
"All Saints Parish Church Northallerton 1951"
"Centenary Souvenir Brochure 1866 – 1966" Northallerton Methodist
    Circuit

Hospitals
"Rutson Hospital 1877 – 1977"
"Call Me Matron" Cassie M Harker 1980
"The Official History of the Canadian Medical Services 1939 – 45"
"Royal Air Force Hospital Northallerton Operations Record Book
    1943 to 1947
"Northallerton Hospitals Management Committee Reports"
"League of Friends of Northallerton Hospitals – Annual Reports"
    1958 – 2000

461

"Friarage and Rutson Hospitals Nurses Handbook" 1950
"The Friarage Story" Michael Riordan 1990 HMSO

The World Wars
"The Green Howards 1914 – 19" Colonel HC Wylly 1926
"The History of the Green Howards" Geoffrey Powell. Cassell 1992
"The Story of the Green Howards 1939 – 45" Captain WAT Synge
    1952
"Baptism of Fire – St Julien April 1915" Mark Marsay 2000
    Great Northern Publishing
"Action Stations – 4 Military Airfields of Yorkshire"
    Bruce Barrymore Halpenny 1990
"Aerodromes in North Yorkshire and Wartime Memories"
    David Brown 1996
"Halifax File" RN Roberts   Air Britain Histories Ltd
"Battle of Britain Remembered" Vol 1 Nov 1999 Battle of Britain
    Historical Society
"Royal Air Force Leeming Operations Record Book July 1940 to June
    1946
"Royal Air Force Catterick Station Diary" 1939 – 45
"Royal Canadian Air Force Croft Station Diary" December 1943
Operations Record Book RCAF Squadron 427 (Lion) Squadron" 1943
    to 1946
Operations Reord Book RCAF Squadron 429 (Bison) Squadron" 1943
    to 1946
"Yorkshire at War 1939 – 45" Leo Kessler & Eric Taylor
"A History of 7th Field Company RE 1939 – 45"
    Thomas Riordan MM edit Squadron Leader MH Riordan 1984

Northallerton Published
"Smithson's Almanack" 1900 – 1912
"Northallerton in Old Postcards" Vol 1 C Narramore P Turner
    European Press
"Northallerton in Old Postcards" Vol II Michael Riordan European
    Press
"Northallerton in Old Postcards" Vol III Michael Riordan European
    Press
"Northallerton in Old Photographs" Vol I Michael Riordan 1996 Sutton
    Publishing
"Northallerton in Old Photographs" Vol II Michael Riordan 1998
    Sutton Publishing

"Swan Feather" Sheona Lodge   Flambard Press 1993

"Greenhorn – A Twentieth Century Childhood" Anne Tibble 1973

"From Middle Ages to Millenium – Northallerton Grammar School and College 1322 to 2000" Michael Riordan 2000 North Yorkshire County Print

Northallerton – Unpublished

"Archaeological Priorities and Needs – Northallerton" North Yorkshire CC Report – AJ Tyler 1985

"Northallerton from 1926 to 1939" George H Kelley 1985

"Wartime in Rural Yorkshire" Lieutenant Colonel BV Riordan 1996

"Steaks in Winnipeg" Arnold Pearson DSO DFC Ed Joanne Pearson 1990

"Anatomy of an Air Crash – K King's Last Flight" Michael Millar Ontario 1993

APPENDICES

Northallerton – Population   (Census Returns)

1791 -	1960	
1801 -	2138	
1811 -	2234	
1821 -	2626	
1831 -	3004	(Romanby 325)
1841 -	3092	(Romanby 350)
1851 -	3086	(Romanby 406: Brompton 1491)
1861 -	2870	(Rom 362: Brompton 1398)
1871 -	3164	(Rom 410: Bromp 1364)
1881 -	3692	(Rom 414: Bromp 1295)
1891 -	3802	(Rom 421: Bromp 1265)
1901 -	4616	(Rom 474: Bromp 1352)
1911 -	4806	(Rom 537: Bromp 1487)
1921 -	4794	(Rom 649: Bromp 1452)
1931 -	4786	(Rom 841: Bromp 1440)
1951 -	6087	(Rom 1486: Bromp 1632)
1961 -	6726	(Rom 3920: Bromp 1765)
1971 -	8753	(Rom 3962: Bromp 1784)
1981 -	9622	(Rom 4302: Brom 2064)
1991 -	9628	(Rom 5333: Bromp 2064)

Vicars of Northallerton
(from the earliest times to which they can be traced)

Before the Reformation
(Roman Catholic)

12 ..	Gilbert de Vere
1231	Robert _____
1267	John de Derlington
1302	Peter de Killawe
1311	Peter de Fishburn
1323	Alan de Chiredon
....	Richard Askeby
1332	Edmund Cruer
1335	Robert Dighton
13..	John de Haytor
1382	John de Gilling
1393	William Kamell
1396	Robt Redmereshill
1403	John Staynfield
14..	John Corbridge
1421	William Barker
1422	William Middilton
1437	John Thornton
1455	John Treyndon
1465	Robert Walker
1471	Bart Radclyff
1474	R. Rolleston BA
1475	William Halyman
1491	John Fisher DD*
1494	Robert Clay
1522	Leonard Hutchinson
1533	Robert Askew

After the Reformation
(Church of England – Protestant)

1547	Lancelot Thornton
1561	Mark Metcalfe MA
1593	Francis Kaye MA
1624	John Cradock **
1628	Th. Blaikeston MA ***
1640	Thomas Mann
1669	Dr John Neile DD
1675	William Neile MA
1686	John Harper
1694	Charles Neile MA
1718	Chr Hunter MA
1725	Thomas Rudd MA
1729	John Balguy MA
1748	Robert Pigot MA
1775	Benj Walker MA
1814	Reynold Gideon Bouyer LLB
1826	G Townsend DD
1839	Theodosius Burnett Stuart MA
1850	Tho W Mercer MA
1877	Benj Caffin MA
1894	Dr J Barmby DD
1897	Samuel Thompson MA
1925	Canon J T Brown MA
1931	Wm A Blackwell MA
1935	Frederick John Talbot Baines MA
1951	Stephen S Thistlewood MA
1963	Canon John Castledine MA
1985 -	Canon Ian James Fox MA

*	Afterwards Bishop of Rochester, beheaded on Tower Hill 1535
**	Died by poison 1627
***	Ejected by Thomas Mann 1640

Northallerton Grammar School and College
Headteachers and Principals   (1322 – 2002)

1322	R Colstan	1651	T Smelt
1349	R Drybeck	1687	J Todd
1377	J Podesay	1734	W Dawson
1385	William of Leeds	1771	J Wilkinson
1426	T Bubwith	1820	J Bowness
1440	J Levesham	1844	J Horner
1547	J Foster	1874	J Williams
1573	G Dobson	1874	WFN Allen
1576	J Clarkeson	1877	WE Scott
1584	W Gregson	1880	RCD Nugent
1585	S Lawcock	1894	SD Crawford
1613	R Sandeman	1899	HJA Wimberley
1615	R Harrison	1904	WW Raynor
1618	H Youill	1909	JW Bearder
1623	R Fowbray	1921	HT Palmer
1624	M Warton	1943	H Davies
1638	J Lindsay	1947	AT Richardson
1640	J Smith	1969	D Wright
		1979	L Harrison

Principals

1984	J Bell
1997	J Slater

Northallerton Members of Parliament (1298 – 1832)
Before the 1832 Reform Act – Two Members Returned

1298	John le Clark	1707	Sir William Hustler
	Stephen Maunsell		Roger Gale
	_____	1708	Sir William Hustler
Privilege of political representation			Roger Gale
In abeyance.		1710	Roger Gale
	_____		Robert Raikes
1640	Thomas Heblewaite	1713	Henry Peirse
	Sir Henry Cholmley		Leonard Smelt
1658	George Smithson	1714	Cholmley Turner
	James Danby		Leonard Smelt
1660	Sir F Hollis	1722	Henry Peirse
	George Marwood		Leonard Smelt
1678	Sir Gilbert Gerrard	1727	Henry Peirse
	Sir Henry Calverley		Leonard Smelt
1681	Sir Gilbert Gerrard	1734	Henry Peirse
	Sir Henry Calverley		Leonard Smelt
1685	Sir Davis Foulis	1740	William Smelt
	Sir Henry Marwood		Henry Peirse
1688	William Robinson	1741	Henry Peirse
	Thomas Lascelles		William Smelt
1690	Sir William Robinson	1745	Henry Lascelles
	Thomas Lascelles		Henry Peirse
1695	Sir William Hustler	1747	Henry Peirse
	Thomas Lascelles		Henry Lascelles
1698	Sir William Hustler	1752	Daniel Lascelles
	Ralph Milbank		Henry Peirse
1700	Sir Ralph Hustler	1754	Edward Lascelles
	Ralph Milbank		Daniel Lascelles
1701	Sir William Hustler	1761	Edward Lascelles
	Robert Dormer		Daniel Lascelles
1702	Daniel Lascelles	1768	Edward Lascelles
1702	Sir William Hustler		Daniel Lascelles
	John Aislabie	1775	Daniel Lascelles
	Robert Dormer		Henry Peirse
1705	Sir William Hustler	1780	Henry Peirse
	Roger Gale		Edwin Lascelles

1784	Henry Peirse	1814	J B S Morritt
	Edwin Lascelles		Henry Peirse
1790	Henry Peirse	1818	Henry Peirse
	Edward Lascelles		Henry Lascelles
1796	Henry Peirse	1820	Henry Peirse
	Edward Lascelles		Hon.W Lascelles
1802	Henry Peirse	1824	Lt.M Beresford
	Edward Lascelles		Hon.W Lascelles
1806	Henry Peirse	1826	Hon. H Lascelles
	Edward Lascelles		Sir J P Beresford
1807	Henry Peirse	1830	Hon. H Lascelles
	Edward Lascelles		Sir J P Beresford
1812	Henry Peirse	1831	Sir J P Beresford
	Edward Lascelles		Hon.W Lascelles

Northallerton Members of Parliament (1832 – 1885)
(Northallerton Elections – One Member Returned)

1832   Captain J George Boss RN (Independent) 108   W B Wrightson (Liberal) 97

1835   William Battye Wrightson (Liberal) Unopposed

1837   William B Wrightson (Liberal) Unopposed

1841   William B Wrightson (Liberal) 129   Edwin Lascelles (Conservative) 114

1847   William B Wrightson (Liberal) Unopposed

1852   William B Wrightson (Liberal) Unopposed

1857   William B Wrightson (Liberal) 129   Egremont Lascelles (Conservative) 126

1859   William B Wrightson (Liberal) 138   C H Mills (Conservative) 136

1865   Charles Henry Mills (Conservative) 239   Jasper W Johns (Liberal) 190
(C H Mills disqualified for bribery, treating and undue influence)

1866   Egremont W Lascelles (Conservative) 224   W B Wrightson (Liberal) 201

1868   John Hutton (Conservative) 385 Jasper W Johns (Liberal) 373

1874   George W Elliot (Conservative) 387   W B Wrightson (Liberal) 378

1880   George W Elliot (Conservative) 484   Albert O Rutson (Liberal) 384

(1885   Northallerton lost its Member and was merged with Richmond into the Richmondshire constituency)

Richmondshire Members of Parliament (1885 – 2002)

1885	Sir Frederick Milbank – Thorp Perrow Hall (Liberal)
1886 – 1895	Sir George W Elliot – Langton Hall (Conservative) Re-elected 1892 Succ to knighthood 1893
1895 – 1905	John Hutton – Solberge Hall (Conservative) Re-elected 1900 Concurrently Chairman North Riding Quarter Sessions. Chairman North Riding County Council
1906 – 1910	Francis Dyke Acland (Liberal) Subsequently received knighthood
1910 – 1918	Hon. W G Agar Orde-Powlett – Bolton Hall (Conservative) Unopposed Dec 1910 Subsequently Lord Bolton
1918 – 1929	Sir Murrough J Wilson – Cliffe Hall Darlington (Conservative) Unopposed 1922 1923 and 1924 Knighthood 1928
1929 – 1958	Sir Thomas L Dugdale – Crathorne Hall (Conservative) Unopposed 1931 Re-elected 1945 1950 1951 1955 Knighthood 1945 Minister of Agriculture 1951 (Cabinet) Lord Crathorne 1959
1959 – 1983	Sir Timothy PG Kitson –Leazes Hall Leeming Bar (Conservative) Re-elected 1964 1966 1970 1974 1979 Knighthood 1974
1983 – 1988	Lord Leon Brittan (Conservative) Re-elected 1987 Home Secretary 1983 (Cabinet) Ministry for Trade and Industry 1985 (Cabinet) Subsequent Knighthood 1989 Elevation to Peerage 2000
1989 – 2001 onwards	William Hague (Conservative) Re-elected1992 1997 2001 Secretary of State for Wales 1995 (Cabinet) Leader of the Opposition 1997 to 2001

Chairmen – Northallerton Urban District Council   (1895 – 1974)

1895 – 96	Chr. Palliser		1934 – 35	Tho. Woodhead
1896 – 97	Geo. J Robinson		1935 – 36	John Avey
1897 – 98	James Guthrie		1936 – 37	Anthony Howard
1898 – 99	Ernest Gardner		1937 – 38	William Watson
1899–1900	Herbert Clidero		1939 – 39	Arthur E Skelton
1900 – 01	John Walker		1940 – 41	Tho. Woodhead
1901 – 02	Robert Jameson		1941 – 42	Tho. Woodhead
1902 – 03	Henry Hird		1942 – 43	John Avey
1903 – 04	James Guthrie		1943 – 44	John Avey
1904 – 05	John Weighell		1944 – 45	C F Atkinson
1905 – 06	Robert Jameson		1945 – 46	C F Atkinson
1906 – 07	Walter G Eaton		1946 – 47	Arthur E Skelton
1907 – 08	James Guthrie		1947 – 48	George East
1908 – 09	James Guthrie		1948 – 49	Alastair Carter
1909 – 10	G E Hamilton		1949 – 50	John L Swain
1910 – 11	Herbert Clidero		1950 – 51	John L Swain
1911 – 12	John Weighell		1951 – 52	Arthur E Skelton
1912 – 13	Robert Jameson		1952 – 53	G C Wrigley
1913 – 14	Walter G Eaton		1953 – 54	G C Wrigley
1914 – 15	Herbert Clidero		1954 – 55	John L Swain
1915 – 16	Walter G Eaton		1955 – 56	Richie C Pick
1916 – 17	Francis Boynton		1956 – 57	Tho. M Lightfoot
1917 – 18	Robert Jameson		1957 – 58	William L Prest
1918 – 19	Walter G Eaton		1958 – 59	Roy W Moody
1919 – 20	Tho. Woodhead		1959 – 60	William Wake
1920 – 21	George Cotton		1960 – 61	William L Prest
1921 – 22	Walter G Eaton		1961 – 62	Kenneth Hird
1922 – 23	Francis Boynton		1962 – 63	Charles Sawdon
1923 – 24	Ernest Place		1963 – 64	Alwyn Cockerill
1924 – 25	Lewis W Atlay		1964 – 65	H D Walkland
1925 – 26	Henry Hird		1965 – 66	Charles Sawdon
1926 – 27	Francis Kettlewell		1966 – 67	Alwyn Cockerill
1927 – 28	Tho. Woodhead		1967 – 68	M J G Wilson
1928 – 29	George Cotton		1968 – 69	K Parkinson
1929 – 30	John Walker		1969 – 70	D M Willoughby
1930 – 31	Charles Fowler		1970 – 71	Alan W Herbert
1931 – 32	F. Woodhead		1971 – 72	Kenneth Calvert
1932 – 33	Lewis W Atlay		1972 – 73	David J Cole
1933 – 34	Tho. Woodhead		1973 – 74	W A R South

Mayors of Northallerton (1974 – 2002)

1974 – 75	Alwyn Cockerill
1976 – 77	J E Mainwaring-Taylor
1977 – 78	Harold Walkland
1978 – 79	William Wake
1979 – 80	R F (Bob) Tennant
1980 – 81	George Kelley
1981 – 82	Jean Tennant
1982 – 83	John Bacon
1983 – 84	Harold Walkland
1984 – 85	Brian Allison
1985 – 86	Bernard Kirk
1986 – 87	Jane Harvey
1987 – 88	Jennifer Davies
1988 – 90	John Segger
1990 – 91	Linda C Gibson
1991 – 93	John Coulson
1993 – 94	John Michael Southwell
1994 – 96	Jane Harvey
1996 – 98	James Stafford
1998 – 99	Steve Merritt
1999 – 99	Roy Ashman
1999 – 2000	Steve Merritt
2000 – 01	Jack Dobson
2001 – 02	Sally Anderson
2002 – 03	Jack Dobson

Leaders of Hambleton District Council (1985 – 2002)

1985 – 1992	D John Dennis
1993 – 2002	June Imeson

Chairmen of Hambleton District Council (1974 – 2002)

1974 – 76	Alan W Herbert
1976 – 78	Anne Ward Thompson
1978 – 80	Norman Atkinson
1980 – 82	John R Bumby
1982 – 84	Matthew W Cook
1984 – 86	M C W Peter Consett

1986 – 87	Derek E Davies
1987 – 89	Bertram Bosomworth
1989 – 91	Mary Potter
1991 – 92	Charles A Thompson
1992 – 94	R Gordon Horner
1994 – 96	Leonard H Groves
1996 – 97	D John Dennis
1997 – 98	Ralph I Andrew
1998 – 99	Betsy Walkington
1999 – 2000	Geoffrey W Ellis
2000 – 2001	Denis Howey
2001 – 2002	John Prest
2002 – 2003	Percy Featherstone

North Riding Registrars of Deeds (1736 – 1960)

1736	William Turner
1757	Thomas Robinson
1771	Samuel Butterwick
1774	George Crowe
1783	Matthew Butterwick
1821	Richard W C Peirse
1844	Captain Richard Peirse
1872	George A Cayley
1885	Charles A L Ringrose
1916 onwards	Hubert G Thornley (Knighthood 1958)

NB All these gentlemen resided at the Registry House, Zetland Street, Northallerton.

Chairmen North Riding County Council (1889 – 1974)

1889 – 1892	The Hon. John Charles Dundas
1892 – 1895	The Hon. George Edwin Lascelles
1895 – 1915	John Hutton
1915 – 1926	Sir Henry Beresford-Peirse Bart.
1926 – 1938	Major Robert Bell Turton
1938 – 1942	William Fry Whitwell
1942 – 1956	Benjamin Owen Davies
1956 – 1960	William Robinson Burrill-Robinson
1960 – 1974	James Thomas Fletcher CBE.

**North Riding County Council Clerks
and Clerks to the Justices of the Peace (1889 – 1973)**

1889 – 1895	Thomas Lawrence Yeoman
1895 – 1915	William Charles Trevor
1916 – 1960	Sir Hubert G Thornley
1960 – 1973	Robert Wotherspoon

Leaders of North Yorkshire County Council (1974 – 2002)

1974 – 1977	Colonel RJL Jackson CBE DL
1977 – 1981	Ted Dennison
1981 – 1993	John Clout
1993 – 2001	David Ashton
2001 onwards	John Weighell

Chairmen of North Yorkshire County Council (1974 – 2002)

1974 – 1977	J T Fletcher, CBE JP
1977 – 1981	Colonel R J L Jackson, CBE DL
1981 – 1984	Major T H Ives, CBE DL
1984 – 1985	Lt Col M J B Burnett, DSO DL
1985 – 1989	Laurie Backhouse
1989 – 1990	Lt Col Herbrand Vavasour Dawson DL
1990 – 1991	Ken Cooper DL
1991 – 1992	Angela Harris, JP, DL (The Baroness Harris of Richmond DL)
1992 – 1993	Squadron Leader James F Donaldson
1993 – 1994	Fred Robson
1994 – 1995	Beth Graham
1995 – 1996	John Clout, CBE
1996 – 1997	T Ken Hull
1997 – 1998	John Marshall
1998 – 1999	William F Barton, OBE
1999 – 2000	Lt Col John H Jacob, MC
2000 – 2001	Roy Wilson
2001 – 2002	Geoffrey Rennie
2002 – 2003	David Ashton

Chief Executive Officers – North Yorkshire County Council (1974 – 2002)

1973 – 1989	H J Evans
1990 – 1994	Ronald Leyland
1994 – 1999	John Ransford
1999 – onwards	Jeremy Walker

Honorary Citizens of Northallerton

William Wake	October 1992
John Brendan Archer MBE	December 1996
Norman Cuthbert Bryning MBE	June 1997
A. Elizabeth Eleanor McDougle (Nancie) MBE	June 1999
George Henry Kelley	September 2001
George Kenneth Hird	September 2002

Index

Illustrations are indicated in **bold** type

478

479

North Riding Bank 113
North Riding Constabulary 150, 151, 156, 227, 348
North Riding County Council 150, 153, 224, 225, 228, 245, 249, 270, 274
North Riding Court House 131, 159, 227
North Riding Highways Dept 337
North Riding Hotel 436
North Riding House of Correction 156, 157
North Riding Police Headquarters 152, 224, 348
North Riding Quarter Sessions 62, 71, 75, 76, 155, 156, 157, 227, 281, 350, 351
North Riding Red Cross Association 221
North Riding Registry of Deeds 100, 160, 274
North Riding Rural Nurses Association 221
North Riding Traffic Headquarters 348
North Riding War Agricultural Committee 292
North Yorks Farmers Mart 252
North Yorkshire Police Force 379-81
Northallerton Agricultural Show 234, 267, 334
Northallerton Agricultural Society 163, 267
Northallerton Amateur Theatricals 236, 286
Northallerton and Brompton Burial Board 178
Northallerton Bridge **48**
Northallerton Carnival 236, 241
Northallerton Castle **23**
Northallerton CC 361
Northallerton Church **87**
Northallerton College 399, 423, **424**
Northallerton Cycling Club 237
Northallerton Electric Light and Power Company 239
Northallerton Gaol 159, 194, 298, 351, **352**, 382
Northallerton Grammar School 41, 65, 69,190, 225, 315, 316, 345, 346, 422, 431 442
Northallerton Harriers 209
Northallerton Male Voice Choir 236,

435
Northallerton Market 164
Northallerton National Reserve 244
Northallerton NHS Trust 409
Northallerton Parish Church 9, 11, 40, 41, 43, 60, 102, 181-186, 340, 411-12
Northallerton Poor Law Union 173, 174
Northallerton RUFC 439
Northallerton Savings Bank 168
Northallerton Show 267
Northallerton Station **338**
Northallerton Temperance Society 196
Northallerton Town Council 368, 370, 378, 433
Northallerton Town FC 439
Northallerton Urban and Rural District Councils 150, 154, 179, 272, 319, 322, 323, 367
Northallerton Volunteer Rifle Corps 160, 161
Northallerton War Memorial 260, 262, 325
Northallerton War Savings Committee 296
Northallerton Water Bill 179
Northallerton YFC 335
Northallerton, parish 30
Northallerton, Viscount 125, 445
Northallerton-Wensleydale branch line 395, 397, 398
Northdale Horticulture 431
Northern Electricit & Gas 391
Northgrave, Mary 434
Northumberland, Duke of 125
Northumberland, Earl of 62
Nowell, Ralph Bishop of Orkney 19
NRCC Town Plan 326
NSPCA 430
NSPCC 430
NUAgW 334

O'Malley, J 290
O'Malley, Pte T 259
Oak Mount 168
Oak Tree 324
Oakdale 178, 179
Oakdale 220
Oakley, D 264, 274, 278, 348
Odericus Vitalis 14
Ogilby, John 95

487

Sports 199, 288
Sportsman's Club 200
Springwell Lane 285, **307**
Squatters 321, 322
Squire, Will 121
St Bartholomew's Fair 67
St Cuthbert 14
St Cuthbert's, Durham, church 15
St George's Fair 32, 164, 265, 404
St James Hospital 33, 35, 57, 180, 321
St James Estate 386
St Laurence, chantry 59
St Mary's Hospital 36
St Matthew's Fair 32, 84, 270
St Thomas Church 182
Stafford, Cllr J 415
Stafford, PO A 305
Stage coach 95, 96, 114-16, 138-40
Standard House 379
Standard Monument 23
Stanley Court 386
Stanley, T 386
Station Mart **145**, 166, 233, 234, 334
Stead, PO P 305
Steere, Sgt 310
Stephen, King 17
Stephenson, William 128
Stockdales 377
Stocks 65
Stone Cross 383
Stone, E 364
Stonefall Cemetery 308, 311
Straingwaise, judge 61
Strangways, Henry 50
Strangways, Sir James 47, 52, 56, 66
Strangways, Sir Thomas 51, 52, 53
Streete House 76
Strickland, Col Sir Roger 81
Strickland, Sir William 56
Strikes 169
Stringer, Anne 98
Stroyan, A 351
Stuart, Rev TB 176, 192
Stubbins, W 189
Stukeley, Dr W 4, 9
Sun Beck 99, 194, 285,
Sunbeck House 175
Sunday Schools 121
Sunflower charabanc 279
Sunters 331, 389, **390**
Supermarkets 375

Sussex, Earl of 63
Suttle, Robert 76
Swain Court 386
Swain, T & W 253, **254**
Swain's farm 243
Swale and Bedale Brook Navigation 117
Swale, River 1, 10, 116
Swinithwaite estate 88
Swinton, Countess 377
Sykes, M 271
Symeon of Durham 14

Tan yards 168
Tanning 82
Taylor, FO W J 307
Teal 365
Teesdale J 330, 388
Temperance Hotel 196
Temperance Band 202
Temple, Dr W Archbishop 278 282
Tennant, Cllr B 378
Tennant, John 122
Tennis club 439
Terry, B 345
Tesco 6, **375**, 376
The Sun 196
The Swan inn 67
Theakston's of Masham 236
Theatre Royal 189, 199, 200
Thimbleby 112
Thirsk 10, 78
Thirsk Rd 222, 282
Thistlewood, Rev S 340
Thompson, Lt C J M 264
Thompson, P 386
Thompson, R 283
Thompson, Rev S M 224, 235, 262
Thompson, Sir R 194
Thompson, T 194
Thompson, Walter & Son 294, 322, 325, 331-2, 340, 347, 386
Thompsons (butchers) 376
Thomson, Archbishop of York 182, 187
Thorn Gapp 100
Thornley, H 257, 280, 288, 315, 341, 342, 350
Thornton-Berry, C 406, 408
Thornton-le-Beans 52, 66
Thornton-le-Moor 78, 266

489